Curriculum Models and Early Childhood Education

Appraising the Relationship

Stacie G. Goffin

Ewing Marion Kauffman Foundation

Merrill, an imprint of
Macmillan College Publishing Company
New York

Maxwell Macmillan Canada
Toronto

Maxwell Macmillan International
New York   Oxford   Singapore   Sydney

Editor: Linda A. Sullivan
Production Editor: Colleen Brosnan
Art Coordinator: Peter A. Robison
Cover Designer: Robert Vega
Production Buyer: Patricia A. Tonneman
Electronic Text Management: Marilyn Wilson Phelps, Matthew Williams

This book was set in Bitstream Swiss 721 and Garamond by Macmillan College Publishing Company and was printed and bound by R. R. Donnelley & Sons Company. The cover was printed by Phoenix Color Corp.

Table 5–1 from *Social Class, Race, and Psychological Development* by Martin Deutsch, Irwin Katz and Arthur R. Jensen, copyright © 1968 by Holt, Rinehart and Winston, Inc., reprinted by permission of the publisher.

Macmillan College Publishing Company
866 Third Avenue
New York, NY 10022

Macmillan College Publishing Company is part of the
Maxwell Communication Group of Companies.

Maxwell Macmillan Canada, Inc.
1200 Eglinton Avenue East, Suite 200
Don Mills, Ontario M3C 3N1

Library of Congress Cataloging-in-Publication Data
Goffin, Stacie G.
     Curriculum models and early childhood education : appraising the
relationship / Stacie G. Goffin
        p.   cm.
     Includes bibliographical references and index.
     ISBN 0-675-21154-9
     1. Early childhood education—United States—Curricula.
    2. Curriculum planning—United States. I. Title.
    LB1139.4.G64   1994
    372.19—dc20   93-26064
                                       CIP

Printing: 1 2 3 4 5 6 7 8 9   Year: 4 5 6 7

To Sabra, Bruce, and Marguerite

Foreword

Lilian G. Katz, Ph.D.

Every teacher, at every level of education has to answer at least these two questions: What should be learned? and How is it best learned? Although the first question is fairly easy to answer in theory, it is surprisingly difficult to answer in terms of specific practices. Should young children in St. Louis be studying oceans? Should 4-year-olds in Miami be making snowflakes out of Styrofoam? Should preschoolers in Ohio be learning about rain forests? Is a daily calendar ritual appropriate for 4- or 5-year-olds? Why not? Or why? And whose answers to these questions should carry the most weight?

Teachers rarely have time to ask these questions explicitly; their lives are usually too hectic to ponder the deep and long-term implications such questions raise! However, they often ask: What shall I do on Monday morning? As soon as we turn to making decisions about actual curriculum and teaching practices, our confidence in the answers tends to waiver. The answers might be based on tradition—"We have always had these activities." They might be based on assumptions about children's enjoyment, or on a holiday or seasonal observance. They might be based on expediency, habit, state or district curriculum guides, upcoming tests, parents' preferences, philosophy, or any of an infinitely long list of other bases—perhaps mixed together in unspecified proportions. Answers to the question of how something is best learned might also have a similar variety of sources, including assumptions about how young children learn.

Curriculum models are sets of answers to these questions developed by creative and thoughtful educators based largely on their own experience, theories, and ideologies. In this book, Stacie Goffin offers us a much-needed contemporary analysis of the issues and implications of five such models, and helps us understand why these models were developed and how their developers addressed these two questions. The historical and contemporary forces that gave rise to the development of each of the models and shaped them are examined closely and deeply. Readers will surely find help in making their own decisions about where curriculum models fit into their own practices and philosophy.

Summarizing the detailed analysis of five contemporary early childhood curriculum models, Dr. Goffin presents us with a dilemma. By definition, a dilemma is a predicament in which each of two alternative courses of action—one of which must be taken—is equally desirable or undesirable, and in which taking one course undermines the potential benefits and values that might have been derived if the other "horn" of the dilemma had been chosen. What is the nature of the curriculum models dilemma?

One way to describe the dilemma is to define it as a choice between the *standardization* of teaching practices through adherence to a curriculum model, versus *professionalization* that, by definition[1] means the exercise of the professional's own judgment based on advanced training and specialized knowledge, not typical of early childhood practitioners at the present time. As Goffin points out, each of these two "horns" of the dilemma carries its own advantages and its own errors. The advantage of standardization, accomplished by setting standards of practice, is that it can elevate the overall quality of early childhood provisions. However, on the one hand, the potential error of standardization through curriculum models is it might also inhibit the development and exercise of the practitioner's own judgment in response to the specific context of her own practice. On the other hand, if we set aside curriculum models, and the standards and standardization they inevitably give rise to, the many current practitioners who have not had the benefit of professional preparation and specialized knowledge may have to struggle alone to find their own ways—for better or for worse. Without the standardization inherent in adopting curriculum models, the range of quality is likely to be very wide—excellent, innovative, and imaginative practices at the upper range, and some seriously deficient practices at the low end of the range.

One possible alternative to the dilemma is to develop and adopt a body of basic *principles of practice* based on cultural, ethical, developmental, and psychological criteria. The term *principle* is used here to refer to generalizations of sufficient reliability that they are worthy of consideration when deciding what practices to adopt. The development and continual refinement of this body of accepted principles of practice is one of the most important functions of professional associations and societies for all professions, and distinguishes professions from crafts and trades and other occupations. Professional associations like the National Association for the Education of Young Children and the Association for Childhood Education International are laying the foundation for this ultimate goal through position statements and a variety of other publications and projects.

As this work progresses, another approach to this dilemma might be to take a developmental view of the role of curriculum models; namely, to encourage neophyte practitioners who have not had the benefit of specialized training to adopt a curriculum model to their liking *as a beginning basis* on which to launch their careers, as a "survival" kit, so to speak. Then encourage them to the view that once

---

1 See Katz, L. G. (1988). The nature of professions: Where is early childhood education? In L. B. Katz (Ed.), *Current topics in early childhood education* (Vol. 7, pp. 1–16). Norwood, NJ: Ablex.

they pass through the "survival" stage of development,[2] they should adopt the habit of seeking greater knowledge, of becoming eclectic, of experimenting with their own ideas, of seeing themselves as developing professionals, and of adapting practices to suit their own particular pedagogical needs.

In this work, Dr. Goffin gives us a solid basis for enriched dialogue about the issues raised: issues of appropriate curriculum, the status of the profession, the nature of specialized training, the role of professional judgment, and the entire future of our field. The work to be done is hard and long, but can contribute substantially to the well-being of all our children.

---

[2] See Katz, L. G. (1977). Teachers' developmental stages. In L. G. Katz, *Talks with Teachers* (pp. 7–13). Washington, DC: National Association for the Education of Young Children.

Acknowledgments

I always enjoy reading a book's acknowledgments because they provide an entree into an author's personal and intellectual life. This is no less true for me as I gratefully acknowledge those individuals and institutions who have nurtured me and my work during the writing of this book. Writing this book provoked an intense, intellectual journey that ultimately transformed the original intentions for this book. Because this intellectual journey was so influential in determining the purpose and design of this book, the first chapter summarizes the route of my journey and its impact on the book's evolution into its current form. These acknowledgments recognize those who have supported my journey during the past 3 years.

This book was conceived while I was a faculty member in the School of Education at the University of Missouri-Kansas City. Without their support, especially the gift of time, this book would never have come to fruition. I am especially grateful for the year-long sabbatical during which time the major work for this effort was conducted.

Fortunately, this generous support was extended when I began my work at the Ewing Marion Kauffman Foundation. The foundation not only accepted my request to begin my new position several months after we concluded our negotiations, but they also encouraged me to assimilate the labor needed to complete this text into my plan of work. Their support enabled me to see this book through to its completion.

Then there was the support that came from those who read, and reread, the various versions of the chapters herein. These friends and colleagues always managed to share their comments in ways that permitted me to improve my thinking and writing. Deserving special mention are Harriet Cuffaro, David Day, Linda Edwards, Lilian Katz, Marguerite Myers, Doug Powell, Edna Shapiro, and Catherine Wilson. Appreciation is also due for the comments provided by the following reviewers: David E. Day, SUNY–College at Buffalo; Elizabeth A. Eddowes, University of Alabama at Birmingham; Kathy Fite, Southwest Texas State University; Stevie Hoffman, University of Missouri; Sally Lubeck, The University of Michigan; Daniel Walsh,

University of Illinois at Urbana-Champaign, and C. Stephen White, The University of Georgia. The affirmation provided by all these individuals went a long way toward sustaining the self-discipline and commitment a text of this magnitude requires. My debt to Marguerite Myers's intellectual prowess and endless encouragement is especially deep.

I am also most appreciative to my editor, Linda Sullivan, for the sustenance she provided. If she ever felt impatient with the length of time it took me to write this book or uncertain about some of my unconventional decisions, she never expressed them to me. Harriet Cuffaro and Edna Shapiro's comments on Chapter 4, "The Developmental Interaction Approach" were especially helpful in assuring its accuracy—both of fact and interpretation. And special gratitude is extended to Lilian Katz for her thoughtful foreword. In addition, I'd like to say "thank you" to my father for his endless queries on the status of each chapter, queries that I know reflected his interest in, and support for, my work.

At one point in the process of writing this book, I found the following note wedged between the keys of my computer. "Mom, something has come between us. The computer! I am not sure that I can love it, too. I do enjoy, like you, but the addiction and love is just not there for me as it is for you. I love you. Please call for help. I care!" Neither my daughter Sabra—who wrote that satirical note—nor my husband Bruce has ever questioned the legitimacy of my commitment to writing this book. Their acceptance permitted me to devote untold hours without ever doubting their knowledge of my commitment to them and my roles of wife and mother. I hope they know that I never took this support for granted.

Brief Contents

Part I   *Early Childhood Curriculum Models in Context*   1

Chapter 1   Setting the Stage: A Very Personal Introduction   3
Chapter 2   Curriculum Models and Early Childhood Education: A Historical Framework   11

Part II   *Early Childhood Curriculum Models: A Contemporary Review*   35

Chapter 3   The Montessori Method   37
Chapter 4   The Developmental-Interaction Approach   65
Chapter 5   The Direct Instruction Model   97
Chapter 6   Two Models Derived from Piagetian Theory   125

Part III   *An Examination of the Underpinnings of Curriculum Models in Early Childhood Education*   163

Chapter 7   In Pursuit of Answers: Comparative Evaluations of Early Childhood Curriculum Models   165
Chapter 8   Reemergence of Essential Questions: Identifying the Source of Early Childhood Curriculum   187
Chapter 9   Curriculum Models and Early Childhood Education: Some Final Thoughts   209
References   215
Index   239

Contents

Part I: *Early Childhood Curriculum Models in*
Context   1

Chapter 1
Setting the Stage: A Very Personal Introduction   **3**
    Probing the Concept of Curriculum Models: Why Now?   5
    An Outline for What Follows   6

Chapter 2
Curriculum Models and Early Childhood Education: A Historical
Framework   **11**
    Early Childhood Programs and Public Policy   11
    An American History of Curriculum Models in Early Childhood
    Education   14
        The Early Childhood Context   14
        The Emergence of Systematic Variation   16
        The Political Setting   18
        The Influence of Shifting Psychological Insights   19
        Development of Curriculum Models   21
        The Ending of an Era   25
    Contemporary Backdrop for Early Childhood Curriculum Models   27
        Changing Societal Context   28
        Changing Configuration of Early Childhood Education   29
        Changing Knowledge Base   30
    Conclusion   31
    For Further Reading   33

Part II: *Early Childhood Curriculum Models:*
A Contemporary Review   35

Chapter 3
The Montessori Method   37

The Montessori Method: An American Chronology   39
    In the Beginning   39
    From Italy to the United States   43
    The Resurrection   46
Montessori's Method   48
    Essential Conceptual Elements   49
    The Montessori Program   55
The Importance of Timing   60
For Further Reading   62

Chapter 4
The Developmental-Interaction Approach   65

Evolution from Experimental Nursery Program to the Developmental-Interaction Approach   69
    The Beginning: The Bureau of Educational Experiments   71
    Emotions as a Prominent Theme: The Influence of Psychodynamic Theory   75
    The Explosion of Preschool Education: The Bank Street Approach as Defender of "Traditional" Early Childhood Ideals   78
The Developmental-Interaction Approach   80
    The Psychological Rationale   80
Essential Tenets   84
    Value Priorities   86
    Educational Goals: A Vehicle for Promoting Developmental Processes   86
    Teaching Strategies   89
    Organization   92
From Reflective Practice to Theory into Practice   93
For Further Reading   96

Chapter 5
The Direct Instruction Model   97

The Psychological Framework for Direct Instruction   100
    The Tenets of Behaviorism   100
    Science, Method, and a Science of Education   104
Teaching Disadvantaged Children in the Preschool: The Bereiter-Engelmann Model   107
The Direct Instruction Model   111
    Program Content   113
    Programmatic Design   113
    Teaching Methods   115

Explaining the Unanticipated Success of Academically Oriented
Curricula   116
    The Timing Was Right   116
    A Justification for Academic Early Childhood Programs   118
    A Changing Relationship Between Early Childhood and Elementary
    Education   119
    Developmentally Appropriate Practice: Reclaiming Traditional Early
    Childhood Education   121
    Explaining the Unanticipated Success of Developmentally Appropriate
    Practice   122
For Further Reading   124

Chapter 6
Two Models Derived from Piagetian Theory   125

Early History: Applying Piagetian Theory to Early Childhood
Education   128
The Piagetian Mystique   129
The Kamii-DeVries Approach   131
    Deriving Educational Implications from Piaget's Theory of Cognitive
    Development   134
    Curriculum and Activities   141
    Expectations for Teachers   147
The High/Scope Curriculum Model   148
    The Preschool Curriculum Framework   154
    The K–3 Curriculum Framework   157
    Serving as Change Agents Through Program Dissemination   158
For Further Reading   160

Part III: *An Examination of the Underpinnings of Curriculum Models in Early Childhood Education*   163

Chapter 7
**In Pursuit of Answers: Comparative Evaluations of Early Childhood
Curriculum Models   165**

Empirical Evaluations of Early Childhood Curriculum Models   166
    Initial Findings: Short-term Effects   167
    Follow-up Findings: Long-term Impact   170
    Using the Findings from Program Evaluations   173
    Explaining Program Effects   174
A Changing Picture: An Emergent Pattern of Differential Impact   175
    The Policy Connection   182
For Further Reading   185

Chapter 8
Reemergence of Essential Questions: Identifying the Source of Early Childhood Curriculum   187

Developmental Theory and Early Childhood Curriculum   189
   Questioning Old Assumptions and Making New Ones: Changing
   Understandings about Child Development   190
   Child Development Theories and Early Childhood Curriculum:
   Challenges to the Status Quo   198
   Research on Teacher Effects: New Judgments on the Nature of
   Teaching   202
   New Judgments about the Nature of Teaching   204
Beyond a Search for Efficacy   206
For Further Reading   207

Chapter 9
Curriculum Models and Early Childhood Education: Some Final Thoughts   209

An Expanded Agenda for Early Childhood Education   210
   Changing Societal Context   211
   Changing Professional Context   211
Curriculum Models and Early Childhood Education: A Dilemma   213

References   215

Index   239

Part I

Early Childhood Curriculum
Models in Context

Part I comprises two chapters that present a personal and historical context for the investigation of enduring early childhood curriculum models. Chapter 1 describes the interpretative framework that has shaped the book's overarching questions and presents an overview of the book's organization and content. The second chapter explores the circumstances that have supported the systematic promotion and development of curriculum models, first in the 1960s and then again in the 1990s.

■ ■ ■ ■ ■ ■

Chapter 1

Setting the Stage

A Very Personal Introduction

■ ■ ■ ■ ■ ■

When I first proposed writing this book over 3 years ago, I wanted to create a textbook for my graduate course on early childhood curriculum models. I had taught this course at least once a year for almost a decade, but I had been struggling for several years to find an up-to-date text. Frankly, I kept waiting for Ellis Evans to write an updated, third edition for his classic text, *Contemporary Influences in Early Childhood Education* (1975). When that expectation never materialized, I confidently proposed to write the needed text myself! I realize what follows risks exposing my intellectual naivete; yet sharing some of the pathways I have traveled during the last 3 years in my journey toward this book's completion can provide insight into the struggles that have helped shape this book and defined its objectives.

My original intention was to write the survey text Evans had not. The second edition of Evans's text provided not only a comprehensive overview of prominent curriculum models but also situated their descriptions within the theoretical context (usually developmental theory) that supplied a conceptual basis for the model. The chapter describing behaviorally based programs, for example, first explained behavioral theory and then described several curriculum models derived from the same theoretical foundation.

Evans's presentation of various theoretical frameworks enabled readers to appreciate how early childhood curriculum models have been constructed from diverse conceptual frameworks. His approach also highlighted how various model developers have selected different aspects of the same theory as the focal point of their program design. The text prospectus that I sent to Merrill promised a similar format.

I was accepting, of course, the idea that curriculum models provided a sound framework for organizing teaching and curriculum in early childhood education. But, even then, I already was conscious that developmental theories provided a shaky knowledge base for curriculum development because their meaning for curriculum design was open to multiple interpretations. But, when students kept prodding for the source of educational goals for early childhood curriculum derived from behavioral theory (and not for other theoretical foundations), I also became cognizant of the fact that, despite the supposed objectivity of theoretical descriptions of children's development, desired end points for children's growth were, in fact, implicit within each theory. With this new insight, I began to think more critically about the various sources of early childhood curriculum.

At this point, however, I simply considered this attribute of developmental theory an imperfection problematic to model-building. Nor was this characteristic yet a potential challenge to curriculum models as a framework for curriculum development. In fact, I incorporated these theoretical variations as a critical component of my curriculum models course. Following a fairly factual description of models that had emerged from a particular theory, students and I would analyze and compare models in terms of the various interpretations they had made of their shared theoretical base.

Curriculum models are idealized descriptions of programs that can be copied or emulated (Spodek, 1973). As a referent, models are frameworks for decision making about educational priorities, administrative policies, curriculum content, instructional methods, and evaluation. Through classroom discussions that scrutinized models in terms of these purposes, I found myself becoming increasingly dissatisfied with existing curriculum models. (In other words, no model quite addressed all the educational priorities that mattered to me or did so as I would have!) And then, the curricular content of models began to appear dated, either because it failed to address educational and/or developmental concerns that had arisen since its initial construction or because it described developmental events in ways that differed from prevailing understandings—or failed to describe them at all. Although these dissatisfactions also were classified under the heading of imperfections, they prodded me more deeply into study and reflection. By this time, however, I was beginning to question more than the ability of curriculum models to incorporate current content. I was finding it difficult to classify my concerns as interesting ambiguities; they were becoming more troublesome, and, in the process, so was the notion of curriculum models.

What finally undermined my trusting acceptance of curriculum models was a mounting disgruntlement with the role of developmental theory—rather than educational purpose—as a primary determinant of what was educationally worthwhile. At this point in my intellectual evolution, I was questioning not only the content of curriculum models but also their structural limitations.

My response was to propose an enlarged conceptualization for models, one that I hoped would rectify these limitations. I created a programmatic distinction between curriculum models and program models. In contrast to curriculum models, program models had multiple informants. Curriculum decisions were determined by purpose (versus developmental theory) and informed by understandings of child development, family dynamics, and the impact of different environmental circumstances. I thought the focus on program purpose, such as early intervention or family support—versus a specific theoretical framework, such as Piagetian theory—also would provide program models the flexibility to incorporate new knowledge. For a short while, this more encompassing configuration of models quelled my discontent.

Ultimately, however, my concept of program model was too general to be useful. Probably more significant to my intellectual evolution, however, was an ever-increasing puzzlement regarding the purpose of curriculum models. As I continued to delve deeper and deeper into this investigation, the very notion of curriculum models became enigmatic; by now, my questioning extended beyond the source and currency of their content. I also had begun to ponder their purpose and function within early childhood education. Pondering this question eventually became a constant companion. Ultimately, this became the question that shaped my examination of individual curriculum models and my contemplation of curriculum models as a theoretical construct.

Thus, my interest in understanding the purpose and function of curriculum models, in general, and their impact on early childhood education in particular, expanded my initial intention for this book. In addition to being a contemporary survey of prominent early childhood curriculum models, it also became an investigation of the role of early childhood curriculum models within the context of current, as well as historical, issues and concerns. This investigation, in turn, revealed the extent to which, as a theoretical construct, curriculum models have influenced the early childhood profession—and the extent to which their influence might yet be felt.

■ *Probing the Concept of Curriculum Models: Why Now?*

Whereas my questions regarding the purpose, function, and impact of early childhood curriculum models could accompany me throughout the process of writing this book, the question of their relevance could not. After all, my initial intention in writing this book had been to provide a contemporary discussion and comparison of curriculum models. Once their usefulness came into question, however, I was plagued by self-doubts. Why bother to spend endless hours researching and describing various early childhood curriculum models if I was uncertain about their merit? Without an answer to this question, my commitment and enthusiasm to the arduous task of writing a textbook repeatedly waxed and waned.

But my reading and thinking about the questions I was raising for myself did not cease, and eventually, I came to better understand my concerns. I finally was able to resolve my struggle when I thought beyond curriculum models and considered these questions in terms of their relevance to current issues of curriculum development and professionalism confronting early childhood education. The irony of my intellectual saga is that this text resumed its professional importance when I finally began to think that these questions, in and of themselves, were of importance.

When I finally disentangled these concerns, I recognized more clearly that I had been struggling with questions revolving around how early childhood curriculum is determined—and by whom. I have journeyed from dissatisfaction with the content of early childhood curriculum models to deliberating their structure and then finally to recognizing that both of these concerns are part of a larger question regarding the purpose and function of curriculum models. It was when I began to consciously recognize my questions as meaningful beyond curriculum models per se that the puzzle pieces in my thoughts began to interlock.

■ *An Outline for What Follows*

Schubert (1986) defines a synoptic curriculum text as one that attempts to summarize the state of the art of curriculum studies as a guide for reflection on issues, problems, ideas, and procedures that curriculum developers should be aware of in order to inform curriculum development. He notes that any text that brings knowledge together from diverse sources also provides interpretations that lean in one direction or the other and thus provides new ways of viewing the curriculum field. "Every book is an interpretation. . . . As authors study a topic or phenomenon, they interact with it; their writing about it portrays both themselves and the phenomenon under study" (p. 3).

Following Schubert's definition, I think of this book as a synoptic text of curriculum models in early childhood education. This very personal introduction is an open acknowledgment of the interpretative framework that has informed my investigation. Its inquiry into the purpose, function, and impact of curriculum models within early childhood education distinguishes this book from the synoptic texts that have preceded it. Consequently, this text does not focus only on presenting an extensive array of curriculum models for informational purposes, nor does it attempt to provide detailed comparisons among models (see Day, 1977; DeVries & Kohlberg, 1987; Mayer, 1971 for comparative analyses).

The focus of my inquiry has been different and, to my knowledge, unique. In addition to a comprehensive, historically situated examination of a prominent set of curriculum models, this text ponders the purpose and function of curriculum models in early childhood education. It accomplishes this objective by investigating the life course of each model and, in the process, contemplates their impact, individually and collectively, on early childhood education.

Curriculum Models and Early Childhood Education: Appraising the Relationship is organized into three sections. Each chapter concludes with recommendations "For Further Reading." A textbook can only hope to highlight selected ideas and issues. The possibilities suggested for additional reading are presented to encourage readers to further study and discuss issues in more depth.

In addition to this introduction, the second chapter in this first section places early childhood curriculum models in a historical context. This overview examines the circumstances that supported the promotion and development of curriculum models in the sixties and again in the nineties. It also identifies the changed circumstances that provide a different context for their continued development and implementation.

Knowledge of this context is of more than historical interest; both past and present support for curriculum models in early childhood education stems from societal expectations for early childhood education—expectations that surface from the intersection of particular historical events. Chapter 2 shares important information for understanding the conditions that have nurtured the growth and development of curriculum models in early childhood education.

Part II, which includes Chapters 3 through 6, examines what I call enduring curriculum models: the Montessori Method (Chapter 3), the Developmental-Interaction approach (Chapter 4); and models derived from behavioral (the Direct Instruction model; Chapter 5) and Piagetian theory (the Kamii-DeVries approach and High/Scope Curriculum model; Chapter 6). These have been identified as enduring models because they have, in fact, endured into the present and have been implemented in multiple locations. Clearly, there are many other curriculum models that could have been selected, but these five models are ones well known within the early childhood profession, have remained popular choices for those who "shop" for curriculum models, and are accompanied by an extensive literature describing their educational objectives, content and structure, and assessment procedures. They also provide contrasting examples of conceptual frameworks for interpreting the character of learning and development during early childhood. These curriculum models also have endured long enough to have histories of their own. Thus, they are particularly informative examples for an exploration of the purpose, function, and impact of curriculum models in early childhood education.

Each of these five curriculum models initially was developed for preschoolers (3- and 4-, and often 5-year-olds) in out-of-home settings. With the advent of Project Follow Through, several of the curriculum models were restructured to extend into the primary grades. (See Chapter 2.) Others, specifically the Montessori Method and the Developmental-Interaction approach, already had curricula extending into the primary grades. With the exception of the Kamii-DeVries approach, each of these five curriculum models now encompasses curriculum for children preschool through third grade. Although infant and toddler programs also fit into the professional definition of early childhood education, curriculum models specific to this age group are not part of this exploration. This decision was made because infant and toddler programs necessitate investigation of very different developmental and educational issues (Bredekamp, 1987; National Association for the Education of Young Children & National Association of Early Childhood Specialists in State Departments of Education, 1991).

Because, by definition, curriculum models are conceptual frameworks, discussion and comparison rely on written materials that detail their assumptions and premises. To be as fair and accurate as possible, only books and articles written by the primary architects are used in describing individual models. For the same reasons, as well as to better convey the flavor of individual curriculum models, I rely heavily on the use of quotes. Curriculum analysis, however, draws on multiple perspectives, including my own.

Throughout the second section, curriculum models are interpreted as creating unique learning environments or cultures for learning; hence, descriptions and discussion consider not only the learning objectives of various models, but also the nature of a model in terms of socializing children to understand themselves, their environment, and others in their world in particular ways. It also is assumed that teachers are being socialized, as well, to understand children and their growth and the teaching profession in particular ways.

Presentation and discussion of each model is embedded within its particular social and historical context. This frame of reference highlights the extent to which each curriculum model is a product of its time, a finding accentuated by the fact that the extent to which a particular model is accepted, lionized, and/or rejected largely has been determined by its alignment with larger societal concerns.

The historical factor also informed the sequence in which the curriculum models are presented. The Montessori Method, described in Chapter 3, is the oldest enduring curriculum model, whereas the models derived from behavioral and Piagetian theory are among the newest. Readers are encouraged to read the chapters in the order presented; the sequence of chapters highlights the history of curriculum models in early childhood education, enables readers to better appreciate interactions among their proponents, and fosters understanding of the purpose, function, and impact of curriculum models within early childhood education. Each chapter, as it examines the life course of an individual curriculum model, brings further clarification to this overarching interest.

The book's last section moves beyond examination of individual models to investigate curriculum models in early childhood education from the perspectives of program evaluation and curriculum development. Specifically, Chapter 7 reviews findings from comparative evaluations of early childhood curriculum models and the effect these findings have had on the perpetuation of curriculum models and public polices related to early childhood education. The discussion in this chapter highlights issues that have been of particular interest to researchers, educational decision makers, and legislators regarding early childhood programs. It also raises questions regarding the capacity of curriculum models to be responsive to differences in children, teachers, and program sites.

Chapter 8 reviews, with broad strokes, some of the significant shifts in thinking that have occurred within child development theory and research since the mid-sixties. Research on and deliberations about teacher effects, which have experienced a similar upheaval, also are examined. This latter body of research is pertinent to this discussion because it challenges conventional thinking about the role of teachers in relation to curriculum development and implementation. In particular, it challenges the notion of teachers as curricular technicians, as practitioners who primarily are expected to implement the knowledge of others. New understandings about child development, reassessment regarding the relationship between child development knowledge and early childhood curriculum, and research on teacher effects are considered in terms of the challenges they elicit for early childhood curriculum models as tools of education.

The overarching question of this book—"What is the purpose, function, and impact of curriculum models in early childhood education?"—is addressed directly in Chapter 9. Understandings that emerged from investigating individual curriculum models and current thinking in program evaluation, developmental psychology, and research on teaching are summarized and examined in light of current expectations for early childhood education.

This book, however, should not be misconstrued as providing a definitive answer to the question of the usefulness or appropriateness of early childhood curriculum models—not only because such an answer would be premature, but also because such a conclusion would be contrary to the intention of this book. Curriculum models have potential for instigating both positive and negative consequences, for children as well as the early childhood profession. And, as I hope readers will anticipate, this ambiguity derives from contemporary characteristics of early childhood education and their intersection with current societal needs and expectations.

This book has been written for graduate students, teachers and teacher educators, and instructional leaders and administrators. It is especially relevant for readers who are interested in analyzing early childhood curriculum within the confines of curriculum models and in contemplating the educational and professional implications of bounding curriculum in this way. I realize, of course, that at the level of graduate study, many readers may, in fact, belong to more than one of these categories.

Writing this book has provoked me to think very deeply about issues of early childhood curriculum. My experience also represents a living example of learning as a developmental process; I hope my journey provides similar stimulus for thoughtful and provocative discussion by others.

■ ■ ■ ■ ■ ■

Chapter 2

Curriculum Models and Early Childhood Education

A Historical Framework

■ ■ ■ ■ ■ ■

The intensity of interest in early childhood education since the mid-1980s recalls the explosion of interest during the 1960s that launched Head Start, a national program for disadvantaged preschoolers. Once again, expansion of early childhood education is being driven by changing social, political, and economic circumstances and faith in its capacity to effect change. Once again, early childhood education is being promoted as a solution for many of society's social and economic problems. And, once again, there is a resurgence of interest in finding—and defining—the most effective early childhood programs for achieving these ends.

Powell (1987a) attributes renewed interest in early childhood curricular issues to three factors: (1) questions being raised about the education of 4-year-olds in public schools; (2) the successful efforts of national professional associations in promoting appropriate educational practices for young children; and (3) reports describing results of longitudinal research that challenge earlier conclusions that differences among curriculum models were nonexistent. According to Powell, "The question of *which curriculum* to use in educating young children has regained its prominence in public and professional interest in early schooling" (p. 192, emphasis added).

■ Early Childhood Programs and Public Policy

The coupling of social and political concerns with interest in early childhood education, in the sixties and again in the nineties, reveals the vital connection between early childhood issues and public policy. Connections between social and political concerns and children's issues have existed throughout the history of governmental policies benefiting children (Pizzo, 1983). But, analysis of this relationship has increased significantly since President Johnson's initiation of "The Great Society," a time during which the federal government issued a series of policies designed to help eradicate poverty and social inequality (see, for example, Grubb & Lazerson, 1988; Steiner, 1981; Zigler, Kagan, & Klugman, 1983).

Policies made by the federal government, in state capitals, and in city halls may seem far removed from the lives of children and early childhood educators. The problems decision makers confront, however, are the problems children and early educators are living, and the solutions they devise become the programs and practices early educators are asked to implement on behalf of children and families (Goffin & Lombardi, 1988).

Public policies are governmental solutions to societal concerns. Consequently, they are part of the broad, cultural context influencing children's development (Bronfenbrenner & Weiss, 1983). Public policies help define the social and economic circumstances that determine the range of choices parents, early childhood educators, and others can make on behalf of children.

Low-income parents' options for their children's early education, for example, are expanded because of the existence of Head Start, a federally supported early education program for disadvantaged preschoolers. Yet, access to Head Start is restricted because insufficient federal appropriation limits enrollment to fewer than 30% of eligible children (Children's Defense Fund, 1991).

In addition, the absence of national standards for child care quality engenders a wide range of health and safety regulations across the states, which, in turn, affects the nature of children's daily experiences, the range of choices available to parents, and the working conditions of child care teachers. And the absence of sufficient and stable financial support for early childhood programs influences the overall quality and stability of early childhood education.

Historically, government involvement in children's issues has been crisis oriented, available only for specific, narrowly defined problems and targeted groups of individuals (Goffin, 1983). The onset of early intervention programs, which provided the impetus for curriculum model development in the 1960s, was prompted by such a crisis. The crisis was America's "discovery" of rampant poverty; the problem was disadvantaged children's lack of school success. Low-income preschoolers and their families were the targeted population. Preschool education was the proposed solution. Based on psychological premises regarding environmental impact and the concept of critical periods (which justified targeting early childhood), preschool programs were supposed to ameliorate the effects of disadvantaged circumstances, thus enabling poor preschoolers to enter schooling as well prepared as their middle-class counterparts.

Changing social circumstances have again provided a rationale for advocating government policies on behalf of children and families. Concerns about growing numbers of impoverished children who are at-risk for school failure, increasing numbers of teenage parents and employed mothers requiring child care for their children, and the competitive capabilities of our country's future labor force have coalesced to generate a new sense of national urgency. Public policy initiatives emerging in response to these concerns repeatedly propose early childhood programs as vehicles for addressing these issues.

The current focus on early childhood education as a means for resolving these new social concerns is augmented by successful early intervention programs initiated during the sixties, including Head Start, and longitudinal findings from experimental curriculum models (Kagan, 1987). These same successes also have positioned early childhood programs as a critical component of educational reform efforts (Committee for Economic Development, 1987; U.S. Department of Education, 1991).

These larger issues swirling around early childhood programs are pertinent because they affect public interest and support (including financial resources) for early childhood education. They also help shape public expectations (which are often different from those held by professionals) regarding what early childhood programs should achieve. Bettye Caldwell, a prominent early childhood researcher and advocate, succinctly states an opinion held by many: "It has consistently been economic and social needs that provided the force to move the field forward. This is just as true today as it was 200 years ago" (1989, p. x).

In contrast to the 1960s, however, focused attention on early childhood education and curriculum models now comes primarily from the state, rather than federal, level. At least half the states currently fund prekindergarten programs. According to Mitchell, Seligson, and Marx's (1989) study of early childhood programs provided by public schools, recent public school interest in early childhood education originates from state involvement with the school reform movement. The primary motivation for this interest, however, is reminiscent of that generated during the 1960s: concern for children's school readiness and a search for the curriculum that will best prepare children for school success. Furthermore, this focus has been intensified by national attention directed toward The National Governors' Association and former President Bush's number one educational goal: "that by the year 2000 every child should enter school ready to learn"[1] (U.S. Department of Education, 1991). Significantly, this interest is still—for the most part—based on the assumption that children need to be readied for schooling, and that children, rather than schools, are at-risk for success.

Since the 1960s, there have also been changes in societal conditions and the character of early childhood education. Understandings of child development and curriculum have also undergone significant change, and these changes have ramifications for content analysis of early childhood curriculum models.

More than 25 years have now passed since curriculum models were a focal point in early childhood education discourse and practice. Although no longer a central issue in the field, the idea of curriculum models has been woven securely into the

---

[1]   Then-governor Clinton chaired this task force of the National Governors' Association, and this educational goal has remained an educational priority with his presidential administration.

fabric of early childhood education. A central question of this text is: Should their return to a prominent position in deliberations of early childhood curriculum, as forecast by Powell (1987a), be encouraged? The investigation of this question begins by exploring the circumstances that supported the creation and dramatic growth of curriculum models during the late 1960s and early 1970s.

■ An American History of Curriculum Models in Early Childhood Education

The Early Childhood Context

Prior to the onset of early intervention programs beginning in the late 1950s, *systematic* variation in early childhood programs was minimal. Differences that did exist were primarily a result of differences among sponsoring agencies rather than curriculum distinctions generated by different goals and theoretical orientations (Spodek, 1973; White & Buka, 1987).

This had not always been the case, however. The early history of early childhood education was dominated by the growth of kindergartens that were primarily informed by the work of Friedrich Froebel, who opened his early childhood program in Germany in 1837 and is credited with the creation of kindergarten education. But, at the turn of the century, some early childhood educators began to question Froebel's philosophy and practice, initiating an intensive, 10-year public debate (1903–1913) within the International Kindergarten Union between those, such as Susan Blow and Elizabeth Peabody (prominent leaders of kindergarten education in the United States), who argued the continued validity of Froebelian tenets and educators who contended his curriculum was too structured, rigid, and unscientific (see Weber, 1969, for a description of this debate).

Eventually, the ideas put forth by progressive early childhood educators, such as Patty Smith Hill, a colleague of philosopher John Dewey and learning theorist Edward Thorndike, won the day. The culmination of their deliberations was reported in *The Kindergarten* (Committee of Nineteen, 1913). To a large extent, the early childhood curriculum that emerged from this debate dominated early childhood practice (with the exception of day nurseries/child care; see pp. 16–18) until the 1960s.

Current interest in early childhood curriculum models surfaces some of the same issues/questions confronted by the Committee of Nineteen in their deliberations. Do curriculum models need to remain faithful forevermore to their original tenets? Should they? Must curriculum models remain self-contained or can they accommodate to changing educational understandings and expectations? If curriculum models are responsive to changing conceptualizations of children and education, can they still legitimately be defined as curriculum models?

According to Froebel's proponents, the answer to these questions was "no." According to his advocates, Froebel had designed the ideal play materials for young children. "True, these leaders recognized that in the hands of some kindergartners[2] Froebel's program had become excessively formal, but the cure for these adverse tendencies was to be found in a greater understanding of the spirit and philosophy behind Froebel's educational principles. Deviation from Froebel's program was not to be countenanced" (Weber, 1969, pp. vii–viii).

A closer examination of the term *model* supports their conclusion. By definition, models are "a standard or example for imitation or comparison, a representation to show the structure or serve as a copy of something" (The Random House College Dictionary, 1988, p. 857). The term *curriculum model* refers to a conceptual framework for decision making about educational priorities, administrative policies, instructional methods, and evaluation criteria (Evans, 1982). Curriculum models identify the essential, idealized elements of a program and serve as a referent or standard from which to judge the extent to which a program, as implemented, approximates the ideal (Spodek, 1973). They organize philosophies and/or theories of child development and learning into templates for educational programs.

According to Evans (1982),

> A curriculum model provides an ideal representation of the essential philosophical, administrative, and pedagogical components of a grand education plan. It constitutes a coherent, internally consistent description of the theoretical premises, administrative policies and instructional procedures presumed valid for achieving preferential education outcomes. (p. 107)

Thus, any investigation of the effect of curriculum models must contemplate the consequences of relying on a template (regardless of how elastic) for determining curriculum and teacher-child, child-child interactions.

In early childhood education, theories of child development have served as the dominant foundation for curriculum model development (Day, 1977; Silin, 1987, 1988; Spodek, 1988; Weber, 1984; White & Buka, 1987). Early childhood curriculum, especially in programs implemented outside the public schools, has been largely informed by the belief that early childhood education should be directly derived from child development research and theory (Caldwell, 1984; Elkind, 1989; Weber, 1969; White & Buka, 1987). Chapter titles in Part II of this book reflect the acceptance accorded this belief in curriculum model development.

Variations among curriculum models reflect differences in value commitments concerning what is more or less important for young children to learn as well as the process by which children learn and develop, even though these value commitments frequently are not made explicit. Curriculum models in early childhood education also have varied in terms of the flexibility they grant teachers for interpreting the cur-

---

2   "Kindergartner" was a term applied to kindergarten teachers and those training kindergarten teachers.

riculum's conceptual template. But, according to Mayer (1971), regardless of these variations,

> All curriculum models have been conceived so as to yield interactions among teachers, children, and materials in a way that is believed to facilitate the objectives of the design . . . the type of interaction(s) stressed by a program are logically related to the high priority objectives of that program and to theoretical notions about how children learn best what the program considers most important. (p. 291)

Curriculum models also attempt to foster a conviction that one approach is better than an alternative view (Nuthall & Snook, 1973). This conviction is reinforced by definition of a curriculum model as an *ideal representation.* Comparing models in terms of their effectiveness in achieving *similar* outcomes provides the competitive aspect of curriculum model development (Evans, 1982).

The models approach to developing early childhood curriculum became prevalent during the 1960s with the advent of early intervention programs, including the initiation of Head Start, and the infusion of federal funds into their research and development (Clarke-Stewart & Fein, 1983; Evans, 1975; Osborn, 1980; Powell, 1987a). Consequently, the history of early childhood curriculum models is tightly interwoven with the history of early intervention programs, especially Head Start and Project Follow Through.

The Emergence of Systematic Variation

Prior to the onset of Head Start in 1965 (a national, federally funded preschool program for children considered at-risk for school failure), early childhood education was characterized by its three discrete branches: kindergartens; day nurseries (now called child care); and nursery schools.

Kindergartens were viewed as children's first experience with formal education. Although kindergarten history, especially since the mid-1920s, has responded to changing conceptualizations of school readiness, prior to the onset of Head Start, kindergartens were primarily oriented toward nurturing positive social-emotional development (Spodek, 1986). This focus reflected not only a programmatic emphasis, but also the prevailing consensus that intellectual development was not amenable to environmental influence. Even though most public schools did not offer kindergartens, they were considered an extension of public school education (Day, 1983).

Day nurseries and nursery schools served preschoolers. Day nurseries (some of which served children younger than 2 years) began their history in the United States in the late 1800s and were full-day programs for children whose mothers were employed outside the home. Although their purpose underwent several changes during their early history, day nurseries provided primarily custodial care and were created in response to the necessity of maternal employment. By the early 1930s, due to less positive societal attitudes toward maternal employment, only mothers who *had* to work were employed. As a result, day nurseries were developed primarily to serve lower income groups and were influenced primarily by the social work, rather than education, profession (Cahan, 1989).

In contrast, nursery schools, which began to flourish in this country at the start of the 1920s, were half-day programs, mostly attended by children from affluent families, and designed primarily to provide child-rearing advice and social-emotional enrichment to a child's home life. The expertise surrounding nursery schools came largely from university-based child development researchers (Cahan, 1989). "Nursery schools were established for educational experimentation, for demonstration of methodology, or for purposes of research, but not for the relief of working mothers or neglected children" (National Association for the Education of Young Children [NAEYC] Organizational History and Archives Committee, 1976, p. 463). According to Abigail Eliot, a pioneer in the development of nursery schools, the major difference between nursery schools and day nurseries, aside from parental choice versus parental necessity, was program. "In the new nursery school, the children were active . . . alive . . . choosing . . . gay, busy, happy. *That* was the difference" (Hymes, 1978, p. 16).

These various characteristics made nursery schools most popular among child psychologists, educators, and affluent families (Cahan, 1989). Nursery schools, consequently, remained limited in scope and influence, because they were primarily of interest to the middle class and supported by private funds, unless included as part of university curricula (Biber, 1979a).

Kindergartens, day nurseries, and nursery schools, therefore, each lived individual histories prior to the 1960s, served different populations of children, and developed distinctive purposes. Their curricular focus, although primarily centered on social and emotional nurturance (a focus reinforced as the ideas of Freudian psychology were assimilated into early childhood practice), ranged from custodial to enrichment to school readiness.

These programmatic distinctions co-existed when Head Start exploded on the scene in 1965. It might be argued that the absence of a coherent view of early childhood education was a critical and necessary contextual factor that supported the emergence of early childhood curriculum models. The conceptual stratification that existed within the field insinuated that no curriculum existed for half-day "educational" programs for economically disadvantaged preschoolers. Hence, it was a niche easily perceived as wide open for educational experimentation. In contrast, it had taken three decades (1890–1920) of passionate debate for progressive educators to topple Froebel's dominance of kindergarten education (see Weber, 1969). If curriculum models had entered a setting where broad agreement regarding acceptable early childhood goals and practices pre-existed, the proliferation of new models of preschool education might have met greater resistance.

Furthermore, in the sixties, unlike the early twentieth century, there was no single arena or organization for debating the issues and developing new consensus. In contrast to the unifying role played by the International Kindergarten Union, which had been organized in 1892, the early childhood leadership in the sixties was divided among the National Association for the Education of Young Children (NAEYC, which was only reorganized as such in 1964; until then, it had been the National

Association for Nursery Education or NANE, which officially organized in 1929), the Association for Childhood Education International (ACEI, which was an outgrowth of the International Kindergarten Union), and a former department from within the National Education Association (NEA) (Weber, 1969).

The curriculum upheaval in early childhood education during the early twentieth century restructured early childhood curriculum and practice and set the direction of the field for most of the next 50 years. In contrast to the professional consensus forged by the Committee of Nineteen, the curriculum upheaval of the sixties left the field fragmented and without a mandate regarding appropriate curriculum and practice for young children.

The Political Setting

Head Start and other early intervention programs were created as centerpieces for the War on Poverty. As part of the nation's belief in its ability to eradicate poverty and minimize social inequality, early childhood programs became vehicles for helping young children gain needed skills and understandings that would enable them to take better advantage of the public school system, and thus escape poverty. The first summer of the program, 652,000 children participated in 2,500 centers employing 41,000 teachers (when first initiated in 1965, Head Start was organized as a 6-week summer program) (Osborn, 1980, p. 149). Head Start and related early intervention programs dramatically increased the number of preschoolers who experienced early childhood education (both in reference to overall numbers and program [educational versus custodial] focus). This summary of events, however, fails to convey the intense sense of purpose, optimism, and excitement that this initiative generated.

Faith in the ability of early childhood programs to achieve such dramatic outcomes was based on two critical and interrelated assumptions regarding the significance of early childhood and its contribution to later development: (1) that the first 5 years of life were a critical period in a child's development and (2) that the character of children's early experiences was predictive of their later capabilities. An underlying presumption accompanying these beliefs was that the experiences of children from low-income families were "inadequate" experiences and that providing enrichment could compensate for their disadvantaged home environments (Evans, 1975; Horowitz & Paden, 1973; Zigler & Anderson, 1979). Hence, early childhood programs developed for this purpose were frequently labeled compensatory education.

A major premise underlying program interventions is the intent to bring recipients closer to "normal" functioning. In this instance, the expectation of normality usually referred to social and academic behaviors consistent with middle-class norms (Horowitz & Paden, 1973; Sigel, 1990). Thus, it seemed logical to target the solution for eradicating future poverty toward its youngest victims. It was also politically acceptable. "In an effort to eradicate poverty while preserving the structure of the American economic system, economic deprivation was construed as cultural deprivation. The early experience paradigm was embraced by policy makers" (Ramey, Bryant, & Suarez, 1985, p. 248).

The significance of political acceptance should not be underestimated. As part of the War on Poverty, Head Start was initially viewed not only as a program of educational intervention, but also as a catalyst to help poor people become more actively involved in advocating for their own needs. Based on this reasoning, Head Start was originally housed in the Office of Economic Opportunity and was viewed as a community action program. In *The Devil Has Slippery Shoes* (1969/1990b), Polly Greenberg vividly describes the dramatic political reaction when the first Head Start program in Mississippi acted more like a community action program than a straightforward program for early education. White and Buka (1987) even suggest that Head Start's eventual treatment by the federal government as primarily an educational program (what they called a "tacit political simplification of the program," p. 74) might have been what saved it from the terminal fate accorded other poverty programs.

The Influence of Shifting Psychological Insights

Conclusions regarding the critical nature of children's early lives were informed, in part, by Hunt's (1961) and Bloom's (1964) extensive analyses of existing empirical evidence concerning the contributing role of environment (versus heredity) in stimulating mental development. Especially pertinent to the onset of early intervention programs was their argument that intellectual development was particularly receptive to environmental stimulation during early childhood. According to Zigler and Anderson (1979), Bloom's (1964) conclusion that the first 5 years of life were a critical period of intellectual growth quickly became "gospel among the popular press" (p. 7).

The notion that human intelligence could be modified was a new idea in the 1960s (White & Buka, 1987). Hunt's and Bloom's conclusions were repeatedly cited in support of early childhood intervention programs; their work was used as scientific justification for the federal government's support of Head Start (White & Buka, 1987). Departure from the long-standing belief that intelligence was totally determined by one's heredity helped generate optimistic anticipation for the possibilities environmental intervention might trigger. It also set the stage for a re-examination of existent early childhood curriculum.

This "marshalling of scientific data" (Evans, 1975, p. 2) and popular support helped legitimize public attention to early childhood education. A focus on classrooms was assisted by the 1954 desegregation ruling, *Brown v. The Board of Education of Topeka,* which directed attention toward low-income, black children (Gray, Ramsey, & Klaus, 1982) and the launching of Sputnik in 1957, which fostered a national self-consciousness about falling behind in the "race to conquer the frontiers of space. . . . Almost overnight, a curriculum revolution penetrated all levels of American schooling" (Weinberg, 1979, p. 912).

Research on the effects of educational programs for young children became a vehicle for examining the plasticity of intellectual development. In fact, the possibilities of environmental intervention already were being explored by a small number of experimental early intervention programs that had been initiated 5 to 10 years earlier, in the mid- to late fifties. (These research-oriented programs were to assume critical importance during the mid-seventies when the existence of Head Start became jeopardized; see page 26 and Chapter 7.) But the advent of Head Start propelled this exploration to a national, and highly public, scale.

Developmental psychologists were interested in exploring the limits of Hunt's and Bloom's findings (Clarke-Stewart & Fein, 1983; Day, 1983). This interest was intensified by Skeels's (1966) timely publication of the longitudinal findings from his early intervention study, which had been initiated in the late 1930s (Gray, Ramsey, & Klaus, 1982; Horowitz & Paden, 1973). Skeels and his colleagues had transferred a small group of children, all of whom were judged to be mentally retarded, from an orphanage to an institution for the mentally retarded, where the children were cared for by residents and staff. In contrast to the relative neglect these children had experienced in the orphanage, they now were the recipients of extensive affection and stimulation. Skeels's first follow-up study, about $2\frac{1}{2}$ years following the end of the experimental period, found significant gains in children's IQ (Skeels & Dye, 1939). These initial findings, however, were largely ignored, in part because of the strength of existing belief in the immutability of IQ (Gray, Ramsey, & Klaus, 1982; Zigler & Anderson, 1979).

Reconnecting with his subjects 20 years later, Skeels (1966) found that as adults, all 13 children from the experimental group were self-supporting and independent. In contrast, members of the comparison group, who had remained in the orphanage, had a median education of less than third grade and were institutionalized, unemployed, or employed at menial jobs.

The research of Skeels and his colleagues demonstrated that a group of initially retarded infants, when provided an enriched environment, could function at normal levels as adults. Horowitz and Paden (1973) point out that, in contrast, the maturational approach of Gesell, which represented prevailing beliefs, recommended that retardation was best diagnosed during infancy, at which point parents should be helped to understand that their child would never be normal. Gray, Ramsey, and Klaus (1982), whose Early Training Project, initiated in 1959, was one of the first formal early intervention programs, described the impact of Skeels's 1966 monograph as "electric" (p. 9). Its timing was certainly fortuitous.

Within this context of changing ideas regarding environmental impact and intellectual plasticity, Head Start and related early intervention programs provided developmental and educational psychologists the opportunity to discover whether early childhood was, in fact, a critical period for intellectual development and whether early childhood programs could compensate for disadvantaged environments (Clarke-Stewart, 1988).

The dominant involvement of developmental psychologists, rather than early childhood educators, in creating these new early childhood programs perhaps can be explained, at least partially, by the historical relationship between nursery schools and developmental psychology. During the 1920s and 1930s, the Laura Spelman Rockefeller Memorial Foundation awarded significant sums of money to establish child study institutes at several universities and colleges. Nursery schools were an integral part of these institutes, providing an enrichment program for preschoolers and a site for research on child development for developmental psychologists (Cahan, 1989; Hymes, 1978; White & Buka, 1987).

Another important mission of these institutes was to translate child development research for use in parent education. "The institutes would study children, maintain exemplary forms of preschool education, and serve as a vehicle for the transmission of the fruits of such study to parents" (Siegel & White, 1982, p. 276).

Consequently, when national concern with the ravages of poverty focused on early childhood, many developmental psychologists simply shifted their interests. They needed merely to switch their research focus from middle- and upper-income children in preschool settings to children from low-income families.[3] Significantly, however, their involvement during the era of curriculum models extended beyond child development research to include curriculum development.

The social agenda of the early sixties, in conjunction with new ideas about the environment's impact on intellectual growth, provided motivation for such a change in focus and attracted the interest of educational, as well as developmental, psychologists (Lavatelli, 1971). The diversity of experimental curricula devised by these psychologists reflected the intense theoretical debates occurring within the field of psychology. These debates, in turn, became the source of controversy within early childhood education regarding appropriate early childhood curriculum. As the thinking of developmental and educational psychologists came to dominate early childhood curriculum development, many nursery educators questioned why their substantial knowledge regarding early childhood education was largely ignored (Biber, 1977; Biber & Franklin, 1967; Dowley, 1971; Greenberg, 1987; White & Buka, 1987). The dynamics behind their question were especially important to the evolution of Bank Street's Developmental-Interaction approach (see Chapter 4), whose curriculum represented nursery school practice.

Development of Curriculum Models

With the advent of Head Start in 1965, the benefits of nursery education were no longer confined to middle-class preschoolers. As a result, the population of children that had been separately served by different streams of early childhood education began to merge. The prevailing wisdom of established nursery school programs, especially as communicated by the Bank Street College of Education, was designated the official Head Start orientation toward preschool education. The notion of curriculum models would not emerge for yet another 2 years.

Basic assumptions of the prevailing child development approach included responsibility for developing the "whole child" and creating an environment conducive to exploring, manipulating, constructing, thinking, symbolizing, and talking

---

[3] Additional evidence for this conclusion comes from George Stoddard's opinion that the National Association for Nursery Education (NANE, the forerunner of NAEYC) helped unite the efforts of the new child study centers "on behalf of this great movement to secure a better educational environment and a better educational experience" (p. 465, as cited in NAEYC Organizational History and Archives Committee, 1976; Stoddard was NANE president from 1931–1933).

(Biber, 1979a). According to Biber (1979a), a major figure in American nursery education and primary architect of the Developmental-Interaction approach, "Those of us who crossed the lines between private preschool education and day-care programs in our professional lives welcomed Head Start as a fulfilled wish—the chance to provide the best for the children who need it most" (p. 155). Eventually, this initial approach toward providing compensatory education came to be labeled the "traditional model" (Miller, 1979).[4]

The development of new curriculum approaches for early childhood programs was fueled by an evolving consensus, most often promulgated by psychologists, that a "traditional" middle-class nursery school curriculum could not effectively help children from low-income families to develop needed competencies (Miller, 1979; Powell, 1987a). Especially being challenged was the nursery school emphasis on social-emotional development. Both the new belief in intellectual malleability and the programmatic emphasis on school readiness propelled psychologists to refocus early childhood curriculum on cognitive and academic development. According to Day (1983), psychologists "had an important influence on early education because they dared to suggest that children under the age of six should have special academic training" (p. 61).

So, with support from federal and private agencies during the late sixties and early seventies, psychologists and others created a wide variety of experimental preschool programs. A survey commissioned for the Office of Child Development in 1972 reviewed approximately 40 preschool models and another 200 in various stages of development, the majority of which were used in Head Start programs (Miller, 1979).

New programs were constructed primarily from theories of learning and development. Reflecting the lack of consensus within psychological theory, differing and often opposing theoretical interpretations of child learning and development became the basis for program development. Researchers hoped to discover which types of programs would best encourage cognitive development (Clarke-Stewart, 1988; Miller, 1979; Powell, 1987a). Implicit in this focus was the belief that school readiness was primarily a cognitive undertaking. Early childhood curriculum models varied around this cognitive focus. In order to remain competitive, more traditional preschool programs drew on new theoretical ideas, such as those of Jean Piaget, to support the value of play and creative endeavors for cognitive development. They also began to search for ways to use play more explicitly for developing cognitive concepts (Lavatelli, 1971).

When Project Follow Through was established in 1967, the search for the curriculum best able to advance cognitive and academic development became directly associated with specific curriculum models. Project Follow Through, a federally

---

4   Biber's (1984) reaction to this label is worth noting. "We could not imagine that what to us was a steady course of experimentation directed toward basic change in the philosophy of early education would come to be designated as 'traditional.' The ideological fundamentals that we assumed would gradually gain general acceptance came upon hard times in the 1960s when a narrow scholasticism dominated experimental programs in search of single-trace solutions to the pervasive damage of poverty in early childhood" (p. 25).

sponsored educational project, was designed for children in kindergarten through grade three in hopes of extending the anticipated benefits of Head Start.

The Westinghouse Ohio study, an early follow-up study of children enrolled in Head Start programs, found that initial gains in children's school achievement began fading after children's entry into public schools (Cicirelli, 1969). Based on the possibility that schools were at fault for the erosion of children's gains, Follow Through was instituted as a vertical expansion of Head Start into kindergarten and the primary grades (Bissell, 1973).

At the same time, the federal government wanted to evaluate the effectiveness of these programs to determine which approaches to early childhood education were most beneficial. To help respond to this question, Project Follow Through was organized as a study of planned variation.

The program was administered by the U.S. Office of Education (USOE), even though project funds were provided in the legislation for the War on Poverty through the Office of Economic Opportunity. Local communities were invited to design, carry out, and evaluate various approaches to early education (kindergarten through third grade) in hopes of learning which approaches would work best (Hodges et al., 1980; Rivlin & Timpane, 1975). In order to compare their effectiveness, Follow Through was implemented using 13 different curriculum models at 80 different school sites across the country. Models of early childhood education were chosen by USOE and the developers of those models became Follow Through model sponsors. The majority of the models were sponsored by universities and educational laboratories. By 1971, 22 models were operational in 173 local projects. At Project Follow Through's peak in the early 1970s, 84,000 children and their parents were being served in 4,000 classrooms in every state of the nation. As of 1980, there were 19 model sponsors; the number of local projects per sponsor ranged from 1 to 19 (Hodges et al., 1980). (See Table 2–1.)

Shortly thereafter, a similar research effort was launched within Head Start involving 12 curriculum models (Rivlin & Timpane, 1975). (See Table 2–2.) According to Miller (1979), a prominent researcher involved in evaluating the differential effectiveness of curriculum models, experimental programs varied in their assumptions about education, interpretations of the developmental process, and beliefs about the effects of culture, especially poverty, on a child's cognitive development. Curriculum models ranged in focus from didactic, drill-oriented programs of instruction in school-specific content to programs emphasizing child discovery and enrichment. Model development was heavily influenced by a developer's beliefs regarding poverty's impact on cognitive development and the type of environment that would ameliorate its effects.

The growth and evaluation of early childhood curriculum models, therefore, accompanied the federal government's investment in Head Start. Head Start was, and continues to be, one of the federal government's most significant, continuous, and direct investments in early childhood education. In the late 1960s, the federal government's support of various curriculum models was, in part, a search for the best way to structure its investment. It was assumed there would, in fact, be one best approach. According to Weikart (1983), the primary architect of the High/Scope

Table 2–1
Participating Models: Project Follow Through

1. Bank Street College of Education Model, Bank Street College, New York
2. Behavior Analysis Model, University of Kansas, Lawrence
3. Bilingual/Bicultural Model, Southwest Educational Development Laboratory, Austin, TX
4. High/Scope Cognitively Oriented Curriculum Model, High/Scope Educational Research Foundation, Ypsilanti, MI
5. Cultural Linguistic Approach, Northeastern Illinois University, Chicago
6. Culturally Democratic Learning Environmental Model, University of California at Santa Cruz, Santa Cruz
7. Direct Instruction Model, University of Oregon, Eugene
8. EDC Open Education Program, Educational Development Center, Newton, MA
9. Florida Parent Education Model, University of Florida, Gainesville
10. Home-School Partnership Model, Clark College, Atlanta
11. Individualized Early Learning Program, University of Pittsburgh, Pittsburgh
12. Interdependent Learning Model, Fordham University, Bronx, NY
13. Mathemagenic Activities Program, University of Georgia, Athens
14. New School Approach, University of North Dakota, Grand Forks
15. Nongraded Model, Hampton Institute, Hampton, VA
16. Parent Supported Diagnostic Model, Georgia State University, Atlanta
17. Prentice Hall Personalized Learning Model, Prentice Hall Developmental Learning Centers, Inc., West Paterson, NJ
18. Responsive Education Program, Far West Laboratory, San Francisco
19. Tucson Early Education Model, University of Arizona, Tucson

Curriculum model and a participant in both Project Follow Through and Head Start Planned Variation, the quest for a superior curriculum was consistent with the American search for "best" solutions. It was also consistent with American beliefs that science could provide the means for improving society.

Given the high stakes involved, this competitive environment spawned not only innovation but also discord. Controversy between programs that emphasized children's social-emotional development and those programs that prepared more structured learning environments focused on advancing cognitive development was especially intense (Osborn, 1980; see, for example, Biber, 1969, 1979b; Moore, 1977). In assessing the impact on the profession, Butler (1976) lamented, "On the one hand, the effect on the field has been positive inasmuch as new programs have been created and rethinking of all programs has been stimulated; however, the lack of agreement among professionals has created a certain amount of divisiveness when unity of purpose might be a definite asset" (p. 6).

Table 2–2
Participating Models: Head Start Planned Variation

1. Bank Street College of Education Approach, Bank Street College, New York
2. Behavior Analysis Model, University of Kansas, Lawrence
3. EDC Open Education Program, Educational Development Center, Newton, MA
4. The Enabler Model, U.S. Office of Human Development, Office of Child Development
5. Englemann-Becker Model, University of Oregon, Eugene
6. Florida Parent Education Model, University of Florida, Gainesville
7. High/Scope Cognitively Oriented Model, High/Scope Educational Research Foundation, Ypsilanti, MI
8. Individualized Early Learning Program, University of Pittsburgh, Pittsburgh
9. Interdependent Learning Model, Fordham University, Bronx, NY
10. Responsive Educational Program, Far West Laboratory, San Francisco
11. Responsive Environments Corporation Early Childhood Model, Englewood Cliffs, NJ
12. Tucson Early Education Model, University of Arizona, Tucson

The Ending of an Era

Intense interest in developing and comparing diverse curriculum models for preschool and primary education continued for approximately a decade. Interest declined during the late 1970s and early 1980s, and attention shifted to other early childhood issues. The disappointing findings of the Westinghouse Ohio study on the effects of Head Start helped shift debate from a question of which type program was most effective to whether early childhood education programs were beneficial for economically disadvantaged children. Failure to find significant differences in program effects for children who participated in distinctive programs, the difficulty in designing and implementing large-scale comparison studies, and the decline in federal support for such efforts also contributed to the decreased investigation of early childhood curriculum models. Finally, dramatic increases in maternal employment and numbers of children in child care, which still bore its custodial, welfare label and value-laden association with maternal employment, shifted concern toward study of the impact of full-day care (Clarke-Stewart, 1988; Clarke-Stewart & Fein, 1983; Powell, 1987a).

Perhaps because child care was associated with a different purpose and still carried its custodial label, curriculum models, with their educational emphasis and linkage with federally financed programs, were having little if any impact on this fastest growing segment of early childhood education. Rather, as more and more middle-class women entered the work force and child care programs emerged in response to the demand, the first wave of child care research, reflective of child care's distinctive history, focused not on its educative value but on whether or not child care was harmful to children's development, especially in the emotional realm (Belsky, 1984; Clarke-Stewart, 1987a).

Yet, even as interest was shifting away from curriculum models, a group of investigators who had implemented some of the first experimental early intervention programs were tracking down and assessing the school success of their original participants, who were by then in upper elementary grades and high school. Their endeavor represented a collaborative attempt to justify public faith—and public investment—in the power of early intervention. The results of their efforts, collectively and individually (which began to be published in the late seventies and continued to be reported throughout the first half of the eighties), demonstrated positive effects for children who experienced early childhood education (Berrueta-Clement, Schweinhart, Barnett, Epstein, & Weikart, 1984; Consortium for Longitudinal Studies, 1983; Gray, Ramsey, & Klaus, 1982). These findings (which are reviewed in Chapter 7) restored public optimism, rejuvenated public support for early childhood education, and generated renewed interest in early childhood curriculum models.

The following quote, taken from a chapter written by Spodek and Walberg in 1977, seems to capture the emotional roller coaster that must have been experienced by those who shared in the excitement of the sixties and the letdown of the seventies:

> The mid-1960s and just beyond seemed to represent an era of plenty in the field of early childhood education. It was characterized by unparalleled activity. Programs were provided for children not served in the past. New curriculum models were developed and evaluated. There was research relating to the characteristics of early childhood and to the impact of environmental variables on achievement and development based on naive notions concerning the power of early childhood experience and the ability of educational programs to right social wrongs. The range of goals ascribed to the programs was broader than the goals conceived earlier.
>
> The era of abundance seems to have ended, and we face the years of scarcity. Resources that sustained earlier activities have evaporated. Service programs still in operation have been cut back by the effects of inflation. There seems to be an absence of support for the type of research and development activities that characterized the earlier period, and the optimism of that period seems also to have waned. (pp. 1–2)

Spodek and Walberg's words highlight as well the fact that development of curriculum models occurred during a unique time in the histories of the United States and early childhood education. Their development was bolstered by considerable financial support and a sense of larger purpose.

The context that nourished early intervention programs, in general, and the development of curriculum models in particular, is important to understanding their impact. Gray, Ramsey, & Klaus (1982) and Woodhead (1988) caution that the effects of early intervention programs during the 1960s, including well-researched curriculum models, should not be solely attributed to the benefits of early childhood education. They attribute much of the success of early intervention programs to the hopeful, optimistic times of which they were a part; they even question whether similar results could be achieved in a different era.

■ *Contemporary Backdrop for Early Childhood Curriculum Models*

As findings regarding the long-term effects of early intervention became available to educators and policy makers, interest in early childhood education and curriculum models re-emerged. Renewed interest can be attributed not only to the positive findings produced by longitudinal research of early childhood programs, but also to studies renewing the debate regarding the differential effectiveness of curriculum models (for example, DeVries & Goncu, 1987; DeVries, Haney, & Zan, 1991; DeVries, Reese-Learned, & Morgan, 1991; Schweinhart, Weikart, & Larner, 1986; see Chapter 7), and the focus on early childhood education in educational reform efforts (Mitchell, Seligson, & Marx, 1989; United States Department of Education, 1991; Warger, 1988).

The interaction of these three factors appears to be sustaining the competitive relationship among proponents of different early childhood curriculum models. The search by public schools for the most effective curriculum for their early intervention programs has spawned a lucrative market for early childhood curriculums and aggressive claims regarding their effectiveness. In addition, focus on early childhood programs within public school settings has reframed the debate between social-emotional and cognitive programs to one between developmental versus academic curricula. The controversy originally debated between preschool educators and psychologists has been extended to include heated discussions between early childhood and elementary educators, with kindergarten curriculum frequently the field of battle. Thus, the curriculum debates that proliferated during the era of curriculum models have endured.

Although educators and policy makers have renewed their search for the most effective ways to prepare young children for school success, researchers assessing different approaches to early childhood education have determined that they need to go beyond global questions that ask, "What works best?" Their research is now more likely to question how early childhood programs might be tailored to maximize the learning potential of children with differing characteristics (Clarke-Stewart, 1988; Miller, Bugbee, & Hybertson, 1985; Powell, 1987a).

Parallel to the pattern etched by research on the effects of child care (see, for example, Belsky, 1984; Clarke-Stewart, 1987a; Phillips & Howes, 1987), research on the effects of varied curricula moved beyond global questions of effectiveness to questioning effectiveness for whom and under what conditions. Then it moved into a third wave of research effort that has examined the intersection of program effects and children's family environments. Following the first wave of studies, evaluators attempted to address the differential impact of diverse curriculum models on individual children. But the limitations of examining program effects in isolation from other, simultaneous aspects of children's lives eventually became apparent, and researchers began to extend their investigations to include the impact of early childhood programs (including curriculum models) in conjunction with other significant contributors to children's educational and developmental outcomes. Researchers seem to be increasingly sensitive to the need to ask questions that try to disentangle the various elements of early childhood programs, and how, individually and in association with each other, these elements interact with and affect children who bring different characteristics and personal circumstances to programs (Clarke-Stewart, 1987a, 1988; Miller, Bugbee, & Hybertson, 1985; Powell, 1987a). These types of questions more clearly match the complexity of the educational enterprise, and challenge the notion that any single "ideal representation" might be most effective for all children under all circumstances.

The re-emergence of curriculum models, however, is confronted by more than reformulated research questions and deeper understandings regarding the effects of early education. They resurface to a changed set of social circumstances, a shifting focus within, and away from, developmental psychology as a primary determinant of curriculum, and the field of early childhood education in transition. Equally notable, interest in curriculum models has re-emerged at a time when the notion of packaging curriculum is being debated. These changes create a developmental context for early childhood curriculum models that is different from the one that existed in the 1960s. Each of these issues is discussed briefly below in order to provide a contextual framework for the chapters that follow. These issues will surface yet again in the last three chapters.

Changing Societal Context

In the 1960s, public interest in early childhood education united around concern for the economically disadvantaged, an issue embedded within the civil rights movement. Current interest in early childhood education, however, reflects contemporary demographics, and social and economic circumstances specific to the 1990s.

During the 1990s, renewed preoccupation with early childhood education reflects the increasing numbers of mothers with young children in the work force, the national spotlight on educational reform, concern with anticipated labor shortages by the year 2000 along with the country's accompanying need for skilled labor, as well as continued concern with the unequal school success of children from economically disadvantaged circumstances. Concerns for school success are accentuated by frustration with the social cost of school failures.

Unlike the 1960s, when interest in early childhood education primarily revolved around the single issue of school readiness for economically disadvantaged children, attention to early childhood education activated during the 1980s has coalesced around the diverse concerns just listed. Although early childhood education is still viewed as a vehicle for resolving societal problems, the list of concerns is more differentiated, targets a larger proportion of young children, and involves a broader constituency than government officials and social reformers. The receptivity to early childhood education as a policy solution to these various problems, however, can be attributed largely to positive regard for Head Start and the findings from longitudinal studies on the positive, long-term effects of early childhood education.

Increasingly, early childhood education is seen as critical not only to minimizing the impact of poverty but also as essential to the success of public schools and the international competitiveness of American business. Public schools are recognizing that their success in educating children is tied in important ways to children's well-being when they begin formal schooling (National Association of Elementary School Principals, 1990). And national business groups, such as the Committee for Economic Development (1987, 1991), have targeted early childhood education, especially for children identified as being at risk of school failure, as a strategy for addressing their concerns regarding future business productivity. The broadened constituency concerned with early childhood programs also includes the larger population of parents employed outside the home who are dependent on the availability of child care. This expansion of interest, although certainly not universal, has enlarged the child population being targeted and expanded the public's expectations for early childhood education.

Changing Configuration of Early Childhood Education

Since the 1960s there has also been a tremendous increase in the number of young children served by early childhood programs. In 1965, approximately 47% of 5-year-olds were enrolled in kindergartens; in 1986, 90% of 5-year-olds attended kindergarten, which had become almost universally available in public schools (Spodek, 1986). Head Start now serves over 450,000 children (Silver Ribbon Panel, 1990), and the majority of 3- and 4-year-olds with nonemployed mothers participate in half-day programs (Hofferth & Phillips, 1987).

The most dramatic growth in early childhood education, however, has occurred in full-day early childhood programs or child care. Since the early 1970s, the proportion of children younger than 6 with mothers in the work force has increased by nearly 80% (Hofferth, 1989). Political interest in child care programs has been heightened by the fact that a majority of this increase can be attributed to entry of middle-class mothers into the work force. If the trends from 1970 to 1985 continue, Hofferth (1989) predicts there will be almost 15 million preschool children with mothers in the labor force by 1995.

Increased attendance in early childhood programs of all types has sparked conception of an elaborated and less fragmented interpretation of early childhood education. Recall that at the onset of the Great Society, nursery school programs, kindergartens, and child care were distinctive in purpose and clientele. Now the early childhood profession is arguing that the care and education of young children, regardless of program sponsorship, are inseparable components. Early childhood advocates try to capture this emergent integration between the care and education of young children by using the phrase "early childhood care and education."

Kagan (1989) attributes this coalition building among early childhood education's various strands (nursery education, kindergartens, child care, and most recently Head Start) to the success of the National Association for the Education of Young Children position statement on developmentally appropriate practice (Bredekamp, 1987). This document, which identifies pedagogical characteristics of developmentally appropriate early childhood programs, regardless of sponsorship, has functioned as a consensus document, presenting a description of early care and education practices around which the field can coalesce. Although only in its infancy, this emerging sense of professional cohesion contrasts with the separateness that marked nursery schools, kindergartens, and child care during the 1960s.

In addition, the early childhood profession has returned to its historical roots (see, for example, Gregory, Merrill, Payne, & Giddings, 1908) and retrieved the belief that early childhood education encompasses children birth to age 8 (Bredekamp, 1987). This educational age span encompasses programs that serve children in infancy through third grade. Consequently, discussions of early childhood education now explicitly embrace nursery schools, kindergarten through third grade, child care for children infancy through school age, and early intervention programs. These programs are organized for diverse purposes, serve children and their families in a variety of ways, and confront different internal and external challenges. Furthermore, they are provided by various sponsors: community and government agencies, for-profit groups, employers, churches and synagogues, public schools, private institutions, and individual providers.

Mitchell, Seligson, and Marx (1989) label this mixture of programs the early childhood ecosystem, even though organization of these various programs into a coordinated system is still embryonic (Kagan, 1990). The daunting task of constructing a coordinated system of early childhood care and education is propelling the field to deliberate professional issues that transcend age of child served, length of program day, program sponsorship or program type.

Moreover, early childhood programs serve an increasingly ethnically diverse population of children, many of whom are educationally at-risk because of inadequate health care, family instability, and insufficient economic resources (Children's Defense Fund, 1991; Kagan & Garcia, 1991; National Commission on Children, 1991). This demographic information gains further educational meaning when joined with new understandings regarding the critical role of parent involvement and community support to the effectiveness of early childhood programs for children living in disadvantaged circumstances. These new understandings are helping to fuel a growing movement for early childhood programs, especially those organized for children at-risk, to expand their programming to include support services for children and their families (Committee for Economic Development, 1991; Kagan, Powell, Weissbourd, & Zigler, 1987; Silver Ribbon Panel, 1990).

Early childhood education during the 1990s, therefore, provides a very different setting for the development and implementation of early childhood curriculum models. But, it is the changing knowledge base that supplies the critical catalyst for reassessing the content of enduring early childhood curriculum models.

Changing Knowledge Base

The knowledge base undergirding education in general, and early childhood education in particular, has expanded and shifted in focus since the 1960s. Studies of human development since the sixties, which, of course, include child development, also have generated new understandings and assumptions about the developmental process. In general, these new understandings are based on much more complex, context-bound explanations of development and education (see Chapter 8 for detailed discussion).

The changing child development knowledge base has been influenced by research on early childhood program effects. The expansion of publicly supported early childhood education during the 1960s and the increasing numbers of children in child care in the seventies and eighties generated considerable research on the impact of early childhood programs on child growth.

These studies also spawned criteria for program quality (for example, Weikart, 1989). When comparative evaluations initially failed to find significant differences between curriculum models, attention turned to delineating the characteristics associated with program quality (such as group size, teacher-child ratio, and the existence of a well-developed curriculum), independent of program type or curriculum content. This change in focus reflected an attempt to understand the effect of early childhood programs in terms of characteristics associated with quality, rather than in terms of the differential effectiveness of curriculum models. And as the need for improving the overall quality of early childhood programs became apparent, this distinction assumed increasing importance. Still, findings from program evaluations that focused on child outcomes specific to different early childhood curricula highlighted the complexity of child development, disputed simplistic interpretations of environmental impact on children's development, and stressed the challenge of consistently implementing early childhood curriculum models.

Findings from early childhood program evaluations and recent understandings about human development spark new questions about the content and implementation of curriculum models. The necessity for asking these questions is elevated by current debate regarding the extent to which theories of learning and development can or should serve as sources of educational goals, and whether such theories should prescribe what to teach (Egan, 1983; Kerr, 1981; Kessler, 1991a, 1991b; Silin, 1987, 1988). This debate is enriched by recent conceptualizations of teaching as dynamic and uncertain and classroom teachers as reflective practitioners (see, for example, Elliott, 1989; Kerr, 1981; Schon, 1983; see Chapter 8 for more detailed discussion). These new perspectives induce further insights into the assumptions that undergird early childhood curriculum models and implicitly structure their purpose and function.

■ *Conclusion*

Early childhood education seems to be at a critical juncture in its professional evolution. Early childhood education prior to kindergarten and first grade increasingly is being recognized as children's first encounter with formal education. In addition, there is growing acceptance of early childhood education as extending until third grade. At the same time, public awareness of the ways early educational experiences can contribute to children's success with later schooling and future productivity is placing increasing pressure on early childhood programs to meet societal expectations.

Simultaneously, the demand for program availability, especially from employed parents and their employers, has escalated. And the number of new and expanded public programs seeking to serve 3- and 4-year-old children identified as at-risk has increased dramatically.

The preparation of early childhood personnel has not kept pace with demand, however, not only because predictions of demand went unheeded, but more importantly, because caring for children has not been perceived by the general public as an educational and/or professional enterprise. Therefore, professional preparation of early childhood educators primarily has served those who teach within public schools, where professional certification is required—though even this preparation is not always informed by an early childhood knowledge base.

As expectations for quality have begun to accompany demands for program availability, competition for qualified early childhood personnel has been intensifying. Preparing and keeping qualified personnel, however, is undermined by the inferior compensation offered early childhood educators (Willer, 1987), especially those who work outside the public school system. It is confounded further by the profession's struggle to define the prerequisite knowledge base for entering the profession (see, for example, Bredekamp & Willer, 1993).

David Weikart, a primary architect and proponent of the High/Scope Curriculum model, recently proposed a solution to this quandary (1992). He has recommended the institutionalization of early childhood curriculum models as a mechanism for assuring early childhood program quality. His recommendation advances the use of curriculum models as a strategy for professionalizing early childhood education.

Thus, in the nineties, the profession of early childhood education confronts a number of contradictory demands and expectations. Increasing public demand for quality early childhood programs co-exists with inadequate financial support and public understanding of early childhood education, whether provided within or outside public school settings. Public expectation that investment in early childhood education should produce immediate high yields co-exists with a field attempting to move toward a coordinated system for providing early childhood programs and a clearly conceptualized, coordinated system of professional preparation and development.

Renewed interest in early childhood curriculum models has materialized, in part, because of demand for consistent program quality and accountability. Still unresolved from the upheaval of the sixties, however, are issues surrounding early childhood curriculum and its development. Simultaneously, educators are debating the source and characteristics of professionalism in teaching. This debate and these issues place an investigation of early childhood curriculum models within a unique sociohistorical framework and locates it at the intersection of a critical juncture in early childhood education.

■ *For Further Reading*

Cahan, E. D. (1989). *Past caring: A history of U.S. preschool care and education for the poor, 1820–1965.* National Center for Children in Poverty, Columbia University (154 Haven Avenue, New York, NY, 10032).

> This very readable, short but thorough examination of the dual histories of child care and nursery schools documents the creation of a two-tiered system of care and education for America's preschoolers.

Evans, E. D. (1975). *Contemporary influences in early childhood education*, 2nd ed. New York: Holt, Rinehart & Winston.

> This classic textbook provides a review and analysis of curriculum models during a time of intense support for early childhood curriculum models. Extensive research findings and bibliographies relevant to various models are provided. Consistent with its date of publication, emphasis is given to half-day early childhood programs designed for economically disadvantaged preschoolers.

Goffin, S. G. (1989). Government's responsibility in early childhood care and education: Renewing the debate. In C. Seefeldt (Ed.), *Continuing issues in early childhood education* (pp. 9–26). New York: Merrill/Macmillan.

> This chapter provides an overview of government involvement in early intervention programs, child care, and parent education and support programs. It concludes with a rationale and framework for government responsibility in early childhood care and education.

Weber, E. (1969). *The kindergarten: Its encounter with educational thought in America.* New York: Teachers College Press.

> Weber provides a detailed examination of the growth of kindergarten education from its beginnings in the United States until the mid-sixties. Much is also said about the growth of nursery schools. Weber's reliance on historical primary sources and detailed analysis makes this an especially informative review of early childhood education's formative years in the United States.

Weber, E. (1984). *Ideas influencing early childhood education: A theoretical analysis.* New York: Teachers College Press.

> In historical sequence, Weber describes the evolution of early childhood education in the United States and the significant ideas that have influenced its growth. Weber's review emphasizes the need to recognize the values inherent in different theoretical interpretations of child development applied to early childhood education.

White, S. H., & Buka, S. L. (1987). Early education: Programs, traditions, and policies. In E. Z. Rothkopf (Ed.), *Review of research in education* (Vol. 14, pp. 43–91). Washington, DC: American Educational Research Association.

> This scholarly review documents the diverse influences on early childhood education during its 200-year history. White, a Harvard psychologist who helped shape Head Start policy, incorporates tidbits of history from the perspective of an insider.

Part II

Early Childhood Curriculum Models

A Contemporary Review

Part II comprises Chapters 3 through 6. These chapters examine five enduring early childhood curriculum models: the Montessori Method, the Developmental-Interaction approach, the Direct Instruction model, the Kamii-DeVries approach, and the High/Scope Curriculum model. The description of each curriculum model is embedded within its particular social and historical context. Because historical factors also influenced the sequence in which the five curriculum models are presented, readers are encouraged to read the chapters in the order they are introduced.

■ ■ ■ ■ ■ ■

Chapter 3

The Montessori Method

■ ■ ■ ■ ■ ■

For man, who has formed a new world through scientific process, must himself be prepared and developed through a new pedagogy.

Maria Montessori, The Montessori Method, 1912/1964

From minds thus set in order, . . . come sudden emotions and mental feats which recall the Biblical story of Creation. The child has in his mind . . . , the first flowers of affection of gentleness, of spontaneous love for righteousness which perfumes the souls of such children and give promise of the "fruits of the spirit" of St Paul.

Maria Montessori, The Secret of Childhood, 1937/1966

Credit for being the first architect of an early childhood curriculum model belongs to the German educator, Frederich Froebel. His method of kindergarten education involved precise procedures and specially developed materials that could be replicated in other settings. According to Weber (1969), Froebel's ideas found easy acceptance in the United States in the mid-1800s because their idealistic base was consistent with the philosophy of a number of American educational leaders. In addition, many German immigrants living in America had been directly trained in Froebel's educational methods and, thus, were available to explain and demonstrate his procedures.

Froebel's ideas dominated kindergarten education in the United States until they were challenged by progressive educators in the early 1900s. The Montessori

Method entered the American scene at just this time, when there was considerable disenchantment with Froebel's approach to early education, and American early childhood educators were deliberating approaches to early education that were less philosophic in their orientation and more in line with new scientific thinking.

The Montessori Method, which is the second curriculum model created expressly for early childhood education, was first implemented in Rome, Italy, in 1907. It retains the singular title of being the oldest enduring model. In contrast to Froebel's experience, Montessori's approach to early education has endured the passage of time despite challenges to its basic assumptions and practices.

As a result, examination of the Montessori Method and its 86 years of American history provides a unique opportunity to explore professional and public reactions to a specific curriculum model in relation to changing historical and societal circumstances and shifting educational thought. It also permits consideration of the circumstances that support a model's continuation over time.

Since its first introduction to the United States early in the twentieth century, the Montessori Method has undergone two documented revivals, in the mid-sixties and again in the late seventies–early eighties, attesting not only to its enduring allure, but also to the power of timely matches between educational models and societal needs and expectations. Montessori's commitment, and that of her son following her death, to retaining the purity and integrity of her methods also juxtaposes the tension of sustaining a model's "purity" and consistency alongside a changing society and knowledge base that serves as context for educational programming.

Montessori made a full-time commitment to disseminating her ideas and to training teachers in her method at the age of 40. Although Montessori follows Froebel in a chronology of curriculum models, her method appears to be the first curriculum model carefully and intentionally mass-marketed for dissemination and replication. Furthermore, of the curriculum models to be reviewed in this text, the Montessori Method is the only one in which a single individual is responsible for developing both the conceptual framework *and* the template for its implementation. Hers is the only model bearing "a designer name."

The designers of other enduring curriculum models have relied on the ideas of others, primarily developmental theorists, for their conceptual frameworks. Although each of these program designers has striven to retain the integrity of his or her model, Montessori's "ownership" of both the conceptual framework and program design, plus the program's implementation, perhaps helps explain her undiminished attempts to retain total control over the method's dissemination and the use of her didactic materials, to which she devoted herself from 1916 until her death in 1952.

When Montessori began advocating her method full time in 1916, she gave up her other roles as physician, university professor, and classroom teacher. E. M. Standing, Montessori's official biographer, wrote in a passage Montessori herself approved, "Her mission in life had crystallized. . . . She felt the duty of going forth as an apostle on behalf of all the children in the world, born and as yet unborn, to preach for their rights and their liberation" (as cited in Kramer, 1976/1988, p. 156).

This quote begins to reveal the challenge of any attempt to explain and understand the Montessori Method. Montessori was a physician, anthropologist, educator, and mystic. She claimed to be both a scientific educator and a missionary. These two roles, in particular, conjure up seemingly contradictory characteristics, contradictions that also imbue her writings. Yet, it is these apparent contradictions that help explain the model's endurance: Montessori's method embraces the prestige and presumed validity of a scientific approach to early education plus the emotional fervor that accompanies what Kramer (1976/1988) and Cohen (1969) both have deemed cultist.

■ *The Montessori Method: An American Chronology*

In the Beginning

Mention of Maria Montessori and her Method is almost always accompanied by a statement of the fact that she was the first Italian female physician, a feat of courage and perseverance that can only be imagined. (Some of what her experience must have been like is described by biographer, Rita Kramer, 1976/1988.) Montessori was also a feminist and a crusader for children's rights. She was especially determined to liberate children from the rigidity of early twentieth century Italian public education "where the children are repressed in the spontaneous expression of their personality till they are almost like dead beings" (Montessori, 1912/1964, p. 14). She believed that her approach to early education could revolutionize society by producing a new generation of children prepared for, and capable of, creating a better world.

Fifteen years prior to the opening of the first Casa dei Bambini ("Children's House"), Montessori served as an assistant doctor at the Psychiatric Clinic at the University of Rome and visited insane asylums to study the sick. It was this work that led to her interest in "idiot" children (children whom we would today identify as mentally retarded and perhaps developmentally delayed), who were, at that time, housed in general insane asylums. Her conclusion that the needs of these children were pedagogical rather than medical led to the creation of the State Orthophrenic School.

At the State Orthophrenic School, Montessori was able to try out her pedagogical ideas, which were largely based on the work of Jean-Marc-Gaspard Itard (known for his attempts to educate the "wild boy of Aveyron") and Edward Sequin, who had developed a specialized method and didactic materials (instructive, self-correcting apparatus) for working with "deficient" children. Montessori directed this program, which served children for the full length of the day, for 2 years. During these 2 years (1898–1900), she prepared teachers for a method of observation and education targeted to children with special learning needs. Eventually, Montessori, herself, worked directly with the children from 8:00 AM until 7:00 PM. During this time, Montessori modified Sequin's materials and began to produce her own. She also drafted the beginnings of her method of reading and writing that would be a source of great excitement to educators and others around the world.

Montessori considered her method more rational than others currently in use. She became convinced that if her method could succeed in enabling "an inferior mentality" to grow and develop, it would "set free (the) personality" of normal children (Montessori, 1912/1964, p. 33).

The opportunity to apply her method to "normal" children came in 1906. In part, this opportunity presented itself because of her successful 2-year tenure at the State Orthophrenic School. Her method for working with retarded children had succeeded so well that the children under her care successfully passed the public school examination alongside their typical peers, an event that generated considerable public attention and excitement. Montessori realized, however, that this success reflected the deficiencies of public school education as much as the validity of her method (Montessori, 1912/1964).

The opportunity to try her techniques with normal children also surfaced because of changing social circumstances throughout Italy. An awareness of these circumstances highlights not only the context of Montessori's achievement, but also begins to illuminate the missionary zeal she felt for her work. Montessori was a multi-faceted individual. She was obviously an amazing educational innovator; but she was also a feminist and an impassioned social reformer.

Because of economic distress, the late 1890s was a period of widespread social disorder throughout Italy. In 1903, a new prime minister initiated a series of social, economic, and financial reforms. These initiatives, especially in housing and education, were at their height in 1906 (Kramer, 1976/1988; Montessori, 1912/1964) and set the stage for the first Casa dei Bambini, which opened in 1907.

Within this context, Rome was a city that had undergone a dramatic population increase, especially of immigrants from the countryside. This population growth fueled a tremendous building fever. This construction boom, however, was essentially an economic venture for Roman banks; no standards of health and safety guided the construction of new apartment buildings. When the economy shifted, uncompleted and rundown apartment houses dotted the city landscape. Abandoned structures quickly became occupied by beggars, criminals, and the homeless (Kramer, 1976/1988; Montessori, 1912/1964).

One such tenement was the Quarter of San Lorenzo, which became the first site where Montessori applied her innovative educational ideas with normal children. "With no sanitation and no policing, (the Quarter of San Lorenzo) became a hellhole of infection and prostitution, an abode of the dead as well as the living" (Kramer, 1976/1988, p. 109).

Eventually, a group of wealthy bankers decided to undertake an urban renewal scheme that could reap them both public good and financial profit. They began their venture with the renovation of apartments in the Quarter of San Lorenzo and chose employed, married couples, many of whom had children, as tenants. When parents left in the morning for work, however, their children who were under school age were left unattended and began defacing building walls and stairs. Following on her success at the State Orthophrenic School, Montessori was invited by the Roman "Good Building" Institute, which administered the remodeled tenements, to develop an infant school for children 3 to 7 years of age; the invitation was extended in hopes that such a program would reduce the vandalism and thus protect the bankers' investment (Kramer, 1976/1988; Montessori, 1912/1964).

Montessori, however, saw larger possibilities. The Roman "Good Building" Institute owned more than 400 tenements in Rome, and each apartment house was to have its own school. Montessori envisioned the Children's Houses as having both social and pedagogical significance. "From the very first I perceived, in all its immensity, the social and pedagogical importance of such institutions, and while at that time my visions of a triumphant future seemed exaggerated, today many are beginning to understand that what I saw before was indeed the truth" (Montessori, 1912/1964, p. 48).

In the early twentieth century (as well as 86 years later!), the Children's House was an amazingly progressive idea that served not only the needs of children and their parents, but the community and its business interests as well. As initially envisioned by Montessori, the Children's House was the core of what we might today call a family resource center, providing not only comprehensive child care services that addressed children's nutritional and health care needs as part of the educational program (which she contrasted with the custodial care provided in the insane asylums), but also public baths, hospitals, and a "house-infirmary" for sick child care.

Montessori also saw the Children's Houses as realizing the educational ideal of linking family and school around educational aims. Although her frame of reference for low-income families was more judgmental than many of us might wish, her ideas demonstrated sensitivity to the need for families and educators to work closely together if children were to truly benefit. Montessori recognized the advantages to be derived from the Children's House being inside the tenement, thus making it available to parents for observation at any time; she also felt parents' financial support of the program via their rent promoted a sense of parent ownership. The teacher even lived in the same tenement building as did the children and their parents, enabling her to be accessible to parents (Montessori, 1912/1964).

Parents, however, had accompanying obligations. Mothers were obliged to send their children to the Children's House clean and to co-operate with the teacher in the educational work. The regulations (see Table 3–1) required mothers to meet with the teacher at least once a week to learn the progress of their children and to accept helpful advice. If children came to school unclean or unruly, then they were sent home to their parents.

The first Children's House opened under Montessori's guidance and direction on January 6, 1907. A second opened in the same quarter on April 7, followed by a third in Milan in the fall of 1908. In November, 1908, a house was opened for middle-class children in an affluent section of Rome. By 1916, the Montessori Method was an international phenomena.

Almost from the very beginning, then, despite its initial target population, the Montessori Method served both poor and affluent children, and in so doing, the comprehensiveness of its initial approach to early childhood education began to wane. When the method was implemented with children from more affluent families, many of the health and nutrition and family support components were omitted.

The shift from a comprehensive program to one with a more narrow curricular focus was reinforced further by the emphasis of Montessori's followers on her methods and materials, rather than on her insightful understandings about children and

Table 3–1
Rules and Regulations of the "Children's Houses"

The Roman Association of Good Building hereby establishes within its tenement house
  number _____, a "Children's House," in which may be gathered together all children
  under common school age, belonging to the families of the tenants.
The chief aim of the "Children's House" is to offer, free of charge, to the children of those
  parents who are obliged to absent themselves for their work, the personal care which
  the parents are not able to give.
In the "Children's House" attention is given to the education, the health, the physical and
  moral development of the children. This work is carried on in a way suited to the age of
  the children.
There shall be connected with the "Children's House" a Directress, a Physician, and a
  Caretaker.
The programme and hours of the "Children's House" shall be fixed by the Directress.
There may be admitted to the "Children's House" all the children in the tenement
  between the ages of three and seven.
The parents who wish to avail themselves of the advantages of the "Children's House"
  pay nothing. They must, however, assume these binding obligations:
  (a) To send their children to the "Children's House" at the appointed time, clean in
      body and clothing, and provided with a suitable apron.
  (b) To show the greatest respect and deference toward the Directress and toward all
      persons connected with the "Children's House," and to co-operate with the
      Directress herself in the education of the children. Once a week, at least, the
      mothers may talk with the Directress, giving her information concerning the home
      life of the child, and receiving helpful advice from her.
There shall be expelled from the "Children's House":
  (a) Those children who present themselves unwashed, or in soiled clothing.
  (b) Those who show themselves to be incorrigible.
  (c) Those whose parents fail in respect to the persons connected with the "Children's
      House," or who destroy through bad conduct the educational work of the
      institution.

From Montessori, M. (1964). *The Montessori Method* (pp. 70–71). New York: Schocken. (Originally published in 1912)

families. One could also speculate that this shift was facilitated by the complexities
associated with program replication and different community contexts. In the mid-
sixties, when the Montessori Method was resurrected in the United States as an early
intervention program for economically disadvantaged preschoolers, the model was
characterized by the visible artifacts of the method: the prepared environment,
didactic materials, and prescribed teacher-child interactions. The sense of community created by locating a program within the tenement complex and the linkages initially fostered among child, family, and schooling had paled behind an emphasis on
academic preparation. This academic thrust was propelled by the method's cognitive
emphasis and its success in teaching children behavioral self-control and reading and
writing prior to first grade, accomplishments that align easily with the focus of most

early intervention programs, in and out of public schools, on preparing children for formal schooling.

When the first Children's House opened in Rome in 1907, Montessori was 37 years old. She was an established professional and a distinguished scientist and academic; she was highly regarded by her colleagues and Roman civic and social leaders. Montessori was also a charismatic and inspirational figure and a dynamic speaker (Cohen, 1969; Kramer, 1976/1988). The strength of her personality and convictions, plus the dramatic growth in printed mass media and international communication (Kliebard, 1986; Kramer, 1976/1988), helped assure the rapid interest in, and transmission of, her ideas—not only to educators, but to the general public. Within the United States, the explosion of print materials also helped increase public consciousness of the changes being wrought in American society by urbanization and industrialization (Kliebard, 1986).

From Italy to the United States

Montessori made her first trip to the United States in December, 1913. When she arrived, she was at the peak of her career, one of the most famous women in the world. Her arrival shared headlines with the activities of Pancho Villa in Mexico and President Wilson's refusal to make a public statement on the question of women's suffrage (Kramer, 1976/1988). The beginning of World War I was only a year away. There were an unprecedented number of affluent Americans and poor immigrants. The affluent of America were interested in education as a means for assimilating new immigrants and enriching the lives of their own children. According to Kramer (1976/1988),

> The Montessori system offered a program of reform to a reform-minded age. Through a new kind of educational institution—which seemed to have proved itself beyond anyone's wildest expectations in an unbelievably short period of time—it would be possible to mold a new generation of children—independent, productive members of society— and at the same time solve many of the problems of the day, social inequities of class and sex among them. (p. 154)

Shifts toward an industrialized, urban economy and concerns with the "hordes" of immigrants helped create a receptive climate for Montessori's visit among America's socially minded. Changing views about early childhood education, however, furnished a less positive reception from early childhood leaders. The year of Montessori's arrival in the United States, 1913, was also the year the Committee of Nineteen[1] was preparing to publish its final report. Their report culminated a decade of professional, often acrimonious, debate between Frobelian and progressive educators regarding the proper nature of early childhood education. This report pre-

---

[1] This committee, it will be recalled (see Chapter 2), was convened by the International Kindergarten Union to resolve the conflict between advocates of Frobelian education and those wishing to develop early education programs aligned with new scientific thinking.

sented the new wave of thinking regarding early childhood curriculum. The Montessori Method was quickly determined to be out of step with the new zeitgeist.

The first discussion of Montessori's work in an American publication was in a series of articles by Jenny Merrill in *The Kindergarten-Primary Magazine*, beginning in December 1909. Reports of visits to Montessori schools and discussions of the method, its philosophy, and implications for American kindergartens (nursery schools did not begin to flourish in the United States until the 1920s) appeared in newspapers and popular and professional magazines. Early visitors to the Casa dei Bambini included professional luminaries such as William Heard Kilpatrick of Columbia University (and a disciple of John Dewey), G. Stanley Hall of Clark University, who pioneered the child study movement, prominent child psychologists Arnold and Beatrice Gesell, and Jane Addams, the pioneer of settlement houses. But the American visitors who really made an impact for Montessori were not scholarly professionals but influential individuals such as S. S. McClure, one of the most powerful journalists of his time, whose magazine published a series of articles on Montessori in 1911 and 1912, and Mary Hubbard Bell, the wife of Alexander Graham Bell, who set up a Montessori classroom for her two grandchildren in the spring of 1912 (Hunt, 1964; Kramer, 1976/1988).

Anne George, the first American Montessori-trained teacher, opened the first Montessori school in America in the fall of 1911 with 12 children from upper-middle–class families in Tarrytown, New York. By the end of 1911, arrangements had been completed with an American company for the manufacture and sale of the Montessori didactic materials. An American edition of her book, *The Montessori Method*, translated by Anne George, was published in 1912. The first edition of 5,000 copies sold out in 4 days (Kramer, 1976/1988).

The popular enthusiasm for Montessori's work, however, was not duplicated within the early childhood profession. Early childhood educators expressed concern for the method's lack of interest in children's creative self-expression, the formality of activities, the exact way in which children had to use the didactic materials, and the curriculum's narrow scope (Weber, 1969), concerns that continue to be expressed by early childhood educators. The fact that the Montessori Method was mostly compared to the rigid American Frobelian kindergarten rather than more progressive programs was prophetic. According to Weber (1969), kindergarten teachers were just beginning to free themselves from "the curricular domination of one set of materials" and were less than eager to substitute a new set (p. 79).

Educators philosophically allied with progressive education especially rejected the method's failure to promote children's initiative or motivation to create and solve problems of their own making and its lack of attention to the social and emotional life of the child (which also remain concerns to many contemporary early childhood educators). Also problematic was the almost passive teacher role prescribed by the Montessori Method; the limited role of the teacher, which was in sharp contrast with the "center-stage" role enacted by Frobelian educators, was simply not acceptable to many teachers, a factor noted by Montessori herself—though in her case the contrast was with conventional Italian public school educators (Hunt, 1964; Kramer, 1976/1988; Montessori, 1912/1964; Weber, 1969). Plus, according to

White and Buka (1987), Montessori's ideas entered American discussions at a time when Americans were eager to reduce their reliance on European ideas and influence.

The death knell, however, was sounded by William Heard Kilpatrick, a disciple of John Dewey and one of the country's most influential progressive educators (Hunt, 1964; Kramer, 1976/1988; Weber, 1969). Kilpatrick (1914) contended that Montessori's ideas were tied to an outmoded theory. He wrote,

> We conclude . . . that Madame Montessori's doctrine of sense-training is based on an outworn and cast-off psychological theory; that the didactic apparatus devised to carry this theory into effect is in so far worthless; that what little value remains to the apparatus could be better got from the sense-experience incidental to properly directed play with wisely chosen, but less expensive and more childlike playthings. (p. 52)

Within 5 years of her visit to the United States, Montessori was all but forgotten by the American public. Montessori continued disseminating her method throughout Europe and other parts of the world, but American early childhood professionals returned to the issue that had been the focus of their attention before being diverted by the "new kid on the block"—developing a new, American approach to early childhood education (Cohen, 1969; Kramer, 1976/1988; Weber, 1969).

Montessori's rapid descent was further assisted by her unwillingness to permit anyone other than herself to prepare Montessori teachers and by her insistence that her system be bought as a whole package, or not at all, thus blocking its sustenance from within the early childhood profession. For similar reasons, her popular support waned as well (see Cohen, 1969; Kramer, 1976/1988).

The commercialism involved in patenting an educational method also was greeted with skepticism (Kramer, 1976/1988). Only one company in America was given the right to sell and distribute her didactic materials. To try and further assure only authorized dissemination of her ideas, Montessori created the Association Montessori Internationale (AMI) in 1929 to supervise the training of teachers and to oversee the activities of Montessori schools and societies around the world.[2]

Montessori justified these decisions based on concern that her ideas would be distorted if not practiced exactly as she had translated them for classroom practice,

---

[2]   The AMI, which is located in Amsterdam, has approximately 400 affiliated schools in the United States and 14 training programs, including one for elementary educators and one for infants and toddlers. The North American Montessori Teachers Association is affiliated with the AMI.

The American Montessori Association, with ties to the AMI, was formed in 1960 by Nancy Rambusch and has 45 affiliated training programs across the country. Because Mrs. Rambusch attempted to Americanize the method, the AMI removed its seal of approval in 1963. According to an interview with Mario Montessori, "Nancy's grasp exceeded her reach; she thought she knew better than Dr. Montessori" (Cohen, 1969, p. 324). The National Center for Montessori Education is the most recently created American organization for teacher education (Chattin-McNichols, 1992b).

and to protect her name and method from exploitation. Yet her singular focus on these concerns is open to speculation, because in the process of giving up her other professional roles and creating a following outside the framework of any existing institution, Montessori also had eliminated any consistent stream of financial support. Thus, she became financially dependent on students' fees and royalties from books and materials for her livelihood (Kramer, 1976/1988). Furthermore, as pointed out by Kramer (1976/1988), patenting the Montessori Method via its materials promoted, and helped institutionalize, the idea that they, rather than Montessori's principles, would become the central focus of the method.

The Resurrection

J. McVicker Hunt, in his influential introduction to a new American edition of *The Montessori Method* issued in 1964, attributed Montessori's decline to the fact that her ideas were too dissonant from those emerging in the early 1900s. Hunt's introduction not only placed the dissonance in historical perspective but also espoused that Montessori's moment in history had at last materialized. Accompanying the dominance of developmental and educational psychologists in early childhood education in the mid-sixties, changing psychological notions (versus educational ones) provided justification for Montessori's re-emergence as a viable model for early childhood education, even though early educators, such as Pitcher (1966), expressed concern with the evangelical nature of advocates and with the academic focus of the program.

Hunt identified four psychological conceptions that minimized acceptance of Montessori's ideas when first introduced. First was the notion that school experience for 3- and 4-year-olds could be important for later development. Prior to the 1960s, children's development was believed to be predetermined by heredity. Adherence to this notion was aided by the fact that, to many, educating very young children outside the home was considered an infringement on the functions and rights of families.

A second deterring opinion was belief in fixed intelligence. Montessori's conception of mental retardation as amenable to pedagogical intervention contradicted this notion. Her focus on cognitive development, including her encouragement of children learning to read, write, and count, also differed from the emphasis of the times on social development. Based on acceptance of the concept of predetermined, normative development, the teaching of reading, writing, and counting to children before they were about 8 years was seen as a waste of time, and even potentially harmful.

Third, the belief that all behavior was motivated by instincts or by painful stimuli, sex, or the need to achieve homeostasis (an internal balance) could not accommodate Montessori's belief that education should be based on children's spontaneous motivation for learning. Fourth, the behavioral emphasis in the early 1900s on the response side of learning and its variations in different settings made Montessori's contention that generalizable knowledge could be abstracted from sensory training appear out-of-step with current psychological thinking. This was the referent for

Kilpatrick's (1914; see above) contention that the Montessori Method was based on "an outworn and cast-off psychological theory."

Hunt suggested that revised thinking about each of these ideas made the Montessori Method especially appropriate for early childhood education in the mid-sixties. And, in fact, his analysis not only validated many of Montessori's ideas (in terms of 1960s thinking) but demonstrated just how revolutionary her thinking 65 years earlier had been.

Furthermore, Hunt's (1961) synthesis of the then-current empirical data, along with Bloom's work (1964), had recently provided scientific validation for the contributing role of environment (versus heredity) to intellectual development and argued the special receptiveness of intellectual development to environmental stimulation during the early years of a child's life. Consequently, Hunt's enthusiastic introduction to the reissue of *The Montessori Method*, and his suggestion that the method provided a potential solution to the "problem of the match" (an optimum discrepancy between what an individual already knows and what is being learned), was significant.

His endorsement provided not only the aura of his prestige but also reinforced Montessori's contention that her method was based on scientific pedagogy. As expressed by McDermott in his introduction to the reissue of Montessori's *Spontaneous Activity in Education* (1917/1965), "It is Montessori, above all others, who holds to entwining of empirical method, scientific data, and human aspiration as the irreducible elements in any theory of education" (p. xv). Hence, interest in the Montessori Method in the mid-sixties coincided with America's search for a scientific approach to early childhood education.

Renewed enthusiasm for the Montessori Method was also fostered by the fact that the Children's House had been organized for "the culturally deprived" of the Quarter of San Lorenzo. "From the observations of Americans who visited Montessori's Houses of Children, one gathers they were successful at precisely this business of counteracting the effects of cultural deprivation on those symbolic skills required for success in school and in an increasingly technological culture" (Hunt, 1964, p. xxvi).

Intense interest in early childhood curriculum models, including the Montessori Method, diminished during the late seventies and early eighties, however, as federal support for diverse approaches to early education waned, program evaluations disappointed, and new social needs surfaced (see Chapter 2 for further discussion). Individuals who continued to use the Montessori Method practiced primarily in private early childhood programs. So, it is perhaps somewhat unexpected that the most recent surge of interest in the Montessori Method comes from the public schools (Chattin-McNichols, 1992b; Weiss, 1992).

According to Weiss (1992), national director of the American Montessori Society, the first public school Montessori program was established in the late 1960s, but public school programs only began to multiply with development of the magnet school concept in the mid-seventies. Magnet schools usually are created to help school districts comply with federal desegregation requirements, and especially to draw white, often middle-class families, into city public schools. In 1989, more than

100 school districts were serving children from infancy through adolescence. According to Chattin-McNichols (1992b), this increase demonstrates that the Montessori Method has proven its "salability" (p. 208) to parents.

■ *Montessori's Method*

The review of Montessori's method is organized into two parts: an examination of her essential pedagogical premises and a descriptive overview of the program and its practices. This organizational framework was selected so emphasis would be placed on the ideas that help explain Montessori's thinking. It also is an attempt to portray the relationship between Montessori's philosophical framework and her method. Isolating the specifics of her method from their philosophical underpinnings diminishes not only an understanding of her intent but also decreases appreciation of the coherence in her thinking.

Montessori's method and her writings about it, however, are very detailed. Not only was she concerned with every aspect of a child's life, but also because her method was based on scientific pedagogy, she was obligated to specify every particular in order to ensure accurate replication. Consequently, it is simply not possible for a single chapter to provide a comprehensive, thorough overview. Readers, therefore, are encouraged to read at least one of Montessori's publications directly, especially those noted in "For Further Reading."

I rely on Montessori's own writings for descriptions of her method. Chattin-McNichols (1992) has challenged this decision when made by other authors because he feels reliance on Montessori's original publications ignores changes that have occurred over the years. Yet, by his own admission, additions have been "small changes and adjustments" (p. 21), primarily modifications to sequence or content, not reformation of any of the basic premises that define the Montessori Method. Thus, to try and most accurately present Montessori to others, it still seems valid to minimize the number of interpretations between the original Montessori and the reader.

Because of the redundancy found in her publications, it can be assumed that the ideas discussed here can be found throughout her writings, unless otherwise indicated. Words and phrases placed in quotes unaccompanied by a citation reflect wording consistently used by Montessori. By the frequent use of her own words, I have attempted not only to better represent her thinking, but also to corroborate my interpretations.

It should be pointed out that Montessori only wrote five of the many books that bear her name as author. Four of these works were written and translated into English prior to 1920: *The Montessori Method*, which was published in English in 1912; *Pedagogical Anthropology*, published in English in 1913; and *The Advanced Montessori Method: Spontaneous Activity in Education*, Volume 1, and *The Advanced Montessori Method: The Montessori Elementary Material*, both published in English in 1917. Montessori was directly responsible for the content of these books and supervised their translations from Italian into English. The fifth work, *Dr. Montessori's Own Handbook*, appeared originally in English and was published in 1914 after her return from the United States. These five publications, which describe her method and didactic materials, also contain most of what is essential and original in Montessori's thinking, a fact also noticed by reviewers of her later writings (Kramer, 1976/1988).

Other works by Montessori, such as *The Absorbent Mind* (1949/1963), *The Discovery of the Child* (1948), and *The Secret of Childhood* (1937/1966), are published translations of her many lectures and did not directly involve Montessori (although Montessori did rewrite *The Absorbent Mind* into Italian after its initial publication, which, in turn was retranslated into English). These publications are problematic because Montessori always delivered her presentations in Italian, which, in turn were translated by an interpreter, recorded by listeners, and *then* retranslated into the language of publication. Furthermore, Montessori always spoke extemporaneously and never used notes; thus, there is no way of checking the various translations against an original (Bentley, 1964).

Essential Conceptual Elements

Montessori's writings are dominated by five recurring, interlocking beliefs: (1) that her method represents a scientific approach to education; (2) that the "secret of childhood" resides in the fact that through their spontaneous activity, children labor to "make themselves into men"; (3) that mental development, similar to physical growth, is the result of a natural, internally regulated force; (4) that liberty is the imperative ingredient that enables education to assist the "complete unfolding of (a child's) life"; and (5) that order, most especially within the child, but also in the child's environment, is prerequisite to the child becoming an independent, autonomous, and rational individual. (See, for example, Montessori, 1912/1964, 1917/1964, 1949/1963; 1937/1966; 1936/1970.)

These beliefs were embedded in Montessori's conviction that her method would revolutionize society by creating an educational environment that responded to children's innate nature and nurtured the child's complete spiritual and psychic actualization; this anticipated outcome, in turn, defined the purpose of education. Montessori's method was directed to the development of the individual child and to the purposeful and useful contributions made by individuals to the social collective, thus contributing to society's enhanced functioning.

The Montessori Method as Scientific Pedagogy.   The original title of the Italian version of *The Montessori Method* was *The Method of Scientific Pedagogy Applied to Child Education in the Children's Houses*. Montessori emphasized repeatedly that her method was an approach for putting new principles of science into practice. "My method is scientific, both in its substance and in its aim. It makes for the attainment of a more advanced stage of progress. . . ." (Montessori, 1917/1965, p. 8).

Montessori drew directly from the experimental psychology, pedagogical anthropology, and medicine of her time. She advocated the potential of a scientific approach to pedagogy by describing the progress medicine had made since becoming scientific in dramatically improving the physical well-being of individuals. Similarly, scientific pedagogy would assure the spiritual and intellectual well-being of children and, in so doing, transform the future of civilization. Scientific pedagogy was a means toward "the science of forming man" (Montessori, 1912/1964, p. 2).

Montessori credited Guiseppe Sergi, her teacher from medical school, for proposing the idea that the scientific principles of anthropology could be applied to studying pupils (Montessori, 1913; 1912/1964). In the early 1900s, which also marked the beginning of the scientific movement in psychology and education, the methods of anthropology involved measurements of human features to determine ideal racial characteristics and physical anomalies. Although Montessori did, in fact, regularly measure children's physical characteristics, the significance of pedagogical anthropology came from the shift it facilitated toward directly observing and learning from children. Children and their actions, rather than general principles or abstract philosophical ideas, became the center of pedagogy (Montessori, 1913; 1912/1964).

Naturalistic observations of individual children led to an understanding of children based on their common characteristics, which, Montessori emphasized, were not those of adults reduced to a diminutive scale. "This is precisely the new development of pedagogy that goes under the name of *scientific*; in order to educate, it is essential to know those who are to be educated . . . because we cannot educate anyone until we know him thoroughly" (Montessori, 1913, p. 17).

According to Montessori, it was the naturalistic observation of children within a carefully prepared environment, and the teacher's new role as objective observer, that characterized her method as scientific. It was also this aspect that required specialized teacher training, so that teachers could learn "to divest (themselves) of personality in order to become instruments of investigation" (Montessori, 1913, p. 24). Scientific preparation of the teacher, however, was joined with preparation of the spirit: "But let us seek to implant in the soul the self-sacrificing spirit of the scientist with the reverent love of the disciple of Christ, and we shall have prepared the *spirit* of the teacher" (Montessori, 1912/1964, p. 13).

Scientific pedagogy, natural and rational, was to emerge from her experimentation (Montessori, 1912/1964). The prepared environment, therefore, was initially a classroom organized for the careful observations which "determine experimentally, with . . . a precision not hitherto attained, what is the mental attitude of the child at various ages, and hence, if the fitting material for development be offered, what will be the average level of intellectual development according to age" (Montessori, 1917/1965, pp. 80–81). Once Montessori concluded her 2-year experiment, the prepared environment became the scientifically arranged context, determined by the findings from her experiment, which precisely nurtured children's development.

The liberty of the child, the freedom to develop spontaneously, also possessed scientific importance. Liberty was considered synonymous with an environment free of unnatural inhibitors to the child's growth and the teacher's observations.

Montessori's emphasis, however, was on knowing the child as a member of the species, not as a unique, multi-faceted individual; this frame of reference permitted her to assume that her findings could uniformly apply to all children.

The Secret of Childhood: Spontaneous Activity.   Montessori discovered the "secret" of childhood from her careful observations of children at the Children's House, where children's spontaneous activity emerged and took shape unhampered by adult intervention and imposition. The secret Montessori tried to share with the world was her finding that children were psychic (psychological and spiritual), as well as biological, "creatures" and were endowed with a plan of organic development, which was expressed through their spontaneous activity. However, the formative outcomes of children's spontaneous activity could only be fully realized in a carefully prepared and orderly environment that freed children's natural evolution from external obstructions.

Montessori contended that children's spontaneous activity was especially critical between 3 and 6 years. During these sensitive years, children's spontaneous activity is intrinsically motivated toward bringing their chaotic inner world into an orderly coherence, a prerequisite to the development of rational, intellectual thought. Furthermore, once the sensitive period passes, special proclivity toward the needed developmental activity disappears. In her later writings, Montessori increasingly expressed the belief that the first 2 years of life were the formative years that influenced the entire construct of the child's personality (see, for example, *The Absorbent Mind*, 1949/1963; *The Child in the Family*, 1936/1970).

Although Montessori, unlike most of her contemporaries, believed that the environment was critical in its ability to either help or hinder a child's development, she also strongly believed that the environment could never create. The prepared environment, with its emphasis on liberty, provided an environment where a child could respond to his or her inner forces of growth without being stifled.

This relationship between the child and the prepared environment occurred by organizing for each child "the means necessary for his internal nourishment" (Montessori, 1917/1965, p. 70). These means, which were informed by Montessori's experiments, facilitated a congruence between a child's inner needs and the environment's ability to fulfill those needs. "In order to expand, the child, left at liberty to exercise his activities, ought to find in his surroundings something organized in direct relation to his internal organization which is developing itself by natural laws" (Montessori, 1917/1965, pp. 69–70).

Equally important, in order to be educative, the environment needs to focus the child's activity toward the essential task of self-formation in accordance with the inherited plan. "And the spirit, organized in this manner under the guidance of an order which corresponds to its natural order, becomes fortified, grows vigorously, and manifests itself in the equilibrium, the serenity, the self-control which produce the wonderful discipline characteristic of the behavior of our children" (Montessori, 1914/1964, p. 82).

Montessori's emphasis on children's self-creation in conjunction with liberty necessitated that the well-prepared environment contain the means for self-education. Consistent with Montessori's views regarding scientific pedagogy, however, the process of auto-education was not random. The activities for auto-education had to correspond to the child's emerging inner life, which, in turn, could be determined only by careful study of the child. Montessori created her well-known didactic materials for this purpose. Once Montessori had completed *her* direct study of children, however, teachers' child study occurred in reference to what was already documented about children; the intent of careful observation of children was no longer to learn about children and their unique interests or ways of knowing about the world but rather to ensure the appropriate correspondence between child and material.

Independence was a necessary behavioral accompaniment to Montessori's concern for liberty and auto-education. The meaning of independence referred not only to "freedom to" but "freedom from," freedom *to* take care of one's own needs, and freedom *from* dependency on others. Montessori described the child at birth as helpless, and "circumscribed by bonds which limit his activity" because of social dependency on others. Freedom from these bonds defined individual liberty.

The first phase of Montessori's curriculum, the exercises for practical life, was organized to overcome these limitations and to facilitate a child's independence. The resultant independence not only enabled a child to care for herself but also enabled her to continue to nourish her self-formation through auto-education. Consistent with Montessori's philosophy, the exercises of practical life (described below) are carefully structured to assure that the child's independent movements and actions become increasingly coordinated and orderly.

Montessori's definition of child respect is demonstrated in her intense interest in the child's natural development and her utmost care to avoid intrusions into the child's activity. Respect for the child's spontaneous activity, however, should not be confused with a laissez-faire approach. Montessori prepared the environment to ensure that the environmental liberty provided to children promoted, rather than diminished, their developmental "ascent." When properly prepared, the environment offers children the external means needed for self-perfection—which, according to Montessori, could not be found in a chaotic, unruly environment.

At a more tangible level, the limits of individual liberty are set by the collective interest, represented by "what we universally call good breeding" (Montessori, 1912/1964, p. 87); Montessori discouraged ill-bred acts and annoying and offending behaviors. Teachers' suppression of inappropriate behaviors is also important in helping children come to know the difference between good and evil. Thus Montessori's interpretation of liberty was not synonymous with permitting children to do whatever they pleased.

Teachers' observations of children are critical to securing the method's success. Teachers' careful observations ensure that lessons never provoke "unnatural effort" on the part of the child. Provoking unnatural effort not only alters the child's natural, developmental ascent but also obstructs the teachers' ability to know the spontaneous activity of a child.

Knowledge of the child's spontaneous activity, in turn, is critical to enabling the teacher to determine when individual children are ready for the next step in their formation and for ensuring that the environment provides the needed "nourish-ment." In this subtle fashion, the teacher structures the alignment between the child and the environment (recall Hunt's conclusion that the Montessori Method solved the problem of the match) and shapes the formative sprouts of children's emergent psychic and physiological development in the directions they are predisposed to grow.

This conceptualization of teaching, plus Montessori's negative feelings toward the existing, rigid teaching practices in Italy, led her to name her teachers *directress*. The directress does not directly teach children; instead she ensures that the environment provides what individual children need for their own inner construction.

Because Montessori conceived children's behaviors as innately driven, extrinsic rewards and external punishment are considered not only unnecessary but also harmful, because of their potential to disturb a child's natural development. Children's disruptive behaviors are interpreted as indicators that the innate predis-position for orderly development is being thwarted. Relying on similar reasoning, Montessori interpreted fantasy and imaginative behaviors as characteristic of imma-ture, disorderly minds.

The Child's Labor. The child, according to Montessori, is born in a state of physi-cal and psychological chaos. The primary outcome of positive psychic and physiolog-ical development is growth from disorder to order, which, in turn, leads the child toward more adaptive behavior. Disorder is synonymous with confusion and awk-wardness; order is associated with purposefulness, rationality, achievement, and self-satisfaction. Consequently, work, defined as purposeful and ordered activity toward a determined end, was highly valued, and play, defined as its antithesis, was not. The ". . . achievement of psychic order . . . is the beginning of progressive evolution in the inner life" (Montessori, 1917/1965, p. 90).

Psychic order is created as a by-product of the child's innate ability to become totally absorbed in an activity. This attentive fixation promotes psychic formation by bringing order to internal chaos,

> as if in a saturated solution, a point of crystallization had formed, round which the whole chaotic and fluctuating mass united, producing a crystal of wonderful forms. Thus, when the phenomenon of the polarisation of attention had taken place, all that was disorderly and fluctuating in the consciousness of the child seemed to be organizing itself into a spiritual creation, the surprising characteristics of which are reproduced in every individ-ual. (Montessori, 1917/1965, p. 68)

Internal chaos is behaviorally characterized not only by unfocused/disorderly behavior but also by lack of sensory differentiation (which is also disorderly). Montessori specifically designed her didactic materials to bring order to the child's perceptions of the environment; intimately related to her concern for order, orderly development of the senses was also important because education of the senses was considered the basis of intelligence. The more differentiated (ordered) children's perceptions of stimuli, the more intelligent their behavior.

The ultimate manifestation of internal order, however, was the child's increasing ability to discipline him- or herself toward the accomplishment of a goal, either self-determined or set forth by someone else. The development of active self-discipline represents the development of will, exhibited in focused, self-directed, purposeful actions.

The conclusive sign of active self-discipline, the evidence of mature autonomy, is reflected in a child's ability to so discipline herself that she can submit her spontaneous activity to the will of a higher authority. This achievement requires that a child learn not only to impose self-restraint, but also to actively coordinate her chaotic movements and thoughts and direct them toward a useful purpose.

Montessori's ideas about obedience are frequently challenged. But the meaning of obedience, as discussed by Montessori, is imbued with meaning that extends far beyond passively conforming to someone else's expectations. To the contrary, the true meaning of obedience for Montessori resides in an individual willingly, actively, even joyfully, submitting herself to someone else's will. Chattin-McNichols's (1992b) response to those who criticize Montessori's views on obedience for fostering conformity is especially cogent.

> This notion of obedience is one in which the spiritual side of Montessori and her world view are clearly seen. People who deny the existence of God, feel that it is impossible to enter into a personal relationship with God, or feel that such discussions have no bearing on child development or early education will have trouble understanding Montessori's view on this matter. Such people will not understand how people, including children, can find freedom in obedience to a higher authority. (p. 165)

Once Montessori's interpretations of will, of discipline, of liberty, and of order are situated within her spiritual/metaphysical framework, the seeming contradictions among these concepts, and between her dual roles of scientist and mystic, dissipate. Montessori's pedagogy was predicated on her beliefs in the existence of a Superior Being. The first 6 years of a child's life, similar to the beginning of creation, produce order out of chaos. Functionally, the directress represents an all-knowing, benevolent power; through creation of the prepared environment, she nourishes children's inherent destiny and thus determine the future.

> When the teacher shall have touched in this way, soul for soul, each one of her pupils, awakening and inspiring the life within them as if she were an invisible spirit, she will then possess each soul, and a sign, a single word from her shall suffice; for each one will feel her in a living and vital way, will recognize her and will listen to her. . . . They will look toward her who had made them live, and will hope and desire to receive from her, new life. (Montessori, 1912/1964, p. 116)

Nor did Montessori's belief in scientific, "rational" thinking challenge her framework. For Montessori, science provided a means for verifying her metaphysical constructs. She conceptualized science, as she did her method, as a carefully sequenced technique, not an ongoing process of discovery. Science, like her method, could create order out of disorder and produce absolute truth.

The Montessori Program

Based on her experiments in the Children's Houses, Montessori believed that she had determined a scientific and rational method for facilitating the child's "inner work of psychical adaptation." The method was not amenable to child or teacher modification because, in line with Montessori's thinking, any modification would annul its scientific validity. The method and its materials, therefore, were deliberately devised and were to be precisely used.

In addition to the physical environment of the Children's House, which includes the actions of the directress, Montessori outlined three components to her method for 3- to 7-year-olds who work together in multi-aged groupings: motor education, sensory education, and language education.

Children's care of the classroom environment provides a primary means for motor education. The didactic materials provide for sensory and language education. Montessori described the accomplishments of this formative developmental period as preparation for life: children emerged adaptive and self-disciplined, their personality ordered and equipped for higher order learning. The elementary curriculum builds on the academic skills already possessed by Montessori preschool graduates and is extraordinarily detailed and highly sequenced. The elementary curriculum encompasses the teaching of Italian grammar, reading, arithmetic, geometry and metrics, and drawing and music (Montessori, 1917/1964).

The Prepared Environment.   The learning environment, which might vary if resources were limited, included several rooms plus direct access to a real garden that could be tended by the children. The principal room was the space for "intellectual work," referring to the work with the didactic materials that are described below. Other proposed rooms included a sitting room or parlor for children's casual interactions and a dining room with low, accessible cupboards for dinner and silverware so children could set the tables and return utensils to their place.

The plates were real china and the tumblers glass so children could learn to take care of fragile items and directly understand the consequences of their being treated carelessly. The dressing room contained shelves for each child and wash basins of child height, so children could learn and practice proper hygiene.

Although Montessori apparently should not be credited for originating the use of child-sized furniture (see Hewes, 1983), the frequency with which child-sized furniture is suggested as a Montessori innovation suggests that she must have helped to popularize its use. Perhaps what was unique to Montessori was her emphasis on the classroom design of furniture and its adaptation to children, rather than adults, as critical to the child's healthy development. Now, of course, child-sized furniture and learning materials specially designed for children's intellectual development is an accepted part of early childhood classrooms; Montessori's ideas on this subject now seem commonplace. But, Montessori had reasoned that without such adjustments, children could not learn to socially adapt to their environments; nor could they learn to function independently and responsibly.

The furniture, child-sized tables, chairs, and sofas, was light in weight so it could be moved easily by children and light in color so children could easily wash it.

Montessori also emphasized that the working room had to contain a long, low cupboard with large doors to store the didactic materials. The height of the cupboard helped make the materials easily accessible, thus fostering independence. A second indispensable piece of furniture was a chest of drawers containing several columns of little drawers, each with a bright handle and a small card with a name on it. Each child had his or her own drawer for personal belongings. The room was decorated with pictures hung at children's eye level, and there were ornamental and flowering plants. Montessori believed beauty promoted concentration and refreshed the spirit. Again, it might be hard to read this information with appreciation because today such furnishings are commonplace; but a child-centered environment was quite innovative in the early twentieth century.

Motor Education.   Motor education describes a series of exercises that aid the normal development of physiological movements, such as walking, breathing, and speech, and enable children to care for their own practical needs of dressing and undressing. Montessori divided motor education into two corresponding parts: free gymnastics and educational gymnastics. Free gymnastics did not involve apparatus; it incorporated required and directed exercises, such as marching, to facilitate self-control and poise, and free games with balls, hoops, and kites.

The aim of educational gymnastics was to foster independence and to "give order to (a child's) movements, leading him to those actions which his efforts are actually tending" (Montessori, 1917/1965, pp. 20–21). Educational gymnastics included caring for plants and animals and the practical life exercises, which embraced not only the development of what we would today call self-help skills, but also care for the Children's House, rhythmic movements, gardening, and manual work, which had as its aim production of socially useful objects, such as clay pots.

To teach children self-help skills, Montessori created a collection of wooden frames to which different materials were attached that could be buttoned, hooked, tied together, and so forth. Montessori's description of how the directress should model their use illustrates the way in which Montessori promoted, in careful sequence, the orderly development of children's movements. The teacher, sitting beside a child, "performs the necessary movements of the fingers very slowly and deliberately, separating the movements themselves into their different parts, and letting them be seen clearly and minutely" (Montessori, 1917/1965, p. 22).

As with all the materials, the directress silently demonstrates their appropriate use; Montessori felt words should be kept to a minimum because they distract children from focusing on what they are to learn. Children are taught all movements in this way, including how to sit, rise from one's seat, take up and lay down objects, and offer them to others; wash their faces, polish their shoes, wash the furniture, and set the table. Each exercise is broken down into its component parts and carefully sequenced and analyzed in order to promote the larger purpose of these exercises: the child's coordinated, proficient, and self-restrained movements, all of which are directed toward a useful outcome increasingly under the child's personal control.

Inasmuch as preparing the environment is analogous to a scientist's preparation of instruments, motor education is comparable to the scientist's preparation of subjects. In this instance, preparation of the child primes him

> to exercise himself and to form himself as a man. It is not movement for its own sake that he will derive from these exercises, but a powerful co-efficient in the complex formation of his personality. . . . From his consciousness of this development. . . the child derives the impulse to persist in these tasks, the industry to perform them, the intelligent joy he shows in their completion. (Montessori, 1917/1965, pp. 151–152)

Sensory Education.   The Montessori Method emphasizes methodical education of the senses based on Montessori's belief that education of the senses is the basis of intellectual development. Montessori aimed to refine the differential perception of stimuli by means of repeated exercise. The didactic materials, which are the vehicles for sensory development (see Table 3–2 for a listing of Montessori's didactic materials) were developed so children could *exercise* (versus educate) their senses.

Table 3–2
Montessori Didactic Materials

Didactic Materials for the Education of the Senses
3 sets of solid insets
3 sets of solids in graduated sizes: pink cubes, brown prisms, and colored rods
Geometric solids (e.g., prism, pyramid, sphere)
Rectangular tablets with rough and smooth surfaces
Collection of various stuffs (e.g., velvets, satins, woolens)
Small wooden tablets of different weights
2 boxes, each containing 64 colored tablets
Chest of drawers containing plane insets
3 series of cards on which are pasted geometrical forms in paper
Collection of cylindrical closed boxes (sounds)
Double series of musical bells, wooden boards on which are painted the lines used in music, small wooden discs for the notes

Didactic Materials for the Preparation for Writing and Arithmetic
2 sloping desks and various iron insets
Cards on which are pasted sandpaper letters
2 alphabets of colored cardboard in different sizes
Cards on which are pasted sandpaper numerals
A series of large cards bearing the same figures in smooth paper for the enumeration of numbers above ten
2 boxes with small sticks for counting
Drawings belonging to the Method and colored pencils
Frames for lacing, buttoning, and so forth

From Montessori, M. (1964). *Dr. Montessori's Own Handbook* (pp. 18–21). New York: Robert Bentley, Inc. (Original work published in 1914)

Although the didactic materials are probably the Montessori Method's best known attribute, their use only comprised 1 hour of her proposed daily schedule (see Table 3–3), which, it will be recalled, initially corresponded to parents' working hours (Montessori, 1912/1964).

The didactic materials were designed to develop a child's increasingly refined ability to differentiate qualities of color, form, size, texture, temperature, and weight. They are carefully sequenced/graded so that as a child moves from one material to another, distinctions in size, texture, and so forth are finer and finer.

The didactic materials are auto-educative. They are structured to allow only one correct response; it is this characteristic that makes them self-correcting and allows children to proceed at their own pace, independent of the directress, once a lesson has been received. Children's repetitive use of the same didactic material was evidence, according to Montessori, of the child's work toward self-formation; in turn, it is the activity of self-formation that is the child's work.

The didactic materials represent the primary means by which the environment is prepared, that is, individualized, for each child. A child's progressive use of the didactic materials corresponds to his or her schedule of psychical development; the self-correcting component assures a child's inner development is being appropri-

Table 3–3
Schedule of a Child's Day

Opening at Nine O'clock—Closing at Four O'clock
9–10. Entrance. Greeting. Inspection as to personal cleanliness. Exercises of practical life; helping one another to take off and put on the aprons. Going over the room to see that everything is dusted and in order. Language: Conversation period: Children give an account of the events of the day before. Religious exercises.
10–11. Intellectual exercises. Objective lessons interrupted by short rest periods. Nomenclature, Sense exercises.
11–11:30. Simple gymnastics: Ordinary movements done gracefully, normal position of the body, walking, marching in line, salutations, movements for attention, placing of objects gracefully.
11:30–12. Luncheon: Short prayer.
12–1. Free games.
1–2. Directed games, if possible, in the open air. During this period the older children in turn go through with the exercises of practical life, cleaning the room, dusting, putting the material in order. General inspection for cleanliness: Conversation.
2–3. Manual work. Clay modelling, design, etc.
3–4. Collective gymnastics and songs, if possible in the open air. Exercises to develop forethought: Visiting, and caring for, the plants and animals.

From Montessori, M. (1964). *The Montessori Method* (pp. 119–120). New York: Schocken Books. (Original work published in 1912)

ately directed. A child's eventual disregard for the material reveals successful mastery of the perceptual differentiation inherent in the material.

A child's increasing perceptual sophistication, in turn, epitomizes the child's increasingly orderly representation of the environment. Sequential mastery of the didactic materials forms the foundation of the child's intellectual development by enabling him or her to more accurately gather information through the senses and thus learn from the environment.

> The didactic material, in fact, does not offer to the child the "content" of the mind, but the *order* for that "content." It causes him to distinguish identities from differences, extreme differences from fine gradations, and to classify, under conceptions of quality and of quantity, the most varying sensations appertaining to surfaces, colors, dimensions, forms and sounds. The mind has formed itself by a special exercise of attention, observing, comparing, and classifying. (Montessori, 1914/1964, pp. 82–83)

Language Education.   The language component of the Montessori Method has two parts: the association of language with sensory perceptions, and reading and writing. Language education occurs concurrently with sensory education, and fixes, by means of exact words that are distinctly articulated, the ideas that the mind has acquired.

Writing, reading, and arithmetic are considered later developments that naturally follow education of the senses, emerging around 4 years of age. Sensory education, in addition to its other contributions to children's development, prepares their minds and hands for writing, and for the ideas of quantity, identity, differences, and gradation. Thus, Montessori writes of children's "explosion into writing," which precedes reading, as a natural next-step in a child's intellectual development.

The directress plays a more direct role in this process through the presentation of three-step lessons that accompany the child's use of the didactic materials. These lessons are presented as simply as possible, to avoid placing any obstacles between the child and the experience and to minimize any interference with the child's spontaneous activity. During the first step or period, the directress presents the name of the focal characteristic, for example, "This is red." In the second period, the child is tested on her recognition of the object corresponding to the name: "Give me the red." In the third and final period, the child is asked to identify the name of the object: "What is this?" This sequence, according to Montessori, brings order to children's experience and leads a child from sensations to ideas, from the concrete to the abstract.

Absence of an appropriate response from a child during any of these lessons is interpreted as an indication of his lack of readiness for the psychic association that the directress was attempting to promote. In such circumstances, the directress is expected to retreat quietly and to try again another time. Under no circumstances should the directress try to correct the child, because to do so could lead the child to make an unnatural effort to learn the desired response and thus confound her spontaneous activity.

Montessori presented learning to read and write as extensions of sensory education. The preparatory exercises for writing and reading are embedded within the practical life exercises and sensory education. These program components develop the motoric and perceptual skills needed for writing and reading.

Learning to write and read also is directed by specialized didactic materials. The specially developed didactic materials for writing have children trace outlines and insides of geometric figures with colored pencils, trace sandpaper letters using the fingers and motions associated with writing (which fixes the visual image of letters in muscular memory), and construct words from movable alphabet letters. As the child traces various letters, the directress gives the appropriate letter sound; thus, the child sees a letter, feels it, and hears its sound. Finally, when children begin to construct words, they also learn to sound them out.

Didactic materials for the lessons in reading consist of cards on which are written words and phrases well-known to the children. Children already know from their previous work how to sound out words phonetically. The next step in the sequence involves understanding the sense of the word—giving meaning to the sounds—which the method provokes by giving children opportunities to associate the written word with its representation, for example, the word *ball* with the actual object. Children repeatedly sound out the word written on the card until "finally the word bursts upon his consciousness" (Montessori, 1912/1964, p. 298; it must be noted that Italian grammar and phonology suffer from few of the exceptions that traumatize learners of English). The exercise is concluded by having the child place the word read with the corresponding object.

Montessori found that most children learned to write and read by the age of 5. The ability to make use of written language to express ideas is viewed as an indication that children have achieved the mental maturity to begin elementary work, during which the process initiated in the Children's House is continued albeit with a subject matter focus (Montessori, 1917/1964).

■ *The Importance of Timing*

Initial interest in the Montessori Method in the United States, as well as revival of interest after its "dismissal" in 1916, confirms the significance of historical timing. It also suggests the extent to which preferences for particular educational ideas are linked to cultural, economic, and societal interests and beliefs.

Montessori's arrival in the United States in 1913 certainly found a fertile environment in terms of popular interest and societal need. However, the early childhood profession had just completed a stressful re-examination of its practices, thus, perhaps, making them less willing to open themselves to further debate. Furthermore, despite overlapping beliefs in science as a basis for early education and appreciation for a child-centered approach, Montessori's educational assumptions and method differed in ways that the thinking of the times would not accommodate.

This disjunction was probably exacerbated by the fact that Montessori thought of her method as complete. Her method was based on scientific pedagogy, which, in her thinking, led to the discovery of absolute truth (Montessori, 1912/1964). Even though her results had been based on only 2 years of "experimentation" in the Children's Houses, she did not view her techniques as arbitrary or open to further experimentation (Kramer, 1976/1988; Montessori, 1917/1965. Montessori, 1912/1964, rationalized this short experimental period by proclaiming it the culmination of years of effort that began with the work of Itard and then Sequin). In the mid-sixties, however, Montessori's ideas found not only popular interest, but also a new set of psychological assumptions regarding child development that brought with it scholarly support. Even more important, her ideas not only corresponded with societal needs and interest, they found policy support at the highest levels for re-examining and expanding early childhood education, especially for low-income children. In the mid-sixties, the Montessori Method found its historical, societal, and educational "match."

With the apparent surge of interest from public schools, the Montessori Method is aligned once again at a powerful intersection of societal (desegregation) and educational (academic success for a diverse student population) need. Thus, in the sixties as well as the present, interest in the Montessori Method has swelled in response to the model's capacity, at least rhetorically, to respond to larger societal concerns, rather than to the perceived educational needs of young children. It is noteworthy that at no time in its American history has the Montessori Method been touted by mainstream early childhood education.

Montessori's ardent, longtime followers also deserve credit for sustaining the Montessori Method, including their internalization of Montessori's messianic zeal and fervor. Almost from the beginning of her work, Montessori surrounded herself with a small group of women who devoted their lives to her. On November 10, 1910, this group, along with Montessori, even met in a Roman chapel to dedicate their lives to the cause (Cohen, 1969; Kramer, 1976/1988).

On her death in 1952, Montessori's ideas and methods continued to be tightly controlled by her adherents. Her efforts were sustained by her son, Mario, who served as president of the Association Montessori Internationale until his death in 1981. Today her grandson, Dr. Mario Montessori, Jr., fulfills this role, although he is less involved in the AMI's activities (Chattin-McNichols, 1992b).

These efforts to sustain and control the integrity of the Montessori Method have not been without negative consequence, however. In addition to sustaining the continuation of the Montessori Method, they also have helped assure the isolation of the method from the mainstream of educational thought and limited the intellectual growth of the model (Kramer, 1976/1988), a characteristic further strengthened by the dominance of Montessori's writings in Montessori teacher-training programs (Simons & Simons, 1986).

The tendency toward exclusiveness persists until this day. As recently acknowledged by Chattin-McNichols (1992b), an advocate of the Montessori Method and a Montessori teacher educator and supervisor, many Montessorians feel that their training (which takes about 12 months and on successful completion results in certification as a Montessori teacher) has taught them everything they need to know about children and teaching. Consequently, many feel they have no need to remain current with developments in the fields of child development and early childhood education. According to Chattin-McNichols, there is almost no communication between Montessorians and other educators.

This discussion helps explain Kramer's conclusion that Montessori's ideas "became enshrined in a movement that took on more and more of the character of a special cult rather than becoming part of the mainstream of educational theory and practice" (1976/1988, p. 16). In terms of our investigation of curriculum models, cognizance of these factors adds to the contextual complexity of the exploration by revealing the interplay between the personality of individuals and their models of curriculum.

This discussion also raises questions regarding the viability of static approaches to education. Based on their review of Montessori's ideas and methods, Simons and Simons (1986) concluded "that Montessori education, as practiced today, is misguided in its attempt to keep alive a system of education that may have been effective and appropriate in the past, but which, being fossilized, is inappropriate for the children of today" (p. 218). In attempting to protect the purity of her method, Montessori helped guarantee that it would be challenged as socially exclusive and intellectually out-of-date.

These insights, which benefit from historical hindsight, need not be limited to discussion of the Montessori Method, however. Ideally, hindsight might provoke foresight. Perhaps the Montessori experience illuminates a tension inherent to all curriculum models. If such is the case, the Montessori Method, rather than being an anomaly, might function as one of the clearest illustrations of the potentially restraining character of curriculum models.

■ *For Further Reading*

Kramer, R. (1976/1988). *Maria Montessori: A biography.* Reading, MA: Addison-Wesley.

  Kramer's biography of Montessori places her work within both a historical and personal context. Her conclusions help support the linkages between teaching and autobiography.

Loeffler, M. G. (Ed.). (1992). *Montessori in contemporary American culture.* Portsmouth, N.H.: Heinemann.

  This edited text is based on a series of papers presented at a 3-day symposium held in 1990 and sponsored by the American Montessori Society (AMS). As the book's title suggests, the readings examine Montessori's legacy and contemporary application. Of particular interest is Nancy McCormick Rambusch's chapter, which describes some of the tension between AMS and its European counterpart, AMI, and Lilian Katz's chapter, and the accompanying set of replies, which detail her questions about the Montessori Method.

Montessori, M. (1964). *The Montessori Method* (A. E. George, Trans.). New York: Schocken. (Original work published in English in 1912)

Montessori, M. (1964). *Dr. Montessori's own handbook.* Cambridge, MA: Robert Bentley. (Original work published 1914)

Montessori, M. (1965). *Spontaneous activity in education* (F. Simmonds, Trans.). New York: Schocken Books. (Original work published in English in 1917)

These three books comprehensively describe and explain Montessori's method for 3- to 7-year-olds. Readers interested in her elementary methods should refer to her book on advanced methods, but its content is linked to Italian grammar and phonology, which limits its direct usefulness. *The Montessori Method* is the most detailed and also includes considerable history. *Spontaneous Activity in Education* primarily describes Montessori's philosophical rationale, whereas *Dr. Montessori's Own Handbook* details the prepared environment and the use of the didactic materials. The *Handbook* is the most readable of these three books, perhaps because it was written originally in English.

■ ■ ■ ■ ■ ■

Chapter 4

The Developmental-Interaction Approach

■ ■ ■ ■ ■ ■

There is a central thesis governing the choice of techniques for advancing cognitive proficiency within the developmental-interaction point of view. . . . [T]his thesis maintains, first, that in a coherent system, techniques selected in the interest of a particular educational target should be justified in terms of a comprehensive concept of an optimal learning environment. Second, there needs to be constant weighing of the impact of any given technique on any other established goals for the development of the child.

Barbara Biber, Early Education and Psychological Development, 1984

We thought we were the wave of the future. We could not have imagined the important place that behavior modification as applied to preschool education would attain in the 1960s and thereafter as part of government planning in particular and in academic circles in general. We also could not imagine how much the past would be forgotten or misread, as though "thinking," because it was not called cognition, had no place in the earlier educational designs. We could not imagine that what to us was a steady course of experimentation directed toward basic change in the philosophy of early education would come to be designated as "traditional."

Barbara Biber, Early Education and Psychological Development, 1984

An inquiry into the Developmental-Interaction approach (also known as the Bank Street approach) depicts far more than a particular approach to early education. It also reveals a significant historical slice of early childhood education; the subtle effects of status accorded theory versus practice, researcher versus teacher, and cognition versus affect; and the extent to which a profession and its practice can be influenced by external circumstances. In addition, once again, the pivotal impact of an educational viewpoint colliding with an unsympathetic, historical moment is exposed.

Although the name "developmental-interaction approach" was not officially assigned until the early seventies (Shapiro & Biber, 1972), the beginnings of this approach to early education can be traced to the early 1900s and the advent of Progressivism and progressive education.[1] In contrast to the curriculum models discussed in the next two chapters, the Developmental-Interaction approach evolved from the daily practice of nursery school practitioners (and pioneers), especially Harriet Johnson, Lucy Sprague Mitchell, and Caroline Pratt. Rather than a preferred theory determining the direction of practice, practice within a specified value framework was linked with ongoing research and eventually a theoretical framework.

Yet contrary to the Montessori Method, which similarly grew from the experiences of a practitioner, the details of practice never became prescribed. Until its formalization as an approach to early childhood education, much of what teachers knew and understood about children, child development, and education was personal and individual, even though informed by, and an informant to, practice, research, and theory.

The Developmental-Interaction approach originated with the progressive, experimental, New York City nursery schools of Harriet Johnson and Caroline Pratt, and their collaborative relationship with Lucy Sprague Mitchell, who was a dynamic and influential feminist. Mitchell wanted to foster the development of emotionally secure and healthy children because "'whole' children were the best guarantors of a progressive, humanistic society" (Antler, 1987, p. xviii). In 1916, with the generous financial support of a relative, Mitchell formed the Bureau of Educational Experiments (BEE), which created a supportive, organizational structure for the evolution of an approach to early education and teacher education that rapidly assumed national status (Antler, 1982, 1987). When the Bureau moved its location to 69 Bank Street (still in New York City) in 1930, its approach to early childhood education and teacher education assumed the name "the Bank Street approach," even though the Bureau did not officially bear the name Bank Street College of Education until 1950.

---

[1] The Developmental-Interaction approach, of course, is only one example of an educational approach whose roots extend to the progressive education movement. It would seem remiss, therefore, not to note the British Infant Schools. The British experience of the 1960s and 1970s remains unique in its successful adaptation of progressive ideas on a large scale. As exemplified by the British Infant Schools, which served 4- through 7-year-olds, the British philosophy represented a fusion of many sources, including progressive experiments in Europe and America in the late 19th and early 20th centuries; the ideas of Froebel, Montessori, Margaret Macmillan, Abigail Eliot and Caroline Pratt; plus the educational philosophy of Dewey and developmental theory of Piaget. The Infant Schools were characterized by their respect for the child as a unique individual, family groupings, the use of open classrooms, unstructured days, integrated learning through play and projects, children as agents in their own learning, and concrete, first-hand experiences. In the United States, these ideas were most frequently associated with the open approach to education. For further information, the reader is referred to Rogers, 1970.

In the late fifties, Bank Street staff became interested in placing their cumulative, practical knowledge base within a theoretical framework (spurred in part, perhaps, by the aging of their living informants such as Lucy Sprague Mitchell, who retired from her work at Bank Street in 1956). Although various Bank Street faculty members helped conceptualize and describe the Developmental-Interaction approach, Barbara Biber, who joined the Bureau of Educational Experiments in 1928, is credited with shaping its developmental interaction theory (Antler, 1987; Shapiro & Mitchell, 1992; Zimiles, 1987); she also was its most prolific spokesperson. According to Biber (1977b),

> By 1959, it seemed fruitful to examine critically the rationale—the basic assumptions about learning—that was the foundation for the educational practices presumed to attain the stated values and goals. Knowledge of the growing field of child development and psychology of learning had indeed influenced these assumptions, but they had been primarily derived from the direct experience of observing and teaching children in school. . . . To what extent would formulations and viewpoints in the field of psychology, arrived at independently of the field of education, corroborate these assumptions and thus provide a firmer theoretical base for the practices? (p. 425)

The advent of Head Start in 1965 served as a catalyst for continued pursuit of a more highly developed theoretical rationale for preschool education. At this point in time, Bank Street refined its previous conceptualization and more clearly delineated the distinctions between psychological concepts and their implications for the teacher's role (see, for example, Biber, 1967).

By the early 1970s, the Bank Street approach had been formally renamed the Developmental-Interaction approach. This name change occurred, according to Biber (1977b), because "it is time to be signified by (our) essential theoretical characteristics rather than by a bit of fortuitous geography" (p. 423).[2] This accounting, however, would seem to provide only a partial explanation. The renaming and expanded conceptualization of the Bank Street approach coincides with the 1967 creation of Project Follow Through and the influx of federal dollars for experimental early childhood programs. In contrast to the dynamic character of experimental programs in the early 1900s, however (see, for example, Winsor, 1973), experimental early childhood programs in the 1960s were derivatives of preconceived curriculum models.

Project Follow Through, and eventually a segment of Head Start, was structured to differentiate the effectiveness of early childhood curriculum models. Consequently, Bank Street's participation in Project Follow Through necessitated the formulation of its practice into a curriculum model. Examination of the Developmental-Interaction approach, therefore, presents a singular opportunity to ponder the after-effects of exchanging evolving, dynamic, individualistic practice for practice ordained in terms of a formal theoretical framework.

---

[2]   Shapiro adds that although the approach had been identified with the Bank Street College of Education, its new name was, in part, an attempt to acknowledge the fact that the approach was not limited to the institution. According to Shapiro, "It would be, and would have been, presumptuous, to say the least, to act as if Bank Street was the only source of this way of conceptualizing early childhood education" (personal communication). Even so, Bank Street takes credit for having "a uniquely long-term experience" with putting the theory into practice (Shapiro & Biber, 1972, p. 55; Shapiro & Mitchell, 1992, p. 15).

Current scholarly arguments about the activity of teaching emphasize its emergent nature and the importance of framing teaching in terms of its dynamic qualities (see Chapter 8). Thus, current deliberations regarding teaching provide ad hoc validation for the experimental frame of reference that originally characterized the Bank Street approach. But the experimental tone of the 1960s was not organized around practice; it was organized around the implementation of systematized curriculum models. In the mid-sixties and early seventies, experimentation occurred at the level of program conceptualization—not teacher practice.

Therefore, with the advent of Project Follow Through, adherents of the Bank Street approach needed to direct their attention to assembling the essential components of what became labeled the Developmental-Interaction approach. Rather than an evolutionary educational approach seeking continuous input and undergoing incessant self-assessment, the Bank Street approach—with the onset on curriculum models—unexpectedly became designated a program option. In addition, because the Bank Street approach exemplified existing thinking about early childhood education, advocates were compelled to defend the superiority of this approach relative to the new curriculum possibilities suddenly available for young children (see, for example, Biber, 1988; Franklin & Biber, 1977).

But more than the opportunity to participate in Project Follow Through seems to have been at stake. On the one hand, based on the defensive, sometimes exasperated tone of their writings in the seventies, one suspects that Bank Street's participation in Project Follow Through was actually an attempt to place the Bank Street approach "on the playing field," to assure that it was, in fact, a program option, and to legitimate and validate its long-standing approach to early childhood education for *all* children, regardless of socioeconomic status.[3] (The Developmental-Interaction approach con-

---

3   Greenberg (1987), in an apparent outburst of frustration with the lack of recognition given these early childhood educators, suggests their ideas were ignored because they were women.

> Have we accepted the traditional cultural assumption that child care is "women's work," and is therefore low status, so what's so great about those old nursery school teachers anyway? Are we saying that our field, because a woman's field regardless of the many warm and wonderful men in it, did not count until the male psychologists entered it in the 60s? ... To progressive educators, harsh discipline was anathema, interpersonal interaction was of prime importance, and emotional expressiveness through play and the arts were highly prized. Lack of discipline is soft. Love and friendship are soft. The arts (unlike sciences) are soft. Emotional expressiveness is soft. Children are soft. Little children are softer still. And women are softest of all, as are the areas of work historically allocated to them.... Our cultural ideal, on the other hand, is touch, hard, and masculine. "Hard" science, for example, is far more highly esteemed than a "soft" field such as "domestic science." Is it coincidental that when, in the 60s, the leadership of our field for the first time became suddenly male, psychosocial went out of fashion and cognitive, learning objectives, scientific terminology, and statistical research swooped in? We have managed to overlook the progressives' extensive scientific research not because it wasn't done primarily by males, but because, far worse, it wasn't even done in the male mode—distanced, termed "objective," wreathed in statistics. The progressives "just" observed, recorded, hypothesized, experimented, and did the other things scientists do. (p. 83)

Greenberg's provocative proposition takes on an additional layer of profundity when one realizes that women's choice of careers in such "female" fields as child development and preschool education during the early 1900s reflected their eagerness to participate in their era's social reform efforts. Many of these women, including Lucy Mitchell, were members of the first generation of college-educated women (Antler, 1987).

tended that although the specifics of practice might change when working with children from low-income families, programmatic principles did not.)

In addition, to the extent that the Developmental-Interaction approach synthesized multiple theoretical perspectives, its formalization re-affirmed the historical and contemporary importance of the "whole child." It can be argued, therefore, that Bank Street's efforts also represented an attempt to re-establish a cohesive framework for a field unexpectedly fragmented by diverse and often contradictory approaches to early education (the "evidence" stitched together relative to this last point can be found in Biber, 1979; Franklin, 1981; Shapiro & Biber, 1972; Weber, 1984, Chapter 11).

According to Zimiles (1987), a long-term Bank Street faculty member, Bank Street faculty realized their approach had to be explicated and their method codified in order for it to be disseminated and made more accessible and universal.[4] The Bank Street approach had evolved from the practice and intellect of a handful of people. Its experimental, evolutionary character was well-suited to its intimate setting, and given the relatively small dimensions of nursery education in the United States until the mid-sixties, no pressure existed to do otherwise. But, with the initiation of Head Start, not only did the numbers of children attending preschool programs swell, but so did the unanticipated demand for teachers, the majority of whom were hired without formal preparation as early childhood educators.[5] Thus, the push for codification was not just a theoretical issue; it was also a response to an unprecedented demand for early childhood programming.

■ Evolution from Experimental Nursery Program to the Developmental-Interaction Approach

The history of the Developmental-Interaction approach is a chronology of significant events and shifts in thinking that influenced the evolution of a multifaceted program

---

[4]   In response to my argument, Shapiro contends that there was another goal.

Partly because the writings were scattered and dealt with one issue or another, partly because the teacher's role is extremely demanding, and perhaps also because many people prefer simplicity to complexity, there were many who dismissed the Bank Street approach as a "mystique." Writing the 1971 pamphlet [Promoting Cognitive Growth] and '72 paper [referring to her paper written with Barbara Biber] were strongly motivated by the desire to "demystify"; the goal was not to codify but to clarify. (personal communication)

[5]   This factor eventually led to the creation of the Child Development Associate credential with which Biber was actively involved.

toward a cognitive-affective position. The Developmental-Interaction approach is the only approach/model under consideration that is informed by *multiple* theoretical perspectives assembled in terms of their congruity with preferred values and practice. Furthermore, when officially labeled the Developmental-Interaction approach in the early seventies, the program's conceptual framework reflected six decades of ongoing involvement and leadership in early childhood classrooms and the field of early childhood education. This fact led Biber (1977a) to comment, "To experienced educators many newly structured programs appeared unseasoned in quality and restricted in scope because most psychologists were newcomers to the world of early education . . ." (p. 41).

But, the history of the Developmental-Interaction approach also is linked with the histories of progressive education and the nursery school movement; to understand the subtleties that clarify the Developmental-Interaction approach and its evolution, it is necessary to appreciate the intersection of these three histories. Group, out-of-home care that focused on the "educational" versus "custodial" needs of young children was rare in the early 1900s; despite its dramatic growth through the 1920s, nursery schools remained sparse until the advent of Head Start in 1965. Today, we take the proliferation of preschool programs (a term, by the way, of more modern vintage) for granted, but in 1920, only three nursery schools were in existence; in 1924, there are records of 25 programs, and by 1928, with the expansion of university-based programs, 89 nursery schools were recorded (Goodykoontz, Davis, & Gabbard, 1948).

These nursery schools, however, even though few in number and mostly for white, urban, middle- and upper-class children,[6] were diverse in approach. The Developmental-Interaction approach represents an example of this diversity; its evolution can be chronicled in three loosely configured phases: its experimental, progressive beginnings, from 1916, with the creation of the Bureau of Educational Experiments, through the twenties; its alignment with psychodynamic theory beginning in the thirties and continuing through the fifties; and the period of its formalization as an approach to early childhood education after the advent of Head Start in 1965.

During the first phase, the organizational supports for the Developmental-Interaction approach were instituted, its enduring focus and interests articulated, and its leadership role in early childhood teacher education initiated. During the second phase, the psychological basis for the approach solidified. In the last phase, the Developmental-Interaction approach formally articulated and advocated its educa-

---

[6]   According to Cahan (1989), there is some evidence of the existence of a child development movement, separate from those of whites, among blacks during these years.

tional philosophy and preferred practices, delineated itself as a specific approach to early childhood education, and attempted to combat the "misreading of history" (Biber, 1977a, p. 48) by psychologists newly interested in early childhood education.

By the 1960s, Bank Street's approach, along with those of other progressive experimental programs, was considered mainstream nursery education. Evans's (1975) classic examination of early childhood curriculum models reviewed the Developmental-Interaction viewpoint in six pages, as part of a chapter entitled "The Mainstream of Early Childhood Education." Hence, when the shift in thinking regarding the significance of the early years for intellectual development, new interest in cognitive development, and explosion of concern for young, disadvantaged children erupted, Bank Street's approach to early education represented the status quo.

Despite its experimental character, the Bank Street approach was labeled traditional, which in this instance frequently incurred the connotations of outmoded and resistive to change. When nursery education finally was recognized as an appropriate educational beginning for young children and extended to preschoolers from low-income families, the political context, theoretical representations, and educational expectations had shifted. (Chapter 2 discussed this shift in greater detail.) Consequently, after almost 50 years of leading the way for others, the Bank Street approach was placed on the defensive, especially with respect to its emphasis on social-emotional development and its ideas regarding how best to promote children's intellectual development.

The Beginning: The Bureau of Educational Experiments

The beginning of the Developmental-Interaction approach took root in the early 1900s and was closely intertwined with the progressive education movement, especially the views espoused by John Dewey. Progressive education, in turn, was part of the Progressive movement, which sought political and social reforms in response to societal changes wrought by industrialism. Progressive education attempted to improve society through the reform of public education.

According to Cremin (1961/1964), progressivism in education meant broadening the program and function of the school to include direct concern for health, jobs, and the quality of family and community life, applying pedagogical principles derived from new scientific research in psychology and the social sciences to classrooms, and tailoring instruction to the different kinds and classes of children increasingly part of the public schools (pp.viii–ix). Cremin explains that, especially in the beginning of the progressive education movement, there was an inextricable relationship between social reform, reform through education, and the reform of education.

Progressive ideas affected the direction of early childhood education in at least two significant ways: the "overthrow" of Froebelian kindergartens and the establishment of experimental nursery schools. In reference to the dominant kindergarten ideology of the late 1800s and early 1900s, the ideas associated with progressive education provided the impetus for confrontation between adherents to Froebelian-inspired curriculum, which was founded on philosophical idealism, and those who advocated a more progressive, scientifically informed approach to kindergarten education. As already discussed in Chapters 2 and 3, the more progressive-minded kindergarten educators emerged victorious.

Furthermore, about the same time and beyond, kindergarten advocates also were seeking to establish kindergartens in public schools in order to establish a secure financial base. Attempts to institutionalize kindergartens in public schools were accompanied by efforts to increase teachers' professional status through increased training, alliance with other professionals, and reliance upon "scientific" practice (Bloch, 1987; Cremin, 1961/1964; Weber, 1969). These aspirations helped frame kindergarten education's particular, and separate, historical course. Bloch (1987) further suggests that the kindergarten's move toward the age-graded primary school system helped pave the way for nursery schools to forge a separate and autonomous movement.

The nursery movement, which began to flourish after 1920, actually encompassed different type programs; each type program had different principles, practices, and underlying goals (Biber, 1984; Greenberg, 1987; White & Buka, 1987). Experimental nursery schools provided one of the distinctive strands within the nursery school movement, even though they, in turn, varied from each other (Antler, 1982; Biber, 1984; Greenberg, 1987). According to Biber (1984), the experimental preschools shared a common commitment to an experimental approach to early childhood education, rebellion against the rigid methods dominating education, new concepts of childhood and the learning process, and a dedication to recording and analyzing their educational experiments.

Experimental nursery schools, in contrast to research-based programs sponsored by universities and colleges, were linked with the progressive education movement and its mission to alter the practices that dominated public schools (rather than child development research). Experimental nursery schools contended they were a suitable beginning for children's education *and* a lever for basic change in education, "a way of making a breakthrough toward a whole new philosophy of education. This conception of nursery school education was a built-in phase of the progressive education movement with a common body of basic principles and purposes" (Biber, 1984, p. 14). In her 1919 Chairman's report, Mitchell stated, "We think of all our work ultimately in relation to public education" (as cited in Antler, 1987, p. 285).

The Developmental-Interaction approach, therefore, was directed from its very beginning toward school-age children, as well as preschoolers. Educational practices associated with progressivism were seen as appropriate for students of all ages (Biber, 1977b).

Concurrently, progressive nursery school programs saw their experimental efforts as generating a knowledge base about practice that would help operationalize this new philosophy of education. Existing knowledge regarding developmental information about young children and conventional practice in early childhood education was, for the most part, nonexistent when these experimental and research-based programs began. It is their knowledge and experiences that form the core of our current expectations for and about early childhood education, and it was created as a result of intense interest in generating and applying what were then new scientific understandings to the process of education.

The nursery school of Harriet Johnson, which cared for children from 14 months to 3 years of age (later the Harriet Johnson Nursery School and then the Bank Street School for Children, which serves as a laboratory and demonstration center for the Bank Street College of Education and encompasses preschool through eighth grades), and Caroline Pratt's Play School, attended by children 3 years of age through elementary school (later renamed the City and Country School and, according to Greenberg [1987], probably one of the first nursery schools in the United States reflecting what we now call developmentally appropriate practice), became the Bureau's sites for gathering scientific data concerning children's growth and studying educational factors in a school environment. These two programs, which were relocated to the same building, served as the Bureau's laboratory; the practice of teachers in these two programs, in collaboration with Bureau researchers, shaped the beginning of the Developmental-Interaction approach (Antler, 1982; Biber, 1977a).

The research focus of Lucy Sprague Mitchell and her colleagues contrasted, however, with that of university-sponsored child development lab schools. University lab schools were research centers focused on the scientific application of developmental theory to classroom settings and abstracting these principles for enhancing child development or supplying the content for parent education. The BEE's primary purpose, in contrast, was to develop ways to create a functional relationship between research and schooling that would inform planning within the school environment (Antler, 1982, 1987).

This mission was embedded within the humanistic and reformist ideals of progressive education; more fully developed individuals would be more capable of being caring, productive citizens who could create a force for effecting social change. And, consistent with the tenor of progressive education (and in contrast to the behavioristic tendencies informing the habit training curriculum of kindergartens during the 1920s), interest in finding ways to stimulate intellectual development was holistically integrated with physical, emotional, and social development (Antler, 1982; Biber, 1977a, 1984; Cremin, 1964; NAEYC Organizational History and Archives Committee, 1976; Weber, 1969).

In contrast to other progressive experiments, however, the Bureau also placed a strong emphasis on scientific measurement to assist teachers in planning the learning environment for children (Antler, 1982). The new science of psychology and scientific orientation to education was generating interest in observing and documenting children's behaviors, but the BEE's interest was not in understanding children per se. They used their data to inform practice. "We are working on a curriculum, checking it by our growth records; and working on how to record growth, evaluating our records by the children's reactions to our planned environment" (1919 Bureau Annual Report, as cited in Antler, 1982, p. 571).

The major programmatic thrust during this early period, according to Biber (1977a, 1977b, 1981) came from John Dewey's image of schooling as a world where young children could be active questioners and experimenters and thus free to develop their thinking and reasoning powers more fully.

> If we were to free the child's intellectual capacity, we had to make learning an active, self-generating, searching experience; if we were to be responsive to the goal of educating the whole child, we had not only to stimulate independent thinking and reasoning processes but to open avenues toward creative reorganization of experience as intrinsic to the learning process; if education was ultimately to effect social change, we had to bring the reality of how the world functions into the classroom curriculum; if we expected children to become awakened to the advantages of a democratic society, we had to provide the experience of living democratically in the social setting of the schoolroom, of being part of a cooperative structure characterized by egalitarian interpersonal relations. (Biber, 1984, p. 309)

Thus, the Bureau's educational and experimental emphasis was on developing the "whole child," nurturing children's individual knowledge of themselves and their world through a curriculum of experiences (a new notion at that time), and a variety of ways, most especially play, to express and represent the experiences they had encountered. Given their long-standing commitment to intellectual development, it is easy to appreciate Biber's consternation over charges launched during the sixties and seventies that the Developmental-Interaction approach was devoid of intellectual fiber.

Mitchell and her colleagues were unique in seeing the bi-directional relationship between research and practice. They were also atypical in emphasizing the importance of "observing (children's) natural behavior in situations planned for children's development" (Mitchell, 1925, as cited in Antler, 1982, p. 575) at a time when their colleagues in university lab schools were more involved in learning about children by testing them.

Both as an essential program premise and a distinctive characteristic, this broader conceptualization of measurement, including what was worth measuring, was significant. Almost 40 years later, it resurfaced as a divisive issue when advocates of the Developmental-Interaction approach protested the assessment of early childhood curriculum models, especially their own, based on narrow measurements of intellectual ability (see Chapter 8 for further discussion on this point; see also Gilkeson, Smithberg, Bowman, & Rhine, 1981; Zimiles, 1977).

During the last half of the 1920s, Mitchell began to reassess the Bureau's priorities, in particular the relationship between its educational and research functions. Significantly, this questioning arose, in part, from doubts about the usefulness of its research efforts for informing educational practice. According to Antler (1982), by the end of the 1920s,

> the bureau was ready to abandon its faith that quantitative measurement could provide the functional indices of children's growth that could guide educational planning. . . . Moreover, Mitchell came to fear that the very formulation of exact standards of normal growth might in fact distort individual variation in development and lead to the promulgation of mechanistic, uniform norms, which if applied as educational guides could deaden rather than enhance children's impulses to learn. (p. 581; this issue reasserted

itself again after Bank Street's formalization as an approach to early childhood education though, this time, relative to the loss of individuality within theories of development; see, Shapiro & Wallace, 1981)

Although an emphasis on research was maintained, it became addressed in a separate division under the leadership of Barbara Biber, who had joined the Bureau in 1928. Then, in 1931, the Bureau, at the request of numerous experimental schools sharing a similar philosophy and in need of teachers who could teach in their experimental programs, established the Cooperative School for Student Teachers (later called the Cooperative School for Teachers) to train nursery, primary, and elementary school teachers for work in schools with a progressive emphasis (Antler, 1982). At this point, the program for teacher education became the Bureau's primary thrust, and their thinking about the way children learned was extended to teacher education. As expressed by Mitchell in the first school catalog:

> Our aim is to help students develop a scientific attitude towards their work and towards life. To use this means an attitude of eager, alert observations; a constant questioning of old procedures in the light of new observations; a use of the world as well as of books as source material; an experimental open-mindedness. . . . We are not interested in perpetuating any special "school of thought." Rather, we are interested in imbuing teachers with an experimental, critical and ardent approach to their work. (as cited in Antler, 1982, p. 583)

By the beginning of the 1930s, the outlines of the Developmental-Interaction approach had been drawn: its child-centered approach; its attention to the nature of the learning environment; a focus on individual development as a conduit for social reform; a complex perception of the teaching role; and an experimental, experiential approach to education.

Moreover, this review of the early history of the Developmental-Interaction approach highlights that, from the very beginning, its architects carved an approach to early childhood education that was distinctive from its contemporaries by uniquely mingling the critical intellectual thinking of the era. The holistic, process-oriented approach to early childhood and teacher education that emerged during these formative years eventually became problematic, however. During the sixties and seventies, when competitive assessment of curriculum models turned precise program implementation and outcome-based evaluations into focal points, a dynamic conceptualization of teaching and learning became a liability because it impeded rapid dissemination and resisted conventional program evaluations.

Emotions as a Prominent Theme:
The Influence of Psychodynamic Theory

According to Cremin (1961/1964), when World War I ended in 1918, the progressive education movement increasingly became disassociated from its original, political concept of social reform. Rather than a more radical notion of schools as vehicles for societal change, the notion of social reform became refashioned around the belief that each individual has uniquely creative potential and that a school attentive to helping children develop their potential is the best guarantee of a society truly devoted to human worth and excellence. Following this shift, two major intellectual streams of thought converged to form the two prongs of child-centered pedagogy: expressionism (which centered on the importance of the arts and the significance of multiple modes of imaginative self-expression) and Freudianism (Cremin, 1961/1964).

The educational efforts of the BEE reflected this shift toward a focus on individual potential and a child-centered pedagogy vitally interested in children's self-expression. Interest in self-expression, however, was embedded within the context of psychodynamic theory, which provided the Developmental-Interaction approach its first *theoretical* parameter (as opposed to its previous reliance on value statements, research, and practice). Although the primary source was Freudian theory, according to Biber (1977a), the nursery school world moved more toward neo-Freudianism, giving more attention to the impact of sociocultural influences and placing less emphasis on determinism.

> New sensitivity to the undersurfaces of behavior, to the depth and power of emotional responsiveness became part of educational thinking. . . . There was increased understanding of the inner struggles of growing up: the management of overwhelming emotion; feelings of ambivalence, conflict, and guilt in relationships with loved figures; the pull between impulse and adaptation, between the lingering comfort of dependence and the siren call of independence. (Biber, 1977a, pp. 47–48)

Previously, and consistent with their progressive leanings, curriculum concerns had centered on providing a learning environment "rich in possibilities for direct contact and interaction with things, people, and ideas—one in which emerging symbolic skills would gain salience by being tested, tried out, and enjoyed in natural functional contexts" (Biber, 1977a, p. 43). Teachers were challenged to find experiences in which children were engaged with thinking and questioning in order to operationalize Dewey's vision of creating a thinking person as a means for effecting social change.

Concern with emotional processes and personality development added a new dimension to the BEE's interest in the "whole child"; attention to how emotions condition the ways children interpret their school experiences now became a primary concern. In addition, the perceived value of free play was expanded beyond its contributions as a mode of thinking and vehicle for symbolic representation to include an appreciation for its role in supporting children's expression of diverse emotions, for synthesizing the subjective and objective aspects of experience, and providing a vehicle for symbolically resolving personal conflicts that could not be faced directly (Biber, 1981).

Thus, this second phase was one of evolution beyond the initial perspective of the early progressive school movement toward a cognitive-affective position. This evolution was informed by concepts from psychodynamic psychology of changing drives, energies, and conflicts at different stages of development (especially as informed by the writings of Issacs (1930/1966) who was attempting to do the same [Biber, 1981]); increased knowledge from developmental psychologists such as

Piaget[7] and Werner about cognitive development, plus parallel effort by educators "who chose to continue and develop the ethos of the progressive school movement" (Biber, 1981, p. 18). According to Biber (1981), during this second phase "What seems to have come together . . . is the earlier ideal image of a curious, creative, problem-solving, socially sensitive individual and the contemporary interest in the life of feeling, the condition of the self, the inner processes and opportunity for personal integration of meanings and purposes in both spheres" (p. 22).

This conceptual extension created a natural alignment with the mental health movement, which assumed national importance during the fifties and sixties. The mental health movement was interested in investigating ways to prevent mental illness by conceptualizing a healthy course of individual development and learning how to make social institutions, such as schools, more supportive (Biber, 1979). Not surprisingly, Biber did considerable writing about the Bank Street approach using the lens of mental health during this time.

Although a unique opportunity to promulgate Bank Street's views, this relationship with mental health helped deepen professional perceptions that the Bank Street approach was a program concerned solely with social-emotional development (versus the whole child). A critical error of the sixties, according to Biber (1984),

> was the misperception of the highly developed discipline of early childhood education as being a socialization-mental health model, seriously neglectful of cognitive stimulation, with more serious consequences for the disadvantaged than for the middle class child. . . . Educators identified with these purposes and programs at Bank Street and elsewhere, felt seriously misunderstood by the critics from academe. (p. 97)

---

7 Given the dominant influence that Piagetian theory exerted on early childhood curriculum in the sixties when interest in cognitive development erupted, digressing to the reactions of Mitchell and others to Piaget's theory in the thirties effectively highlights the significance of timing relative to professional acceptance of new ideas. Mitchell, who earned considerable fame for her children's books, criticized Piaget's assumption that the exclusive function of children's language development was the expression of logical thought and communication, to the exclusion of its function as an "art form" (Antler, 1987). Susan Issacs, whose practice and reflection were important informants to the Bank Street approach during this time, challenged Piaget for his total lack of reference to the contribution of children's psychological experiences to intellectual development, his lack of awareness of children's reasoning ability expressed within the context of their everyday experiences, and the absence of attention to the developmental effect of continuous experiences (Issacs, 1930/1966). And, according to Margaret Pollitzer, co-founder of the Walden School (a pre-1920 progressive school),

> Piaget didn't say anything about creating cooperative children to be citizens in a democracy; that was a big part of our focus as progressive nursery and primary educators.... Piaget examined how children absorb and process information from the external world—but we knew that—we all had lab schools going long before he wrote ... Piaget wasn't at all interested in one of our biggest excitements—the wealth of creativity within a young child that is shaped by feeling and imagination, and bursts out in marvelous language and art.... Piaget was investigating mental mechanics. Progressives were concerned with developing "the whole child" [another of Lucy Mitchell's terms]. Our goal was to create great people (as cited in Greenberg, 1987, p. 75).

The Explosion of Preschool Education: The Bank Street Approach as Defender of "Traditional" Early Childhood Ideals

When Head Start was announced in 1965, it took the Bank Street approach as its prototype (Biber, 1979, 1984; Greenberg, 1987). To some extent, this decision was influenced by economic considerations; there was concern that fewer children could be served with the cognitive-based research programs being promoted by developmental psychologists (Greenberg, 1990a). In addition, there apparently was resistance to "model program clones being mechanically planted in widely diverse settings" (Greenberg, 1990a; p. 45). But according to Greenberg (1987), a member of the government staff who helped formulate the Head Start program during the summer of 1964, the selection primarily reflected the staff's curriculum preference.

> The words "The basic Head Start classroom should work like a Bank Street College elementary classroom for nursery/kindergarten" are in the earliest staff-written concept paper in the Head Start historical files.
>
> It is interesting to note that neither Montessorian nor Piagetian philosophies were prominent in the minds of national staff people designing the Head Start educational component at headquarters. . . . Office of Economic Opportunity staff had collected information about the research being done by people newly interested in enrichment for "disadvantaged" young children: Susan Gray at Peabody, Cynthia and Martin Deutsch at the Institute for Developmental Studies, David Weikart at the Perry Preschool Project which he had begun in 1962, and so on. But the "ideal" was Bank Street style.[8] (Greenberg, 1987, p. 76)

A question that naturally arises at this point is why the Bank Street approach was viewed as "the ideal." One possibility could simply be the fact that Bank Street's approach represented the existing prototype for nursery education and therefore was simply the obvious choice. This possibility is further supported by the fact that many graduates and admirers of the Bank Street approach, including Edward Zigler (who is recognized as a key architect of Head Start), were involved with Head Start's development. But, a stronger explanation can be advanced by taking note of the philosophy and values shared by Head Start and Bank Street.

To begin with, there was compatibility between Head Start's emphasis on health care and social services and Bank Street's advocacy, originating from their progressive roots, for an expanded conceptualization of education. But, an even more vital bond between Head Start and the Bank Street approach resided in their mutual belief that education could provide a vehicle to reform society.

---

8 Williams (1977) suggests a slightly different scenario. Based on her acquaintance with members of the original research and demonstration staff at DARCEE (Susan Gray's program at Peabody and one of the early experimental compensatory programs), Williams contends that it had been the original intent of Project Head Start planners to derive Head Start's educational program from the early experimental, research programs. This plan was not carried out, however, because some educators denounced the behavioral orientation of the demonstration projects and successfully lobbied for use of the "traditional" nursery school approach. "The advocates of reduced structure won their point, and the original Head Start adopted nursery school strategies and content" (p. 62).

Head Start was created as the centerpiece for the War on Poverty. It relied on the optimistic belief that early education could help eradicate the poverty of individuals and minimize inequality by enhancing children's success with public school expectations. Its initial placement in the Office of Economic Opportunity was based on the belief that Head Start was more than "just" an educational intervention for poor children; it was also a community action program with the intent of helping poor people improve their lives through the availability of new resources and technical assistance (Greenberg, 1990a). Head Start's mission was clearly harmonious with the progressive history, affiliations, and values of Bank Street.

According to Biber (1984),

> Head Start represented revolutionary change in the dominant concepts of learning in early childhood and in the relation of school to family and community—revolutionary meaning here that knowledge and principles that had been developed in a sector of society with a small voice were to be applied in the encompassing public sphere. There were conflicting ideal images. Was the Headstart experience to be the most efficient route for children of poverty toward adaptation to the expectation and ideology of the existing public educational system? Or, was Headstart, as it developed as a movement, to be a stimulant toward incorporating new concepts of learning and socializing experience into the public school system? The challenge was social as well as educational. (p.27)

It was more than politically significant, therefore, when Head Start's community action component was minimized, and the program became redefined as primarily an educational intervention. Although this "tacit political simplification of the program" (White & Buka, 1987, p. 74) may have helped save Head Start from the terminal fate experienced by other poverty programs during the early seventies, in narrowing its political definition to an educational program with the mission of preparing children for existing school practices, Head Start became disassociated from its reformist beginnings and emerged an appropriate arena for educational manipulation by psychologists eager to apply their various theories regarding effective early intervention.

With the heightened interest in cognitive development, new-found optimism regarding intellectual malleability, and the diversity of theoretical perspectives, psychologists were eager to test their theories. The Bank Street approach was challenged not only because of its "conventional" thinking, but also because, from the perspective of interested psychologists, its social-emotional emphasis failed to address cognitive development adequately. Furthermore, the fact that the program had historically served white, middle-class children of mostly professional parents led psychologists to contend that the Bank Street approach was a mismatch for the unique intellectual needs of economically disadvantaged children (Miller, 1979).

This interpretation probably was fueled further by existing negative attitudes toward progressive education. According to Cremin (1961/1964), 1957 marked the end of the progressive education era.

> What was already apparent in 1952, and what became ever more apparent as the decade progressed, was the presence of a large and articulate public ready for educational reform

of a nonprogressive variety. . . . When the Russians launched the first space satellite in the autumn of 1957, a shocked and humbled nation embarked on a bitter orgy of pedagogical soul-searching. (Cremin, 1961/1964, pp. 343, 347)

As expressed by Admiral Hyman G. Rickover (1959),[9] "Parents are no longer satisfied with life-adjustment schools. Parental objectives no longer coincide with those professed by the progressive educationists. I doubt we can again be silenced" (pp. 189–190). And, thus was the stage set for the back-to-basics movement and more "scientific" approaches to education.

Consequently, Bank Street's emphasis on social-emotional development as the most appropriate context for nurturing the whole child collided not only with psychologists' focused attention on cognitive development, but also society's new frame of mind. As lamented by Biber (1984), "The ideological fundamentals that we assumed would gradually gain general acceptance came on hard times in the 1960s when a narrow scholasticism dominated experimental programs in search of single-track solutions to the pervasive damage of poverty in early childhood" (Biber, 1984, p. 25). The backlash against progressive education, combined with Head Start's retreat from its original community action agenda, further estranged the values and perspective of the Developmental-Interaction approach from those of its contemporaries.

During the expansive sixties and early seventies, therefore, proponents of the Developmental-Interaction approach were placed on the defensive. Through their involvement as one of the Follow Through curriculum models and their ongoing promotion of Head Start's original intent, they became the standard bearers for educating "the whole child," resisting a constricted focus on children's cognitive development regardless of a child's socio-economic status, and preservers of progressive education's legacy.

■ *The Developmental-Interaction Approach*

The Psychological Rationale

Their self-appropriated name, *Developmental-Interaction approach,* reflects Bank Street's historic concern with the whole child and the complexity such a comprehensive approach entails. Concern with the whole child entails appreciation of the child as both an intellectual and emotional being; respect for the complexity of development implies sensitivity to the complex, interactions between the child and her environment and the complicated, internal interactions between cognition and affect. As defined by Shapiro and Biber (1972) (and continually restated in later writings without revision):

---

9   Admiral Rickover's status as the principal architect of the U.S. Navy's nuclear-powered fleet added enhanced credibility to this conclusion.

> Developmental refers to the emphasis on identifiable patterns of growth and modes of perceiving and responding which are characterized by increasing differentiation and progressive integration as a function of chronological age. Interaction refers, first, to the emphasis on the child's interaction with the environment—adults, other children, and the material world, and second, to the interaction between cognitive and affective spheres of development. The developmental-interaction formulation stresses the nature of the environment as much as it does the patterns of the responding child. (Shapiro & Biber, 1972, pp. 59–60)

Discussions of the Developmental-Interaction viewpoint consistently identify it as an "approach" to early childhood curriculum rather than a model. Avoidance of the term *model* carries semantic importance because it conveys the strong and continuing belief that, despite the formalization of a conceptual framework, the daily practice of education should retain its experimental character. For example, in describing the contribution of the Bank Street School for Children to off-site Follow Through personnel, Biber (1977b) wrote, "It is utilized not only as a live image of a learning environment based on given principles, but also as an example of the 'goal in sight' and as evidence that the 'ideal' and the 'optimal' in all educational designs are matters of continuous study and trial, under any circumstance" (p. 453).

Their belief that education is an experimental, versus applied, undertaking is an important premise to understand because it directly informs the way in which the approach is explained to others, the scope of the teacher role, and the conceptualization of teacher-child interactions. Because the Developmental-Interaction approach has such a personalized interpretation of individual change and views the educational process as dynamic exchanges between the child and every facet of her environment, it cannot, by definition, present a predetermined curriculum and description of teacher strategies and still remain conceptually consistent. One of the side-effects of such a conceptualization, however, is greater reliance on a teacher's knowledge and her ability to recognize and skillfully respond to the individuality of each child and his or her interests, which "is not readily come by" (Franklin & Biber, 1977, p. 26) and requires a special kind of teacher preparation.

This level of teacher sophistication was, in fact, clearly envisioned by those who developed the Developmental-Interaction approach (see, for example, Biber, Gilkeson, & Winsor, 1959; Biber & Snyder, 1948). But the result is an approach more vulnerable to the personal abilities of individual teachers.

> Stated simply, the teacher we are asking for is aware of the complexities of the interaction between intellectual development and affective experience in the developing years. Further, the ideal teacher is aware of the differences in the social codes and styles of interaction among young children from widely different cultural groups. Finally, we are looking for a teacher who can maintain healthy, cohesive group functioning which is so flexibly enacted that individual needs can be sensed, understood and met, with suitable adjustment. (Biber, 1988, p. 46)

The lack of programmatic precision contrasts with the specificity found in the Montessori Method described in Chapter 3 and that of behavioral methodology to be described in Chapter 5. This contrast results not only from their stance toward the practice of early childhood education but also from the fact that the Developmental-Interaction approach conceptualizes research and theory as informants to early childhood education, rather than as determinants of educational goals and/or educational practice. Developmental theory, according to Biber, is not synonymous with educational theory. Developmental theory can provide a rationale for educational practice but not its justification. (This interpretation contrasts most strongly with the Kamii-DeVries approach, which is discussed in Chapter 6.)

The dynamic quality of the Developmental-Interaction approach is intensified further by its bond with psychodynamic theory. Psychodynamic theory characterizes individual development as highly dynamic and personalized; an experience can be understood only in terms of the intellectual and emotional interpretation/reaction an individual provides it, interpretations that are highly charged by emotional substrates.

The Developmental-Interaction approach's strong identification with psychological processes is a distinctive and distinguishing characteristic. No other curriculum model presented in this book claims an allegiance to psychodynamic principles or heavily relies on psychological constructs to rationalize its interest in social-emotional variables, even when such interest exists.

But it is important not to overestimate the interest in promoting healthy personality development because the Developmental-Interaction approach also distinguishes itself from early education programs wholly aligned with psychodynamic theory (Biber, 1984; Franklin & Biber, 1977). Progressive-based programs such as the Walden School, which based its educational efforts on psychoanalytic theory, believed that progressive ideals could best be achieved through resolution of the largely unconscious problems intrinsic to the maturational process; these programs adapted the teacher-child relationship to respond to these unconscious events (Biber, 1984). Biber and others, however, considered a wholly psychodynamic viewpoint as restrictive as an overly cognitive emphasis; in this instance, though, cognitive processes are given the peripheral position (Franklin & Biber, 1977).

In contrast, the Developmental-Interaction approach stresses the importance of the "whole child"; it recognizes and appreciates the continuous entanglement of the cognitive and social-affective parts of development. "It can be suggested that the 'whole child' is not only a guiding concept in this approach but a powerful image, an almost concrete embodiment of ideas and sentiments that serves a central generative function in elaborating theory and thinking about practice in the context of a value system" (Franklin, 1981, p. 71).

Reflecting these assumptions, formal presentations of the Developmental-Interaction approach usually begin with a statement of its progressive values, followed by a delineation of six theoretical principles acquired from psychodynamic and developmental theory. General educational goals and teaching strategies are then derived from these principles. Educational goals and teaching strategies, in turn, provide the parameters for the inclusion and promotion of possible learning experiences (see, for example, Biber, 1977b; Biber & Franklin, 1967; Shapiro & Biber, 1972).

Thus, explanation of the Developmental-Interaction approach proceeds deductively, from encompassing principles to specific practices. However, specific practices can be understood only in light of the overarching principles and only as these principles, which exist independently in their written form only, are being experienced by a particular child during a particular circumstance. "A competent teacher needs to know why, not only what and how. That is the only guarantee that she can make sound adaptations to differing situations" (Biber, 1979, p. 157). Figuratively, the Developmental-Interaction approach can be visualized as a nested design, with each superordinate component setting the conceptual boundaries for the next element. Architects of the Developmental-Interaction approach intentionally kept their conceptualization complex in order for it to better match their perception of the actuality of development. But, as a result, it is a model whose implementation is dependent on conceptual understanding rather than skillful replication.

The ultimate conceptualization of the Developmental-Interaction approach evolved from diverse sources during their 60 years of operation. In their efforts to integrate methods and understandings about the learning process into a new educational paradigm, adherents strived to create a comprehensive and internally coherent educational approach. They concluded that their concern with the whole child necessitated the integration of multiple theories in order to comprehensively reflect the complexity of development and to support its totality (Biber, 1977b, 1984; Franklin, 1981).

> It is a basic tenet of the developmental-interaction approach that the growth of cognitive functions—acquiring and ordering information, judging, reasoning, problem solving, using systems of symbols—cannot be separated from the growth of personal and interpersonal processes—the development of self-esteem and a sense of identity, internalization of impulse control, capacity for autonomous responses, relatedness to other people. (Biber & Shapiro, 1972, p. 61)

This reasoning helps explain why Biber and her colleagues, despite numerous commonalities with cognitive-developmental approaches (see Chapter 6), rejected the various, derivative curriculum models from Piagetian theory. They denounced their preponderant emphasis on developing cognitive structures (versus intellectual processes), the separation of cognitive and affective development, and insufficient attention to intuitive processes, feelings, and fantasy "as they reflect and feed into the child's aesthetic as well as his inter- and intrapersonal development" (Franklin & Biber, 1977, p. 16; see also Biber, 1984, 1988). The Developmental-Interaction approach values nonrational and intuitive understandings as well as the more rational, logically oriented ones promoted by cognitive-developmental models.

The concept of a "family of theories," as proposed by Reese and Overton (1970), was found to be particularly useful in rationalizing the notion of theoretical variation built on a shared, common base (Biber, 1984; 1988; Franklin, 1981). The concept of a family of theories proposes that theories can be grouped according to shared assumptions, with members of a given family differing in certain respects but sharing a set of views that is clearly distinct, and often opposed to, the shared assumptions of other groupings. This concept provided those articulating the Developmental-Interaction approach a supportive rationale for relying on multiple theoretical perspectives, as long as each new "family member" added to the comprehensiveness and coherence of their psychological rationale.

Articulating the relationships between practice and multiple theoretical perspectives within an integrated conceptual framework evolved over a period of several years within a context of careful consideration of relationships between practice and theory and a desire for internal consistency among values, learning-teaching practices, and psychological theories of motivation and development (examples of the evolution can be found in Biber, 1967, 1977b; Biber & Franklin, 1967; Biber, Shapiro, & Wickens, 1977; Shapiro & Biber, 1972; Shapiro & Weber, 1981). Those involved in the process recognized that finding congruence among educational assumptions and psychological theories required choices, and this realization reinforced their historical concern with clearly explicating and elevating their educational values as educational guides (for example, Biber, 1977b; Biber & Franklin, 1967; Franklin & Biber, 1977; Shapiro & Biber, 1972).

In contrast to the Montessori Method, belief in the interplay between theory and practice as an ongoing interaction has sustained the fluidity of the Developmental-Interaction approach. This characteristic is reinforced further by the way in which the Developmental-Interaction approach has been formalized—it is the conceptual framework, rather than practices, that has been prescribed.

■ *Essential Tenets*

The Developmental-Interaction approach has been informed by three main sources: (1) the dynamic psychology of Sigmund Freud and his followers, including Anna Freud, Erik Erikson, Heinz Hartmann, and Harry Stack Sullivan, especially as their ideas relate to the understanding of motivation and autonomous ego processes; (2) gestalt and developmental psychologists who have been concerned with cognitive development, especially Max Wertheimer, Kurt Lewin, Heinz Werner, and Jean Piaget; and (3) educational theorists and practitioners who either have been influenced by these psychologists or developed their own approach, specifically John Dewey, Harriet Johnson, Susan Issacs, Lucy Sprague Mitchell, and Caroline Pratt (Shapiro & Biber, 1972; Shapiro & Mitchell, 1992).

The internal consistency among these various theories comes from the fact that both psychodynamic processes and developmental theory rely on stage theories of development that conceptualize development in terms of qualitative shifts in modes of experiencing and reacting, which occur in an invariant sequence, the earlier being necessary precursors for the later (Biber, 1977b; Shapiro & Biber, 1972). Stage theory serves as an informant in terms of providing a framework for understanding and interpreting children's changing behaviors, however, rather than as a literal informant of what children can be expected to do—or should be expected to know—at various points in their development.

Additional coherence is established by linking the values implicit within chosen theories with those explicitly promoted by the Developmental-Interaction approach. "A common purview of optimal human functioning establishes kinship between the educational practices and the psychological theories" (Biber, 1977b, p. 426). Thus, it is assumed that theories of development are not value free.

Presentation of the specifics of the Developmental-Interaction approach follows an outline used by Biber (1977b): value priorities, developmental-educational goals, teaching strategies, and organization. The essentials of this approach, however, already have been described. It is still a child-centered, experience-based, process-oriented early childhood program focused on promoting every aspect of a child's development in the direction of optimal human functioning.

It also is still a program organized for children from the early preschool years through the elementary grades. So much of the work published about the Developmental-Interaction approach particularizes principles relative to the preschool years because that's the level at which its proponents have experienced the most pressure to explain and defend their approach. The essential elements of the approach, however, are not age specific. And finally, it is still an approach to early childhood education that believes advancing a child's total psychological functioning—social and emotional, as well as intellectual—should define the school's overarching aim and function.

What is different about the Developmental-Interaction approach from what already has been presented about the Bank Street approach is the expanded breadth, depth, and detail that have been created by embedding and substantiating long-term practices and understandings within a comprehensive theoretical framework. Now there is a comprehensive, articulated formulation of the Developmental-Interaction approach that can be provided as a framework and psychological rationale for influencing the practice of others.

This formulation, moreover, represents an important, historical shift in focus. At its beginning, ongoing practice and ongoing research informed each other; then, gradually, practice was related to theory. With the advent of the Developmental-Interaction approach, theory now informs practice.

Given the character of the Developmental-Interaction approach, specifics are, in fact, distilled conceptual principles/guidelines for informing teacher practice and decision making, not particulars of implementation. As noted by Evans (1975), these guidelines are a "set of profound, variously abstruse principles" (p. 73). Because Biber has attempted to rationalize every program element and elucidate the multiple interconnections among them, program descriptions often require attentive reading—and rereading. It is impossible for summaries, including the one that follows, not to oversimplify the approach's detailed operational statements. Most frustrating is the extent to which overviews dilute the complex psychological conceptualization of the educational process. The frequent use of quotes has been an attempt, in part, to convey the intricacies of the approach's psychological rationalizations.

Value Priorities

According to Biber (1981, 1984), the preferred values of the Developmental-Interaction approach have remained constant throughout the curriculum's evolution. The stated values are those humanistic views of optimal human functioning "generally acceptable across the broad sweep of Western culture" (Shapiro & Biber, 1972, p. 61) and are linked with John Dewey's philosophy of democratic living. These values are grounded in the progressive ideals of individuality and social potential. Educationally, this dual focus generates a continuing search for the kinds of educational experiences that will promote optimal development of individuality as well as ongoing exploration for the "images of society" that should inform the classroom's social dynamics (Biber, 1981, p. 11). Biber (1981) has also stated that "[i]n the broadest sense, the basic value system is an amalgam of ideas about social change, process of maturing, and selection of preferred learning-teaching strategies" (p. 11), thus highlighting that every aspect of the Developmental-Interaction approach is related to its expressed values.

Educational Goals:
A Vehicle for Promoting Developmental Processes

The program's psychological rationale, which provides the underpinnings for practice, is drawn from psychodynamic and cognitive-developmental theory. Even though the Developmental-Interaction approach is not based on the belief that psychological theories, in and of themselves, can specify what the immediate or ultimate purposes of education shall be, it does view them as important screening devices when organizing curriculum and making decisions about experiential content and choice of methods and strategies. Six theoretical formulations, reflecting overarching beliefs about the developmental process (see Table 4-1), provide "the channels through which to navigate toward selected educational goals" (Biber, 1977b, p. 428).

These six formulations, in turn, are reduced to four primary psychological constructs that determine the program's developmental-educational goals and teaching strategies: competence, individuality, socialization, and integration. It is assumed that growth in each of these four areas proceeds developmentally and will be actualized differently by children in different stages of their development.

Therefore, the educational emphasis of the Developmental-Interaction approach is the child's developmental progress (as informed, and particularized, by various stage theories) toward increased competence, individuality, socialization, and integration by supporting the developmental processes *underlying* these four constructs. This emphasis is in intentional contrast with discrete, concrete behavioral achievements sequenced toward a specified accomplishment.

The teacher, consequently, is primed to be sensitive to children's individual behaviors in terms of the underlying developmental processes that they reflect—because it is the development of these underlying processes, rather than specific behaviors, that are the focus of the teacher's educational efforts.

Table 4–1
Six Essential Theoretical Formulations

---

1. The autonomous ego processes of the growing organism synchronize with increasingly strong motivation to engage actively with the environment, to make direct impact upon it and to fulfill curiosity about it.
2. The course of development, characterized by qualitative changes or shifts in the individual's means of organizing experience and coping with the environment, may be viewed overall in terms of increasing differentiation and hierarchic integration. This general line of development can be discerned within different stages and with regard to the pattern of growth in various spheres (for example, motor activity, emotional development, perceptual-cognitive functioning).
3. Progress from earlier to later levels of functioning in any domain (emotional, intellectual, or social) is characterized by moments of equilibrium in which the individual's schemata are adequate for the task at hand, and by moments of instability in which currently operative structures are breaking down but new ones are not sufficiently developed to take over completely.
4. An individual does not operate at a "fixed" developmental level, but manifests in his behavior a range of genetically different operations. Earlier or more "primitive" modes of organization are not eradicated, but become integrated into the more advanced modes of organization.
5. The self is both image and instrument. It emerges as the result of a maturing process in which differentiation of objects and other people becomes progressively more refined and self-knowledge is built up from repeated awareness and assessment of the powers of the self in the course of mastering the environment. The shape and quality of the self reflect the images of important people in the growing child's life.
6. Growth and maturing involve conflict. The inner life of the growing child is a play of forces between urgent drives and impulses, contradictory impulses within the self and demanding reality outside the self. The resolution of these conflicts bears the imprint of the quality of interaction with the salient life figures and the demands of the culture.

These statements are quoted from Biber, B. (1977b). A developmental-interactional approach: Bank Street College of Education. In M. C. Day & R. K. Parker (Eds.), *The preschool in action: Exploring early childhood programs* (2nd. ed.), pp. 426–28. Boston: Allyn & Bacon. They can also be found in Biber, B., & Franklin, M. B. (1967). The relevance of developmental and psychodynamic concepts to the education of the preschool child. *Journal of the American Academy of Child Psychiatry, 6* (1–4), 5–24.

Educational goals (see Table 4–2), therefore, do not define behavioral end points. Instead, they are construed as informants regarding how to support, stimulate, and guide developmental processes in individual children in the direction of actualizing each child's optimal functioning. Given the complementary concern for social potential, these goals also help establish priorities for the social organization of the classroom.

The emphasis on underlying developmental processes also means that the approach's educational aims are extended developmentally. As a result, program effectiveness cannot be validly assessed in terms of short-term objectives. This particular factor contributed to the defensiveness of proponents of the developmental-interaction viewpoint because their approach was placed at a distinct disadvantage

Table 4–2
Developmental-Educational Goals

---

1. To serve the child's need to make an impact on the environment through direct physical contact and maneuver
2. To promote the potential for ordering experience through cognitive strategies
3. To advance the child's functioning knowledge of his environment
4. To support the play mode of incorporating experience
5. To help the child internalize impulse control
6. To meet the child's need to cope with conflicts intrinsic to this stage of development
7. To facilitate the development of an image of self as a unique and competent person
8. To help the child establish mutually supporting patterns of interaction

---

These developmental educational goals are excerpted from Biber, B. (1977b). A developmental-interaction approach: Bank Street college of Education. In M. C. Day & R. K. Parker (Eds.), *The preschool in action: Exploring early childhood programs* (2nd ed.), pp. 435–445. Boston: Allyn & Bacon.

when competitive evaluations of curriculum models focused on short-term gains in cognitive functioning. (This is discussed further in Chapter 7).

Competence.   The primary learning associated with this developmental construct involves bringing a child's individual potential to its highest possible realization— becoming competent in body and mind. Functionally, this includes concern for how the child uses her knowledge and skills in negotiating the environment and in interactions with others.

Individuality.   The enhancement of individuality focuses on promoting the child's sense of self as unique— "a distinct, thinking, feeling being capable of emotional investment, with a sense of worth based on knowledge and feelings of his own competence as much as on reflections of himself in people around him" (Biber, 1977b, p. 430). High priority is placed on autonomous functioning, which in this instance (in contrast to Montessori's conceptualization of autonomy [see Chapter 3] and Kamii and DeVries's [see Chapter 6]) refers to the ability to make choices, develop preferences, take initiative, risk failure, set an independent course for problem solving, and accept help without sacrificing independence.

Socialization.   This developmental process, when framed in terms of an educational goal, involves assisting children to learn control over individual impulses in order to participate in classroom life, adapt their behavior to a rational system of controls and sanctions, and become self-regulating. This goal also addresses extending oneself in relationship to others.

Integration.   The goal of integration is concerned with helping children merge disparate experiences, both personal and impersonal—"to integrate thought and feeling, thought and action, the subjective and the objective, self-feeling and empathy with others, original and conventional forms of communication, spontaneous and ritualized forms of response" (Shapiro & Biber, 1972, p. 62). When teachers respond to children with this goal in mind, they attempt to help children see the connections among their various reactions to an incident, to appreciate a situation more completely. Functionally, this means teachers avoid strategies that fragment learning. The process of integration is seen as especially critical to creativity and maximum engagement in learning (Biber, 1977b; Shapiro & Biber, 1972).

Teaching Strategies

Teaching strategies are viewed as an intermediate construct between the developmental principles and developmental-educational goals and the specific content and organization of the program experienced by children. Teaching strategies have been carefully deliberated based on the assumption that chosen strategies influence the selection of program content and learning experiences.

Teaching strategies are composed of three programmatic components: the nature of the teacher-child relationship, curriculum content and instructional principles, and motivation (Biber, 1977b). These components of the learning environment are the same elements emphasized by Shapiro and Biber in their elucidation of the term *interaction* (see page 81). These programmatic components are seen as essential to achieving developmental-educational goals because they describe the characteristics of the learning environment that either facilitate or impede a child's actualization of his potential. The Developmental-Interaction approach, however, does not limit its focus to learning within the classroom; it also emphasizes extending children's learning opportunities into the community (i.e., field trips) and actively seeks continuity between home and school environments.

Teacher-Child Relationship.   The primary task of the teacher in the teacher-child relationship is to establish a mutually trusting relationship. Such a relationship is seen as foundational because it enables the teacher to become effective as a mediator of children's learning experiences, provides a reflective surface for the child's developing self-concept, assures the child's identification with the teacher (which is prerequisite to a child taking as his own the learning goals that the teacher holds for him), and serves as a model for human interchange.

The nature of the teacher-child relationship, therefore, is one of the defining, interactional elements of this approach. It is the teacher, however, who is given theoretical and actual responsibility for structuring and nurturing this relationship. The teacher's delineated responsibilities designate her as the respondent and activator; the child's active influence on the teacher, other children, and the learning environment is mentioned less frequently.

In order to establish and sustain a trusting relationship, teachers are expected to be able to: listen in order to understand a child's underlying thinking when immature verbal discourse may deflect it; help formulate and channel children's semiformed intent into a realizable activity; establish herself as a resource for meeting problems of confusion, fear, loss of direction, anger, or loneliness; understand behavior in the context of the characteristics of the stage of development; and establish a personalized, differentiated relationship with each child (Biber, 1977b, p. 431; these descriptors were chosen from a listing of 19 expectations).

Curriculum content and instructional principles refer to the program of activities and the nature of the learning experience. Biber (1977b) provides a listing of 18 statements to describe instructional principles for preschool children. These principles are meant to inform what knowledge and skills children should be expected to master at this stage of development, the role of the child in the mastery process, and the most effective organization of learning experiences. Examples of these principles include the following:

- intellectual mastery is conceived in terms of the organization of knowledge and an active stance toward learning;

- children's varied ongoing experience in the classroom is the primary material for advancing the functional use of language and the thinking processes;

- curriculum content reflects two dominant themes of this period: the "how" processes of making, doing, and fixing; and the questions of origin—where things come from, where they end, what is to be born, and what it is to die;

- optimal learning is active learning in which the child is given the role of questioning, probing, exploring, and planning;

- the curriculum is organized flexibly so as to provide many opportunities for children to make choices, select from alternatives, and determine their own course within an established program;

- the teacher uses every appropriate opportunity to encourage differentiated observation and comparison, the search for causes and origins, and the organization of experience in terms of continuity and transformation;

- ideally, thinking becomes part of continuous experiencing, in the same stream with doing, feeling, and imagining. (p. 432)

The teaching role envisioned here . . . requires the capacity to empathize with the mental processes of young children, to deal without anxiety with the ambiguity necessarily associated with exploration-search patterns rather than right-wrong paradigms, to deal with variations not only in rate of mastery but in cognitive style, and thus to carry a multiple series of evaluative criteria by which to judge when learning is being productive for different children. (Biber, 1967, p. 120)

In Bank Street's most recent dissemination effort, the role of social studies is emphasized as the core of the integrated curriculum for children 4 through 8 years old (see Mitchell & David, 1992).[10] This recent statement adds to the program-

---

[10]   Bank Street's new curriculum guide is accompanied by a companion videotape entitled "Social Studies: A Way to Integrate Curriculum for Four and Five Year Olds." The guide, however, emphasizes its relevance to teaching children to 8 years of age.

matic alignment between practice in the preschool and elementary grades, where social studies has long provided a vehicle for integrating themes of concern and subject matter knowledge (Cuffaro, 1977; Gilkeson, Smithberg, Bowman, & Rhine, 1981).

Gilkeson, Smithberg, Bowman, and Rhine (1981), for example, describe a primary grade project where students explored Weeksville, a community of former slaves located where the school in question now stands. Children dug up artifacts, read historical records, and re-created the clothing, tools, and activities of Weeksville, acquiring a "host of skills" (p. 258) throughout the project's completion. Furthermore, as implied in this last statement, at the primary level, academic skills are interconnected and integrated throughout children's learning activities.

It is noteworthy, within this context, that despite continuous reference to John Dewey's influence, the Developmental-Interaction approach fails to incorporate his strong concern for teachers' knowledge of subject matter. Consistent with its psychological emphasis on developmental processes, interest in intellectual development focuses on processes such as reasoning and problem solving; but little attention is given to what children should think about beyond what they are immediately experiencing and/or are interested in knowing—even in their most recent curriculum guide (Mitchell & David, 1992). The issue of subject matter knowledge is rarely addressed.

Yet, as Dewey (1938) has pointed out, the critical question for progressive education is, "What is the place and meaning of subject-matter and of organization *within* experience?" (p. 20). The Developmental-Interaction approach does not address this question. Extensive expectations for teachers relative to their psychological knowledge of the child is not joined by similar expectations for a thorough familiarity with organized knowledge as represented in the disciplines. This tilt toward the child, and away from Dewey's dual and integrated thrust, is consistent, however, with the direction taken by many educators during the progressive education era (Cremin, 1961/1964).

It logically follows, given its process orientation and concern with integrated developmental processes, that advocates of the Developmental-Interaction approach oppose programs in which stimulation of cognitive development is disassociated from meaningful experience and occurs apart from consideration of other interacting developmental processes (Biber, 1981, 1984). Behavioral curriculum models with this focus dominated the compensatory education movement, however, and thus were a consistent irritant to advocates of the Developmental-Interaction approach (see Chapter 5). Their objection to direct cognitive instruction, however, was of long standing; as a teaching strategy, direct instruction is consistent with conventional public school practices, which contributors to the Developmental-Interaction approach have railed against throughout its history.

Finally, *motivation* as a program factor refers to what constitutes positive motivation within this approach. It is framed by six statements that emphasize children's intrinsic drive toward competence, the intrinsic satisfaction of meaningful learning, and the linkage between motivational concepts and the child's development as an autonomous individual (Biber, 1977b, p. 433).

Organization

One of the challenges to discussing the Developmental-Interaction approach stems from the fact that, for so many of us "later generation" early childhood educators, characteristics of this approach have, in fact, become mainstream practice. When they are so pervasive in present practice, it is difficult to ferret out the approach's distinguishing characteristics.

Depiction of classroom organization and materials is an especially good example of this predicament. The classroom organization developed by the Bank Street position and integral to the Developmental-Interaction approach has become standard description in undergraduate, early childhood textbooks.

Yet, organizational characteristics represent a critical component of the learning environment and are necessary for fulfilling program goals. The essential aspect is that the classroom arrangement allows children to speak and move about freely, to work individually and in groups, to choose their activities, and to have access to a variety of materials. In a typical preschool classroom, there are clearly marked areas for painting, water play, block building, dramatic play, and looking at books. Table groupings serve as places for snacks, art-related activities, table games, and lunch. The organization of primary classrooms is based on similar tenets, though, obviously, available materials would reflect the interests of older children as well as teacher concerns with basic skills (Gilkeson, Smithberg, Bowman, & Rhine, 1981).

Criteria for material selection are derived from the developmental-educational goals and teaching strategies. In general, priority is given to open-ended materials, such as blocks, paints, sand, clay, wood, planks, jungle gyms, animal and people figures, dress-up clothes, and housekeeping set-up, that offer multiple and varied opportunities for child-initiated exploration, experimentation, and representation. More structured materials, such as pegs, form boards, and puzzles, are provided to strengthen perceptual discrimination and manipulative problem solving. For primary children, written materials, such as books, catalogs, and magazines, and math and science equipment, such as kits, scales, thermometers, attribute blocks, geoboards, and Cuisenaire rods, plus games become the classroom staples.

Materials, mass-produced and home-made, are arranged functionally on open shelves where children can have easy access, and are labeled with pictures, symbols, or written labels, depending on what children can understand. Children are given responsibility for properly using materials and returning them to their appropriate location. Finally, for preschoolers, activities are scheduled in a regular sequence so children know what to expect and can develop a sense of temporal order.

All these organizational aspects are also intended as statements about how the room is to be used and the way in which the teacher expects children to be engaged in learning. The classroom is planned not only in terms of practical needs but also in terms of the teaching value (Biber, 1977b; Gilkeson, Smithberg, Bowman, & Rhine, 1981).

The teacher plans activities to achieve predetermined learning goals for individual children and the children as a group, but most especially, she will be a careful observer of children and their activities and will be responsive to the learning possibilities embedded within children's ongoing experiences with classroom materials, with each other, and in interaction with her. Ultimately, therefore, it is the teacher who operationalizes this carefully integrated conceptual framework, who sensitively responds to children's underlying motivations, recognizes the sources of confusion, seizes opportunities for new insights, and optimizes moment by moment interactions. "The teacher is the most important figure in the developmental-interaction approach because it is she who creates the climate in the classroom, the physical and psychological learning environment of the young child's life in the school" (Shapiro & Biber, 1972, p. 68).

■ *From Reflective Practice to Theory into Practice*

The Developmental-Interaction approach is the most comprehensive enduring approach to early childhood curriculum because of its encompassing concern with social-emotional and intellectual development. It is also among the most flexible because as an approach *to*, rather than a model *for*, early education, it chose to develop principles that are intended to inform practitioners' daily decision making rather than provide them specifics of practice.

Yet, even so, evolving to the form and status of a formalized approach has significantly, even if subtly, transformed its historical approach to early childhood education. Biber (1988), herself, unwittingly identified the most significant "after-effect" of formalizing an approach to early childhood education, of exchanging evolving, dynamic, individualistic practice for practice prescribed within a formal theoretical framework.

In a paper addressing the challenges of professionalism in early childhood education, Biber (1988) identifies the integration of theory and practice as the paramount difficulty. Notably, before ultimately placing this challenge at the feet of teachers, she reminisces the contributions of Lucy Mitchell and Harriet Johnson as pioneers of a new form of education for young children. And then she laments, "Theory and practice were woven together. Today, theory and practice are separate provinces; seldom does the same individual operate in both. Often they don't even talk to each other. New lines of connection and communication must be built from both domains" (p. 37).

Yet, formalizing an approach to curriculum, in effect, creating a curriculum model, regardless of how flexible and dynamic, promotes this very detachment of theory from practice, of teaching from research and theorizing, and teachers from researchers and theoreticians. It undermines relationships between teachers and theoreticians/researchers as equal partners and co-informants, which *had* characterized the Bank Street approach; it promotes a relationship of dependency, where practice becomes dependent on research and theory "to tell it what to do"; and it encourages teachers to become recipients of others' knowledge and know-how, rather than co-creators.

Biber and her colleagues seem to be unaware of these repercussions, however. Their critical sensitivities have been directed more toward the theoretical impact of having formalized their conceptual framework. They question, for example, "To what extent does adherence to a given psychological theory as the basis of an educational design restrict the comprehensiveness of the program—the extent to which it provides for the multiple aspects of learning, ego development, and socialization?" (Franklin & Biber, 1977, p. 25). And Biber (1984) asks, "Is it spurious or at least premature to posit a body of theory or theories sufficiently comprehensive to be the foundation for the multitudinous aspects of an educational design?" (p. 303).

Those espousing the Developmental-Interaction approach recognized, as well, that how one arrives at the formation of a value system is problematic (Biber, 1981), and they pondered the lack of articulation between individual variation and developmental theory. They questioned whether developmental theories direct attention toward characterizing behavior in terms of what it has not yet become, and whether developmental stage theories divert attention from the uniqueness of the individual (Shapiro & Wallace, 1981).

Yet, there is no apparent awareness of a movement, in which they have unintentionally participated, that has shifted the balance between theory and practice. Biber (1984, 1988) has urged theorists to interact with teachers as a source for greater understanding of how individual children, from year to year, function within the educational sequence, and she has argued, "Theory should not be insulated from application, nor should practice be allowed to escape responsibility for articulating theoretical foundations since cross-fertilization is essential to sound progress in both spheres" (Biber, 1984, p. 304). But despite these expressions of concern for collaboration between theory and practice, the subtle shifts in Biber's analyses of the Developmental-Interaction approach indicate a different kind of relationship.

When Biber (1977b) wrote about the decision in 1959 to begin to critically examine the rationale for their practices, she said,

> Knowledge of the growing field of child development and psychology of learning had indeed influenced these assumptions (about learning), but they had been primarily derived from the direct experience of observing and teaching children in school. . . . To what extent would formulations and viewpoints in the field of psychology, arrived at independently of the field of education, corroborate these assumptions and thus provide a firmer theoretical base for the practices? (p. 425)

In contrast, when justifying their change in name to the Developmental-Interaction approach more than a decade later, Biber (1977b) argued it was time to be known by their essential *theoretical* characteristic.

And, when writing retrospectively about the era of the seventies, there is no longer any mention of corroborating the relationship between theory and practice.

> By the seventies, our thinking was directed toward clarifying the developmental-interaction point of view: the implications for education of perceiving identifiable successive pat-

terns of growth as a function of chronological age, of placing emphasis on the child's interaction with the social and physical environment within the context of preferred values, and, finally, of recognizing the interaction between cognitive and affective spheres of experience. (Biber, 1984, p. 310)

Lucy Mitchell's contention that Bank Street's teacher education program would not perpetuate any particular "school of thought" (as cited in Antler, 1982, p. 583) now seems debatable.

Since its formalization as an approach to early childhood education, the Developmental-Interaction approach is no longer infused with the conjectural, experimental practice that characterized it during the era of progressive education. Its rationalization now relies mostly on the thoughtful deliberations of theorists such as Biber, rather than the reflective practices and ideas of practitioners. Although Biber's writings continue to rely on the pioneer insights of practitioners such as Harriet Johnson, Lucy Mitchell, and Susan Issacs, their contemporary counterparts are conspicuously absent. Similar to other curriculum models developed during the sixties, the notion of experimental practice became associated with how to implement a preconceived conceptual framework.

One only need read *I Learn from Children* by Caroline Pratt (1948/1990) to appreciate the energy, commitment, and intellectual vitality that came from practitioners and researchers mutually creating and re-creating the meaning and purpose of an educational setting. Even though the Developmental-Interaction approach has maintained an experimental quality to daily practice and avoided mechanizing the acts of teaching, by shifting its attention away from practice, and toward theory, as a primary stimulus for decision making, the teacher's role also shifted from that of creator to implementer—even though as noted throughout the chapter, the complexity of its implementation is daunting and therefore problematic to a field in desperate need of "qualified" practitioners.

Furthermore, the existence of a formalized conceptual framework, by definition, constrains the possibilities considered and subtly redirects teacher thinking and behavior from contemplating how to maximize individual and group potential to how to best implement a chosen approach. Silin (1986), in his review of Biber's book *Early Education and Psychological Development,* speaks to this particular point.

> One would wish [that Biber's] command of the psychological literature and her openness in assimilating new research findings were matched by an equal willingness to deal with developments in sociological and political theory. Biber would never limit her psychological insights to the work of one person, yet this is exactly what she does in the realm of sociopolitical analysis by relying so completely on John Dewey. The developmental-interaction approach claims to be a comprehensive one, yet its knowledge base is confined to developmental psychology; its politics to the liberal, democratic view of a large faction within the progressive movement; and its social vision to the description of individual personality traits deemed desirable for an ill-defined world of the future. (p. 615)

There is no way of knowing if the Bank Street perspective would have been formalized as the Developmental-Interaction approach if the external pressures that were present during the sixties had not existed: concern with the nation's capacity to respond to international competition; discouragement with the educational status quo; and an incredible demand for early childhood programs co-existing with the early childhood profession's insufficient capacity to respond. Nor is there any way to forecast what might have happened to an appreciation of, and concern for, the "whole child" if Biber and others had stayed outside the fray.

The pressures faced by the Bank Street approach during the sixties are not unlike the ones the field of early care and education currently confront. These shared historical factors make the experience of the Developmental-Interaction approach especially informative to current deliberations concerned with how to assure increasing numbers of children consistently high quality early childhood care and education in ways that also elevate the professional knowledge and expertise of those who provide it.

■ *For Further Reading*

Biber, B. (1984). *Early education and psychological development.* New Haven: Yale University Press.

> In this book, Biber presents many of her original writings, extending from 1939 until 1977, and then reassesses her thinking, sometimes validating it anew, other times extending it to reflect her current interests or thinking. As such, it is a comprehensive theoretical and personal review of Biber's thinking over five decades.

Biber, B. (1977a). Cognition in early childhood education: A historical perspective. In B. Spodek & H. Walberg (Eds.), *Early childhood education: Issues and insights* (pp. 41–64). Berkeley, CA: McCutchan.

> Because changing perspectives on cognition are so integral to the history of the Developmental-Interaction approach, I found this historical review by Biber to be especially informative.

Biber, B. (1977b). A developmental-interaction approach: Bank Street College of Education. In M. C. Day & R. K. Parker (Eds.), *The preschool in action: Exploring early childhood programs* (2nd ed., pp. 421–460). Boston: Allyn & Bacon.

> Although focused on its preschool program, this chapter presents a detailed discussion of the Developmental-Interaction approach that, more than other descriptions, reveals the intricacy of the approach and its psychodynamic underpinnings.

Greenberg, P. (1987). Lucy Sprague Mitchell: A major missing link between early childhood education in the 1980s and Progressive Education in the 1890s–1930s. *Young Children, 42*(5), 70–84.

> Greenberg uses her review of Antler's (1987) biography of Lucy Sprague Mitchell not only to describe Mitchell's contributions to the early childhood profession but also to provide a historical review of early childhood education prior to the 1960s. Greenberg presents a passionate review of early childhood education's U.S. history from the 1930s to the 1960s.

Chapter 5

The Direct Instruction Model

It seems to me somewhat misleading to go on treating the traditional approach as one among a host of alternative approaches to teaching young children. It is better seen, not as a distinctive approach to teaching, but as a system of custodial child care that may incorporate to a greater or lesser extent various educational components similar to those found in instructional programs for young children, but that is primarily distinguished by its minimization of teaching. The true issue between the traditional approach and the various instructional approaches in not *how* young children should be taught but *whether*.

Carl Bereiter, "An Academic Program for Disadvantaged Children:
Conclusions from Evaluation Studies," 1972

In the beginning, there was the response. And the behaviorist looked at the response and saw that it was good. At least it was real, and the behaviorist was weary of creativity. There had passed considerably more than six days, during which numerous psychologists had invented even more numerous souls, minds, instincts, feelings, drives and mediating mechanisms, all to explain the response. But the behaviorist who had started with the response because it was clearly there, began to explain the response with what was also clearly there, which was the external environment. And indeed, the response proved responsive to the external environment, indicating that the word was good, too. Therefore, another word was made to name those parts of the clearly there external environment to which the response was responsive; and the new word was called stimulus. And together the two words were functional, and begat many new words, such that the land was filled with them.

Donald M. Baer. "In the Beginning, There Was the Response," 1975

The Bereiter-Engelmann preschool, which was the forerunner to the Direct Instruction model, was one of the first curricula expressly developed as an early intervention model after the advent of Head Start. As the tone of the first introductory quote suggests, the Bereiter-Engelmann preschool served as a critical, and often belittling, protagonist to early childhood programs with a "traditional" focus. Hence, examination of the Bereiter-Engelmann preschool continues the drama that unfolded when academically oriented models challenged early childhood programs that advanced intellectual development as an untutored process.

As detailed in Chapter 4, the Developmental-Interaction approach was placed in a defensive posture almost from the onset of the curriculum model era. In this chapter, an "assailant's" viewpoint is presented. In the process, the competitive climate created by the curriculum model era and its search for the most effective early childhood programs becomes more visible.

The experiences of the behaviorally grounded Bereiter-Engelmann and Direct Instruction models during this era are almost the complete reversal of those encountered by advocates of the Developmental-Interaction approach. Whereas proponents of the Developmental-Interaction approach were placed on the defensive because of the contrast between their holistic, child-centered viewpoint and that of more cognitively oriented programs, the Bereiter-Engelmann and Direct Instruction models were catapulted to center stage by the alignment of their curricular premises with educational norms and societal expectations.

This alignment sustained the prominence of their and other academically oriented models despite shifts occurring in behavioral theory toward more cognitively oriented interpretations of learning (Case & Bereiter, 1984; White, 1970; Wittrock & Lumsdaine, 1977) and in spite of impassioned challenges by members of the early childhood profession. As expressed by one detractor, the Bereiter-Engelmann model created

> an environment in which work and play are polar opposites, in which the pleasurable interpersonal affective factors in learning are avoided while material (cookies) rewards are permitted. It is, in short, an atmosphere of puritanical zeal in which difficult tasks are dutifully pursued, while delight in an original expression, deviation, personal view or recounting are devil's pleasure. (Moskovitz, 1968, p. 27)

The Direct Instruction model built on the approach developed by Bereiter and Engelmann. Developed as a part of Project Follow Through, the Direct Instruction model, which targets kindergarten through third grade, has endured as an active curriculum model. Even though only the Direct Instruction model remains a viable program, both models serve as the focus of this chapter, for two reasons. First, and most obvious, as a precursor to the Direct Instruction model, knowing the Bereiter-Engelmann model helps our understanding of its successor. Second, as a leading advocate for intense and direct academic instruction as the most appropriate curriculum for disadvantaged preschoolers, review of the Bereiter-Engelmann model provides a graphic example of the opposing perspectives that came to inhabit early childhood education during this era.

In contrast to the Montessori Method and the Developmental-Interaction approach, the Bereiter-Engelmann model, and then the Direct Instruction model, grew out of and were nurtured by the particular tenor of the sixties. As a result, examination of these two models also provides a chance to consider the influences that shaped model development during this time. Finally, as a new, and radical,[1] addition to curriculum possibilities in preschool and kindergarten education, these two models also furnish an opportunity to examine the impact wrought by the onset of curriculum models.

The degree of support for an approach that "shocked early childhood education establishmentarians" (Evans, 1975, p. 141) was apparently unanticipated. According to Biber's (1984) reflection, "We thought we were the wave of the future. We could not have imagined the important place that behavior modification as applied to preschool education would attain in the 1960s and thereafter as part of government planning in particular and in academic circles in general" (p. 25). Appreciating the history and impact of these two models requires an understanding of how this level of support came to be.

The Bereiter-Engelmann and Direct-Instruction models, in conjunction with other academically oriented models spawned during this period, brought the tensions between developmental and academic orientations heretofore deliberated in elementary education into the arena of kindergarten and preschool education. In the arena of early education, however, with its established child-centered focus, the tensions quickly escalated into warfare.

The downward movement of this debate from elementary to preschool, in turn, further exacerbated the prevailing distinction between the (child) care and education of young children. The advent of Head Start not only affirmed the educational purpose of nursery schools, it spurred its acceptance as an appropriate beginning of children's out-of-home education, regardless of socio-economic background. Thus, no longer was the argument whether or not nursery programs were educational but rather how their educational purpose was best achieved and whether or not educational purpose differed for children of different socio-economic status (see, for example, Elkind, 1970; for a contemporary version of the same issue, see Sigel, 1991).

Kindergartens were undergoing a matching evolution for similar reasons (Weber, 1969); as a result, the historically separate pathways of nursery and kindergarten education began to merge in their opposition to academic curricula for young children (Chapter 2 details the beginning of this history). Child care, however, continued to carry the burden of its history and its negative character as a substitute for mothering; its custodial focus remained intact and outside the purview of educational institutions. By the end of the zenith of the curriculum model era in the early seventies, the educational purposes of preschool and kindergarten education often were juxtaposed against the custodial function of "day care."

---

1   Heretical might be a better word choice!

Debate regarding how educational purpose was best achieved in early childhood programs was operationalized in the diversity of curriculum models that emerged during the 1960s. Until the mid-sixties, *systematic* variety in early childhood curricula for nursery schools and kindergarten programs had been minimal. Programmatic differences reflected the differences among sponsoring agencies rather than conscious decisions to vary curriculum in terms of specified learning goals and objectives (Spodek, 1973; White & Buka, 1987). Propelled by the search for the most effective educational interventions for disadvantaged preschoolers and the infusion of federal dollars into their research and development, the models approach to early childhood education flourished during the sixties and early seventies. The 1967 initiation of Project Follow Through, and its method of planned variation among curriculum models, systematized the effort, intensified the competitive overtones of the search for the best model, and framed the problem of which curriculum was best as one to be resolved by science.

The concept of curriculum models, therefore, emanated from outside the field of early childhood education. Both in concept and in practice, they were imposed on the field. Moreover, no other educational level, other than early childhood education, uses curriculum models as blueprints for complete programs (Goffin, 1989). Examination of the Bereiter-Engelmann and Direct Instruction models begins to uncover how the advent of curriculum models in early childhood provoked not only the creation of diverse curriculum possibilities but also initiated curricular repercussions that are still reverberating.

■ *The Psychological Framework for Direct Instruction*

The Tenets of Behaviorism

The Bereiter-Engelmann and Direct Instruction models are based on learning principles derived from behavioral psychology. Derived from the stimulus-response psychology of Edward Thorndike and John Watson, who is usually credited as the father of behaviorism, behavioral psychology substituted observable stimuli and responses for mentalistic ideas and images.

In contrast to the other curriculum models under discussion, the Bereiter-Engelmann (B-E) and Direct Instruction (DI) models are not built from a theory of child development. Behavioral changes and individual differences are explained in terms of learning, not development. As defined by Hilgard and Bower (1975), learning "refers to the change in a subject's behavior to a given situation brought about by repeated experiences in that situation, provided that the behavior change can not be explained on the basis of native response tendencies, maturation, or temporary states of the individual (e.g., fatigue, drugs, etc.)" (p. 17). Learning, therefore, is understood as the result of an external event. Consistent with its dismissal of mentalistic ideas and images, behavioral psychology views the child as a recipient of, rather than participant in, learning.

According to White (1970), learning theories can be characterized by five statements:

1. The environment is characterized in terms of stimuli.
2. Behavior is characterized in terms of responses.
3. Stimuli called reinforcers, when applied contingently and immediately following a response, increase or decrease the response in measurable ways.
4. Learning can be understood in terms of the associations among stimuli, responses, and reinforcers.
5. Unless there is evidence to the contrary, all behavior is learned, manipulable by the environment, extinguishable, and trainable. (pp. 665–666)

The B-E and DI models are based on the application of these behavioral principles and laws of learning to instruction. Movement from learning in theory to prescribing learning in practice means that the structure of the subject matter content being taught also has to be considered (Case & Bereiter, 1984; Hilgard & Bower, 1977). Siegfried Engelmann, who helped design both curriculum models, is credited with employing learning principles and programming strategies to construct the programmed lessons in reading, arithmetic, and language (Becker, Engelmann, Carnine, & Rhine, 1981; Bereiter, 1968).

The efforts of Bereiter and Engelmann and their colleagues are part of what is variously labeled theories of instruction, instructional psychology, instructional design (Case & Bereiter, 1984; Glaser, 1990; Hilgard & Bower, 1975; Wittrock & Lumsdaine, 1977), and, more recently, educational learning theory (Bereiter, 1990). According to Case and Bereiter (1984), a behaviorist technology of instruction emerged primarily as a result of B. F. Skinner's work in conceptualizing the notion of shaping or successive approximations. Whereas the principle of reinforcement deals with strengthening behaviors that already are part of an individual's repertoire, the shaping process conceptualizes a means for modifying existing behavior by reinforcing behavioral variations that are in the direction of a desired behavior. With this behavioral principle, it became possible to promote new (versus merely reinforce existing) behaviors.

Individuals involved with this field of study are predominately educational and behavioral psychologists, rather than developmental psychologists. In an examination of the relationship between the learning theory tradition and child psychology, White (1970) points out that no learning theory has ever been constructed from studies of children or been specifically directed toward them.

Consequently, many of the educational psychologists developing early childhood curriculum models had limited knowledge of, or experience with, early childhood education. Nor, given their underlying assumptions about learning and their disinterest in the construct of development, was such knowledge or experience needed. Based on the assumption that all behavior is learned and is subject to predictable laws of learning, the architects of the B-E and DI models created an instructional environment designed to teach young children directly and systematically the prerequisite skills in reading, arithmetic, and language believed necessary to securing their future academic achievement.

The early childhood community, however, was aghast. Based on her observation of the B-E classroom, Weber (1970) wrote,

> As a total learning theory, operant conditioning, dependent as it is upon the key words "operants" and "reinforcement" can be accepted only by those who are willing to view the learner as passive and non-purposive and who tolerate the assumption of determinism. . . . This mechanical approach leaves no place for feelings, sensitivities, creativity, or a sense of autonomy in learning.[2] (p. 27)

Bereiter countered in terms consistent with behaviorists' fundamentally different approach to children and the purposes of education.

> On the contrary, we cared about the children, and we considered their emotional future as carefully as we considered their academic future. Concern for the children's emotional stability was the justification for such careful programming of skills—to make learning a less frustrating experience. (Anderson & Bereiter, 1972, p. 341)

Finally, the B-E and DI models also were informed by the thinking prevalent during the sixties regarding the learning needs of young children from economically disadvantaged home environments. In particular, their decisions regarding program content and instructional design were heavily influenced by their acceptance and interpretation of the notion of cultural deprivation.

The notion of cultural deprivation was constructed in the mid-sixties in an attempt to understand why low-income children, in contrast to their middle-class counterparts, were unsuccessful learners in public schools. The widely accepted interpretation was that children from low-income families were deprived of adequate learning experiences, especially in language development; their "culture" deprived them of the adult-child interactions and stimulating experiences common for their middle-class peers, and thus they arrived at school intellectually unprepared to learn.

This interpretation was a prevalent explanation for the different performance levels of low-income and middle-class children. Variation among curriculum models resided not in their acceptance of the concept but in their programmatic responses to this presumed deficiency. Whereas the Developmental-Interaction approach, for example, assumed the same underlying developmental processes needed nurturing and support, regardless of a child's socio-economic status (Biber, 1967, 1984), the

---

2   Although Weber's comment was directed toward the Bereiter-Engelmann preschool, it should be noted that Bereiter and Engelmann did not view their program as based on operant conditioning. According to Bereiter (1986), their model "was not a Skinnerian behavioral management program. It was . . . a rationalist program of concept teaching not even remotely Skinnerian in theory" (p. 290). This distinction was explained further in the earlier discussion about theories of instruction. For examples of curriculum models based on operant conditioning, the reader is referred to Bushell, 1973, 1982, and Ramp and Rhine, 1981.

architects of the B-E and DI models developed a program based on the premise that preschoolers and kindergartners from low-income backgrounds enter school with fewer skills and concepts than their advantaged peers. From their way of thinking, delaying academic instruction because children are not "ready" only serves to widen the gap. Given their adherence to behavioral theory, it was logical that they would advocate minimizing the gap in achievement through direct means.

Understanding the disparity between these two views is relevant because it further clarifies their differing approaches. In addition, although the concept of cultural deprivation has been discarded, debates regarding the most appropriate curriculum for young children identified at-risk still revolve around similar issues—do all children thrive with similar learning experiences, or do the "needs" of low-income children necessitate an academic curriculum?

The following two quotes, the first by Biber and the second by Bereiter and Engelmann, effectively contrast the difference in approach. According to Biber (1967),

> What the child misses . . . is not only a model of spoken language but, much more fundamentally, a lack of rich, meaningful communication beyond just the necessities of practical living. These lacks are deterrents for language use, indeed. Eventually, they become deterrents for learning to read. But, more than that, more deeply, they are deterrents for being able to learn in general because it is through the active relationship with people, it is through being known and felt and understood as a person, that the child's basic curiosity and interest in the world begins to flower and develop. (p. 112)

In contrast, Bereiter and Engelmann (1966b), who identified the B-E model as a remedial course for preschoolers deficient in language and verbal reasoning, asserted,

> From the beginning there is a lag in learning that must be overcome if disadvantaged children are to emerge from school with the same skills and knowledge as more privileged children. If the lag is to be made up during the school years, then schools for disadvantaged children have to provide higher quality and faster-paced education than that provided for advantaged children. Another possible solution is to provide this kind of education before the school years—the motivating idea for preschool education for disadvantaged children. (p. 6)

Thus, Bereiter and Engelmann's creation of an academic curriculum model was based on the belief that the critical issue confronting disadvantaged children was their learning deficit, which increased in magnitude as low-income children progressed through grade school (this was known as the cumulative deficit). The most effective way to remedy this deficit, according to proponents of the B-E and DI models, was by directly and systematically teaching the skills children needed in order to succeed in school (Bereiter & Engelmann, 1966b; Carnine, Carnine, Karp, & Weisberg, 1988; Gersten, Darch, & Gleason, 1988; Gersten & George, 1990).

Twenty-seven years later, it is difficult to read *Teaching the Disadvantaged Preschooler* wherein Bereiter & Engelmann provide a detailed rationale for, and explanation of, the B-E curriculum model. Their 1966 interpretation of cultural deficit, in light of our changed understandings about cultural diversity in 1993, is unnerving. According to their interpretation, cultural deprivation and language deprivation were synonymous. As explained by Horowitz and Paden (1973), based on a conclusion that disadvantaged children did not speak and think clearly,

> [Bereiter and Engelmann] worked from a deficit model which could almost be described as a dismissal model. In the area of language, for instance, they sometimes have appeared to assume that for all practical purposes the "disadvantaged" child has no language, that he cannot think, and that he has nothing to think about. . . . They argue that whatever his language, it is insufficient for functional operation in the middle-class, mostly white culture where the child must ultimately operate. (pp. 374–375)

At this point, it is important to note that even though the Direct Instruction model builds on the Bereiter-Engelmann model, it does not speak to the issue of "cultural deprivation." Instead, it rationalizes the effectiveness of its direct instruction and "catch-up" approach by arguing that low-income, at-risk students should be prepared "to enter first grade with a similar knowledge base in reading, mathematics, and language concepts as children not at risk" (Gersten, Darch, & Gleason, 1988, p. 228).

Science, Method, and a Science of Education

Science and Method.   With its emphasis on observable behaviors and environmental manipulation, the history and practice of behavioral psychology is closely aligned with experimental methodology (Hilgard & Bower, 1975; White, 1970). Experimental designs attempt to impose environmental control over the experimental situation and to manipulate single variables in search of quantifiable cause and effect relationships. The theoretical linkages between behavioral psychology and experimental research assumed practical and political significance for the B-E and DI models when evaluations of early childhood curriculum models determined program effectiveness by assessing children's learning in terms of their scores on standardized tests, tools of assessment particularly well matched to the learning objectives and teaching style of these two models.

The outcomes desired from curriculum model development were directly linked with belief in the tenets of experimental research and the ability of science to provide data from which a solution to the problem of educating economically disadvantaged children could be found. First funded as part of Project Follow Through (and then Head Start Planned Variation), the systematic creation, dissemination, and scientific evaluation of curriculum models was instituted to determine the most effective curriculum for equalizing the academic success of low- and middle-income children. Curriculum models were regarded as whole units; thus, the curriculum model itself was the environmental manipulation, in effect the "treatment," which then was evaluated in terms of educational impact. In turn, program evaluation results were to provide an objective, scientifically derived answer to the policy concern regarding how to most effectively improve the school success of low-income children. As a result of the theoretical consistency between behavioral psychology and experimental research design, the B-E and DI models had a competitive edge in comparative evaluations, which, in turn, reaped their models of early education political advantage.

Until recently, experimental research designs were the unquestioned hallmark of objective, scientific practice and the most valued source of confirmation for specified practice and policy. This belief gave the empirically validated practices of the Bereiter-Engelmann and Direct Instruction models an added aura of validity. Later, it also augmented their boasts of programmatic superiority, assertions that were (and are) based on the superior test scores and academic performance of children attending their programs (see, for example, Becker, Engelmann, Carnine, & Rhine, 1981; Carnine, Carnine, Karp, & Weisberg, 1988; Gersten, Darch, & Gleason, 1988).

Method and Science of Education.   A basic premise of the B-E and DI models, both of which rely on direct instruction as the most efficient means of teaching, is that the *how* of teaching is as important as the *what* (Becker, Engelmann, Carnine, & Rhine, 1981; Bereiter & Engelmann, 1966a, 1966b). Bereiter and Engelmann felt most early childhood programs were focused on the issue of program content to the exclusion of teaching method. They contended that failure to develop "more effective teaching methods is perhaps to fail completely in equalizing the educational attainment of children from different cultural backgrounds" (Bereiter & Engelmann, 1966a, p. 55).

In the B-E and DI models, the *how* of teaching and *what* is taught are intimately correlated. In reference to the Bereiter-Engelmann model, Bereiter (1972) boasted that no other preschool program presented instructional goals in such a clear-cut fashion or had procedures so exclusively devoted to achieving those goals in the most efficient manner. "I would assert that the program is . . . at bottom distinguished entirely by the degree to which content and method are combined into a fully engineered instructional program" (Bereiter, 1972, p. 5).

Reliance on direct instruction to teach carefully structured academic content is consistent with behavioral psychology's emphasis on observable behaviors, systematic manipulation of environmental input, and attention to quantifiable outcomes. This is reflected in the belief of program architects that "children can be taught competencies more rapidly if teachers are provided with well-planned educational procedures, including pretested curriculum materials" (Becker, Engelmann, Carnine, & Rhine, 1981, p. 96).

Both the reliance on direct instruction and focus on academic content affronted traditional early educators who trusted and valued children's interests as sources of curriculum content. This discrepancy, however, indicates more than difference in style and beliefs about the nature of children and their learning. It also reveals a fundamental difference in educational purpose.

Whereas both the Montessori Method and the Developmental-Interaction approach saw their efforts as part of a larger reform of public education, the B-E and DI models did not challenge existing objectives and practices. "Certainly, the emphasis was not on changing the society and schools to fit the disadvantaged but on changing the disadvantaged to fit the school" (Anderson & Bereiter, 1972, p. 339).

Designers of the B-E and DI models did see their efforts as aimed at improving schooling, however. Rather than wanting to restructure public schooling, though, their interest was in making public school curriculum more effective and efficient. The most frequent point of comparison made by proponents of these two direct instruction models concern the basal series that schools traditionally use to teach language skills, reading, and arithmetic. They consistently attack the limitations of basal readers and highlight the organizational and structural advances found in their programmed lessons. Their goal has been to improve upon the status quo by doing it better—by providing increased consistency and efficiency in procuring greater academic achievement for all children.

This goal, and the method chosen to achieve it, provides the connection necessary to link the scientific method conceptually and pragmatically with a science of education. A science of education strives to systematically apply the findings of science to the problems of education and thereby improve its predictability, efficiency, and effectiveness. This same intention is inherent to the purported function and research of theories of instruction.[3]

Psychology's vision of a science of education can be traced to Thorndike's work in the early twentieth century (Cremin, 1961/1964). The vision also was shared and reinforced by early twentieth century curriculum theorists. These curriculum theorists, categorized as social efficiency educators by Kliebard (1986), were inspired by the power of the scientific method and the possibility of using it to devise curricula that efficiently prepared individuals for their future roles as adults.

Emerging at the same time as the United States's rapid growth as an urban and industrial nation, social efficiency educators similarly strived for efficiency, social utility, and scientific management (Kliebard, 1986).[4] Amazing correspondence exists between the axioms of social efficiency educators and those of Bereiter[5] and

---

3   Although Bereiter (1986) credits *Teaching the Disadvantaged Child*, published in 1966, with being the first explicit formulation of direct instruction, direct instruction has by no means been limited to these two curriculum models. It has been a central component of the teacher effectiveness movement (see, for example, Brophy, 1979) and popularized by educators such as Madeline Hunter (1976, 1977, 1979). DI proponents like to point out that direct instruction received official support from the United States Department of Education in the 1986 publication *What Works*. As noted earlier, though, theories of instruction have been shifting their reliance on behaviorism to cognitive theory. To the extent that these theories now contemplate learning in less mechanistic ways, their interpretation of its applicability seems less mechanistic as well. For a recent discussion of some of these changes, see Iran-Nejad, McKeachie, and Berliner (1990b).

4   It is generally agreed that the curricular views associated with social efficiency educators dominate public schooling.

5   Actually, Carl Bereiter's views about learning and instructional design have evolved in dramatic ways since 1966. In one of his recent articles, for example, he wrote,

the distinctive requirement of an educational learning theory [would seem to be] to explicate the students' role as intelligent agents in the learning process, to take account of the variety of resources that may come into use in achieving difficult learning objectives, and to embed explanations of particular learning processes within larger descriptions of the cognitive structures by which people adapt to various contexts so that they can achieve personal goals within them. (Bereiter, 1990, p. 619)

Engelmann and their associates.[6] As architects of the B-E and DI models, they approached the ideals of efficiency, social utility, and scientific management by focusing on clearly stated academic objectives and by standardizing teaching strategies and curriculum.

Teaching Disadvantaged Children in the Preschool: The Bereiter-Engelmann Model

The Bereiter-Engelmann preschool was established by Carl Bereiter and Siegfried Engelmann at the University of Illinois at Urbana-Champaign in the mid-1960s. A 2-hour per day program, it was designed to provide intensive direct instruction in reading, arithmetic, and language to disadvantaged children, 4 to 6 years of age (Bereiter & Engelmann, 1966b).

According to Anderson & Bereiter (1972), the decision to develop their model for preschoolers was a strategic one. It was anticipated that the preschool would be more amenable to change because it had fewer educational commitments, fewer explicit goals, fewer ties to the educational establishment, and fewer years of existence. The age of the children also was considered a plus because they were willing to learn, "more teachable," and not yet tainted by the arbitrary nature of the school system. Finally, Bereiter and Engelmann also felt they would be more likely to find cooperative adults who wanted to help children. "And, if changes seemed impossible within the schools themselves, then early education was the *only* place to prepare children for what they had in store" (Anderson & Bereiter, 1972, p. 340).

The choice of an academic program that taught skills in language, reading, and arithmetic was based on their belief that these were the skills disadvantaged children needed to succeed in public school. Each of these three subjects was taught as a separate class, each with its own teacher. Children circulated in groups of five from class to class, each session lasting 20 minutes. The only other major educational activity was singing. The teachers sung specially written songs to give children further practice in skills being taught in the classes. During the other hour of the day, the whole class participated in "minor activities," including snack time and a semi-structured activity.

Curriculum.   Two different strategies were used to determine curriculum content (Bereiter, 1970). First, Bereiter and Engelmann looked at the kinds of things children were expected to know when they encountered first grade curriculum materials, and second, they worked backward from the content of the Stanford-Binet intelligence test to define a "universe of conceptual content" (p. 205). From these exercises, they determined that the conceptual content of the program should include concepts of

---

6   Interested readers should read Chapter 4 of Kliebard's (1986) text.

color, size, shape, location, number, order, class, action, use, material, and part-whole relations as applied to concrete objects and events.

The B-E model identified 15 goals (Bereiter & Engelmann, 1966b). The first nine goals pertained to words and constructions that occur in ordinary speech, such as "ability to use both affirmative and *not* statements in reply to the question, 'What is this?'" and "ability to use the following prepositions correctly in statements describing arrangements of objects: on, in, under, over, between." Objectives 10 to 15 addressed numerical and reading skills, including "ability to count objects correctly up to ten," and "ability to recognize and name the vowels and at least 15 consonants." These goals, in turn, were carefully analyzed to determine the prerequisite learning for their achievement.

Teaching Methods.   According to Bereiter and Engelmann (1966a), their instructional method had five distinguishing characteristics:

1. It was fast paced. During a twenty minute period, five or more different kinds of tasks would be presented and as many as 500 responses might be required of each child.
2. Task irrelevant behavior was minimal. The efforts of both the teacher and the children were task-oriented; spontaneous exchanges were intentionally minimized by the teacher.
3. There was a strong emphasis on verbal responses. Children often produced them in unison so that each child's total output could be maximized.
4. The curriculum was comprised of carefully planned, small-step instructional units and continuous feedback. Although the teacher discouraged "irrelevant exchanges," she was to be sensitive to possible difficulties, quickly correct mistakes, and anticipate and avert misunderstandings.
5. The curriculum placed heavy work demands on children. Children were required to pay attention and work hard and were rewarded for thinking. (pp. 55–56)

Instruction was carried out "in a business-like, task-oriented manner" (Bereiter & Engelmann, 1966b, p. 59). The pace and intensity of the academic instruction led to charges that the program was unhealthy for young children. Bereiter and others associated with the B-E—and DI—models have persistently reiterated, however, that children have experienced no negative emotional side-effects from learning academic subjects in demanding and rigorous ways (Bereiter & Engelmann, 1966a, 1966b; Carnine, Carnine, Karp, & Weisberg, 1988; Gersten & George, 1990).

Despite their reassurances, however, concerns regarding the effects of academic environments in preschool and kindergarten persist, indicating the magnitude and longevity of this debate (see, for example, Gallagher & Sigel, 1987; Rescorla, Hyson, & Hirsh-Pasek, 1991b). Moreover, although the debate has generalized to contrasting declarations about the advantages and disadvantages of developmental and academic curricula, and more recently to comparisons between developmentally appropriate and inappropriate curricula (for example, Burts, Hart, Charlesworth, & Kirk, 1990), as well as contrasting curriculum models (for example, DeVries, Reese-Learned, & Morgan, 1991; Schweinhart, Weikart, & Larner, 1986), the opposing claims have remained relatively unchanged.

The language program was based on five basic teaching "moves" (the term "moves" is Bereiter's; see Table 5–1). Actually, these moves are less teaching strategies than articulation of various sentence structures that, once mastered, were presumed to enable different levels of reasoning and thinking. These structures progressed from basic statements of object identity to if-then statements and finally language for deductive reasoning.

An underlying assumption was that language structured thought; children could not think logically unless they had the language with which to reason. The B-E language curriculum directly taught disadvantaged children the sentence structures deemed necessary to support their ability to think logically.

Concepts, therefore, were grouped together based on the rules governing their manipulation rather than thematic associations such as the zoo (Bereiter, 1968). This

Table 5–1
Basic Teaching Moves in Terms of Task Difficulty

---

1. Verbatim repetition:

Teacher: This block is red. Say it . . . .
Children: This block is red.

2. Yes-no questions:

Teacher: Is this block red?
Children: No, this block is not red.

3. Location tasks:

Teacher: Show me a block that is red.
Children: This block is red.

4. Statement production:

Teacher: Tell me about this piece of chalk.
Children: This piece of chalk is red.
Teacher: Tell me about what this piece of chalk is **not.**
Children: (ad lib) This piece of chalk is not green. . . not blue, and so on.

5. Deduction problems

Teacher: (with piece of chalk hidden in hand) This piece of chalk is not red. Do you know what color it is?
Children: No. Maybe it is blue . . . maybe it is yellow . . . .

---

is because the objective was not for children to learn about the zoo but, rather, to teach them conceptual strategies for organizing content information. Consequently, strategies were selected based on their capacity to be generalized to other content. By the program's end, the majority of time was spent on deduction problems, although at each new step in the program, teachers and children went through all of the moves, even if in condensed form.

Instruction in reading and arithmetic were similar in conception to the language program. They were highly verbal, with considerable emphasis on learning generalizable rules through the repetitive and patterned practice of tasks that embodied the rule. (This is called learning rules by analogy.) The essential principle to be learned from the example associated with the five teaching moves presented in Table 5–1 is that saying that something is not a member of one set is equivalent to saying that it is the member of another set. And because learning rules by analogy required children to figure things out, designers of the B-E model disavowed the criticism that children's academic achievement was the result of rote memory.[7]

Bereiter (1970) credited his efforts, along with others in the compensatory education movement, with formulating a common content for preschool programs and initiating consensus regarding instructional goals. He characterized pre-existing early childhood programs as sharing a common set of activities, but lacking in a shared set of learning expectations.

> Their commonality resides not in what they are trying to get children to learn but rather in a set of activities, such as free play, certain games, story reading, painting, housekeeping and dress-up, field trips, etc, that constitute the traditional school fare.
>
> When Project Head Start began, this fund of common activities was about all there was to draw upon in forming a compensatory educational program for young children. Since then, in an effort to put wheels under one or another view of the cognitive needs of disadvantaged children, educators have begun to introduce new elements into the preschool curriculum that were not merely considered to be good things for children to do but that were intended to produce particular effects. Now, regardless of what long-range effects one wishes to produce, it is necessary to have children doing something in the short run that entails learning.[8] (pp. 204–205)

Teacher Characteristics.   The B-E model designated three teachers for every 15 children. Teachers taught particular subjects, not groups of children. Their ability as managers was of paramount importance. "In a preschool that is concerned with

---

7   As part of its evolution toward the Direct Instruction model, the original B-E curriculum model was replaced with DISTAR (the instructional programs in reading, arithmetic, and language), which was written by Engelmann and others (and is described as part of the DI model), the Conceptual Skills Program written by Bereiter and other associates, and the Open Court Kindergarten Program written by Bereiter and Hughes—all of which, according to Bereiter (1972), differ from each other and the program set forth in *Teaching Disadvantaged Children in the Preschool.*

8   In explaining why academically trained psychologists might have missed the important emphasis given to thinking in traditional preschools, Biber (1977a) suggested, "They may not have recognized attention to cognitive processes when these did not appear as specifically structured lessons but were, instead, interwoven with the total experiential scheme of learning" (p. 49).

enabling every child to extract the maximum amount of learning from every minute of the school day, efficient and intelligent management becomes of the utmost importance" (Bereiter & Engelmann, 1966b, p. 66).

Teachers also had to master the teaching strategies associated with the model. The teacher acted as a clinician; her responses were always to be premeditated and purposeful. They were also scripted.

> Slight variations can make the difference between successful learning and discouraging confusion. This is not to say that there is only one way to present a concept, any more than there is only one way to perform a surgical operation. But it takes a very sophisticated practitioner to know which variations are optional and which are dangerous. (Bereiter & Engelmann, 1966b, p. 104)

Consequently, teachers were encouraged to study the chapters depicting basic teaching strategies and to use them as they "would a detailed cookbook, recognizing that it is possible to be a very good cook without being an expert in the science of cookery, but that when one is not a thorough master of the science of cookery, it is necessary to stay close to the recipes if one is to avoid failures" (Bereiter & Englemann, 1966b, p. 104).

Bereiter and Englemann identified elementary school teachers as preferable teacher candidates because they "more or less" spoke the language of the intensive preschool. They found elementary teachers more inclined toward direct instruction, to work toward specific learning goals, and to maintain discipline. Furthermore, they discouraged hiring nursery-school teachers because they "must usually unlearn a great deal before they can become effective. . . . Their conception of child development and the emergence of skills is usually diametrically opposed to the viewpoint on which the intensive preschool rests" (Bereiter & Englemann, 1966b, p. 69).

■ *The Direct Instruction Model*

It is unclear when the Direct Instruction model received its current name, but it appears to have been in place by 1981. Wesley Becker, who strengthened several behavioral components of the program, joined Engelmann in 1967, following Bereiter's departure earlier that same year. At that point, the model became known as the Engelmann-Becker Model; in a 1980 discussion of Follow Through models, it was identified as the Engelmann-Becker Direct Instruction Model, and in a 1981 publication, the designers labeled it the Direct Instruction Model. The model and its staff left the University of Illinois at Urbana-Champaign and moved to the University of Oregon in 1970.

The DI model is designed for children in kindergarten through third grade. Because recent research findings indicate the model achieves greater success with children who begin the program as kindergartners, the designers contend that it is very important that children begin the program before first grade (Gersten, Darch, & Gleason, 1988).

The designers suggest the kindergarten year is so important because it represents a gradual, but systematic transition between a child-centered, "accepting" preschool and the structured environment of most first grades (Carnine, Carnine, Karp, & Weisberg, 1988; Gersten, Darch, & Gleason, 1988). The DI kindergarten year builds, step-by-step, the skills and knowledge necessary for student success in first grade. Proponents argue that program evaluations document that even extremely disadvantaged 5-year-olds can be taught to read in kindergarten, without negative side-effects (Carnine, Carnine, Karp, & Weisberg, 1988; Gersten, Darch, & Gleason, 1988). This advocacy for academic kindergartens and direct instruction for low-income students (Carnine, Carnine, Karp, & Weisberg, 1988; Gersten, 1991; Gersten & George, 1990; Gersten, Darch, & Gleason, 1988) continues their historic role as protagonists to traditionally oriented early childhood programs.

The short-term goal of the model is to help students achieve grade level performance on major school achievement test batteries by the end of third grade. The program's long-term goal is to teach basic academic skills to low-income students "that will equip them to compete with their more advantaged peers for higher education and the opportunities available in our society" (Becker, Engelmann, Carnine, & Rhine, 1981, p. 109).

Although the program's primary focus is children's achievement in cognitive academic areas, the designers acknowledge an interest in promoting children's affective and social development and suggest students receive "instruction in these areas" in ways appropriate to local circumstances (Becker, Engelmann, Carnine, & Rhine, 1981). Usually 3 hours of a 5-hour day are devoted to teaching academic skills, with the remaining 2 hours designated for other activities.

Advocates contend (with accompanying evaluation data) that their instructional methods engender positive self-esteem. Their reasoning is that as children become more academically competent, they feel better about themselves and others respond to them more positively. "From this perspective, a positive self-concept occurs as a by-product of good teaching" (Becker, Engelmann, Carnine, & Rhine, 1981, p. 109).

The Direct Instruction Model[9] is built on two basic premises: (1) that the rate and quality of children's learning in the classroom is a function of environmental events and (2) that educators can increase the amount of children's learning in the classroom by carefully engineering the details of students' interactions with that environment. "When these details are chosen and sequenced according to a rational plan, efforts to improve the rate at which children learn are likely to be successful" (Becker, Engelmann, Carnine, & Rhine, 1981, p. 98).

---

[9]   Becker, Engelmann, Carnine, and Rhine (1981) provide a complete description of the Direct Instruction model, including detailed analysis of its program design and curriculum content. Their chapter served as a primary informant for this review of the model's program and design.

Program Content

The instructional programs in reading, arithmetic, and language are the core of the model and are published under the trade name DISTAR. Each program contains objectives for three curriculum levels, creating a total of nine programs. These nine programs, in turn, contain programmed lessons derived from learning principles and programming strategies that were field-tested to ensure their empirical validity.

Teachers focus first on decoding skills and then on comprehension in DISTAR Reading I and II. In Reading III, students learn to read to obtain and use new information. In DISTAR Arithmetic I, students learn basic addition and subtraction operations and their related story-problem forms. In DISTAR Arithmetic II, they are introduced to multiplication and fractions along with further instruction in addition, subtraction, and various measurement concepts. Then in Arithmetic III, students receive instruction in algebra, factoring, and division, as well as continued practice in addition, subtraction, multiplication, and division.

Finally, the first two language programs teach object names, classes, and properties and relational terms. Children learn to make complete sentences and to describe their world. Language comprehension and language production are stressed. Students learn to ask questions to obtain information and are taught logical processes, including causality, deductions, opposites, and multiple attributes. The third language program expands students' logical use of language and basic grammatical rules. There are also activities designed to improve writing and spelling skills.

During each group session, teachers present six or seven brief 3-minute teaching sequences. These lessons include frequent teacher-student verbal interaction through games and races. Students, therefore, actively participate in lessons; engagement rates might be as high as "ten responses per minute, with 80 to 90 percent of the responses being correct" (Carnine, Carnine, Karp, & Weisberg, 1988, p. 75).

In addition, students spend 30 minutes a day in academically related independent activities. Supplementary gamelike activities provide additional practice and mastery of key concepts (Gersten, Darch, & Gleason, 1988).

Decisions regarding which concepts to include were heavily weighted in terms of a skill's generalizability and its success quotient. According to Gersten, Darch, and Gleason (1988), a central image that guided the conceptualization of the DI model was of students learning new concepts and skills in such a way that they "experienced unremitting success" (p. 229).

Programmatic Design

Three primary sources informed the construction of the DI model: (1) empirical behavior theory, (2) logical analysis of the use of classroom resources, and (3) logical analysis of concepts and tasks (Becker, Engelmann, Carnine, & Rhine, 1981).

Empirical Behavior Theory.   Behavioral principles that informed the model are reinforcement, conditioned responses, stimulus control, prompting, shaping, punishment, extinction, and fading. (Each of these learning principles refers to strategies that increase or decrease the presence of desired behaviors.) These learning principles were utilized in the construction of the DISTAR programs and in developing teaching procedures for eliciting and maintaining students' attention, securing their responses, and dispensing reinforcers. These behavioral principles also guided organizational decisions and management procedures for regulating the verbal behavior of teachers and students, monitoring students' academic progress, and using praise and other reinforcers to encourage students' acquisition of desirable behaviors.

Logical Analysis of the Use of Classroom Resources.   In response to limited resources, the DI architects used logical analyses to determine potential benefits and costs of alternative choices in the use of classroom resources. The results of their analysis informed such decisions as the choice of small group rather than individualized instruction; the use of parents as paraprofessionals rather than employment of more teachers; giving priority to academic instruction over play, art, music, or some other activity; and the use of scripted lessons over permitting teachers to select their own instructions.

Logical Analysis of Concepts and Tasks.   According to Becker, Engelmann, Carnine, and Rhine (1981), identifying the structural relationships that exist among concepts and tasks is a prerequisite for designing efficient educational programs. For example, the concepts hot-cold and wet-dry are sets of polar concepts that share a common characteristic; they are two-member groups. If this structural relationship is understood, then you know that if something does not have one characteristic, it must have the other. Becker, Engelmann, Carnine, and Rhine (1981) also identified various hierarchial structures that illustrate the characteristics shared among concepts; for example, collies are dogs; dogs are mammals; mammals are animals; animals are living things, and so forth. In addition, the variable of complexity was analyzed so that teaching could progress from simple tasks to more difficult ones.

The findings from these analyses were used to design the DISTAR programs. Objectives were analyzed into sets of related problems that children could solve by using a common strategy; concepts were identified that could be taught as general cases. This was the information program designers used to create systematic lessons in reading, language, and arithmetic. This information also was used to devise strategies for teaching basic concepts, teaching systematically related concepts, teaching rules, and teaching cognitive operations, which, in the DISTAR program, represent four different classes of tasks. The assumption was that student mastery of these lessons would result in their learning designated skills and concepts that in turn could be generalized and transferred to new learning situations.

Finally, as students progress through kindergarten and the primary grades, the teaching and task requirements shift in terms of six dimensions (Becker, Engelmann, Carnine, & Rhine, 1981). At first glance, these teaching strategies might seem commonplace, yet they specify the application of learning principles. Their systematized and systematic application distinguishes them from conventional classroom practices.

1. From overt to covert problem-solving. When teachers use an overt problem-solving strategy, they make every step in the strategy explicit. Eventually, via the application of appropriate learning principles, the problem-solving process becomes covert until only the response is overt. Covertization provides an essential link between the work that students perform under close supervision and their eventual independent effort.

2. From simplified contexts to complex contexts. In simplified contexts, when teachers introduce a discrimination, they emphasize the relevant features of the task. In more complex contexts, students are expected to apply their knowledge in a variety of settings characterized by a wide range of irrelevant detail.

3. From providing prompts to removing those prompts. Early in instruction, a teacher may use modified examples or special wordings to focus the learner's attention on relevant features. Later, these prompts are removed.

4. From massed practice to distributed practice. Massed practice is designed to bring about mastery and occurs when new skills are being learned; distributed practice (in other words, less frequent practice) aids retention of what has already been learned.

5. From immediate feedback to delayed feedback. As learners become more capable, teachers reduce the amount of feedback they provide.

6. From an emphasis on the teacher's role as a source of information to an emphasis on the learner's role as a source of information. As learners increase their repertoire of skills, teachers decrease their role as providers of information and become more of a guide to assist students in using information previously acquired. The learner must decide how to apply previously learned skills and information in a variety of problem solving situations. (p. 102)

Teaching Methods

Each DISTAR program includes instructions or scripts indicating exactly what the teacher should say and do during classroom instruction. Proponents discourage deviation from the script because it has been found that teachers lose their effectiveness when they attempt to individualize instruction for individual students (Gersten, Carnine, Zoref, & Cronin, 1986). Individualization does occur, however, in terms of a student's entry level, motivating procedures, techniques for making corrections, and the number of practice trials to mastery.

Scripts provide teachers with directions, sequences of examples, and sequences of subskills and wordings that all have been tested for effectiveness. Scripted presentations are also valued because of the amount of time saved from supervising and training teachers when everyone uses the same program. Under these circumstances, a supervisor need only pinpoint a teacher's deficiency and then provide appropriate remedies. In one of their case studies, Gersten, Carnine, Zoref, and

Cronin (1986) found that although kindergarten teachers initially resisted changing their teaching style because they thought the model too academic, they changed their minds once they saw the program's effects.

In order to have several groups working simultaneously, teachers are assisted by classroom aides. Aides are usually students' parents and are specially trained to perform teaching activities. Similar to the B-E model, teachers and aides become specialists in one of the three subject areas.

Small-group instruction is considered a central feature of the model. A class is usually divided into four groups of four to seven individuals, and students rotate through subject areas and seat work. Small-group instruction lasts about 30 minutes in each subject area at levels I and II. At level III, each 15 minutes of instruction is followed by 30 minutes of self-directed practice in workbooks.

Top ability groups are expected to complete 1.5 lessons per day and the lowest ability groups .7 lessons per day. Teachers systematically use positive consequences such as behavior-specific praise and point systems to strengthen students' motivations for learning.

Finally, parents are actively involved not only as teacher aides, but also as progress testers (monitors of student progress). Parents also work with their children at home using home practice books to reinforce skills students have recently mastered; as parent workers, they teach other parents to use the language training materials.

■ Explaining the Unanticipated Success of Academically Oriented Curricula

To understand the rapid acceptance of the B-E and DI models as a valid approach to early childhood education (acceptance promoted primarily by individuals outside the field), it is necessary to reinsert these two models into the sociopolitical context that birthed them so successfully during the 1960s. An appreciation of this context also helps explain their staying power, even though two significant interim occurrences, which are discussed in a later section, have created a more level playing field for the competition between academic and developmental programs.

The following discussion of the B-E and DI models shifts to focus on their position as significant and powerful representatives of, and advocates for, academic early childhood programs—rather than as discrete models. This discussion begins to disclose some of the ways in which the introduction of curriculum models in the mid-sixties has influenced the professional evolution of early childhood education.

The Timing Was Right

Prior to the onset of Head Start and other early intervention programs, most preschool and kindergarten programs were child-centered and nonacademic.

Although considerable activity in the learning theory tradition had been occurring in psychology, it had had little if any impact on child development theory/child psychology (White, 1970).

Preschool programs, as exemplified by the Bank Street approach, were heavily influenced by psychodynamic theory and focused on nurturing children's development. Kindergartens, after an early alliance with Thorndike's behavioral theory and his notion of habit-training (Bloch, 1987; Weber, 1969), became a program almost totally maturational in approach, using the then-new normative data about child growth being generated by child study centers. This normative data, according to Weber (1969), was used "to define those conditions that would foster growth organismically—including physical, intellectual, social, and emotional development. These were developmental needs formulated by adults who then used them to formulate a program" (p. 184).

The programmatic emphasis in preschool and kindergarten education in the mid-sixties, therefore, even with their differences, was on assuring the appropriate environmental conditions, deduced from child development theory, for nurturing each child's potential. Thus, when the B-E model burst onto the early childhood scene, it represented an approach to early education diametrically opposed to the status quo. The question is, why, under these circumstances, did it not only survive, but also succeed in changing the landscape of early childhood education?

The answer seems to lie in the timely convergence of at least six factors that emanated almost simultaneously from psychology, education, and societal dissatisfaction.

1. challenges to the notion of fixed intelligence;
2. the "discovery" of widespread poverty in the United States;
3. the 1957 Russian launching of Sputnik which punctured America's pride;
4. the escalation of interest in cognitive development nurtured by the rediscovery of Piaget's theory of cognitive development; Piaget's theory, in turn, was positively reassessed, in part, because of society's concern with re-establishing its competitive intellectual edge;
5. dissatisfaction with the educational status quo; and
6. the additional potency of applied learning theory following B. F. Skinner's "discovery" of operant conditioning.

Most of these factors, of course, are the same ones that helped launch Head Start in 1965. The nation's search for a solution to the problem of poverty, in conjunction with optimism that modifying the experiences of young children could change the trajectory of their development and success with schooling, at a time when Americans were embarrassed by the apparent inferiority of their educational system, converged in enthusiastic public support for compensatory education. (Chapter 2 discusses these changes in more detail.)

It would be easy to argue that the focus on academically oriented programs might be explained merely by the fact that once the purpose of Head Start was narrowed to enabling children to achieve greater success in schools, program designers, such as those who developed the B-E and DI models, thought it most logical to accomplish this purpose by focusing on the academic skills disadvantaged children needed to learn. This apparently simple explanation, however, *only* achieves its explanatory value when understood in terms of the forces that made this approach to compensatory education appear more valid than others. In fact, adoption of a behaviorally defined academic approach to early education rested on three supports: (1) re-establishment of academic development as the mission of schooling, (2) behaviorism's focus on changing behavior through modifying the environment, and (3) the interface between these two factors and school practices.

A Justification for Academic Early Childhood Programs

Americans were in the mood for effective academic solutions. "While American schoolchildren were learning how to get along with their peers or how to bake a cherry pie . . . Soviet children were being steeped in the hard sciences and mathematics needed to win the technological race that had become the center piece of the Cold War" (Kliebard, 1986, p. 265). The "scientific" language of behaviorism fit right in with America's search for technological superiority, and programmed learning made sense as the most effective means for alleviating the consequences of disadvantaged environments.

In addition, according to Egan (1988), behaviorism's discussions of process and product and teaching as a technological enterprise is analogous with the notion of assembly lines, thus aligning it in powerful ways with some of America's most deeply held beliefs about progress and how to achieve it efficiently. According to historian Michael Zuckerman (1987), Americans' mechanization of their ideas of the world and of themselves are very deep. "It is that mechanization of our apprehension of experience that impels our recurrent readiness to seek technological escapes from technologically induced dilemmas, that mechanization of our very imagination that promotes our presumption that the only way out is forward" (p. 262).

Now, link these insights with the underlying assumption of the first early intervention programs—that providing disadvantaged children with a changed environment would alter the course of their future academic development. Behavioral psychology was premised on exactly the same notion—that the determining factor in changing behavior resided not within the individual, but within the environment. In contrast, traditional early childhood programs placed their faith in defining "those conditions that would foster growth organismically" (Weber, 1969, p. 184). Thus, when the political and educational search for environmental changes that would stimulate intellectual development erupted, the learning theory tradition was positioned to respond.[10]

---

10   White (1970) chronicles a similar development in child psychology. He explains learning theory's lack of impact on child psychology until the mid-fifties by the fact that a genetic point of view dominated child psychology.

Watson's behaviorism, and the subsequent elaboration of learning theories, did not have a significant influence on child psychology in the early decades of this century because child psychologists had a rival theoretical scheme, more or less implicit and unrehearsed, in the genetic-rationalist tradition. (p. 665)

The final and critical element in understanding the unanticipated success of behaviorally derived academic programs was their alignment with the practice of most schools. Unlike the Developmental-Interaction approach, or the Piagetian-based models to be discussed in Chapter 6, the B-E and DI models created a first-time, close alliance between the curriculum of early childhood programs and that of the public schools. Even the Montessori Method, which shares B-E and DI's academic focus, structures its program very differently from conventional classrooms.

The relationship between early childhood and public school curricula is an important consideration because a major purpose of Head Start and Follow Through has been to improve public schooling (Hodges et al., 1980; Maccoby & Zellner, 1970; White & Buka, 1987). In contrast to early childhood curriculum models that proposed alternative views on curriculum and the purposes of education, the B-E and DI models sought to help schools do a more efficient job of teaching basic academic skills. The improvements sought for the primary grades by the B-E and DI models and similar academically oriented curricula were theoretically and pragmatically consistent with existing school practice and certainly less threatening to the status quo.

A Changing Relationship Between Early Childhood and Elementary Education

Since the onset of compensatory education, a critical transformation in the relationship between preschool and kindergarten education and elementary schools has materialized. Although conceptually subtle, cognizance of this transformation seems critical for understanding the success of academic curriculum models. Simultaneously, it also reveals reverberations from the curriculum model era on the subsequent progression of early childhood education.

This change in relationship has emerged from the reality that, despite programs and rhetoric to the contrary, most early intervention programs have focused on enhancing the ability of low-income children to succeed at the next level of the educational system. In actuality, if not in theory, a majority of early intervention programs have understood their purpose in terms of school readiness rather than child development.

Consequently, it was not the persuasiveness of progressive early educators and their arguments regarding nursery education as a lever for promoting educational change that convinced the public about the importance of early education. Rather, it was dismissal of the notion of fixed intelligence, designation of the preschool years as the most susceptible to redirection, and a societal reason for using this knowledge that has leveraged public acceptance regarding the significance of early education as a counteragent for children's disadvantaged circumstances. Contemporaneously, public appreciation for the benefits of nursery education extended to children from middle-income families. And, once nursery education became appreciated as preschool education, and was recognized as an "educational" program, it became subjected to the same struggles as other parts of the educational system regarding curriculum priorities.

This deduction is supported by the work of Kliebard (1986), who argues that four competing interest groups (humanists, social efficiency proponents, developmentalists, and social meliorists) have been struggling for control of the American public school curriculum since the 1890s. In the case of early childhood education, however, the appearance of various educational factions vying for control over the curriculum did not emerge and evolve over an extended period of time; instead, the struggle was introduced and systematized through the medium of curriculum models.[11]

The advent of curriculum models, of course, cannot be credited as the sole cause of this transformation. But, both as a participant in, and an artifact of, this transformative process, the emergence of curriculum models has affected early childhood education in at least two significant ways. First, the development and evaluation of curriculum models has furthered the notion of a science of education within early childhood education. Second, competition among curriculum models, within the changing context of early education, unexpectedly thrust early childhood education into the struggle for control of the American curriculum that Kliebard (1986) has described.

In the specialized realm of early childhood education, this struggle has pitted developmentalists against social efficiency educators. The fact that early childhood's participation in this decades-long struggle did not occur until recently, rather than during the early 1900s when the developmental faction first emerged, supports the catalytic value being attributed to the onset of early intervention programs and the systematic variation of curricula. At the same time that the four factions identified by Kliebard were emerging, kindergartens were dismantling their connection with Froebel, and progressive and laboratory-based nursery schools were emerging. The interest group labeled developmentalist was shaping, almost single-handedly, the notion of early childhood education (see Bloch, 1987, 1991; Weber, 1969).

Nursery schools, of course, were almost totally separate from public schools in the early and mid-1900s, and public school kindergartens, which were limited in number, developed a curriculum derived primarily from maturational theory (although their allegiance to maturation theory only developed after an initial interest in aligning their curriculum with the public schools; Bloch, 1987; Weber, 1969). Elementary school, in the minds of most educators, began with first grade.

Thus, discussions about preschool and kindergarten curriculum were usually separate from those about primary schools and, as a result, were unaffected by the struggle described by Kliebard (1986). However, after the launching of Project Head Start and similar early intervention programs, this relationship began to change. Preschool education slowly but surely was reconceptualized as an appropriate beginning for primary schooling (especially for low-income children). This alteration had

---

11 In a recent attempt to understand the challenges currently confronting kindergartens, Walsh (1987) used a similar line of reasoning to conclude that kindergartens have become integrated into the elementary school. He argues that the inconsistent changes confronting kindergartens reflect the fact that they have become entangled in the ongoing struggle over which position shall have control over the curriculum. His title question of "Why here? Why now?" is misleading, though. According to the reasoning just presented, this conflict was instigated over 25 years ago when the purpose of nursery schools was reinterpreted as preschool education.

escalating ramifications as public school programs for 4-year-olds began to prolifer-
ate during the 1980s. This change in relationship between preschool and elementary
education illuminates why interest in curriculum models now comes from state
departments of education and public schools (Powell, 1987a) and why their interest
is articulated in terms of effective preschool curricula.

Developmentally Appropriate Practice:
Reclaiming Traditional Early Childhood Education

Early childhood education's entry into the public struggle over the structure and
content of school curriculum has sustained the conflict between developmental and
academic curricula (and opens early childhood education to criticism from curriculum theorists; see Chapter 8). Early childhood educators and developmental psychologists continue to frame the debate in child development terms (e.g., Elkind,
1986; Rescorla, Hyson & Hirsh-Pasek, 1991a; Sigel, 1991), and social efficiency educators, such as Gersten and his associates (Carnine, Carnine, Karp, & Weisberg, 1988;
Gersten, Darch, & Gleason, 1988; Gersten & George, 1990), remain focused on
issues related to school learning.

Reflecting this distinction, early childhood educators now frame the controversy
between academic and developmental programs as a battle between developmentally appropriate and developmentally inappropriate curricula. The change in terminology, however, reflects more than a particular ideological stance; it points to a critical alteration in the way the issues currently are being debated.

Since the mid-1980s, early childhood advocates for a developmental curriculum
have moved from a defensive to offensive position. With what some may consider sweet
irony, programs characterized by what is currently labeled developmentally appropriate
practice have begun to place academically oriented (i.e., developmentally inappropriate)
programs on the defensive. Now, for example, proponents of the Direct Instruction
model contend that there need not be a dichotomy between programs that address academic skills and those that address socialization; they argue that kindergarten programs
for economically disadvantaged children should include not only effective academic
instruction but also child development experiences (Carnine, Carnine, Karp, & Weisberg,
1988; Gersten, Darch, & Gleason, 1988; Gersten & George, 1990). Of interest to this discussion is the changing circumstances that have supported this reversal of positions.

Few would disagree that the most successful challenge to the validity of academic early childhood programs has been the 1986 position statement of the National
Association for the Education of Young Children (NAEYC) entitled "Developmentally
Appropriate Practice in Early Childhood Programs" (DAP; Bredekamp, 1987; the document was expanded in 1987 to address children from birth to age 8). According to
Bredekamp (1991), the escalation of public school programs for 4-year-olds provided
a major impetus for the document's development. In response to membership
request, and in hopes of influencing public school prekindergarten and kindergarten
programs, the NAEYC Governing Board appointed a Commission on Appropriate
Education for 4- and 5-year-olds expressly for this purpose.

Bredekamp's overview of events, however, takes on a deeper hue when considered in light of the unanticipated success of academically oriented preschools and kindergartens and the increasing numbers of children in these programs. By the mid-1980s when NAEYC first articulated the concept of DAP, 90% of 5-year-olds were attending kindergartens, which, by then, were almost universally offered by public schools (Spodek, 1986). Consistent with the trend begun in the mid-sixties, when only half as many children attended kindergarten, kindergartens had become increasingly academic (e.g., Egertson, 1987), and there was every indication the same trend would characterize the development of the new prekindergartens.

Early childhood educators, consequently, did not want just to exert influence on public school prekindergarten and kindergarten programs; they also wanted to stay the tide of academic curricula. The DAP position statement, therefore, reflected more than just an attempt to influence public school decision making. It represented as well an attempt by the early childhood profession to re-assert—and re-insert—its developmental tradition into the continuing struggle for control of the public school curriculum.

Bredekamp (1991), who edited the position statements, acknowledges the document's political motivation. She also affirms that "[i]t is reasonably safe to say that the developmentalist perspective of the document reflects the consensus position of the early childhood profession" (p. 202).

Explaining the Unanticipated Success of Developmentally Appropriate Practice

NAEYC's stated purpose for developing DAP has been advanced beyond expectations. The DAP position statement has been enormously effective both internally and externally. Internally, the concept of DAP has helped to unify early childhood education's various strands (nursery education, child care, Head Start, and kindergartens; Kagan, 1989). This unanticipated outcome can be attributed to the galvanizing effect of the profession's attempt to reclaim its heritage.

Externally, the concept has become familiar rhetoric in reports commissioned by businesses seeking high quality early childhood programs to help assure the competence of their future labor force (e.g., Committee for Economic Development, 1991) and by educational associations committed to educational reform (e.g., National Association of Elementary School Principals, 1990; National Association of State Boards of Education, 1988, 1991; acceptance by these groups has enabled the concept of DAP to influence the curriculum of primary grades). Even proponents of the Direct Instruction model have reframed their presentation. Now they, too, speak to developmentally appropriate practice and use its terminology, even though, programmatically, the model has remained unchanged. As expressed by Gersten, Darch, and Gleason (1988), "Teaching reading in a developmentally appropriate fashion to [low-income] students is a challenge—but it can lead to enduring benefits to the students involved" (p. 238).

The degree and extent of current support for a developmental orientation to early childhood education is in sharp contrast to the reception given to proponents of the Bank Street approach in the mid-sixties. How did it come to be? What changed to make the public and other educators more receptive to an approach they had summarily dismissed for the preceding two decades? And does this change mean that the dream of progressive early educators to reform schooling "from below" (i.e., via nursery and kindergarten education) may at last be coming to fruition?

A critical turning point in the complexion of the competition between developmental and academic approaches to early education appears to have been the 1984 publication by David Weikart and his associates describing the lasting effects of the developmentally oriented High/Scope Curriculum model (see Chapter 6). Prior to their publication, the Consortium for Longitudinal Studies (1979) had released their findings regarding the long-lasting impact of early intervention programs. The findings of this influential study (discussed in greater detail in Chapter 7), which demonstrated that children who had participated in early childhood interventions were less likely to be retained in grade or to be placed in special education programs and were more likely to graduate from high school, renewed public confidence in the value of early intervention programs, irrespective of the curriculum model.

In contrast, the findings regarding the long-term impact of the High/Scope model not only reinforced the optimistic conclusions of the Consortium study, they also linked the outcomes to a particular curriculum model. Their results credited their preschool model with improving children's cognitive performance during early childhood; improving scholastic placement and achievement during the school years; decreasing delinquency, crime, use of welfare assistance, and incidence of teenage pregnancy; and increasing high school graduation rates, frequency of enrollment in postsecondary education programs, and employment (Berrueta-Clement, Schweinhart, Barnett, Epstein, & Weikart, 1984). Enthusiasm for these findings was augmented by an economic evaluation of the data in terms of cost-benefits, which enabled educators and policy makers to contemplate the value of preschool education in economic terms. (This receives further discussion in Chapter 7.)

These well-publicized findings provided developmentally oriented early childhood programs what years of heated debate had not—namely scientific validity. By verifying the benefits of a developmentally oriented early childhood program in terms of measurable outcomes through "scientific" research, and hailing these outcomes in terms of their cost-effectiveness for society, Weikart and his associates succeeded in aligning a developmental approach with the technological norms of society. This strategy, which has been amazingly successful with policy makers and public school decision makers, in turn, set the stage for NAEYC's unveiling of their position statement on developmentally appropriate practice.

Then, in 1986, High/Scope researchers published results of another longitudinal study that compared outcomes for children who had participated in preschool programs between 1967 and 1970 using the High/Scope model, a traditional curriculum, and direct instruction (Schweinhart, Weikart, & Larner, 1986). Based on participants' self-reports at age 15, Schweinhart, Weikart, and Larner concluded that children participating in the Direct Instruction model were more likely to engage in delinquent acts than children participating in the other two curriculum models. Although the study's methodology has been questioned, the possibility that direct instruction models might have harmful effects has been influential in promoting the concept of developmentally appropriate practice.

With the passage of time, however, advocacy on behalf of developmentally appropriate practice is less frequently couched in terms of achieving holistic educational goals. Rather, traditional early childhood practices now tend to be promoted in terms of their capability to secure conventional educational objectives cost-effectively and to meet societal needs without harmful side-effects, especially when these promotions are addressed to corporate and political decision makers and public school administrators. As a result, curriculum possibilities for young children have been narrowed to achieve more conventional developmental/educational outcomes.

Thus, in response to the earlier question as to whether the dream of progressive early educators to reform public schooling "from below" is at last coming to fruition, the answer seems to be "yes" . . . but "no." The movement toward developmental early childhood programs for children prekindergarten through third grade continues to gain momentum and enthusiasm. Yet advocates for programs described as developmental are more likely to tout children's intellectual (albeit not academic) and social-emotional development than their overall psychological adjustment, are less likely to position their struggle as part of a larger educational effort, and are unlikely to propose revolutionary changes in the goals of education.[12] These latter aspirations, unfortunately, are more difficult to support with scientific justifications and in terms of social efficiency.

◼ *For Further Reading*

Becker, W. C., Engelmann, S., Carnine, D. W., & Rhine, W. R. (1981). Direct instruction model. In W. R. Rhine (Ed.), *Making schools more effective: New directions from Follow Through* (pp. 95–154). New York: Academic Press.

> This chapter is a comprehensive and detailed description of the Direct Instruction model written by its designers.

Gersten, R., Darch, C., & Gleason, M. (1988). Effectiveness of a direct instruction academic kindergarten for low income students. *The Elementary School Journal, 89,* 227–240.

> This more recent description and defense of the Direct Instruction model provides not only a succinct summary of the program but also one "enlightened" by the rhetoric of developmentally appropriate practice.

Kliebard, H. M. (1986). *The struggle for the American curriculum, 1893-1958.* New York: Routledge.

> This book chronicles the struggle among four interest groups to achieve control over the public school curriculum. I found it a fascinating text, not only because of its thesis, but also because the information was presented through the lens of a curriculum theorist.

---

12 These last three outcomes are taken from Zigler's (1984) summary of Barbara Biber's contributions to early education.

Chapter 6

Two Models Derived from Piagetian Theory

So what *do* we do with stages? What is there beyond the rhetoric of generalities and vague long-term goals? . . . what teachers need are not descriptions of stages on Genevan tasks, but descriptions of developmental stages (or levels) in classroom activities—that is, in activities justifiable on the basis of cognitive-developmental theory and research.

Rheta DeVries, Developmental Stages in Piagetian
Theory and Educational Practice, 1984

Evidence of the cost-effectiveness of . . . high quality preschool programs has enabled them to become part of the social "safety net." So, the Perry Preschool Project began as a "suspect" innovation, then became one of a multitude in a surge of public support for such efforts, and has played a major role in legitimating preschool education through the research evidence of its cost-effective nature as a social investment.

David Weikart, In Preface to Changed Lives:
The Effects of the Perry Preschool Program on Youths through Age 19, 1984

This chapter is unique to this book for the fact that it explores two early child-hood curriculum models—the Kamii-DeVries approach and the High/Scope Curriculum model—both of which rely on the theory of Jean Piaget. As a result, the content of this chapter highlights how different interpretations of the same theoretical framework can generate distinctive approaches to early education.[1]

Examination of the Kamii-DeVries approach and the High/Scope model helps illustrate the challenge of deriving definitive educational implications from developmental theory in general, and Piaget's theory of cognitive development in particular. Although these two models—and their three program architects—rely on the same theory to rationalize their practices, they appeal to different aspects and interpretations of the theory to do so.

The extent of the two models' reliance on Piaget's theory also differs. Whereas the Kamii-DeVries approach is almost totally reliant on Piaget's theory, the High/Scope model incorporates the ideas of non-Piagetians as well. As expressed by Weikart in his introduction to the model's first rendition, "While there is a growing congregation of 'high church' Piagetians in preschool education, I would classify this curriculum as the product of 'store front' Piagetian theory utilization" (Weikart, Rogers, Adcock, & McClelland, 1971, p. ix). In contrast, Kamii and DeVries pride themselves on having achieved a coherent, internally consistent curriculum.

These particular two models also present contrasting rationales for creating curriculum models. As the introductory quotes intimate, the Kamii-DeVries approach and High/Scope model emphasize different programmatic concerns.

The High/Scope model, through the efforts of the High/Scope Educational Research Foundation, has generated sustained interest in, and attention to, curriculum models as a vehicle for disseminating a "proven" curriculum that will provide society a payback for its investment in early childhood education. As one of the first experimental early childhood programs initiated in the early sixties (before the advent of Head Start), advocates of the High/Scope curriculum have effectively promoted the positive results of its longitudinal studies describing the long-term effects of the curriculum on program graduates. (See Chapter 7 for reviews of these studies.) The effectiveness of the High/Scope Foundation's advocacy on behalf of early childhood education has demonstrated policy makers' responsiveness to educational programs that can be empirically and economically justified.

Most of the extensive writings by designers and advocates of the High/Scope model argue the importance of early childhood education as part of society's resolution of its many ills and the unique efficacy of the High/Scope model in this regard (see, for example, Berrueta-Clement, Schweinhart, Barnett, Epstein, & Weikart, 1984; Weikart, 1987, 1988, 1992; Weikart & Schweinhart, 1993). In contrast, Kamii and DeVries rarely address early childhood education as a public policy issue. Rather, the bulk of their writings, both individually and collaboratively, mine the educational

---

[1] There are numerous approaches to early childhood education derived from Piagetian theory. Lavatelli's (1970) approach used many of Piaget's experiments as a means for advancing children's cognitive development. Less literal applications include the approach of Forman and his colleagues (1977, 1980) and Copple, Sigel, and Saunders (1979). The High/Scope model and Kamii-DeVries approach were selected for review because they are better known, more systematized, and included in numerous comparative program evaluations.

implications of Piaget's theory, justify the superiority of his theory as a framework for early education, and refine the explication of their approach.

Kamii and DeVries confidently express not only the superiority of Piaget's ideas as a theoretical framework for early education, but they also further contend that their approach represents the most faithful implementation of Piaget's ideas (DeVries & Kohlberg, 1987; Kamii & DeVries, 1978). Thus, the soundness of their approach to early education is highly dependent on the validity of Piaget's theory as an explanation for human development in general, and cognitive development in particular. (Recent critique of Piaget's theory can be found in Karmiloff-Smith, 1992; for critiques accompanied by implications for education see Gardner, 1991; Inagaki, 1992.)

The writings of Kamii (1981a, 1981b, 1985) and DeVries (1984; DeVries & Kohlberg, 1987) advocate not so much the importance of early childhood education, however, but the possibility of a scientifically informed approach to early education, thus continuing, though perhaps not intentionally, the search initiated during the sixties with the advent of Project Follow Through. DeVries's recent efforts, in particular, continue the lengthy effort to develop a science of educational practice and rationalize, conceptually and empirically, the superiority of a Piagetian approach, such as hers, to early education (DeVries, 1991; DeVries & Goncu, 1987; DeVries & Kohlberg, 1987; DeVries, Reese-Learned, & Morgan, 1991). As a result, DeVries's ongoing work reinvigorates discussions regarding the justification for curriculum models in early childhood education.

These two early childhood models, therefore, have been designed with different purposes. Although Weikart and Kamii and DeVries each selected Piagetian theory as a basis for their decision making, they did so with different intentions and for different reasons.

The High/Scope model based its curriculum on Piaget's theory of cognitive development because his theory provided program developers a coherent, cognitively oriented framework for creating a curriculum designed to help ameliorate the scholastic difficulties of disadvantaged youth. The Kamii-DeVries approach relies on Piaget's theory because its coherent explanation of cognitive development provides a framework for creating a scientifically valid approach to early education. As a logical outcome of these choices, the High/Scope model and Kamii-DeVries approach each use curriculum models to achieve different outcomes.

The High/Scope curriculum model has provided the High/Scope Educational Research Foundation a vehicle for widely disseminating its cognitively oriented curriculum and for expanding accessibility to a "proven" early childhood program that promises to improve children's life chances. For DeVries, the structure of a curriculum model is providing a vehicle for designing a theoretically coherent, empirically validated approach to early education—a framework for creating, at long last, "a science of educational practice" (DeVries, 1991, p.547).

Uniquely, these two approaches to early childhood education are still in process. Their architects continue to develop and refine their curricula. The work of Weikart and DeVries, therefore, reveals contemporary thinking regarding curriculum model development. But, at the same time, due to this circumstance, this chapter does not benefit from the kind of historical commentary that has been available for the other four curriculum models.

■ *Early History: Applying Piagetian Theory to Early Childhood Education*

David Weikart and Constance Kamii both became involved with early childhood education during their tenure with the Ypsilanti, Michigan, public schools in the early sixties. One of the impressive facts about the High/Scope and Kamii-DeVries approaches, in fact, is the sustained length of time their architects have committed to curriculum development and program dissemination.

Prior to their entry into early childhood education, David Weikart was a school psychologist and Constance Kamii a diagnostician and adolescent counselor. The Perry Preschool Project was initiated in the Ypsilanti Public Schools in fall 1962 as part of a long-term effort to improve the scholastic performance of Ypsilanti's disadvantaged youth. Frustrated by the lack of alternatives within the existing school system, Weikart decided to explore the potential of preschool intervention for 3- and 4-year-olds. Weikart became the Perry Preschool Project director and Kamii served as a research associate.

The curriculum developed for the Perry Preschool Project evolved into its current form during the ensuing 10 years. The first significant revision occurred during spring 1964 when the Perry Preschool project staff rejected its instructional emphasis on visual-motor skills, number concepts, and language enrichment activities and began focusing its efforts on a curriculum founded on the developmental theory of Jean Piaget (Hohmann, Banet, & Weikart, 1979; Weikart, Rogers, Adcock, & McClelland, 1971). In the foreword to their 1979 curriculum description, the program architects note:

> It is difficult . . . to imagine the dearth of information about preschool curriculum that the Perry Preschool faced. In 1960, when the first planning for the project began, there were few guidelines on how to operate a nursery school. . . . Published discussions of curriculum that the staff turned up stressed group dynamics and physical, social and emotional development, but programs specifically aimed at school success and/or cognitive development were not accessible to us if they were in fact available. (Hohmann, Banet, & Weikart, 1979, p. xii–xiii)

Shortly thereafter, Kamii was awarded a postdoctoral fellowship, and from 1966 to 1967, she studied at the University of Geneva under Jean Piaget and his colleagues. In 1967, she became curriculum director in the Ypsilanti public schools for a separate early childhood program, the Ypsilanti Early Education Program, and began directing the development of another preschool curriculum based on Piaget's theory. Kamii focused her effort on articulating a framework for preschool curriculum based on Piaget's theory.

For both Weikart and Kamii, Piaget's theory of cognitive development offered a structured, theoretical framework for developing a cognitively oriented curriculum. Their separate intentions, however, were already evident. Weikart chose Piaget's theory as a basis for curriculum because, after a frustrating search for a useful conceptual framework, Piaget's theory addressed the issues of cognitive development he and his staff were confronting (Hohmann, Banet, & Weikart, 1979). Weikart's efforts were focused on developing a preschool curriculum to alleviate the academic disadvantages being experienced by Ypsilanti's disadvantaged children; Piaget's theory provided a needed, cognitive conceptual framework. "Piaget offered a conceptual structure around which a preschool curriculum model could be built, an explicit rationale for preschool activities" (Weikart & Schweinhart, 1987, p. 255).

Kamii, however, unlike Weikart, was interested primarily in probing the educational implications of Piaget's theory for preschool education. And, as her understanding and interpretation of Piagetian theory evolved, she became increasingly dissatisfied with her early efforts. In fact, ultimately Kamii cited her early thinking and writings as an example of how one should *not* interpret Piaget for education (see, for example, Kamii, 1971, 1972; Kamii & Radin, 1967, 1970; Sonquist & Kamii, 1967).

As a result of her continuing study, and in contrast to the curricular emphasis of the High/Scope model, Kamii shifted her focus away from Piaget's stages of cognitive development and the overt behaviors characteristic of thinking at various stages and toward the constructive processes that advanced cognitive development and logical reasoning. This shift in focus, and ongoing investigation of the educational implications of Piaget's theory, accelerated when Kamii began her collaborative work with Rheta DeVries at the University of Illinois Chicago campus in 1970 (DeVries also studied at the University of Geneva under Piaget and his colleagues). Prior to pursuing the outcomes of Weikart and Kamii's divergent routes, however, a brief analysis of why, in the 1960s, Piaget's theory of cognitive development generated such excitement in the educational community deserves explanation. Recall from Chapter 4's discussion of the Developmental-Interaction approach, for example, that Lucy Sprague Mitchell and her progressive colleagues had read Piaget in the 1930s and been unimpressed. Barbara Biber and her Bank Street affiliates read Piaget again in the 1960s, and although they thought his ideas useful and incorporated them into their conceptualization of the Developmental-Interaction approach, they argued that his ideas were insufficient as the basis for an entire curriculum. What, then, about Piaget's theory in the 1960s so galvanized psychologists such as Weikart, Kamii, and DeVries (and so many others)?

■ *The Piagetian Mystique*

The phrase *Piagetian mystique* is borrowed from Evans (1975), who credited most of the attention to children's cognitive development in the sixties and seventies to the ideas of Piaget. Weber (1984) attributes the long delay in recognizing Piaget's ideas to three factors, the first two of which are primarily methodological. Weber first explains the delay of interest in Piaget's ideas in terms of the discrepancy between his clinical research method and the scientific, statistical treatment of findings prevalent in the United States. The second methodological factor was Piaget's persistent blending of empirical description with theoretical speculation; this lack of empirical clarity apparently rankled psychologists seeking to build a science of human behavior. It was the reversal of the third factor, however, that set the stage for Piaget's educational (as opposed to psychological) impact. Prior to the 1960s, as already has been stated many times, there was limited interest in intellectual development because it was presumed to be predetermined and fixed by heredity. The reassessment of this long-term judgment shifted psychologists' focus from the role of biology to the role of the environment. And, as we already know, this reassessment, aligned with society's surging concern with alleviating poverty, led to a national focus on early childhood education as a mechanism for assuring school success. In the sixties, therefore, Piaget's theory of cognitive development, which emphasizes intellectual growth as developing from an interaction between the child and her environment, found a psychologically and socially responsive milieu.

This responsiveness was nurtured further by an emerging resurgence of educational interest in intellectual functioning and public expectation that the educational system should promote intellectual prowess, especially in mathematics and the sciences. It may be remembered from discussion in previous chapters that education during the forties and fifties had focused on students' life adjustment; this focus had led to curriculum based on children's perceived psychosocial needs. During the fifties, however, educational criticism focused on once again making the training of the intellect the central function of schools (Kliebard, 1986).

This change in direction became firmly secured when, on October 5, 1957, Sputnik was launched by the former Soviet Union. As described by Kliebard (1986),

> Within a matter of days, American mass media had settled on a reason for the Soviet technological success. Just as Prussian schools were widely believed to be the basis for the victory of the Prussians over the Austrians in the Battle of Konigratz in 1866, so, implausibly, did the Soviet technological feat become a victory of the Soviet educational system over the American. Quickly, life adjustment education was seen as the prime example of America's "soft" education in contrast to the rigorous Soviet system. While American schoolchildren were learning how to get along with their peers or how to bake a cherry pie, so the explanation went, Soviet children were being steeped in the hard sciences and mathematics needed to win the technological race that had become the centerpiece of the Cold War. (pp. 264–265)

Thus Piagetian theory found not only a receptive psychological and social climate in the United States, but also a political one as well. It was not only that Piaget's theory focused on cognitive development at a time when the nation was interested in intellectual development or that his theory saw cognitive development as the result of the child's active interaction with a stimulating environment. Interest in his theoretical ideas was also assured by the fact that his theory specifically conceptualized the development of logical reasoning.

Piaget's theory focuses on the same logical operations that are considered the underpinnings of mathematics and science. Student mastery of these disciplines was going to assure the United States' technological superiority over its competitors and victory in the Cold War competition between the then–Soviet Union and the United States.

Murray (1979) concluded that these converging factors made the adoption of Piagetian theory virtually inevitable. "Given that the content of Piaget's theory and research was largely children's reasoning in mathematics, science, and logic, and the lack of similar content anywhere else in psychology, it was all but inevitable that Piaget would dominate these curricular reforms" (p. 34).

These factors, though, primarily speak to Piaget's acceptance by the general educational community. Murray also notes that Piaget's claim that intellectual development progressed in terms of a hierarchically organized sequence that was rooted in sensorimotor activity ensured, as well, the interest of those concerned with early childhood education. In contrast to the more technical and instructional emphasis simultaneously emanating from behavioral theory, Piaget's theory offered early childhood educators a framework for incorporating cognitive development into early childhood education in a way compatible with their existing notions of teaching and learning as interactive and developmental.

■ *The Kamii-DeVries Approach*

The Kamii-DeVries approach builds on Piaget's distinction between different types of knowledge, incorporates educational implications of Piaget's distinction between heteronomous and autonomous moral reasoning (these terms are defined below), and provides a constructivist perspective on traditional school objectives in number and arithmetic and reading and writing. The first two components are unique to their approach and are the basis for two primary program components: physical-knowledge activities and group games. Kamii and DeVries contend that Piaget's work has educational implications for children's moral, social, affective, *and* cognitive development.

The Kamii-DeVries approach has been developed primarily for preschool, although the work in number and arithmetic and reading and writing that has informed their approach has been extended into the primary grades (for example, Ferreiro & Teberosky, 1979/1982; Kamii, 1985; Kamii & Joseph, 1989). As of 1987, the Kamii-DeVries approach was being implemented in public and private programs in Chicago, Houston, and Homewood, Alabama (DeVries & Kohlberg, 1987). More recently, the Missouri Department of Elementary and Secondary Education has initiated Project Construct (Flynn, 1992; Murphy & Baker, 1990). This initiative, which has been heavily influenced by DeVries and Kamii, is a constructivist approach to education for children in prekindergarten, kindergarten, and first grade. DeVries and Kohlberg (1987) suggest that comprehensive program implementation has been limited by the fact that constructivist program development is fairly well defined only for preschool education, and is well developed for elementary and secondary education only in the area of moral development.

Although Kamii, currently at the University of Alabama at Birmingham, initiated the first curricular components for what now is known as the Kamii-DeVries approach, DeVries, of the University of Houston, framed their collaborative work as a specific approach to early childhood education. DeVries's formal designation of her collaborative work with Kamii as a specific approach to early education became popularized in 1987 with the publication of *Programs of Early Education: The Constructivist View.* In this text, DeVries re-asserts the importance of Piaget's stage theory, in addition to constructivism, and incorporates Kohlberg's stages of moral development and Selman's stages of perspective taking into the curricular framework of the Kamii-DeVries approach (DeVries, 1984, 1992; DeVries & Kohlberg, 1987). These changes reflect a third, still evolving, alteration within the Kamii-DeVries approach—from Kamii's original focus on Piagetian stages, to Kamii and DeVries's shared emphasis on constructivism, to DeVries's current reinsertion of Piaget's stages (structuralism) as an important curricular element.

Until the mid-eighties, Kamii and DeVries had minimized the educational relevance of advancement to the next stage of cognitive development; they had argued that Piaget's stages held little usefulness for teachers in terms of helping them know what to do in their classrooms (DeVries, 1978; Kamii & DeVries, 1977, 1978). Now DeVries has aligned with her colleague Lawrence Kohlberg and champions a carefully delineated definition of development. Specifically, DeVries's endorsement of development as the aim of education refers to children's progression through a sequence of universal stages of intellectual and moral development consistent with Piaget's stages of operational reasoning (DeVries, 1992; DeVries & Kohlberg, 1987). DeVries and Kohlberg (1987) contend that "development as the aim of education is the most legitimate because it avoids the pitfall of value relativity" (p. xii–xiii).

Now that advancement toward the next developmental stage has been reincorporated as programmatically relevant, desired developmental outcomes, as well as preferable practices for their actualization, can be articulated and scientifically validated. Previously, developmental outcomes had been defined in terms of global characteristics. "We advocate development as our educational objective because it is the only way by which individuals can become intelligent, autonomous, mentally healthy, and moral. . . . Curriculum objectives, therefore, can only be stated in general terms" (Kamii & DeVries, 1977, pp. 392–393).

Reinserting Piaget's structuralism into curriculum development is necessary, DeVries (1984; DeVries & Kohlberg, 1987) explains, in order to tighten the interpretation surrounding such general terms. According to DeVries (1984; DeVries & Kohlberg, 1987), the original educational goals she and Kamii promulgated, which had relied on Piaget's constructivism, have become disassociated from his theory. "The generality of constructivist objectives has led to a lack of consensus about the practical definition of constructive activity" (DeVries & Kohlberg, 1987, p. 48).

Omitting the theory's structural component, DeVries argues, makes it possible to justify a variety of loosely connected generalities, such as "hands-on-learning,"

"learning by doing," or "play." Although generally accurate, these generalities lack any guidelines for discriminating the relative value of specific activities and ways of teaching (DeVries, 1984). In other words, because they lack sufficient specificity to guide practice, they are too open to individual interpretation.

By reinserting the theory's structural component (stages of cognitive development), DeVries rectifies this concern. As a curricular informant, Piaget's stages provide tangible boundaries within which curriculum possibilities can be justified in terms of their likelihood for promoting cognitive and moral development in a particular direction; simultaneously, they also provide a specified frame of reference for assessing children's progress (see, for example, DeVries, 1992; DeVries & Fernie, 1990; DeVries, Reese-Learned, & Morgan, 1991). In addition to conceptual and educational implications, therefore, DeVries's re-emphasis on the educational significance of Piaget's stages of cognitive development provides the needed framework for a defined approach to curriculum.

In 1977, Kamii and DeVries asserted, "We do not aim to move children to the stage of concrete operations" (p. 390). At that point in its evolution, the Kamii-DeVries approach emphasized the educational significance of Piaget's notion of constructivism and offered general proposals for improving early childhood curriculum (e.g., Kamii, 1982; Kamii & DeVries, 1977, 1978, 1980). Now DeVries claims that "[t]o deny the aim of concrete operations [is] to rob the rationale of what is uniquely Piagetian" (DeVries, 1984, p. 86). With the re-insertion of Piaget's structuralism, the Kamii-DeVries approach becomes a framework for early education linked to measurable outcomes that are coordinated with Piaget's stages of cognitive development (e.g., DeVries, 1992; DeVries & Kohlberg, 1987).

These revisions place DeVries's thinking at odds with that of Kamii, who continues to emphasize constructivism as the primary educational implication of Piaget's work and autonomy as the indisputable educational goal to be derived from his theory (Kamii, 1984, 1985, 1992). According to DeVries and Kohlberg (1987), although Kamii's goal of autonomy has been a distinguishing characteristic among constructivist programs, "it introduces the difficulty of understanding differences in objectives at less rarified levels of concern" (p. 58) and is too open to multiple interpretations. DeVries and Kohlberg (1987) argue that the goal of autonomy is susceptible to the danger of becoming a vague generality that can be linked with a variety of theoretical possibilities. In their view, "reduction of aims to autonomy is too one-sided, omitting what the notion of structural stages contributes to educational planning" (p. 58).

These alterations to the Kamii-DeVries approach have practical as well as conceptual consequences. No longer is the continuing development of the Kamii-DeVries approach a collaborative effort of its two namesakes, a fact easily overlooked on reading the program name. This state of affairs adds to the challenge of presenting their intricate approach to early childhood education. Sometimes the collective pronoun *they* is accurate when discussing program specifics; but often it is misleading because the statement does not represent the shared views of Kamii and DeVries or, because in some circumstances, the "they" refers to the thinking of DeVries and Kohlberg. This matter is complicated still further by the fact that Kohlberg, who became DeVries's collaborator (and whom she credits for the shift in her thinking

[DeVries, 1984]), died in 1987 just before the publication of their seminal description of the Kamii-DeVries approach.

Because it is DeVries who has anointed the Kamii-DeVries approach and serves as its primary advocate, the description that follows relies heavily on her presentation of the approach, especially as articulated in *Programs of Early Education: The Constructivist View* (later retitled *Constructivist Education: Overview and Comparison with Other Programs*). This text incorporates the previous thinking DeVries had developed with Kamii. It also clearly indicates the ways in which their previous work has been altered to reflect DeVries's more recent thinking, especially relative to Piaget's stage theory, development as the aim of education, sociomoral development, and educational assessment.

Because the most up-to-date version of the Kamii-DeVries approach is being advanced by DeVries, she should be credited with the rationale and justifications that follow, even though her current thinking clearly builds on her earlier collaboration with Kamii; it is their co-authored works (Kamii & DeVries, 1976, 1977, 1978, 1980) that form the core of the Kamii-DeVries preschool curriculum. Finally, because the Kamii-DeVries approach is derived from deep and extensive study of Piaget's theory, an overview of their approach must presume readers have knowledge of his complex ideas.

Deriving Educational Implications from Piaget's Theory of Cognitive Development

The revised version of the Kamii-DeVries approach relies both on Piaget's psychological theory of cognitive development and his epistemologica1[2] framework. Thus, the approach is framed as a cognitive-developmental *and* constructivist approach to early education. DeVries explains her reliance on Piaget's ideas as based on her belief that his work represents the most advanced theory of mental development (DeVries & Kohlberg, 1987). Drawing from Piaget's theory of cognitive development as well as his epistemological framework results in a two-pronged focus: Piaget's structural stages and the concept of constructivism.

Piaget's Structural Stages.   The focus on structural stages emerges from Piaget's theory of cognitive development. Piaget's clinical study of children led him to conclude that intellectual development progressed through four qualitatively different stages from birth through adolescence: (1) sensorimotor, (2) preoperational, (3) concrete operational, and (4) formal operationa1.[3]

Children during the preschool years are characterized by preoperational thinking. Their thinking is different from that of older children and adults not only

---

[2]   Epistemology is concerned with assumptions about the nature of knowledge and how it is acquired.

[3]   Actually, Piaget designated three stages of cognitive development: sensorimotor, concrete operational, and formal operations. The concrete operational stage, in turn, is composed of two subperiods: preoperational and concrete operational. More often, though, the subperiods are ignored, and Piaget's theory is described as having four stages.

because they usually know less but also because they interpret/make sense of what they know differently. Piaget's stage theory shapes his description of the form, content, and sequence of intellectual development/logical reasoning. In turn, this knowledge provides an important underpinning for the educational practices proposed by the Kamii-DeVries approach. Teachers embrace children's preoperational thinking; they plan for it and use it to conceptualize their teaching (DeVries & Kohlberg, 1987).

Following Piaget, DeVries emphasizes development as composed of invariant, sequential, and hierarchial stages in mental evolution. As a result of these characteristics, Kohlberg (1984) has categorized Piaget's stage theory as an example of a "hard" stage model. And, constructivist education, according to DeVries and Kohlberg (1987), aims at hard structural development.

In addition, these stages are presented as universal and structurally whole. Cultural factors may speed up or slow down development, but the sequence remains unchanged, and a given stage represents an underlying thought-organization that a child applies to all her experiences, regardless of the nature of the experiences that have informed her development. Culture and the specifics of one's experiences, therefore, are not significant as explanations of individual development.

Consistent with Piaget's theory, DeVries contends that cognitive organization is present in every area of the child's development "where a self thinks about the physical and social world and its own relation to that world" (DeVries & Kohlberg, 1987, p. xii). Kamii and DeVries (Kamii, 1975; DeVries & Kohlberg, 1987) view cognitive development as explaining and integrating all aspects of development—sociomoral and personality, as well as cognitive development. This conclusion, which permeated Kamii and DeVries's collaborative writings, extended the original parameters of their approach beyond cognitive development to include concern for the whole child.

Kamii and DeVries's interest in the "whole child," specifically children's interests, sociability, character, and general self-esteem, is based on an appreciation that children's active involvement with their environment, which is an essential ingredient for cognitive and sociomoral development, depends on these characteristics of social-emotional well-being. For example, the Kamii-DeVries approach encourages co-operative relationships among children and between children and teachers. The value of co-operative activities, however, rests not so much with concern for creating harmonious, mutually beneficial social relationships or for enhancing children's social skills per se but with the fact that the social context offers possibilities for children to become more aware of differences in perspective (which is essential to cognitive and sociomoral development). And to the extent that children wish to continue a particular social interaction, co-operative activities provide a special motivation to co-ordinate (create relationships among) these differences. The interactions promoted by co-operative activities, in turn, facilitate children's cognitive structures of reasoning. Thus, Kamii and DeVries explain their interest in personality and affective development in terms of its supportive role to cognitive and sociomoral development versus its legitimacy as an equal and uniquely contributing partner in the multifaceted development of children.

Piaget's contention that an individual's thinking becomes more adequate with each stage of cognitive development provides the underpinning for DeVries's conclusion that development, defined in terms of Piaget's stages of cognitive development, should be the aim of education.[4] DeVries acknowledges, however, what has been labeled the psychologist's fallacy.

The psychologist's fallacy is the conviction that educational aims can be derived directly from descriptions of optimum psychological development. The psychologist's fallacy represents an important issue because it confronts the relationship between developmental theory and educational practice—whether developmental theory is most appropriately an informant to, or determinant of, educational goals. (See Chapter 8 for further discussion of this issue.)

DeVries contends that developmental theory, specifically Piaget's theory of cognitive development, can and should determine the identification of educational outcomes. Following Kohlberg's (1981; Kohlberg & Mayer, 1972) classic argument, DeVries averts the psychologist's fallacy and defends acceptance of Piaget's theoretical and developmental outcomes as educational goals by aligning developmental endpoints (e.g., logical reasoning) with philosophical arguments.

> Cognitive-developmental psychological theory postulates that movement through a sequential progression represents movement from a less adequate to a more adequate psychological state. This formal standard is not itself ultimate, but must be elaborated as a set of ethical principles and justified in philosophical and ethical terms. (DeVries & Kohlberg, 1987, p. 9)

The progression of this defense is important to note. DeVries contends that philosophical principles regarding valued behaviors can be stated as educational aims only when they can be expressed psychologically and assessed empirically.

> This means translating [philosophical values] into statements about a more adequate stage of development. Otherwise the rationally accepted principles of the philosopher will only be arbitrary concepts and doctrines for the child. Accordingly, to make a genuine statement of an educational end, the educational philosopher must coordinate notions of principles with understanding of the facts of development. (DeVries & Kohlberg, 1987, p. 10)

To do otherwise, according to DeVries, is to fall prey to arbitrary, often contradictory, objectives that are subject to multiple interpretations.

Thus, DeVries rationalizes transposing the cognitive-developmental outcomes outlined by Piaget into the educational aims of the Kamii-DeVries approach because they represent the "natural" outcomes of cognitive development. In contrast, general societal values are considered arbitrary. Kohlberg and Mayer (1972) coined the phrase "bag of virtues" for their categorization of what they called value relative objectives and contrasted these objectives with developmental progressions that they viewed as natural laws of mental development validated by scientific research.

---

4   This conclusion was actually formulated earlier by Kohlberg and Mayer (1972) and further defended by Kohlberg (1981) in a later publication.

The educational values of the Kamii-DeVries approach are more valid than others, consequently, because they are not arbitrarily drawn from a bag of virtues (DeVries & Kohlberg, 1987; Kamii, 1981).

A summary of DeVries's analysis of the Developmental-Interaction approach helps to clarify her point of view. Recall that adherents of the Developmental-Interaction approach identified educational goals in terms of preferred values and relied on the integration of complementary theories to inform their educational actualization. They argued that this approach to curriculum development enabled them to holistically address the whole child. In contrast, DeVries contends that this approach to selecting goals and theories is arbitrary and fragmented (DeVries & Kohlberg, 1987). Given her belief in the dominant position of cognitive organization in child development, DeVries also argues that the Developmental-Interaction approach lacks a coherent conceptual framework because it draws on multiple theories of emotional and cognitive development. Finally, the contention by Developmental-Interactionists that educational aims, rather than psychological theory, provide unification to curriculum decisions leads DeVries to categorize the Developmental-Interaction approach as eclectic (DeVries & Kohlberg, 1987).

In resurrecting Piaget's structuralism as significant for educational practice, however, DeVries realized that she had to avoid the mistakes of those early education programs that had attempted to directly promote the operational characteristics associated with Piagetian stages. Rather than examine Piaget's stages for their educational implications (DeVries, 1978; DeVries & Kohlberg, 1987), early programs had literally translated Piaget's stage descriptions into educational practice, especially as represented in the experimental tasks Piaget used to identify a child's stage of cognitive reasoning. In these programs, practice with specific Piagetian tasks, such as experiments with conservation of liquid and solids and classification of objects with varying number of attributes, often supplied curricular content (see, for example, Lavatelli, 1970). Programs that organized their curriculum around Piagetian tasks assumed that teaching preschool children how to master these cognitive tasks would promote their development beyond preoperational thought into the next stage of operational thinking.

According to DeVries (1978, 1984; DeVries & Kohlberg, 1987), such literal translation of Piaget's work into educational practice is weakened by three limitations. First, it confuses children's sequential progress on individual Piagetian tasks with the sequence of general cognitive development; this reduces the theory to the development of scientific knowledge and isolated operations (the term *operations* refers to the mental "devices" individuals use to make sense of their physical and social environment). Although Piaget's stages describe children's thinking at various stages of cognitive development, they do not explain how a child moves from one stage to the next. The *how* of development is derived from Piaget's epistemology, in particular, the concept of constructivism.

Second, because progress from one stage to the next occurs over time, practice with Piagetian tasks does not offer pedagogical insights. And, finally, although the Piagetian tasks are useful in demonstrating stages of thought, they do not meet the criteria of good educational activities from a constructivist perspective. Specific

Piagetian tasks are unrelated to children's interests, and children do not advance to the next stages of reasoning through direct instruction. Rather, children advance toward more operational reasoning via the opportunity to directly act on objects and people (the discussion following on constructivism addresses this more fully).

To overcome the limitations of literal translations of Piaget's stages as well as the weaknesses associated with focusing on Piaget's notion of constructivism to the exclusion of the theory's structural features, DeVries (1984, 1992; DeVries & Kohlberg, 1987) has concluded that it is necessary to identify stages or levels of cognitive development *within daily classroom activities.* This focus, according to DeVries, retains the clear and necessary connection with Piaget's structural stages but does so in a way that is meaningful to teachers and their everyday experiences with children.

> The aim is a redefinition of structural stages or levels in terms of signs that are visible to the teacher observing the constructive process as it occurs in classroom activities. . . . The educational integration of structuralism and constructivism requires understanding the structural history and future of a child's present structures as these are observable in the active constructive context. That is, the kind of research with classroom activities and content that Piaget did with his tasks and the broad domains of knowledge needs to be done. . . . This kind of research also may be a vehicle through which the development of the educational translation can progress to more coherence and consensus. . . . *Constructivist education must demonstrate that it facilitates structural progress,* and stages in activities may provide a good focus for both formative and summative evaluation. (DeVries, 1984, p. 87, emphasis in original)

Currently, DeVries is a consultant to Missouri's Project Construct to develop such an assessment technique (see for example, DeVries, 1992). Assessing structural progress in terms of children's daily activities assures the pedagogic meaningfulness of Piaget's theory. "We are looking for indicators observable in classroom activities that not only give the teacher information on the stages of development but also provide a basis for planning further intervention" (DeVries, 1992, p. 19). Furthermore, evaluation of children's structural progress, according to DeVries (1984, 1992; DeVries & Kohlberg, 1987), will validate constructivist education.

In addition, the increased specificity of practice engendered by delineating, through research, the progressive development of logical and moral reasoning in everyday classroom activities will support the development of a behavioral science of education (DeVries, 1984). This possibility is part of DeVries's, as well as Kamii's, long-held belief that early childhood teaching needs to develop a more scientific base for educational practice. Kamii (1981b) has expressed their viewpoint especially cogently.

> Education has developed over the centuries by personal opinions called philosophies, and by trial and error, and by tradition, to meet certain practical needs. To educate the young generation of their society, teachers have used their best common sense. But a profession cannot develop on the basis of common sense alone. . . . Just as agriculture

and medicine advanced with scientific research and theory, education can go forward only by raising fundamental questions once again and getting scientific answers to these questions. (pp. 7–8)

By identifying stages or levels of cognitive development specific to classroom activities, teachers and others will have clear developmental targets to inform their teaching decisions, guide and justify their selection of specific activities, and evaluate individual children's developmental progress. Classroom activities, according to DeVries (1984, 1992; DeVries & Kohlberg, 1987) need to be justifiable in terms of developmental theory and research, and indicators used to assess children's development should be justifiable "in terms of how they fit into a sequential developmental progression" (DeVries, 1992, p. 19). Similarly, DeVries and Kohlberg (1987) suggest that assessing children's developmental understanding of diverse disciplines also will provide an appropriate strategy for determining the sequence for teaching subject matter.

DeVries presently relies on her research of children's progressive strategies in playing Tic-Tac-Toe (DeVries & Fernie, 1990) and the game Guess Which Hand the Penny Is In (1970), her investigation of children's understanding of shadows (DeVries, 1992; DeVries & Kohlberg, 1987), and Selman's (1980) extensive work in chronicling children's growth in interpersonal understanding (DeVries, 1992; DeVries & Kohlberg, 1987; DeVries, Learned, & Morgan, 1991). This developmental knowledge, according to DeVries (1984), will permit a specificity in practice that has been lacking as a result of over-reliance on the constructivist implications of Piaget's theory.

Constructivism.   The concept of constructivism is the second linchpin in the Kamii-DeVries approach. DeVries explains constructivism as the functional aspect of Piaget's theory; it is the process by which cognitive and sociomoral development are facilitated. Stages are the by-products of the constructive process; they are the *results* of development. In turn, children's development of increasingly adequate cognitive structures (i.e., later stages of cognitive development) is the means by which they become more intelligent (DeVries & Kohlberg, 1987).

For this reason, according to DeVries & Kohlberg (1987), constructivism is the heart of Piaget's theory. The curriculum of the Kamii-DeVries approach revolves around creating individual and group activities that mentally engage children in ways that provoke constructivist activity that will facilitate cognitive and sociomoral development. Kamii and DeVries have been both creative and inventive in analyzing the extent to which individual activities can motivate constructivist activity (see, for example, Kamii & DeVries, 1978, 1980). Furthermore, their writings provide not only a clear articulation of their rationale, but also practical principles relevant for teaching and a wide range of activities appropriate for classroom implementation. Depending on the type of knowledge involved (see following) and its associated content, these suggestions range from broad generalities to specific recommendations for sequencing content-specific knowledge.

The constructive process is characterized by two features: (1) children's interaction with their physical and social environments and (2) the internal, mental interaction between children's current way of understanding an event or phenomena and input from a new experience; these interactive processes are formally known as assimilation and accommodation. Through these dual interactions, children progressively reorganize their understandings/interpretations of the physical and social world. In other words, children actively create their knowledge of the world, and a child's cognitive/structural development results from his or her first-hand interactions with the environment. Neither direct biological maturation nor direct learning of external givens from the environment[5] can explain development.

Although the specifics of a child's interactions with the environment are unique to the child and her interests, the cognitive developmental outcomes of these interactions are not. This assumption provides the conceptual and programmatic linkage between constructivism and stage theory.

Constructivism undergirds Kamii's and DeVries's emphasis on children's active participation in learning. Constructive activity, especially during the preschool years, is prompted best by children's spontaneous interactions with their physical and social environments. Cognitive structures develop in the course of children's thinking about their physical actions on objects and interactions with people.

The Kamii-DeVries approach relies heavily, and uniquely, on Piaget's distinction between two types of action that arise from two different types of psychological experience: physical experiences and logico-mathematical experience (Kamii & DeVries, 1976, 1978, 1980; DeVries & Kohlberg, 1987). Physical experience consists of individual actions on objects and leads to knowledge of the objects themselves. For example, when a child drops an object, such as a ball or a piece of glass, a child can observe the object's reaction to being dropped. This type of action is called simple or empirical abstraction. Knowledge that is derived primarily from the physical reactions of objects is referred to as physical knowledge.

In contrast, logico-mathematical experience provokes children to mentally create relationships between and among objects that do not exist directly in the object. For example, number does not exist in an object; it is not a physical property of objects. Children have to mentally put objects into a relationship with each other in order to conclude that, for instance, there are three objects. This mental action, which also is required for spatial and temporal reasoning, is called reflective abstraction.

These two action-types result in two different types of knowledge: physical knowledge and logico-mathematical knowledge. Physical knowledge results from individual action whereas logico-mathematical knowledge results from an individual mentally coordinating two or more actions and reactions. Logico-mathematical knowledge, therefore, emerges from the knower's mental coordination of information; as a result, it cannot be taught directly.

Children's logico-mathematical knowledge is essentially synonymous with their level of cognitive development; this knowledge, according to Piagetian theory,

---

5 General disregard for direct instruction explains their denunciation of didactic approaches such as Direct Instruction.

defines an individual's way of knowing. During early childhood, however, children's ways of knowing still are dependent on direct versus mental action on their environment. Physical experience, therefore, is crucial to preschoolers' cognitive development. "At least for babies and young children, there can be no logico-mathematical experience without objects to put into relationship with one another" (DeVries & Kohlberg, 1987, p. 21).

From an adult's point of view, the relationships construed by children may appear in error, but within a Piagetian framework, such errors are anticipated and appreciated as signs of children's progressive development. Children's early stages of intellectual development are characterized by particular kinds of errors; these errors, therefore, are developmental and reflect children's increasingly sophisticated attempts to make sense of their experiences.

Piaget also discussed a third type of knowledge—social-arbitrary knowledge. This type of knowledge has people, rather than physical or mental action, as its source. Social-arbitrary knowledge refers to those facts and conventions that have been socially accepted, such as the names of objects or the ways in which particular holidays are celebrated.

In actuality, these three types of knowledge are interdependent. All content, whether social-arbitrary or physical-knowledge, must be structured within some logico-mathematical framework. A child's logico-mathematical framework, in turn, is formed from the mental coordination of understandings derived from physical and social-arbitrary knowledge. Kamii and DeVries, however, use these theoretical distinctions to create the core of their curricular approach.

Curriculum and Activities

Kamii and DeVries build on the child development approach as represented by the Developmental-Interaction approach and the classic nursery school text written by Katherine Read (DeVries & Kohlberg, 1987; Kamii, 1981a; Kamii & DeVries, 1977; Read, 1966). Kamii and DeVries value the child development approach's respect for children's pursuits and its insights into children's intrinsic interests, such as block building, painting, play, and table games.

They consider the child development tradition weakened, however, by its dependence on teachers as knowledge transmitters, its largely intuitive methods, and an insufficient appreciation for the nature of preoperational intelligence. They believe that their approach improves on the child development tradition by providing a scientific theory that can contribute greater precision to teacher behaviors. In addition, they believe that Piaget's theory provides teachers a theoretical rationale and more powerful justification for decisions (DeVries & Kohlberg, 1987; Kamii, 1981a; Kamii & DeVries, 1977). The Kamii-DeVries approach, therefore, incorporates the child-centered, child-development approach, much of its daily routine, and a majority of its developmentally oriented activities (Chapter 4 discussed these in detail), but redirects these elements toward an emphasis on children's constructive moral and intellectual activity.

Specifically, children's activity is nurtured and augmented in ways that promote their creation of new intellectual relationships. Meaningful constructivist activities provoke purposeful experimentation. To the extent that children are mentally engaged in an activity, either singly or with others, they are thinking and creating new intellectual relationships that will advance their operational thinking.

Kamii and DeVries primarily use the distinctions among physical, logical-mathematical, and social-arbitrary knowledge as a basis for selecting among activities traditionally associated with nursery education, analyzing their cognitive possibilities, creating meaningful adaptations, and generating new possibilities. So, for example, opportunities for experimentation, especially as incorporated into physical-knowledge activities, are a prominent curriculum component. Group games, based on Piaget's investigation of games with rules and description of moral development, have been given an expanded role. And, what is popularly known as sociodramatic play is retitled symbolic play and encouraged because of its contributions to children's ability to symbolically represent their thinking.

Creating a learning environment that will meaningfully and mentally engage children requires that teachers create possibilities of interest to young children. Piaget designated interest as the fuel of the constructive process (DeVries & Kohlberg, 1987). Kamii and DeVries incorporated the child development approach into their own because it successfully identified many of the activities of natural interest to preschoolers. In the absence of interest, children do not extend the effort to make sense out of experiences (i.e., attempt to assimilate the experience to existing structures) or modify their current way of knowing (i.e., accommodate existing cognitive structures).

Facilitating Moral Reasoning.   The value system of Piaget's cognitive-developmental viewpoint focuses not only on cognitive universals, but also ethical universals. Ethical universals in this instance are operationalized in terms of Kohlberg's stages of moral justice, which were derived from Piaget's early work on moral development. Within this frame of reference, moral development proceeds parallel to cognitive development; increasing adequacy in logical reasoning is necessary, but not sufficient, for attainment of the parallel stage of moral development[6] (DeVries & Kohlberg, 1987).

Piaget distinguished between heteronomy and autonomy. Individuals who are heteronomous rely on the thinking of others, rather than their own, in their decision making. But, if not restricted by adults' overuse of their authority, children naturally evolve toward autonomous thinking and action. In contrast to those who argue that children learn to behave morally through direct instruction the Kamii-DeVries approach contends that moral development is also the result of active mental construction. Moral development, according to this view, is a specific example of logico-mathematical reasoning.

---

[6] Kohlberg's theory of moral development has been extensively critiqued; for examples of this criticism, the reader is referred to Flanagan (1993) and Gilligan (1977, 1988).

As a result, the Kamii-DeVries approach is concerned with what DeVries (1992; DeVries, Haney, & Zan, 1991; DeVries & Kohlberg, 1987) calls the sociomoral atmosphere of the classroom. The term *sociomoral atmosphere* refers to the entire network of interpersonal relations that comprise a child's experiences in school, including children's interactions with their teachers; it includes both social perspective taking and moral judgement (DeVries, Haney, & Zan, 1991; Kohlberg & Lickona, 1987). Teachers' respect for children's thinking, reduction of adult authority, alleviation of arbitrary rules, and opportunities for co-operative, caring interactions necessitating co-ordination of diverse perspectives are each valued for their contributions to children's moral development. So are opportunities for children to create classroom rules and negotiate conflicts with peers and teachers, both of which are seen as characteristic of a democratically run classroom. In each of these instances, the classroom's social life is explicitly appropriated as curriculum. The Kamii-DeVries approach also gives a significant position to group games, which are described shortly. Mention of group games is pertinent at this point in the discussion, however, because Piaget stressed that games, such as Marbles, have a rules component and thus involve attitudes of respect for rules and authority.

Finally, the moral discussion and group decision methods of Selman and Kohlberg (1972a, 1972b; Selman, Kohlberg, & Byrne, 1974a, 1974b) have been incorporated into the Kamii-DeVries approach. This involves setting aside classroom time to view filmstrips presenting hypothetical dilemmas, followed by teacher-facilitated discussion. The presumption is that social and moral reasoning is advanced by providing children opportunities to apply their reasoning to real life situations (Kohlberg & Lickona, 1987).

Physical-Knowledge Activities.   Physical-knowledge activities originate from Kamii and DeVries's use of Piaget's distinction between simple and reflective abstraction and the two types of knowledge—physical and logico-mathematical—with which they are linked (DeVries & Kohlberg, 1987; Kamii & DeVries, 1978). Intelligence, as conceptualized by Piaget, is fostered by action, both physical and mental. Because the preoperational thought of preschool children is still closely linked to physical action, activities to promote the development of thought must be tied to children's interests in figuring out how to do things—in effect, physical-knowledge activities. In turn, the thought instigated by physical-knowledge activities provokes reflective abstraction; coordinating new and existing understandings induces children to mentally re-organize their understandings.

Physical-knowledge activities involve children's actions on objects and their observations of the reactions. Children initiate these actions because they want to see what will happen, want to verify an anticipation of what will happen if they act on an object in a particular way, or desire to experiment in a way that involves some combination of these two reasons (DeVries & Kohlberg, 1987; Kamii & DeVries, 1978). While acting on objects during physical-knowledge activities, children have the possibility of constructing relations of correspondence between actions and reactions, and these gradually evolve into causal, explanatory relations. DeVries (1992; DeVries & Kohlberg, 1987) also presents physical-knowledge activities as an example of how Piaget's structural and constructivist components can be integrated by assessing children's cognitive progress with physical-knowledge activities.

Examples of physical-knowledge activities include activities with rollers,[7] inclines, pendulums, and water play. *Physical knowledge in preschool activities: Implications of Piaget's theory* (Kamii & DeVries, 1978) provides detailed discussion of physical-knowledge activities, guidelines for their creation, and principles of teaching. There is an obvious correlation between physical-knowledge activities and science education, but Kamii and DeVries (1978; DeVries & Kohlberg, 1987) emphasize that the objective of physical-knowledge activities is not to teach scientific concepts, principles, or explanations, but rather to build the foundation for physics and chemistry.

Kamii and DeVries (1978) identified three types of physical-knowledge activities: activities that involve the movement of objects, for example, children's actions on objects to make them move by pulling, pushing, kicking, swinging, and so forth; activities that entail changes in objects, including cooking and mixing paints; and, third, activities, such as sinking and floating objects or shadow play, that share elements of the first two activity types but cannot be neatly categorized.

Good physical-knowledge activities, regardless of which type, are characterized by four criteria that enhance the possibility that children will be able to construct relationships among their actions and an object's reactions: (1) children must be able to produce phenomena by their own actions; (2) children must be able to vary their actions; (3) reactions of objects must be observable; and (4) the reaction of the object must be immediate (DeVries & Kohlberg, 1987; Kamii & DeVries, 1978).

Group Games.   Whereas physical-knowledge activities promote children's construction of knowledge about their physical world, Kamii and DeVries (1980) conceived group games to promote children's adaptation (in the Piagetian sense) to the social world. Group games are geared particularly toward development of the twin objectives of autonomy and co-operation. In conjunction with her revised thinking, DeVries has further elaborated the rationale and objectives associated with group games and begun to describe stages in children's way of playing games (DeVries, 1992; DeVries & Kohlberg, 1987).

The sociomoral objective of the Kamii-DeVries approach is long-term progress in the structure or stage of moral reasoning; these stages outline the developmental construction of inner moral convictions about what is good and necessary in one's relationships with others. Generally,

---

7 Kamii and DeVries (with Ellis and Zaritsky, 1975) have produced a film entitled "Playing with Rollers: A Pre-school Teacher Uses Piaget's Theory," which demonstrates a group of children using rollers in a physical-knowledge activity. This film provides a useful visual explanation of physical knowledge activities. To track down the film's current availability, readers should contact Film Availability, Office of Instructional Resources Development, University of Illinois at Chicago Circle, Box 4348, Chicago, IL 60680.

the sociomoral goal is for children to develop autonomous feelings of obligation (or moral necessity) about relations with others that are not just dictates accepted from adults. Rather, a feeling of moral necessity reflects an internal system of personal convictions. Such a personal system is autonomous in so far as it leads to beliefs and behavior that are self-regulated rather than other-regulated. It is co-operative insofar as it reflects a view of the self as part of a system of reciprocal social relations. (DeVries & Kohlberg, 1987, p. 121)

Within the Kamii-DeVries approach, group games refer to interactions during which children play together according to conventional rules that specify how players relate to each other and the preestablished climax that is to be achieved. The relation between players should be interdependent, opposed, and collaborative (DeVries & Kohlberg, 1987; Kamii & DeVries, 1980). Using their example of the game of Hide and Seek, the roles of "hider" and "seeker" are interdependent; neither can exist without the other. The roles are opposed because the intentions of the hider and seeker are to prevent what the other is attempting to do; and finally, the roles are collaborative because the game depends on the players mutually agreeing on the rules and abiding by them.

Group games promote autonomy by providing a context in which children can voluntarily accept and submit themselves to rules. Importantly, however, these rules are self-imposed by the players rather than dictated by adults (at least as implemented in the Kamii-DeVries approach). Development toward autonomy, and away from heteronomy, is promoted by children's freedom to choose to follow or not follow rules, reflect on the consequences, and eventually grow to understand that the reasons for rules are rooted in maintaining desired relations with others. Group games are particularly facilitative in this regard because the egalitarian relationships among peers removes the force of coercion, permitting autonomous cooperation to emerge and develop, fueled by interest in playing with others.

The Kamii-DeVries approach identifies eight types of group games, which are detailed in *Group Games in Early Education: Implications of Piaget's Theory* (Kamii & DeVries, 1980): aiming games, races, chasing games, hiding games, guessing games, games involving verbal commands, card games, and board games. Educationally worthwhile games provide something interesting and challenging for children to figure out how to do, allow children to judge their own success, and permit children to participate actively throughout the game. Their value is actualized when teachers reduce their use of authority, encourage children to regulate the game, and modify games as needed in terms of how children think so there will be something they want to try and figure out. In addition to their contributions to sociomoral development, each type of group game also promotes cognitive development in distinctive ways.

Traditional School Curricula.   Finally, the Kamii-DeVries approach offers a constructivist perspective on traditional objectives in arithmetic and reading and writing. Piaget and his colleagues have amassed extensive research and theory on children's construction of number. As a result, this aspect of the Kamii-DeVries approach draws from a deep knowledge base and presumes a great deal of theoretical understanding. According to DeVries (DeVries & Kohlberg, 1987), Piaget's work suggests that knowledge of number involves a single system of logical classes and relations that includes conservation of number, class inclusion, and seriation; specific numbers can be understood fully only as a part of this system. Furthermore, the child's construction of number and the development of logic progress in a coordinated fashion; hence, their development is interdependent. Consequently, the general cognitive structures available during concrete operations enable children to understand many specific number and spatial concepts. From an educational standpoint, this implies that by promoting children's cognitive structures, teachers simultaneously are advancing children's construction of number and spatial concepts.

All these aspects of number, however, are logico-mathematical in nature. Thus, numerical reasoning cannot be achieved through direct instruction nor can it be learned from action on objects; rather, children's understandings of number result from a gradual organization of relations that is the result of their mental construction. Based on these understandings, math education should focus on the development of children's general logical ability and cognitive structures before attempting to introduce numerical questions and formal symbolism. In addition, children need opportunities to invent mathematical relations, a possibility that is enhanced within a classroom where the teacher is knowledgeable about the developmental nature of children's mistakes and cultivates an atmosphere conducive to thinking (DeVries & Kohlberg, 1987).

Kamii and DeVries first outlined their approach to the teaching of number in *Piaget, Children, and Number* (Kamii & DeVries, 1976). This work was revised by Kamii in 1982 and then the approach was extended into first grade (Kamii & DeClark, 1985; Kamii has since continued her research into second grade [Kamii & Joseph, 1989]). In general, because construction of number cannot be taught directly or through physical-knowledge activities, the Kamii-DeVries approach promotes children's construction of number through classroom activities of daily living and through group games.[8]

Teachers are encouraged to take advantage of routine situations in which number is a natural issue and to create situations in which children need to think about number in order to accomplish something they want. Examples include the distribution of materials, the division of objects, the collection of things, keeping records, clean-up, and opportunities for voting. In each of these instances, teachers try to avoid providing needed answers (for example, by asking how many napkins are needed so every child at snack has one or how to divide a deck of cards so all the players have an equal number) so children can be confronted with the opportunity to figure out the relationships involved. Similarly, in group games that involve number, such as board games with dice and spinners or aiming games that involve score keeping, children are given the opportunity to devise and negotiate their own system with peers.

---

8   Kamii's work with children's construction of number, as noted previously, extends into the primary grades, but it is not part of the Kamii-DeVries approach, which is a preschool-kindergarten model. DeVries and Kohlberg (1987) acknowledge that Kamii's work substantially extends their own.

DeVries and Kohlberg (1987) rely on the ongoing work by Ferreiro and Teberosky (1979/1982 especially) for their presentation of a constructivist perspective on reading and writing. Ferreiro was a student of Piaget's and Hermaine Sinclair at the University of Geneva. Based on their clinical study of children learning to read and write, Ferreiro and Teberosky have conceptualized how children continually construct and refine their understandings about print and identified some of their constructive errors.

Ferreiro and Teberosky's work suggests that learning to read and write involves an active process of constructing and testing hypotheses about print. From this body of knowledge, DeVries and Kohlberg (1987) identify a list of 14 pedagogical principles, such as begin with what a child knows, respect children's constructive errors and encourage their predictions and self-corrections, support children during times of conceptual conflict, expose children to written language in all its variety, foster social interaction about how to read and write, allow sufficient time for the constructive process, and encourage children to write in terms of their understandings.

For the most part, subject matter knowledge in the Kamii-DeVries approach is located in the content of constructivist activities. Reading, for example, is embedded in group games, cooking, and symbolic play; science is represented in physical-knowledge activities; and elementary arithmetic is developed in group games and daily living activities. DeVries and Kohlberg (1987) contend that further deliberations regarding the teaching of subject matter need to begin with understanding how children think about subject matter, rather than a focus on subject matter analysis. "Teaching informed by Piaget's theory must be based on knowledge of mental development within a subject-matter domain" (DeVries & Kohlberg, 1987, p. 381).

Expectations for Teachers

Kamii and DeVries presume that teachers are child-centered, relate well to children, and understand how to smoothly manage a classroom and provide traditional nursery school activities. To successfully implement the Kamii-DeVries approach, teachers must also be able to execute a number of additional roles. Specifically, DeVries and Kohlberg (1987) have identified four teacher functions: evaluator, organizer, collaborator, and stimulator.

As an evaluator, teachers are expected to have extensive knowledge of children and a thorough understanding of mental development in order to assess children's spontaneous activity, specifically to appraise how a child is thinking about or understanding a particular interaction. And, in order to promote a child's intellectual reasoning, teachers need to be able to coordinate this knowledge with the provision of appropriate learning activities (organizer role) and questions that will extend children's ideas and stimulate their reasoning in ways consistent with the type of knowledge involved (collaborator and stimulator roles). For example, if an interaction involved social-arbitrary knowledge, then the teacher probably would respond with the correct answer, but if the interaction targeted physical knowledge, then the teacher would encourage children to find the answer directly from an object's reaction to a physical action. And, if logical-mathematical knowledge was central, then the teacher would avoid providing any response and, instead, would encourage mental reflection.

> Our view is that when children reason preoperationally, they are usually unable at that moment to correct themselves or to understand correction by others. . . . [O]perational thought evolves out of preoperational thought as the child becomes more and more conscious of new aspects to think about in situations in which interests motivate thinking. (DeVries & Kohlberg, 1987, p. 85)

Thus, a teacher's decision-making skills are consequential; ideally, her decisions result in appropriate catalysts for children's development toward progressively higher levels of reasoning. Teachers, therefore, need to be very knowledgeable about Piaget's theory, especially children's preoperational ways of interpreting experiences, and be able to convert their theoretical understandings into practical knowledge of individual children and developmental progress.

The Kamii-DeVries approach also argues the importance of creating egalitarian relationships with children. Not that teachers never exert their authority, especially when children's safety is in question. But, children's active, mental construction of knowledge, as opposed to their passive acceptance of adults' conclusions, necessitates that teachers minimize their authority and respect children's ways of knowing.

In this context, children are encouraged to take intellectual risks and develop their intellectual and moral autonomy—in effect, to intellectually and morally construct personal interpretations and rules of behavior for self-governance. In addition, their interpretations of the moment are accepted and respected; Kamii and DeVries express concern that when adults impose their answers, children learn to distrust their ability to make sense of their direct experiences (DeVries & Kohlberg, 1987; Kamii & DeVries, 1978).

Without this supportive context, according to Kamii and DeVries, children learn to behave in ways that unthinkingly accept and conform with adult expectations. Piaget identified this type of social reasoning as heteronomous (DeVries & Kohlberg, 1987; Kamii & DeVries, 1978, 1980). Children (and adults) with heteronomous attitudes tend to rely on others to inform their thinking and decision making. Piaget's view, according to DeVries and Kohlberg (1987) is that "following the rules of others through a morality of obedience will never lead to the kind of reflection necessary for commitment to a set of internal or autonomous principles of moral judgement" (p. 31).

◾ *The High/Scope Curriculum Model*

The first version of the High/Scope[9] curriculum model for preschool and K–3 emerged in 1962 and 1978, respectively. In 1964, when the Ypsilanti Perry Preschool

---

9   An interesting aside: the High/Scope name was invented by David Weikart and colleagues to connote "high" aspirations and a broad "scope" of interests. It was first used in conjunction with a summer camp for teens in the early 1960s (Weikart, 1990).

Project came under the influence of Piagetian theory, its curriculum was named the Cognitively Oriented Curriculum. *The Cognitively Oriented Curriculum: A Framework for Preschool Teachers* by Weikart, Rogers, Adcock, and McClelland (1971) describes the curriculum that resulted from this revision. At this point in its evolution, the curriculum began to have its developmental focus. Teachers were still didactic in their interactions with children, however; only now, instead of focusing on specific motor and perceptual skills, teachers taught specific Piagetian experimental tasks in hopes of accelerating children's progress to the next stage of cognitive development (Hohmann, Banet, & Weikart, 1979).

The third revision to the curriculum is presented in *Young Children in Action: A Manual for Preschool Teachers* by Hohmann, Banet, and Weikart (1979). This version replaced the curriculum presented earlier in *The Cognitively Oriented Curriculum.* In this third phase, the notion of children as active learners and constructors of knowledge became central to the High/Scope curriculum. This shift emerged, according to Hohmann, Banet, and Weikart (1979), with the organization of the classroom program around a set of key experiences (described below). This new organization freed teachers from their instructional focus and permitted them to share the development of learning experiences with children. Higher level reasoning in domains of interest to Piaget remain the model's educational target, but now its advancement is fostered through active learning rather than direct instruction.

Young Children in Action[10] provides those wishing to implement the High/Scope curriculum with 3- and 4-year-olds the model's conceptual framework, information on how to organize for the curriculum's implementation, including room arrangement, materials, daily routine, and staffing needs, and activities and teaching strategies associated with each of the ten key experience categories. The importance of working with parents also is emphasized.

The decision to extend the curriculum into the primary grades in 1978 came about because of an invitation from the U.S. Office of Education to participate in Project Follow Through and the urging to do so from several public school districts. Weikart and his associates initially had been hesitant to become involved with Project Follow Through because they questioned the willingness of public schools to change their traditional ways of educating children. Now, however, High/Scope credits their involvement with Project Follow Through as instrumental to the development and expansion of their K–3 curriculum (Wallgren, 1990; Weikart, 1990; Weikart, Hohmann, & Rhine, 1981).

High/Scope's curriculum developers initially focused on revising their preschool program to suit the needs of K–3 children and teachers in public school settings. They quickly confronted the challenge of effecting individual and systemic change. When the funding for Project Follow Through declined, so did High/Scope's involvement with K–3 curriculum development. Their learnings from this experience, though, were carefully considered when interest in developmentally appropriate curricula for kindergarten and primary grades re-emerged in the mid-eighties.

---

[10] As this book goes into production, the forthcoming revised edition of *Young Children in Action* is in press.

Interest in resurrecting and revising their K–3 curriculum primarily came from two sources: agencies implementing the High/Scope preschool curriculum that were interested in extending the curriculum upward and the push toward making developmentally appropriate curriculum available to all children in early childhood programs, not just those living in poverty.

High/Scope staff knew, though, from their experiences with the K–3 Curriculum in Project Follow Through that their existing program needed refinement and expansion. The decision not to simply rewrite *Young Children in Action* using public school vernacular was a strategic one. High/Scope staff consciously chose to extend and reorganize the K–3 curriculum in a way that would be appealing to, and implementable in, public schools; this decision was made in order to increase the possibility of developmentally appropriate practices in school settings (Wallgren, 1990; this is further discussed shortly).

Materials for the updated K–3 curriculum, which were pilot-tested in High/Scope's ongoing Follow Through programs, began to appear in 1990 and were completed in fall 1992. There are now four K–3 curriculum guides: *Language and Literacy* (Maehr, 1991); *Mathematics* (Hohmann, 1991); *Science* (Blackwell & Hohmann, 1991); and a fourth guide, entitled *Setting Up the Learning Environment* (Hohmann & Buckleitner, 1992). These four curriculum guides describe the physical setting, daily schedule, and teacher-child strategies. Each guide, which is accompanied by a video demonstrating the curriculum in action in primary classrooms, presents the theoretical premises of the High/Scope approach, details the supportive research, and describes specific aspects of the curriculum's implementation. Also included are extensive lists of suggested activities. The curriculum's stated thrust is intellectual maturation and conceptual understanding (Wallgren, 1990).

High/Scope's preschool curriculum is probably best known, but both the preschool and primary curricula have been replicated nationally since 1968. The preschool curriculum has been implemented in rural, urban, and suburban settings and has been used with mildly handicapped, economically disadvantaged, and bilingual children, as well as typically developing middle-class preschoolers and primary grade children.

Because of their interest in, and commitment to, dissemination, the High/Scope curriculum developers have been particularly sensitive to the necessity of describing their program in terms that are clear to practitioners (Hohmann, Banet, & Weikart, 1979). The preschool curriculum currently is in use in "thousands of classrooms" throughout the United States and in many foreign countries (Weikart & Schweinhart, 1993).

Both levels of the curriculum are organized around small-group, teacher-initiated interactions and child-initiated activities. The content of these activities and interactions are informed by a set of "key experiences" derived primarily from Piaget's description of cognitive development. Teachers, often in teams of two, use the list of key experiences to help ensure that they recognize and plan for interactions and activities that advance children's cognitive development. The curriculum, however, is not a package with sets of consumable workbooks or prescribed activities—a disclaimer the program architects frequently emphasize (Hohmann, Banet, &

Weikart, 1979; Hohmann & Buckleitner, 1992; Weikart & Schweinhart, 1987, 1993). Rather, the curriculum is a set of recommended activities framed by a daily routine, learning experiences linked to Piaget's theory and description of cognitive development, and a programmatic emphasis on child initiative, problem solving, and representation.

The High/Scope curriculum draws from Piaget's theory of cognitive development and researchers working within a Piagetian frame of reference, plus the instructional techniques of Sara Smilansky (1968), an Israeli psychologist. Smilansky helped the High/Scope staff integrate some of the traditions of early childhood curriculum, especially sociodramatic play, that were being ignored during the sixties because they did not directly address children's cognitive development (Hohmann, Banet, & Weikart, 1979). She also supplied the three-part sequence of children's planning, working, and self-evaluation that became the organizing principle for the daily routine. The architects' years of practical experience are also credited as a critical contributor to the model's development.

Weikart and his associates selected Piaget's theory as a framework because, at the time, it seemed to be the most complete and coherent theory available for addressing cognitive development and assured them of creating a developmentally valid curriculum (Hohmann, Banet, & Weikart, 1979; Weikart & Schweinhart, 1987). They then developed curriculum strategies and goals based on what they saw as Piaget's most salient principles, "rather than on the esoteric, controversial fine-points" (Hohmann, Banet, & Weikart, 1979, p. 2). Piaget's theory of cognitive development is used by the High/Scope curriculum as an overarching, conceptual framework for selecting learning experiences that will enhance children's cognitive development. In contrast to the Kamii-DeVries approach, Weikart and his associates have not extensively and intimately studied Piagetian theory for its educational implications. In fact, they caution just the opposite. "We urge that (our curriculum) not be viewed as a narrowly Piagetian curriculum but rather as a general framework for an approach to education that stresses problem-solving and decision-making by both child and adult" (Hohmann, Banet, & Weikart, 1979, p. vi).

In particular, the High/Scope model extracted two basic principles from Piagetian theory (Hohmann, Banet, & Weikart, 1979; Weikart & Schweinhart, 1987):

1. that human beings develop their intellectual capacities in predictable sequences. The High/Scope curriculum is organized around the notion that learning progresses in terms of stages identified by Piaget's theory of cognitive development and description of the preoperational and concrete operational child (approximately 3–8 years and 8–12 years of age). Piaget's description of age-related cognitive changes helps set programmatic limits on the range of tasks children are expected to master at any given age level, and

2. that changes in logical reasoning occur as a result of changes in a child's underlying thought structures. These changes are not directly teachable; they are the result of children's active construction of new understandings. Weikart and his associates concluded that changes in these underlying

thought structures represented the preparation children required for effective school learning (Weikart, Hohmann, & Rhine, 1981).

These two basic principles, in turn, help define the process and content components of the High/Scope curriculum.

The High/Scope curriculum conceptualizes the teacher's responsibility as supporting children's development. This is accomplished by promoting children's active learning. Children's active learning is so important because it is the catalyst for cognitive restructuring and hence for development. For similar reasons, the High/Scope curriculum also stresses the importance of children's initiative and the shared responsibilities of children and teachers in defining classroom learning experiences. Curriculum developers contend that the curriculum is neither laissez-faire nor directive.

> The central principle of the High/Scope curriculum is that teachers must be centrally committed to providing settings in which children actively learn through construction of their own knowledge. The child's knowledge comes from personal interaction with the surrounding world, from direct experience with real objects, from talking about experiences and ideas, and from the application of logical thinking to these events. The teacher's role is to support these experiences and help the child think about them logically. (Weikart, 1988, p. 65)

The High/Scope curriculum strives to facilitate the "natural development of the child" (Weikart & Schweinhart, 1987, p. 253). It is presumed that facilitating preschool children's natural development will prepare them scholastically for kindergarten and first grade, especially if economically disadvantaged (Hohmann, Banet, & Weikart, 1979; Weikart, 1988; Weikart & Schweinhart, 1987). The K–3 curriculum promotes children's academic growth through developmentally appropriate learning experiences that also help develop problem solving and verbal and written communication skills.

Until recently, the High/Scope curriculum addressed issues of social and emotional development only indirectly. Their reasoning had been that "it's easier and more productive to focus directly on, say, children's planning than on group dynamics, on classifying objects and events than on interpreting fantasies—the one is concrete and intelligible, the other abstract and esoteric" (Hohmann, Banet, & Weikart, 1979, p. 1). Social and emotional development was indirectly addressed through open acceptance of children and their parents and through the curriculum's structure. Positive social and emotional development were appreciated as positive by-products of the model's cognitive orientation. Children's sense of personal responsibility, self-worth, and independence, for example, is nurtured via children's direct involvement in planning and assessing their activities and teachers' concerns with engaging children in meaningful learning opportunities. Now, however, in response to their own research highlighting the significance of positive social and emotional development to later personal and academic success (see Schweinhart & Weikart, 1993; Schweinhart, Weikart, & Larner, 1986), these considerations have been grouped together and targeted as a key experience (see following; Weikart & Schweinhart, 1993).

Identification of the important cognitive changes that occur during the preoperational and concrete operational stages of development provides the content of the High/Scope preschool curriculum. The preoperational child is described as having the ability to mentally represent his actions and experiences, communicate verbally with others, reflect on his own actions, recall past events, predict consequences in familiar cause-and-effect sequences, mentally resolve simple, everyday problems, and distinguish symbols or representations from the things for which they stand. These mental processes, however, still are intuitive and have not yet been organized into the integrated systems characteristic of the next stage of cognitive development.

The many mental operations preoperational children are unable to apply to their experiences are a primary focus of the curriculum. As preoperational thinkers, for example, children have not yet achieved the ability to mentally reverse a process and have difficulty focusing on more than one aspect of a relationship or process simultaneously (i.e., classification; for example, that objects can be blue *and* round). These scientific and mathematical concepts, which also include classes, relations, quantity, and conservation, were recognized as being important for learning science and mathematics.

Finally, in addition to active learning as an important learning mechanism, the High/Scope curriculum recognizes social and communication skills as strategies that facilitate the development of logical reasoning; it also emphasizes the important role of *representation*. Weikart attributes the importance of representation to Piaget's statement that children acquire knowledge through a representational process and to the work of others that linked children's representation of ideas and objects with their cognitive development[11] (Weikart, Hohmann, & Rhine, 1981). Because of its perceived importance, representation was integrated into the model's daily routine, known as "Plan-Do-Review" (which is described under the heading of "Daily Routine"). The High/Scope curriculum emphasizes the representational process as a powerful mechanism for helping children conceptualize and consolidate their understandings across activities and subject matter domains; in addition, representation provides the model an important linkage to traditional academic exercises in reading and mathematics (Hohmann, Banet, & Weikart, 1979; Weikart, Hohmann, & Rhine, 1981).

From these and other characteristics of preoperational and concrete operational thinking, in conjunction with the assumption that active learning, social and communication skills, and representation are essential to promoting development, "key experiences" were identified to serve as guideposts for planning and evaluating the preschool curriculum. Thus, the domains of Piaget's interests plus the elements and

---

[11]   The stress on representation has been criticized by DeVries as a misinterpretation of Piaget's thinking by confusing representational acts with a network of coordinated mental actions underlying specific knowledge and reasoning, in effect confusing representation with mental operations (DeVries & Kohlberg, 1987, pp. 54–55).

precursors of mental operations provide the model's educational content. In addition, key experiences in the K–3 curriculum are derived from the developmental sequence of subject matter. Fundamental skills and concepts in the subject areas are articulated in terms of emerging capacities; these, in turn, provide the sequence of key experiences in each curriculum area (Hohmann & Buckleitner, 1992).

The Preschool Curriculum Framework

Key Experiences.   Key experiences for the preschool curriculum are organized into three categories: social and emotional development, movement and physical development, and cognitive development. Cognitive development is divided into representation, language, classification, seriation, number, space, and time (Weikart & Schweinhart, 1993).[12] These categories are, in turn, further divided into types of learning experiences that will promote cognitive growth within a particular domain. For example, key experiences in social and emotional development, as noted above, include recognizing and solving problems and understanding routines and expectations. Key experiences in using language include talking with others about personally meaningful experiences and expressing feelings in words. And key experiences in classification include investigating and labeling the attributes of things and noticing and describing how things are the same and how they are different (Hohmann, Banet, & Weikart, 1979; Weikart & Schweinhart, 1993)). Teachers are encouraged to sequence activities around the key experiences so the activities move from concrete to abstract, from simple to complex, and from the "here and now" to more distant events.

Activities and interactions involving key experiences are not mutually exclusive; any single activity might incorporate several key experiences. In fact, they are not intended as concepts for direct instruction or individual focus. Rather, the key experiences are designed as reminders to teachers of the content knowledge and intellectual processes inherent in children's activity and accessible to their facilitation. They can be realized through an infinite number of activities across a range of developmental levels and can be initiated either by children or adults. Key experiences provide a way for teachers to think about the curriculum and frees them from the use of workbooks and scope and sequence charts. This permits interactions with children to be more individually responsive (Weikart & Schweinhart, 1987). "The key experiences should each appear many times—they are not goals to 'attain' and check off but are more like vitamins and other nutrients: their repeated presence in many different forms is important for good 'intellectual nutrition'" (Hohmann, Banet, & Weikart, 1979, p. 6). In addition to providing structure to the curriculum, key experiences provide a mechanism for maintaining the model's openness to new possibilities. As new curriculum is added in areas such as computers or music and move-

---

12   In the 1979 version of the High/Scope curriculum, the preschool key experiences were organized into eight categories: (1) active learning, (2) using language, (3) representing experiences and ideas, (4) classification, (5) seriation, (6) number concepts, (7) spacial relations, and (8) time.

ment, High/Scope staff have an existing vehicle for outlining additional experiences (Weikart & Schweinhart, 1987, 1993).

The key experiences also are linked to child and program assessment. They form the basis of the framework an adult uses to observe each child (Weikart & Schweinhart, 1993). The High/Scope Child Observation Record (COR) takes each of the key experience areas and divides it into developmental steps; these are formatted as a checklist that the teacher completes on each child two or three times a year, thereby providing a developmental record of each child's progress.

The COR was revised in 1991; now for children ages 2½ to 6 years, it includes six developmental domains: initiative, social relations, creative representation, music and movement, language and literacy, and logic and mathematics. These domains, in turn, are organized into five assessment levels, sequenced from low to high (Schweinhart & McNair, 1991; Weikart & Schweinhart, 1993). According to Schweinhart and McNair (1991),

> Good measures of child development provide parents and the taxpaying public with information on whether their investment in early childhood programs is paying off. In addition, by mapping out the various dimensions of child development for everyone concerned, good measures present an operational definition of goals for the care and education of young children. (p. 5)

The description of COR sounds very similar to DeVries's notion of assessment. The difference seems to lie in DeVries's desire to develop a measure that is closely aligned with cognitive-developmental theory (versus general cognitive development) and that corresponds to children's developmental understanding of everyday classroom activities and interpretations of subject matter knowledge at various levels of development (versus cognitive abilities characteristic of later-stage development).

Hence, key experiences were designed as an organizational tool for teacher planning as well as program accountability. They provide teachers a framework for planning educational experiences, extending children's involvement with activities, and assessing children's developmental progress, which, in turn, is interpreted as an accountability measure of program success (Weikart & Schweinhart, 1987).

Daily Routine.   Whereas key experiences are the central feature of the curriculum for teachers, the "plan-do-review" sequence is considered the "hallmark of the High/Scope curriculum for the child" (Weikart & Schweinhart, 1987, p. 260). The plan-do-review sequence, in conjunction with small-group time, a large-group circle time, and outdoor play, make up the daily routine.

The plan-do-review cycle is the central curriculum device that permits children to exert their individual choices about activities without excluding the teacher from the learning process. The plan-do-review cycle also is the primary vehicle through which representation is integrated into the curriculum. Regardless of when other parts of the daily routine are implemented, the planning time, work time (including clean-up), and recall are to follow each other in sequence.

Although planning time, work time, and recall are distinct segments of the daily routine, they also can occur throughout children's work time. Depending on her interest, a child might plan, do, and recall several activities with a teacher during a single work time.

During planning time, children tell the teacher of their choice activity and what they intend to do. High/Scope curriculum developers contend that this process helps children form mental images of their ideas and develop a plan of action. "Children make choices and decisions all the time, but most programs seldom have them think about these decisions in a systematic way or help them realize the possibilities and consequences of their choices" (Weikart & Schweinhart, 1993, p. 198). At the same time, planning time provides teachers an opportunity to gauge and extend children's thinking. An indirect learning is a child's perception of herself as someone who can make decisions and act on them.

The "do" part of the cycle is work time. High/Scope classrooms are arranged with learning centers or work areas; a house area, block area, art area, and quiet area are considered the four basic work areas. During work time, which is supposed to be the longest single time period of the day, children are actively involved in implementing their plans in these various areas—following through with a plan in the block area, engaged in the house area, or reading a book in the quiet area. During this time, teachers are observing children and extending their thinking by posing questions that are generated by linking a key experience with the child's ongoing activity.

Clean-up time, which immediately follows work time, is considered an integral part of work time. During clean-up, children return materials to their proper place, often by superimposing an object over a matching visual image (for example, laying a spatula on top of a corresponding paper cut-out). Thus, clean-up time is valued as still another opportunity for children to learn and use many basic cognitive skills.

Recall time occurs with the teacher and a small group of children. During this time, children represent their experiences for their teacher and peers, using a variety of different techniques, for example, verbalizing, drawing, or pantomiming what occurred during their work time. Teachers can choose to focus children's recall on different aspects of their experience, for example, recounting the names of other children involved in their plans, sharing any problems they encountered, or providing an overview of their activities. Recall is intended to bring closure to children's planning and work, create relationships in children's minds between plans and actions, and provide opportunities for children to represent their thinking—in effect, to stimulate children's movement toward concrete operational thinking.

During small group time, teachers present an activity in which all the children participate; this is a time during which children work on teacher-selected activities that incorporate key experiences and offer children learning experiences they might not otherwise be aware of. Usually, there are at least two small-group times occurring simultaneously. Because of the small group size, children can actively participate in the activity, and teachers have a focused time during which they can observe children's capabilities and developmental progress. Circle time is a 10–15 minute whole-group activity and provides each child a chance to participate in a large group. Circle time is a popular time for finger plays, brief games, movement exercises, and another opportunity for planning key experiences.

Throughout the daily routine, teachers are observers, assessors, and guides. Teacher questioning is a key way by which children's logical thinking is extended. To do this effectively, teachers must be able to recognize the key experiences embedded in children's activity, be knowledgeable about a child's current developmental status, and pose open-ended questions that encourage problem solving and independent thinking. Proponents of the High/Scope curriculum argue that these interactions distinguish a cognitive-developmental approach from conventional early childhood programs. Even though children's activities and their organization are derived from a traditional child development approach (similar to the Kamii-DeVries approach), teachers encourage children's active learning during these interactions rather than waiting for it to take place (Hohmann, Banet, & Weikart, 1979; Weikart & Schweinhart, 1987, 1993).

The K–3 Curriculum Framework

The K–3 curriculum is an upward extension of the preschool curriculum. The guiding principles from Piaget's theory remain intact, and the preschool daily routine (plan-do-review and small- and large-group times), classroom design, and manipulative materials are extended into the primary grades. The K–3 curriculum presumes a standard public school class size of 25 children with one teacher. Active learning and child-initiated and individualized learning still is emphasized.

Work areas and key experiences, however, are keyed to the subject matter areas of math, language and literacy, and science, which, in turn, reflect the grade level structure of public schools; in the area of mathematics, for example, almost 100 developmentally sequenced key experiences are identified. In the K–3 curriculum, however, a minimum of six—versus four—activity areas are encouraged. Suggested work areas in first grade include: a reading/writing area, math area, computer area, art area, and construction area; or work areas might be organized around a theme, such as book making. Small-group instruction during small-group workshops (the term used for small-group time)—versus teaching to the whole class—and cooperative projects are encouraged. During small-group workshops, teachers plan activities to present new skills and concepts and introduce projects and problem situations. There may be two or more workshop periods during a day. In addition to mathematics, language and literacy, and science, movement, music, and computers are additional subject areas incorporated into the curriculum (Hohmann & Buckleitner, 1992; Wallgren, 1990).

Key experiences in the K–3 curriculum are presented as detailed sequences of developmental milestones. Similar to key experiences in the preschool curriculum, they are not intended as the content of direct instruction; rather, they are introduced to teachers as "experiences children are expected to encounter over and over again through their classroom interactions with materials, teachers, and other children" (Key Experiences in Mathematics, 1990).

Their detail, though, permits them to serve as a teacher's guide for planning appropriate activities and assessing children's developmental progress. The carefully sequenced detail is seen as especially important for K–3 teachers used to relying on workbooks and instructional guides.

Based on High/Scope's experiences with Project Follow Through and the prevalent criticism that developmental programs lack focus, the key experiences are accompanied by specific activity ideas, teaching suggestions, and instructional strategies. High/Scope staff hope thereby to demonstrate to schools that developmentally sequenced, age-appropriate education can be systematic (Hohmann & Buckleitner, 1992; Wallgren, 1990).

Serving as Change Agents Through Program Dissemination

In his remarks celebrating High/Scope's twentieth anniversary, Weikart (1990) asserted, "We're trying to put in place nationwide a high-quality program that has been validated by 30 years of research. We know the program works; we know we can change children's lives for the better; we *have* to deliver" (p. 14, emphasis in original). The High/Scope Educational Research Foundation is Weikart's vehicle for fulfilling this aspiration.

Weikart founded the foundation in 1970 as the complexities of his project work, and its potential national and international scope, became evident (Weikart, Hohmann, & Rhine, 1981). The foundation is a center for research, curriculum development, professional training, and public advocacy. Its programs focus on children from infancy through adolescence. In addition to its work with the High/Scope preschool and K–3 curriculum, it sponsors, among other things, an adolescent summer camp and the Ypsilanti-Carnegie Infant Education Project.

Through its years of developing the High/Scope curriculum, researching its effectiveness, and implementing it in classrooms, the foundation has acquired extensive knowledge regarding program development, evolution, and implementation. They have been especially sensitive to the value of clearly framing their curriculum's benefits to educational and public policy makers. Their discourse on the economic benefits of well-developed early childhood programs, especially their own model, has capitalized on society's implicit view of early childhood education as an instrument of social reform and has shaped public interpretation of early childhood education as a cost-effective social investment.

Yet, they also know the frustration of trying to effect and sustain change. "A common problem in education," according to Weikart (1990), "is that after a few years, the quality of any program installed diminishes" (p. 14). As a result, finding ways to maintain high quality early childhood programs has become a central thrust for the foundation.

To accomplish this goal, the foundation offers extensive professional training opportunities around its preschool and K–3 curriculum. Following the decline in government funding in the early eighties, these services became an important source of revenue to the foundation. Professional supports include: 2-day awareness activities that introduce the principle elements of their curriculum at metropolitan sites across the country; teacher-training programs that work directly with teachers interested in implementing the High/Scope curriculum; summer institutes; an extended in-service training sequence; consultation and planning; a training of trainers (ToT) program, an annual High/Scope Registry Conference that serves as a network and support system for High/Scope teachers, trainers, and administrators; and extensive publications and videos published by the High/Scope Press, which was established in 1978. The High/Scope Press also publishes a magazine entitled *High/Scope ReSource* and *Extensions,* a subscription newsletter for practitioners.

Although these supports play an important role in informing teachers and administrators about the High/Scope curriculum and in supporting their efforts, it is High/Scope's research accomplishments (which are discussed in more depth in Chapter 7) that have helped propel early childhood education, in general, and the High/Scope curriculum, in particular, into the national limelight and on the agenda of public policy makers and school district administrators. Clearly, the turning point in their dissemination efforts was the 1984 publication of their findings regarding the long-term effectiveness of the Perry Preschool Project. (Weikart, 1990, called it a dream come true.)

The study of the Perry Preschool Project, which lasted from 1962 until 1965, was designed as a classic scientific experiment; it had both a control and experimental group to which children were randomly assigned, and it was longitudinal in design. As a result, its positive finding regarding the effectiveness of preschool education (versus no preschool) can be stated clearly and assertively. The results of their study through age 19,[13] which are reported in *Changed Lives,* document that high quality preschool education can have lasting effects in improving scholastic achievement during the school years; in decreasing delinquency and crime, the use of welfare assistance, and the incidence of teenage pregnancy; and in increasing high school graduation rate and the frequency of enrollment in postsecondary programs and employment. Furthermore, cost-benefit analysis of these findings highlighted the economic benefits derived from investing in preschool education (Berrueta-Clement, Schweinhart, Barnett, Epstein, & Weikart, 1984).

Two years later, this landmark report was followed by findings from their age-15 follow-up of children in the Ypsilanti Preschool Curriculum Demonstration Project. Initiated in 1968, this study compared three different preschool curriculum models—a direct instruction curriculum, the High/Scope curriculum, and a traditional nursery school curriculum—in terms of gains in children's school performance. Although no differences among curriculum approaches had been found initially, High/Scope researchers concluded that, at age 15, children who participated in a direct instruction curriculum were more prone to delinquent behaviors than participants in the other two curriculum models (Schweinhart, Weikart, & Larner, 1986). Due to these findings, High/Scope's focus on child-initiated learning has become

---

[13]   The effects of the Perry Preschool Project through age 27 were recently released; see Schweinhart and Weikart (1993).

even more pronounced and their focus on the social consequences of early education more prominent.

Following the publication of these results, Weikart and his associates have become increasingly vocal about their beliefs regarding the content of early childhood programs—in particular, that they involve child-initiated learning—and the need for more consistent program quality (Weikart, 1987, 1992; Weikart & Schweinhart, 1993). This concern recently led Weikart (1992) to propose a solution to the problem of program quality in early childhood education. And, although it is discomfiting to question Weikart's motives, it must be said that his solution is problematic, not the least because it confounds his concern for high quality programs with the fact that the foundation's services—the training materials and availability as trainers and consultants—are an essential source of revenue.

> There is a strategy that, if fully implemented, may deliver high-quality programs more consistently than current strategies do. Why not commit the field to the finest preservice training it is possible to afford and then have programs operate according to the standards of a model curriculum program? *It was a model curriculum program, after all, that produced the permanent effects on children, families, and the community documented in the High/Scope Perry Preschool Project.* (Weikart, 1992, p. 11, emphasis in original)

Weikart then proceeds to list criteria that curriculum models should possess and the strategies that are essential to effective and efficient program operations—criteria and strategies that few curriculum models other than High/Scope possess. Unfortunately, the perception of conflicting interests is difficult to avoid when advocacy for program quality simultaneously promotes one's own financial interests. Critics of Montessori, it will be recalled, raised similar concerns when, in the early 1900s, she became actively involved with commercially disseminating the Montessori Method.

In the next two chapters, issues that swirl around the notion of early childhood curriculum models—regardless of the curriculum model in question—are explored. These chapters provide additional information that needs to be considered before responding to Weikart's proposal to rely on "proven" curriculum models to increase community access to high quality early childhood programs.

■ *For Further Reading*

DeVries, R., with Kohlberg, L. (1990). *Constructivist education: Overview and comparison with other programs*. Washington, DC: National Association for the Education of Young Children. (Originally published as *Programs of early education: The constructivist view* by Longman in 1987)

This is DeVries's seminal work on the Kamii-DeVries approach. In addition to describing in detail her own approach to early education, she carefully compares it to other curriculum models, including High/Scope, Montessori, and Bank Street. Her lucid writing style makes even difficult Piagetian concepts understandable. Readers interested in pursuing constructivist activities will also want to read Kamii and DeVries's books on physical knowledge activities (1978), group games (1980), and number concepts (1976).

Hohmann, M., Banet, B., & Weikart, D. (1979). *Young children in action*. Ypsilanti, MI: High/Scope Press.

This has been the definitive text on the High/Scope preschool curriculum. A revised edition, however, is forthcoming: Hohmann, M., & Weikart, D. P. (in press). *Young children in action: A manual for preschool educators* (rev. ed.). Ypsilanti, MI: High/Scope Press.

Part III

An Examination of the Underpinnings of Curriculum Models in Early Childhood Education

This final section moves beyond examination of individual curriculum models to investigate curriculum models from the perspectives of program evaluation and curriculum development. Chapter 7 reviews findings from comparative evaluations of early childhood curriculum models and then assesses the impact of these findings on public policies related to early childhood education and the continuing popularity of curriculum models. Chapter 8 reviews, with broad strokes, some of the significant shifts in thinking that have occurred within child development research and theory since the mid-sixties. Research on, and deliberations about, teacher effects are similarly examined. New understandings about child development, reassessment of the relationship between child development knowledge and early childhood curriculum, and research on teacher effects are each considered in terms of the challenges they elicit for early childhood curriculum models as tools of education. Chapter 9 returns to the book's overarching question: "What is the purpose, function, and impact of curriculum models in early childhood education?"

Chapter 7

In Pursuit of Answers

Comparative Evaluations of
Early Childhood Curriculum Models

This chapter reviews research regarding the relative effectiveness of early childhood curriculum models.[1] It returns our investigation of curriculum models in early childhood education to their original purpose—a search for the most effective curricula for children from low-income families. Given our society's focus on results and our strong faith in scientific outcomes, the findings from these program evaluations have been particularly influential with policy and other decision makers.

A chronicle of the search for the most effective curricula reveals more than an answer to the central, competitive question of effectiveness, however. It also exposes the simplicity of evaluators' initial thinking about children, educational programming, and the nature of change. As these assumptions have become more explicit, they have been successfully challenged. Yet, it is these assumptions that have undergirded public support for early childhood curriculum models. Consequently, challenges to the validity and reliability of program evaluations pose similar challenges to the purpose and function of curriculum models in early childhood education.

This review of evaluation findings is organized historically, first in terms of studies investigating the short-term impact of early childhood curricula, followed by more recent findings regarding their long-term effectiveness. Because the histories of early intervention programs and curriculum models are so intertwined, discussion

---

[1]   There is also considerable research on the effectiveness of individual curriculum models relative to various outcomes. It is beyond the scope of this book, however, to review the available empirical evidence on each curriculum model. Readers interested in pursuing this information are referred to Chattin-McNichols (1992a), Evans (1975), Gersten, Darch, and Gleason (1988), and Rhine (1981) in addition to relevant citations referenced in this chapter.

of the former's effectiveness is necessarily included. This historical organization parallels the history of early childhood curriculum models presented in Chapter 2.

Review of curriculum model effects occurs alongside discussion of problems associated with interpreting results of program evaluations. This is done to highlight the sensitivity needed for interpreting these results. Such caution is necessitated, in part, because of a tendency to overgeneralize these particular findings when deliberating federal and state policies regarding early childhood intervention.

Consideration is also given to the extent early childhood intervention programs have accomplished their intended goals: preparing economically disadvantaged preschoolers to enter and/or function in public schools on an equal footing with their middle-class peers. Early childhood curriculum models have competed not only in terms of their relative effectiveness, but also on their conceptualizations of the best way to serve low-income, minority children.

■ *Empirical Evaluations of Early Childhood Curriculum Models*

> The variety among early childhood curricula today enriches the early childhood field. But within this variety lies disputes about educational practice that ought to be resolved. We trust that researchers will continue to seek such resolutions by conducting the necessary curriculum evaluations and fine-tuned research. (Schweinhart, 1987)

Curriculum models, by definition, present ideal representations of education programs. Consequently, they are abstractions. Program implementation, however, converts an abstract program ideal into a practical reality. This reality, in turn, becomes the substance assessed by program evaluation.

One of the major challenges confronting program evaluations is the extent to which a program-in-action accurately reflects its conceptual representation. Failure to accurately implement a curriculum model obscures differences among program types and makes it difficult to assess the extent to which different models may differ in their effects (Barnett, Frede, Mobasher, & Mohr, 1987; Frede & Barnett, 1992; Lawton & Fowell, 1989; Peters, 1977; Rivlin & Timpane, 1975; Travers & Light, 1982).

The findings of a study by Barnett, Frede, Mobasher, and Mohr (1987) highlight the significance of "accurate" implementation. In assessing the impact through third grade of a new public school preschool program for at-risk 4-year-olds in South Carolina, Barnett and his associates found that preschool programs using the High/Scope curriculum model increased children's school readiness *only* when the program's quality of implementation was also assessed. They concluded that if their study had proceeded without measuring accuracy of implementation, it might have been assumed that the preschool program was ineffective.

This difficulty has been a consistent source of frustration in large-scale, comparative studies of curriculum models implemented at different sites (House & Hutchins,

1979; Rivlin & Timpane, 1975; Travers & Light, 1982), but it has also been a source of enlightenment. Variations in implementation of the same curriculum model have helped direct attention to the effects exerted by different settings (Rivlin & Timpane, 1975; Travers & Light,1982).

The term *evaluation* is defined as determining the worth or value of something according to criteria that are clearly explained and justified (House, 1990). Evaluation involves systematic inquiry into the operations of a program, including the services delivered, characteristics of those served, the process by which services are delivered, and program outcomes (Travers & Light, 1982). With respect to early childhood curriculum models, program evaluations have attempted to determine the worth or value of early childhood models in relation to particular outcomes. In practical terms, evaluations have functioned to justify the existence or expansion of programs, improve program functioning, and demonstrate the program's impact on participants (Hauser-Cram, 1990).

Program evaluations can provide information about the overall effectiveness of different curriculum models relative to specified outcomes. This information can be used to compare programs on their relative efficiency and effectiveness; so, policy makers have found this information particularly useful. Yet because of their focus on program outcomes, global program evaluations are less informative for advising practice or for generating understanding of children's lived experience in a particular program. However, evaluations of overall program effectiveness do enable us to compare measured effects of curriculum models with their theorized impact and in relation to other models.

Empirical comparisons of early childhood curriculum models have been dominated by two questions: (1) Are the programs experienced by children really different from each other? and (2) Are some programs better than others in producing desired outcomes? Answers to these two questions primarily come from two sources: experimental preschool programs initiated during the fifties and early sixties and evaluations of early childhood programs that were part of Head Start and Follow Through Planned Variation. The majority of these studies involved experimental preschool programs serving black children from low-income families, with the intention of helping these children begin their formal school careers on an equal footing with their more advantaged peers (Powell, 1987a; Schweinhart & Weikart, 1985).

Initial Findings: Short-term Effects

The most consistent finding from evaluations of preschool early intervention programs has been an immediate increase in IQ scores of program children, as compared to program controls (children who did not attend a preschool program prior to first grade). These increases, however, have consistently faded by third grade (Karnes, Shwedel, & Williams, 1983; Miller & Bizzell, 1983b; Powell, 1987a; Schweinhart & Weikart, 1985; Stallings & Stipek, 1986; Weikart, 1981). Immediate gains in IQ scores were especially pronounced for children in programs with highly structured curricula that had a strong academic focus. But the loss of superiority over children who had not attended preschool occurred for all program children, regardless of the curriculum they experienced. Failure to find significant differences among curriculum models was reinforced by the 1977 evaluations of Head Start and Follow Through Planned Variation (House & Hutchins, 1979; Kennedy, 1978; Rivlin & Timpane, 1975).

Recall that Project Follow Through began in 1967 as a comprehensive educational program for economically disadvantaged children in kindergarten through third grade. Its purpose was to fortify the outcomes achieved by Project Head Start, in order to offset children's declining IQ scores following school entry. Budget problems, however, reduced the project to a small program, and its goals changed accordingly. Follow Through became known for its planned variation of educational approaches; the hope was that study of these variations would increase understanding of program effects (Hodges & Sheehan, 1978; Kennedy, 1978). Head Start Planned Variation was initiated 1 year later. According to Bissell (1973), Planned Variation was designed to explore five issues: (1) the processes involved with implementing various early intervention programs; (2) the nature of experiences provided by different early intervention programs; (3) the effects of different programs on Head Start children and their families; (4) the contributions of intervention programs during preschool versus the primary grades; and (5) the benefits of continuous, sequenced intervention when the same educational strategies were used over several years. In this instance, Bissell's reference to different intervention programs refers to curriculum models.

Head Start Planned Variation incorporated 12 curriculum models, 11 of which were also represented in Project Follow Through. (See Table 2–2.) This made it possible to compare not only a variety of curricula at the Head Start level, but also to follow children interacting with the same curriculum through the early grades.

Children who participated in Head Start Planned Variation classrooms had substantially higher test scores than would be expected of children who did not attend a Head Start program, but they did not perform significantly better than the children with whom they were compared who had attended regular Head Start programs (Rivlin & Timpane, 1975). In addition, no single Planned Variation Head Start curriculum model emerged as significantly better than another (Rivlin & Timpane, 1975).

The cross-model evaluation of Follow Through compared 13 early childhood curriculum models implemented at 80 sites throughout the United States (Follow Through curriculum models are listed in Table 2–1). Curriculum models were organized into categories according to their programmatic emphasis: basic skills, cognitive capabilities, and affective development. Even though, once again, the most academically structured curriculum models produced the greatest academic gain for participating children, this gain was not consistently found at each of their program sites (Kennedy, 1975; House & Hutchins, 1979; Rivlin & Timpane, 1975). In fact, the lack of consistency among program sites for the *same* curriculum models (i.e., within model variation) was the only consistent finding (House & Hutchins, 1979; Kennedy, 1975; Rivlin & Timpane, 1975).

No consistent pattern of differential effectiveness emerged among the curriculum models in comparison to other models or control groups. Based on their reanalysis of the Follow Through evaluation data, correcting for what they saw as statistical flaws in the original study, House and Hutchins (1979) concluded that local conditions, parents, teachers, peers, and the home and school environments had more impact on program outcomes than program type. It should be noted though, that even though Head Start and Follow Through are comprehensive programs, these Planned Variation studies focused only on the educational component and did not assess the effects of the companion health, nutrition, and psychological and social services (Bissell, 1973).

As these and other findings accumulated, they were accompanied by the conclusion that no significant differences existed among early childhood curricula in terms of measured child outcomes (Karnes, Shwedel, & Williams, 1983; Miller & Dyer, 1975; Ramey, Bryant, & Suarez, 1985; Weikart, 1981, 1983). Given less attention at this time were findings that program outcomes were usually consistent with program goals and content (Bissell, 1973; Miller, 1979) or that a relationship existed between curricular approach and ease of implementation. It is noteworthy, for example, that teachers rated highest in terms of program implementation taught in academically oriented programs (Bissell, 1973).

Despite the absence of strong support in favor of any particular curriculum model, highly structured, academic preschool and primary programs were consistently more successful in initially increasing children's IQ scores and promoting academic success in the primary grades. Attention to these findings, of course, was consistent with the high priority being accorded academic development. Not surprisingly, these findings intensified the philosophical debate between those who asserted the priority of social-emotional and general intellectual development and those who advocated academic training during early childhood.

Those program developers whose models emphasized a developmental, and hence less academic, focus argued that the primary measures used to assess program success—IQ scores and gains on academic achievement tests—did not fairly measure their programs' intentions. Proponents of curriculum models, such as the Developmental-Interaction approach (see Chapter 4), which were less structured, and emphasized the importance of social-emotional development and child-initiated activity, argued that their program goals were not fairly or adequately assessed (Cohen, 1975; Hodges & Sheehan, 1978; Takanishi, 1979; Zimiles, 1977). Less personally involved researchers have also pointed out that because program evaluations relied on standardized tests, curriculum models that emphasized the academic skills found on such tests should have been expected to score higher (House & Hutchins, 1979; Stallings & Stipek, 1986).

This problem, to some extent, was inherent to the questions program evaluations were attempting to answer. These early studies of curriculum models were primarily interested in discovering which curriculum model was best for advancing the school success of economically disadvantaged children. In order to conduct a comparison among curriculum models, global measures were needed, measures that could assess program effects on similar outcomes (Clarke-Stewart & Fein, 1983; Peters, 1977; Powell, 1987a). But, as lamented by Rivlin and Timpane (1975), because standardized tests are explicitly designed to give comparable measures of children's academic performance, regardless of curriculum, they are "singularly ill-suited for use as discriminators among curricula" (p. 14).

A second, critical aspect of the problem was the availability of valid and reliable measures of program impact. In measurement terms, validity concerns the extent to which a particular test or other means of assessment accurately measures the behaviors being assessed. Reliability refers to whether or not, on repeated testing, the same outcomes are being measured.

The focus on cognitive abilities as an outcome measure was exacerbated by existing capabilities in the field of measurement. Available measures of children's affective, motivational, and social competence were not sufficiently reliable and valid (Clarke-Stewart & Fein, 1983; Condry, 1983; Gray, Ramsey, & Klaus, 1982; White & Buka, 1987). Cognitive measures were. According to White and Buka (1987), "Since the initiation of the earliest of the modern wave of experimental programs, evaluation efforts have been tethered to the current state of the art of objective measurement of children" (p. 69).

By the mid-seventies, lackluster findings regarding the impact of Head Start programs and curriculum models began to have their effect on policy makers and others. The once exuberant enthusiasm for the possibilities of environmental intervention began to dissipate.

Follow-up Findings: Long-term Impact

Knowledge about the long-term effectiveness of early intervention programs, in general, and curriculum models, in particular, has been heavily informed by the findings from The Consortium for Longitudinal Studies. The Consortium for Longitudinal Studies was formed in 1975 to ascertain whether early education programs had long-term effects on the school performance of children from low-income families (Condry, 1983). Its formation was in response to the threatened demise of Head Start in mid-1970 (Condry, 1983; Lazar, 1980).

The threat materialized, in part, from the disappointing, well-publicized findings of the Westinghouse-Ohio study[2] (Condry, 1983; Lazar, 1980). Given hindsight, this threat to survival should have been anticipated because the theories and programs of early intervention had been overstated and distorted. As a result of these exaggerations, both politicians and the press had assumed that Head Start would eradicate poverty and ignorance (Zigler & Anderson, 1979).

The Westinghouse-Ohio study (Cicirelli, 1969) evaluated the effectiveness of the first 3 years of Head Start (including when it was a summer-only program). As compared with children who had not attended Head Start, the study found few advantages for Head Start participants on standardized tests 1, 2, and 3 years into children's public school careers. The findings from this study spurred the initiation of

---

[2] The Westinghouse Study is frequently targeted for Head Start's loss of public favor at this time. Cicirelli (1984) argues, however, that the study has been maligned.

Project Follow Through, but it also provided a rationale for the Nixon White House to develop a 3-year-phase-out plan for Head Start (Zigler, 1984).

To try and frame a well-informed counterargument to this threat, 11 investigators, who had implemented experimental early intervention programs during the late fifties and early sixties, agreed to collaborate in assessing the long-term effectiveness of early childhood intervention across different program types. As members of The Consortium for Longitudinal Studies, the participants agreed to send their original raw data, plus new data collected from their original subjects, to a group at Cornell University who had no connection with any of the original studies. The group at Cornell then merged the data and provided an independent analysis (Condry, 1983; Lazar, 1980).

The immediate policy need for information regarding the long-term impact of early childhood intervention programs informed the decision to use experimental programs launched during the early 1960s versus initiating a new longitudinal study of Head Start (Condry, 1983; The Consortium for Longitudinal Studies, 1979; Lazar, 1980). The possibility of evaluating existing Head Start programs was also discarded because they lacked the critical elements needed for an experimental research design, such as controls (children who are just like those attending Head Start except for the fact that they are not in the program), base-line measures (knowledge about the children prior to their program experience), and random assignment (children who are arbitrarily assigned to a group that will either become participants or controls) (Condry, 1983; Lazar, 1980).

Without these elements, the outcomes of program evaluation cannot be accurately attributed to children's program participation rather than other factors not controlled by the study design. The use of random assignment in particular is especially critical to being able to conclude that a specific program is directly responsible for changes in participating children (Clarke-Stewart & Fein, 1983; Ramey, Bryant, & Suarez, 1985). Yet random assignment was also becoming a source of tension because of the ethical dilemma of withholding services from eligible participants (the control group) and arbitrarily assigning subjects to control and experimental groups without regard to need (Campbell, 1987; Cohen, 1975; Hauser-Cram, 1990; Seitz, 1987).

The experimental programs that contributed data to The Consortium primarily served children who were eligible for federal assistance, and they contained many of the elements critical to an experimental research design. They thus provided reassurance that the findings might serve as a basis for federal policy (Lazar, 1980).

The Consortium began collecting follow-up data in 1976–77. Each participating program collected parent and youth interview data (children who had participated in the early childhood programs were now between 9 and 19 years of age), school records and achievement test results, and Wechsler Intelligence Test data (The Consortium for Longitudinal Studies, 1979). The study included all major preschool curricula and delivery systems (home-based, center-based, and combination programs). Programs had involved children of various ages, lasted over various periods of time, differed in intensity, and used staff with varying levels of previous training;

this diversity suggested that The Consortium's findings could be broadly generalized (Lazar, 1983).

The Consortium for Longitudinal Studies found that, on average:

1. Preschool programs increased individual scores on standard intelligence tests. These increases remained statistically significant for three to four years after the preschool experience.

2. During most of the elementary school years, arithmetic and reading achievement scores of program graduates were higher than those of controls.

3. Preschool graduates had higher self-esteem, valued achievement, and had higher occupational aspirations than the controls. The parents of preschool graduates also had higher occupational aspirations.

4. Preschool graduates were less likely to be placed in special education or remedial classes than their control counterparts. They were also more likely to meet standard school requirements and to graduate from high school. (Lazar, 1983, p. 461)

The consistency of these findings across curricula led The Consortium to conclude that the search for a "perfect" curriculum was futile. What mattered as far as the outcomes they measured was the implementation of a well-designed, professionally supervised curriculum, with specific goals (Lazar, 1983).[3] David Weikart (1981, 1983), who developed the High/Scope model, concluded that the basic issue for successful early childhood programs was quality of program implementation rather than the particular philosophy of a curriculum model. His frequently cited conclusion was based on the lack of differential effectiveness among curriculum models in promoting sustained increases in children's IQ scores.

Consortium findings, particularly those regarding decreased grade retention and special education placement and increased high school graduation rates, did, as hoped, have significant impact on federal and state policies and helped generate widespread support for early intervention programs. In addition, the use of functional outcome measures, which assessed the effectiveness of early childhood intervention based on criteria of successful school performance, helped undermine reliance on IQ scores and achievement measures as sole indicators of program effectiveness (Condry, 1983). However, given the small differences found among curriculum models on assessed outcomes, the results did little to boost their popularity.

---

3   In attempting to explain why type of program, level of teacher preparation, and intensity of program participation seemed irrelevant, Lazar (1983, 1988), who supervised and directed The Consortium for Longitudinal Studies, speculated that what these programs affected were parents' expectations and the extent to which they valued educational achievement. The important role of parent involvement in the effectiveness of early intervention programs was also suggested earlier in a oft-cited report by Bronfenbrenner (1974). Reynolds's (1992) elaborate analysis of intervening variables, including parent involvement, to explain the influence of preschool intervention is an example of current research attempting to empirically capture the complexity of early intervention.

The findings of The Consortium for Longitudinal Studies were fortified by the independent findings of Weikart and his associates, published in 1984, on the long-term effectiveness of the Perry Preschool Project, which used the High/Scope curriculum model (Berrueta-Clement, Schweinhart, Barnett, Epstein, & Weikart, 1984). A Consortium participant, Weikart had already begun to assess the long-term impact of the Perry Preschool Project when The Consortium was conceived. His findings extended those of The Consortium by addressing not only functional measures of school success, such as special education placement and high school graduation, but also program effects on children's success as members of their communities, including labor force participation, crime and delinquency, and arrest rates.

Evaluations of the Perry Preschool Project, which began when program children were 3 and 4 years old, have assessed children annually from ages 3 to 11, and again at ages 14, 15, and 19[4] (compared with controls who had no preschool experience). Assessment of the results through age 19 credited children's preschool education with improving their cognitive performance during early childhood; improving scholastic placement and achievement during the school years; decreasing delinquency, crime, use of welfare assistance, and teenage pregnancy; and increasing high school graduation rates, frequency of enrollment in postsecondary programs, and employment (Berrueta-Clement, Schweinhart, Barnett, Epstein, & Weikart, 1984). These dramatic findings also focused attention on the High/Scope curriculum and redirected attention to the question of relative effectiveness of different curriculum models.

Using the Findings from Program Evaluations

The decision to investigate the long-term effectiveness of early childhood programs based on especially well-planned and implemented experimental programs, however, made the findings and their policy implications vulnerable to challenges regarding their generalizability to local, nonexperimental programs, which are traditionally supported by federal funding (Evans, 1985; Haskins, 1989; Hebbeler, 1985). The most frequent warning associated with reports of these studies, therefore, is caution in generalizing their conclusions to other than very high quality, early intervention programs for low-income, urban black children (Barnett, 1986; Evans, 1985; Haskins, 1989; Powell, 1987).

The experimental programs evaluated by The Consortium for Longitudinal Studies were implemented under ideal conditions. They were well designed, implemented by skilled practitioners, and evaluated by knowledgeable researchers. As Grubb (1987) observes, the frequent citations of the Perry Preschool Project fail to note that it consistently emerges as the program with the highest ratios, highest

---

4   The effects of the Perry Preschool Project through age 27 were released in 1993. Findings at age 27 for program participants, as compared with the no-program group, found that program participants had higher monthly earnings, higher percentages of home ownership and second-car ownership, higher levels of schooling, fewer arrests, and less usage of social services during the preceding 10 years (Schweinhart & Weikart, 1993).

salaries, and highest costs, "an extraordinarily expensive program by any standard" (p. 42). These concerns have led to questions as to whether the effects of such exemplary programs can be produced by typical programs (Barnett, 1986; Clarke-Stewart & Fein, 1983; Evans, 1985; Haskins, 1989).

Evaluations of more typical early intervention programs have, in fact, found less dramatic outcomes. Evans (1985), in an assessment of urban high school minority students, found no differences between those students who had attended preschool and those who had not. A critical review of early intervention programs by Haskins (1989) concluded that, although there is strong support for the immediate impact of typical Head Start programs on children's intellectual performance, there is "virtually no evidence" (p. 278) of long-term impact on specific measures of life success such as those found for participants in the Perry Preschool Project. This discrepancy has led to calls for the investigation of "ordinary" early childhood programs (Evans, 1985; Haskins, 1989; Jacobs, 1988; Weiss, 1988).

Explaining Program Effects

A consistent lament of researchers involved in evaluation of curriculum models has been the inability to determine which program elements are connected with which program outcomes (Barnett, Frede, Mobasher, & Mohr, 1987; Clarke-Stewart & Fein, 1983; Karnes, Shwedel, & Williams, 1983; Miller & Bizzell, 1983b; Miller, Bugbee, & Hybertson, 1985; Powell, 1987a; Ramey, Bryant, & Suarez, 1985; Sigel, 1990; Travers & Light, 1982). It is difficult to disentangle the effects of content, activities, and materials with teaching techniques (Miller, Bugbee, & Hybertson, 1985). Interpretation of program effects has consistently been thwarted by an inability to link program dimensions, such as type of teacher-child interaction, with program outcomes.

Researchers trying to resolve this issue have attempted to experimentally vary teaching techniques while holding program content constant (Powell, 1987a). The research of Miller, Bugee, and Hybertson (1985), in particular, has helped illustrate the complexity of the relationship among curriculum, instruction, and program outcomes.

Their research attempted to disentangle these three elements. They found that program content varied with technique, and that some teaching techniques were used only with certain tasks (Miller, Bugbee, & Hybertson, 1985); what one teaches, in other words, varies with how one teaches, and how one teaches varies with what is being taught. Similar findings regarding the confounding influence of content and technique have also been described by those involved in research on teacher effects (e.g., Shulman, 1987).

Another difficulty has been identifying a "teaching unit" for purposes of evaluation. Miller, Bugbee, and Hybertson (1985) suggested that some teaching strategies may be comprised of several components and that some teaching elements may only be important in combination with others or be influential only at certain levels of intensity. This uncertainty regarding what comprises a teaching segment makes it difficult to determine what teaching strategies are responsible for which outcomes.

Finally, the determination of which program elements are associated with which program outcomes is confounded by the relationship between the goals of a curriculum and its content and preferred teaching techniques. Program philosophy modifies teachers' implementation of similar teaching techniques (Miller, Bugbee, & Hybertson, 1985). In combination, these findings suggest that understanding the effects of early childhood programs requires conceptualizing early education as something more than a mixture of discrete activities and interactions.

■ A Changing Picture: An Emergent Pattern of Differential Impact

Into the early eighties, it was generally accepted that differences among curriculum models were negligible. In comparison to the absence of significant, differential effects on cognitive growth, findings from Head Start and Follow Through Planned Variation indicating that curriculum models generated outcomes consistent with their program goals received limited attention.

Two experimental programs that were a part of The Consortium for Longitudinal Studies, however, included comparisons of curriculum models within a single study (Karnes, Shwedel, & Williams, 1983; Miller & Bizzell, 1983a, 1983b). This time the finding of consistency between program emphasis and program outcome drew more notice.

A study by Karnes, Shwedel, and Williams (1983) examined the extent to which five different preschool programs for low-income children helped prepare them for public school. It also attempted to determine if any one of these five approaches would be more successful than the others in accomplishing this outcome.

The five programs consisted of two highly structured, didactic programs; two traditional nursery programs that focused on social, emotional, physical, and general language development; and a Montessori program. The impact of the five programs immediately following children's participation and up through third grade were, on the whole, consistent with those discussed earlier, with two exceptions.

First, children who participated in the Montessori program showed continued gains in intellectual functioning through first and second grade. Second, children who participated in one of the highly structured programs *and* received a second year of intensive training showed an increase in IQ scores. Karnes, Shwedel, and Williams (1983) interpreted these findings as evidence of the benefits of sustained intensive intervention, a hypothesis reinforced by the findings from long-term follow-up of students who participated in Direct Instruction Follow Through (Stallings & Stipek, 1986).

Although these students' continuing achievement in the elementary grades is attributed to continued program contact (Stallings & Stipek, 1986), Miller (1979) points out that Karnes, Shwedel, and Williams's findings do not necessarily indicate which programs produce better cognitive results; the study's results might, instead, only indicate the effect of a sustained academic focus. In addition, in both the Karnes and Louisville studies (see shortly), the most detrimental effects on achievement test scores were obtained when children experienced a pre-academic preschool and then attended a program that was either less academic or nonacademic (Miller, 1979).

By the time students who participated in Karnes, Schwedel, and Williams's study graduated from high school, there were no longer significant differences among the groups in terms of school performance. Follow-up data collected after high school graduation showed considerable variability, however. Although there were no statistically significant differences among the five groups, the Montessori and traditional groups contained the largest number of high-school graduates and the Montessori group also had the fewest number of retained students.

The success of children who participated in the Montessori program led Karnes, Shwedel, and Williams (1983) to conclude that task persistence and the ability to work independently, both important elements of the Montessori Method, might be important for long-term school success. Unfortunately, their research could not distinguish which elements of the preschool programs were critical for long-term school success (Karnes, Shwedel, & Williams, 1983).

The Louisville experiment, a stronger study methodologically, attempted to address the question of differential program effectiveness by comparing the effects *and* characteristics of four different preschool programs: Montessori, a traditional preschool, Bereiter-Englemann's direct instruction model, and DARCEE, another highly structured, academically oriented program (Miller & Dyer, 1975; Miller & Bizzell, 1983b). Only the traditional program focused on children's emotional needs, and all but the Montessori program stressed language development (Miller & Dyer, 1975).

The Louisville experiment was designed to (1) assess behaviors that were consistent with program goals, (2) determine if programs so different in goals and philosophies really differed in terms of teacher behaviors and children's experiences, and (3) distinguish which program aspects were crucial to program differences and differential effects (Miller & Bizzell, 1983b).

The researchers were able to answer only their first two questions. They later conducted another study (Miller, Bugbee, & Hybertson, 1985, discussed previously) to determine which program dimensions contributed to which outcomes.

Their classroom observations revealed that the four programs clearly differed from each other in terms of both teacher and child behaviors. Depending on the program in which they were placed, children's experiences also varied. In addition, both the immediate and long-term effects of the four programs differed, and the differences tended to be in line with the program's goals. Miller presented evidence, for the first time, that there might, in fact, be one curriculum model "better" than another in terms of producing academic benefits, that a determination of which was better might vary according to whether a child is male or female, and that the effects of a preschool program may not be revealed until later in a child's schooling (Miller & Bizzell, 1983a, 1983b).

Although immediate program effects on IQ were greater for the didactic programs, they also faded more quickly, especially for children who attended the

Bereiter-Englemann program, a finding that was accentuated for females. Miller and Dyer (1975) concluded that raising IQ might not be a particularly desirable goal for prekindergarten children and that prekindergarten achievement, versus IQ, was a better predictor of first grade success. Miller and Dyer also found a delayed, positive effect for males who participated in the Montessori program, a finding that did not emerge until second grade.

These same children were again compared on IQ and school achievement when they were in sixth, seventh, and eighth grades (Miller & Bizzell, 1983a). This follow-up study found that IQs did not differ significantly among the four program groups. In reading and math achievement, however, there were differential effects in all three grades that related to both the type of preschool program the children experienced and a child's gender.

Males in the two nondidactic programs performed significantly better in reading and math achievement than males who participated in the two didactic programs. Females who participated in didactic early childhood programs achieved slightly better than girls who attended nondidactic programs, but only in reading. Ironically, however, IQ scores of females showed the greatest decline, especially if they attended the didactic Bereiter-Englemann program. The middle school males who attended the Montessori program were consistently in the highest group on school performance. (Several other studies investigating the impact of early childhood experiences have also found program effectiveness to be linked with gender [Evans, 1985; Gray, Ramsey, & Klaus, 1982; Jordon, Grallo, Deutsch, & Deutsch, 1985; Lally, Mangione, Honig, & Wittner, 1988; Larsen & Robinson, 1989; Schweinhart & Weikart, 1993.])

Miller and Bizzell concluded that early childhood programs emphasizing academic skills might require continued intervention in order to achieve maximum impact. They also suggested, as did Karnes, Schwedel, and Williams (1983), that successful school performance might be better achieved by helping children learn strategies that can be generalized to later school experiences, a conclusion, with slight modifications, also advanced by Gray, Ramsey, and Klaus (1982).

In attempting to explain the enhanced effectiveness of the Montessori program for males, Miller and Bizzell (1983a) hypothesized that males, perhaps because of their relative immaturity in comparison to girls, responded better to individualized attention within a structured program format, which is characteristic of Montessori programs. Their findings led them to challenge the appropriateness of drill and didactic instruction in prekindergarten programs. They also hypothesized that children's first school experiences may set different learning paths in motion, depending on what type of program is first encountered (Miller & Bizzell, 1983a, 1983b).

Concern regarding the potential negative impact of highly structured academic preschool programs has been extended by comparative findings reported by Schweinhart, Weikart, and Larner (1986). Their follow-up study included three curriculum models that served children 3 and 4 years old between 1967 and 1970: the High/Scope model, a direct instruction curriculum based on the Bereiter-Englemann model, and a traditional nursery school program.

At age 15, Schweinhart, Weikart, and Larner (1986) found little difference in intellectual and scholastic performance among participants in the three program groups. However, based on participants' self-reports, the researchers found that students who attended the direct instruction program as preschoolers reportedly engaged in twice as many delinquent acts as did participants in the other two curriculum groups. Adolescents from the direct instruction group also reported relatively poor relations with their families, less participation in sports and school job appointments, lower expectations for educational attainment, and less willingness to seek help from others for personal problems.

Designers of the didactic approach have challenged the validity of these findings because of methodological limitations, including small sample size, lack of comparability among students in the three groups, and evaluation and interpretation by a potentially self-interested researcher (Bereiter, 1986; Gersten, 1986). These concerns have caused the findings to be cautiously received by others (e.g., Karweit, 1988; Powell, 1987; Sigel, 1990).

Controversy continues to surround Schweinhart, Weikart, and Larner's (1986) findings, however. Their study renewed the long-standing debate between academic and developmental, child-centered approaches to early childhood education. Their findings also helped to reformulate the academic vs. child development debate of the sixties as one between direct instruction versus child-initiated learning.

In addition, Schweinhart, Weikart, and Larner (1986) intensified competition among models by framing their conclusions as the long-awaited answer to the comparison question regarding the differential effectiveness of early childhood curriculum models. Referring to Weikart's (1981) earlier judgment that limited differences existed among curriculum models of high quality, Schweinhart, Weikart, and Larner (1986) re-ignited the debate by concluding,

> For some years, we interpreted the early findings of the High/Scope Preschool Curriculum study to imply that high-quality early childhood education could be built upon *any theoretically* coherent model. The Curriculum Study, with its age 15 data, no longer permits that conclusion. The latest interpretation from the study, tenuous though the data are, now must be that a high-quality preschool curriculum is based on *child-initiated learning* activities. (p. 43, emphasis in original)

Further evidence of the potential negative impact of intense didactic programs comes from an early study by Stallings (1975). She found that third grade students attending a Direct Instruction Follow Through Program were more likely to attribute their classroom achievement to their teachers rather than to themselves. She also found that these same children scored lower on a test of nonverbal problem solving abilities. In an assessment of this study, as part of a review of research on early childhood programs, Stallings and Stipek (1986) suggested that children's highly structured relationships with teachers and learning materials provided students with little opportunity to experience taking things apart, putting them back together, and seeing how things fit together. They suggested that this lack of experience with concrete materials might have contributed to children's poor performance in nonverbal problem solving.

Stallings and Stipek's (1986) conclusions are augmented by DeVries's recent investigations comparing the level of interpersonal understandings exhibited by children and teachers attending constructivist, didactic, and eclectic (i.e., traditional) kindergartens (DeVries, Haney, & Zan, 1991; DeVries, Reese-Learned, & Morgan, 1991). Children attending a constructivist kindergarten, which stressed problem solving and autonomy, were consistently found to be more advanced in their level of interpersonal understanding with peers and more skillful in their social interactions, as compared to children attending the eclectic and didactic kindergartens.

These findings should be considered in light of the fact that DeVries, who was the lead researcher for both of these studies, is also a primary architect of the Kamii-DeVries approach, which is constructivist in orientation. Nevertheless, in conjunction with Schweinhart, Weikart, and Larner's (1986) study and the accompanying rejoiners to both sets of studies (Bereiter, 1986; DeVries, 1991; Gersten, 1986, 1991), the findings of DeVries and her colleagues contemporize the debate between academically focused and child-centered approaches and raise the ante in the competition among curriculum models.

As noted in Chapter 2, the social context of child care in the United States has induced a different research path for investigations of child care effects (in comparison with investigations of early intervention programs). However, this research can still provide insight into the potential impact of different program structures. Clarke-Stewart (Clarke-Stewart, 1987b; Clarke-Stewart & Gruber, 1984), for example, examined four different types of child care programs: in-home care, family child care, nursery schools, and child care centers. She and her associates found that child care programs with different features presented children with qualitatively distinctive environments. Consistent with this finding, Clarke-Stewart found that program results varied with the type of care.

She concluded that the different types or forms of child care had "distinct patterns of competence" that were consistent with their ecologies (Clarke-Stewart & Gruber, 1984, p. 35). For example, the explicitly educational orientation of the nursery school resulted in children with more advanced cognition whereas children in center care, who had more opportunities for social interaction with their agemates, played more cooperatively with nonfamiliar peers than children with an in-home caregiver. Clarke-Stewart and Gruber (1984) concluded that a child's child care experience was determined by the structure of the child care program. By combining these findings with those described previously, it becomes apparent that different environments do, in fact, foster different child outcomes.

A Critical Missing Element.   Missing from this discussion, however, are children's influences on program outcomes. Program evaluations that ignore child input assume that children are passive recipients of a program's "treatment." Program effects are investigated as if they equally affect participating children, regardless of individual differences, and fail to examine how children experience the program (Clarke-Stewart & Fein, 1983; Powell, 1987; Takanishi, 1979).

Do individual children respond differently to different types of learning environments? Some empirical basis for insight into this question is provided by Miller,

Bugbee, and Hybertson's (1985) study. They noted that most comparisons of program approaches had used classrooms as the unit of analysis. Consequently, little information existed on how individual children functioned in different classrooms.

Their research attempted to investigate the effects of specific teaching techniques and individual child behaviors on child outcomes. They found that children's behaviors in response to the demands of the educational situation were the most significant predictor of what children learned.

Teacher behaviors appeared to be important in terms of how they structured children's responses. But, children's responses to learning experiences, versus the teaching technique per se, was a more significant predictor of child outcomes. Consequently, Miller, Bugbee, and Hybertson (1985) concluded that similar methods could not be expected to have the same effects for all children.

Revised Interpretations of Program Effectiveness.   In combination, these studies provide mounting evidence to challenge earlier conclusions that there are no differences among curriculum models and their effects. These newer findings imply that, even on global outcomes such as IQ or school achievement, curriculum models may have different effects. These revised interpretations, however, still leave open the question of whether any one curriculum model is superior in its ability to promote particular child outcomes; the findings on program effects, however, are still too ambiguous for definitive conclusions (Powell, 1987).

Yet, these findings do bolster the relevance of an educationally significant consideration: learning environments created by different curricula affect program outcomes. Findings that program outcomes tend to be consistent with a program's expressed intent redirects attention to the importance of program goals and content. These findings also supply empirical support for the theoretical contention that particular environmental conditions foster different developmental consequences, depending on the personal characteristics of the individuals living in that environment (Bronfenbrenner, 1989). They also substantiate pleas for research to consider both the learner *and* the learning context (Bronfenbrenner, 1989; Clarke-Stewart & Fein, 1983; Horowitz & O'Brien, 1989; Kessen, 1983; Takanishi, 1979; White & Buka, 1987). Finally, these findings also hint at program differences subjectively experienced by children.

These understandings dispute the long-standing premise that early childhood curriculum can be effective independent of child, teacher, or context. This "new" conclusion is reminiscent of Franklin and Biber's (1977) ardent contention that different approaches "involve children in qualitatively different encounters with people, problems, and ideas in the school setting" (p. 3). Suransky's (1982) vivid portrayal of children's lived experiences in diverse types of early childhood programs underscores the pertinence of this conclusion.

Returning to a Habitual Question: How Is Program Effectiveness to Be Defined?   In a throw-back to criticisms of the first wave of research on curriculum effects, a reconceptualization of program outcomes is repeatedly recommended (Clarke-Stewart & Fein, 1983; Hauser-Cram, 1990; Hauser-Cram & Shonkoff, 1988;

Takanishi, 1979; Travers & Light, 1982). "Past approaches to assessing program impacts on children focused on attributing importance to what was measurable. Future effort must be directed more toward measuring what is important" (Hauser-Cram & Shonkoff, 1988, p. 90).

The demand for change in the conduct of program evaluations appears to be in response to at least two summons from the field:

1. There is increased interest in determining not only the effects of early childhood programs but also in understanding how these effects occur. Joined with recognition of program complexity is interest in discerning how a program affects a child's development, how this effect occurs, and under what conditions (Clarke-Stewart & Fein, 1983; Horowitz & O'Brien, 1989; Jacobs, 1987; Powell, 1987b; Rashid, 1984). Some program evaluators also suggest a retreat from hunting "causes" of program effects to seeking "contributions" (Clarke-Stewart & Fein, 1983; Jacobs, 1988; Phillips, 1987). "The task for evaluation thus becomes one of determining which aspects of a program are valuable, for whom, and in which way" (Hauser-Cram, 1990, p. 589).

2. There is increased recognition of the complexity and dynamic character of early childhood programs *and* program participants. Findings such as those discussed previously have challenged program evaluators to move beyond conceptualizations of programs as single, static treatments (Clarke-Stewart & Fein, 1983; Hauser-Cram, 1990; Jacobs, 1988; Powell, 1987b; Travers & Light, 1982; Weiss, 1988; Zimiles, 1986). "Treatment," according to Clarke-Stewart and Fein (1983), "involves a configuration of factors on multiple dimensions, including personal qualities of the educator, content of the curriculum, its theoretical underpinnings, instructional methods, location, and intensity" (p. 935). As a result of this realization, there are calls to serve children and their families in ways more responsive to their individuality and diversity and the complexity of change. According to Powell (1987a) and many others (Clarke-Stewart & Fein, 1983; Horowitz & Paden, 1973; Miller, 1979; Miller, Bugbee, & Hybertson, 1985), the "bottom line of research on preschool practices . . . is finding an effective match between curriculum and child characteristics" (Powell, 1987a, p. 208).

On the one hand, these conclusions represent an overdue appreciation for the complexity of the educational enterprise. On the other hand, they expose the continuing assumption that early childhood programs can be dissected into component parts for purposes of research and pedagogy.

Similar aspirations were expressed by researchers attempting to establish relationships between elementary school teacher behaviors and measures of teacher effectiveness. Optimism for direct linkages between research findings, teacher behaviors, and teacher effects, however, has been severely undermined by recent arguments that challenge the notion of teaching as a technical undertaking. Findings from the research on teacher effects, consequently, offer little encouragement to

program evaluators seeking to construct, in a composite fashion, an ideal early childhood program (Goffin, 1989; this discussion is continued in Chapter 8).

That construction of an ideal early childhood program can be accomplished
objectively is another assumption that is under assault. (Some would suggest that
the notion of objectivity has been invalidated; see, for example, Barone, 1992, and
Eisner, 1992.) As noted previously, evaluations, by definition, determine the worth or
value of something according to predetermined criteria (House, 1990). Yet, the
value component of evaluations has only recently been confronted.

Initially, evaluators of early childhood curriculum models were assigned the task
of discovering which educational programs worked best (Cohen, 1975; House, 1990;
House & Hutchins, 1979; Rivlin & Timpane, 1975; Travers & Light, 1982) "as a strategy to find grand solutions to social problems" (House, 1990, p. 27). It was assumed,
that as representatives of an impartial science, researchers would be able to identify
causes of social problems and objectively construct and assess best solutions to their
amelioration. The definition of "best," as well as the evaluation process, were presumed to be objective and value-free. The realization that the question was actually
"best for whom and for what purpose" surfaced only recently.

Now, evaluators acknowledge that every aspect of the evaluation process, from
the formulation of initial questions to the development of conclusions, requires
choices that are resolved, even if at an unconscious level, by applying value judgments (House, 1990; Weiss, 1983). The fact that program evaluations are judged
against some criterion of success (expected program outcomes, another program, or
the absence of a program) negates the possibility of program findings ever being
neutral and objective (Apple & Beyer, 1983; House, 1990; Royce, Murray, Lazar, &
Darlington, 1982; Weiss, 1983).

Consistent attempts by advocates to link evaluation findings to policy decisions
have also highlighted the extent to which the meaning of "best" is, in fact, connected
to preferred outcomes—both educational and political (Barnett, 1986; Haskins, 1989;
Royce, Murray, Lazar, & Darlington, 1982; Takanishi, 1979; Weiss, 1983; Woodhead,
1988; Zimiles, 1986). In reference to the early intervention programs initiated during
the 1960s, Horowitz and Paden (1973) acknowledged, "Despite the scientific admoni-
tion against 'belief' and for 'objectivity,' there [was] much faith that environmental
interventions [could] have effects upon developmental outcomes" (p. 391).

To the extent that program evaluations can inadvertently drive program design
(as the availability of cognitive measures drove program outcomes during the sixties
and seventies), this change bodes well for early childhood program evaluation. More
importantly, it hopefully lessens the likelihood that designers of early childhood programs or their evaluators will be able to side-step the question of program values.

The Policy Connection

The majority of evidence for early childhood program effectiveness has been derived
from evaluations on sophisticated curriculum models developed for black, low-
income children identified as at-risk for school failure. As a result, arguments in favor

of preschool education tend to be linked with policy discussions concerned with eradicating the consequences of poverty. Policy makers are asking, "Do these programs prevent major social problems such as school failure, delinquency, and public dependency" (Weiss, 1988, p. 27)?

Of concern is the tendency of policy recommendations to overgeneralize the available research (Clarke-Stewart & Fein, 1983; Haskins, 1989; Kagan & Zigler, 1987). There is no evidence, for example, that the apparent benefits of early intervention programs also accrue for middle-class children (Grubb, 1987; Zigler, 1987).[5] Nor is there convincing evidence that the effects of high quality early intervention programs will materialize for minorities other than African-Americans (Laosa, 1982; Lee, Brooks-Gunn, & Schnur, 1988; Ramey, Bryant, Suarez, 1985).

The extent to which program results can be attributed to the curriculum rather than the additional program supports available to participating families is also being questioned (Haskins, 1989; Zigler, 1987). Clarke-Stewart and Fein (1983) questioned the possibility of still other factors. "If program children do not differ from nonprogram children on measures of school achievement, do positive findings on measures of grade retention or assignment to special education classes mean children's placement is because of reasons other than academic criteria" (p. 941)?

Another concern is the extent to which program achievements are consistent with the original intentions associated with curriculum model development: to assist economically disadvantaged preschoolers enter the public school system on an equal footing with their more advantaged peers. Several researchers have suggested that this question has not been adequately addressed and have investigated how well Head Start graduates perform in school. Hebbeler (1985) and Lee, Brooks-Gunn, and Schnur (1988) both found that, even though participation in Head Start provided advantages, especially in comparison to disadvantaged children without preschool experience, it did not reduce the educational discrepancy between advantaged and disadvantaged children.

After describing her findings, Hebbeler (1985), a school district employee, protested that if "a program has been advertised as capable of eliminating the 'gap' between two groups, citing positive findings which show only improved performance does not prove the program has lived up to its advertising" (p. 214).

Concern for ensuring federal support and funding often drives programs to seek evidence of effectiveness that will please policy makers (Jacobs, 1988; Takanishi, 1979; Weiss, 1988; Zigler & Freedman, 1987). The policy impact of the Perry Preschool Project findings was considerably enhanced by an economic evaluation of the data in terms of cost-benefits because this analysis enabled policy makers to contemplate the worth of early childhood programs in economic terms.

---

[5] Small-scaled research by Larsen and Robinson (1989), however, has found evidence of higher second and third grade achievement scores for middle-class males who attended a preschool program as compared with males who had not. A second study associated with the same longitudinal project concluded that the positive impact could be attributed to the preschool program itself versus the mandatory parent education component (Harris & Larsen, 1989). This particular finding contrasts with the importance attributed to parent participation in programs that target children from low-income families.

Economic evaluation is an assessment of the costs and outcomes of a program for society as a whole, in order to determine a programs's desirability relative to some other alternative (Barnett, 1986). Cost-benefit analysis, in particular, attempts to estimate the monetary value of the resources consumed by a particular program *and* the monetary value of the program's outcomes, such as the monetary worth of avoiding the stigma of being placed in special education, in order to determine the worth of the outcomes relative to the costs of achieving them. This relationship is represented in a cost-benefit ratio. Cost-benefit analysis asks, in economic terms, whether the results of a program are worth more than it costs to achieve them (Barnett, 1986; Levin, 1988; White, 1988).

Cost-benefit analysis of the Perry Preschool Project, based on program impact through age 19, concluded that for every dollar spent for children in 1 year of preschool, there was a savings of $7.00 to society by reducing costs for special education, additional years of schooling, welfare, and the criminal justice system. The benefits also included contributions of future productivity as a consequence of employment. The benefit-cost ratio for 2 years of preschool was $3\frac{1}{2}$ to 1. For every one dollar spent on a child in a 2-year program, society was estimated to save $3.50 (Berrueta-Clement, Schweinhart, Barnett, Epstein, & Weikart, 1984).

Several researchers have cautioned that the extent to which High/Scope's results are directly due to its preschool program, versus the program's heavy parent education component, cannot be determined (Haskins, 1989; Stallings & Stipek, 1986). Still, these cost-benefit findings have been very persuasive with policy makers and have helped build considerable policy support at both the federal and state levels for early childhood intervention programs, in general, and the High/Scope curriculum model, in particular.

However, as noted by several researchers investigating the long-term effectiveness of preschool education, their subjects continue to live in conditions of poverty, and they continue to attend inadequate public schools (Jordon, Grallo, Deutsch, & Deutsch, 1985; Lally, Mangione, Honig, & Wittner, 1988; Lee, Brooks-Gunn, Schnur, & Liaw, 1990). Others emphasize the contradiction of promoting the benefits of high quality preschool education during times of budget retrenchments (Grubb, 1987; Powell, 1987b). "It makes no sense to cite evidence about the educational benefits of exemplary, high-quality programs and then to enact programs with low expenditures, low ratios, low salaries, and inadequate teacher preparation" (Grubb, 1987, p. 42).

Still others question the point of trying to improve the life chances of low-income children during preschool if public school practices that contribute to the process of failure are not also addressed (Horowitz & Paden, 1973; Jordon, Grallo, Deutsch, & Deutsch, 1985; Lee, Brooks-Gunn, Schnur, & Liaw, 1990; Woodhead, 1988). Horowitz and Paden (1973) and Vinovskis (1993) even question whether changing practices in public school classrooms might, in and of themselves, produce desired effects in academic achievement among poor and minority children, thus removing the need for preschool intervention programs as deterrents for public school failure.

Woodhead (1988) asserts that isolated emphasis on the positive effects of early intervention programs places unrealistic emphasis on the early years as a period for effecting permanent individual change, at the expense of distracting attention from other community and school processes that help determine a child's future success, a concern repeatedly expressed by Lazerson during the height of early intervention activity (1970; 1972). Gray, Ramsey, and Klaus (1982), in assessing the impact of their early intervention program on the lives of participants over a 16-year period, also argued the complexity of human experience. They felt the findings of their study could only be understood in terms of "exchanges among changing people with other changing people and institutions during changing times" (p. 267). Woodhead (1988) contends that a narrow focus on preschool education reinforces the nation's political preference for simple strategies and relatively inexpensive educational solutions to complex social and economic problems.

More significant, according to Melton (1987) and Polakow (1986), is that the emphasis on long-term consequences of early childhood deprivation implicitly devalues the well-being of children in the present. When problems of childhood are perceived and promoted as serious only in terms of their long-term consequences, they argue that help is forthcoming only when the effects are expressed in terms of adult nonproductivity and social pathology. The critical political question, according to House (1990) is "Whose interests does the evaluation serve?" And, it might be added, "Whose social values?"

Current measures of long-term effectiveness focus on indicators of school success such as school attendance, retention in grade, and assignment to special education. But Clarke-Stewart and Fein (1983) charge that, "[p]ositive findings may reassure policy makers that the investment in early childhood programs is cost-effective, but they are unlikely to reassure those concerned with broader social values" (p. 941).

As some are beginning to urge, it is important to look at more than program effectiveness in assessing a program's worth. It is also critical to evaluate programs in terms of their relationship to societal values (Apple & Beyer, 1983; Schwandt, 1989; Spodek, 1986; Takanishi, 1979; Woodhead, 1988). As Spodek (1986) pointedly notes, "A program that is effective, but whose goals are not consistent with societal values, may not be considered worthwhile" (p. 35).

■ *For Further Reading*

Barnett, W. S., & Escobar, C. M. (1987). The economics of early educational intervention. *Review of Educational Research, 57,* 387–414.

> This article explains economic analysis with particular reference to early childhood intervention programs.

Clarke-Stewart, K. A., & Fein, G. G. (1983). Early childhood programs. In. P. Mussen (Ed.), *Manual of child psychology* (pp. 917–999). New York: Wiley.

> Clarke-Stewart and Fein have written a comprehensive review of the cognitive and social-emotional effects of early childhood programs, including early childhood curricu-

lum models. Prior to the review, they thoroughly discuss the challenges associated with studying the effects of children's participation in early childhood programs.

The Consortium for Longitudinal Studies. (1983). *As the twig is bent . . . The lasting effects of preschool programs.* Hillsdale, NJ: Lawrence Erlbaum.

This book describes the history of individual early childhood intervention programs and The Consortium for Longitudinal Studies. Chapters written by program developers describe their studies and program effects. Two chapters describe the study conducted by The Consortium and its findings. This book provides a comprehensive overview of The Consortium and the programs that informed its results.

Phillips, D. A. (Ed.). (1987). *Quality in child care: What does research tell us?* Washington, DC: National Association for the Education of Young Children.

This edited volume reviews current research regarding the effects of child care. Introductory and concluding chapters provide integrative reviews and suggest future directions. This monograph provides insight into the different research questions in the worlds of "care" and "education."

Takanishi, R. (1979). Evaluation of early childhood programs: Toward a developmental perspective. In L. G. Katz, M. Z. Glockner, C. Watkins, & M. J. Spencer (Eds.), *Current issues in early childhood education* (Vol. 1, pp. 141–168). Norwood, NJ: Ablex.

Takanishi describes the limitations of traditional early childhood program evaluations that fail to consider the purposes and developmental perspective of nonacademic early childhood programs. Her argument highlights what is needed for program evaluations to become more consistent with the goals and purposes of developmental early childhood programs.

Chapter 8

Reemergence of Essential Questions

Identifying the Source of Early Childhood Curriculum

Noting that this was the sixth edition devoted to early childhood education, Kagan (1991) identified four recurring themes in her preface to the ninetieth Yearbook of the Society for the Study of Education: (1) discerning the relationship between child development theory and educational practice, (2) confirming the appropriate content and method of teacher preparation, (3) defining early childhood education comprehensively and holistically, and (4) using research to define pedagogy. "These fundamental issues," according to Kagan, "transcend time and place, bespeaking a generational continuity of enduring challenges that confront the field" (p. ix). Notably absent from Kagan's list, however, is the issue of curriculum. Its omission, though, accurately reflects the scarcity of debate about early childhood curriculum; nonetheless, curriculum issues are integral to each of these themes.

Curriculum models were developed for the purpose of comparing different approaches to early childhood education. They provide structures for shaping, containing, and transporting early childhood curriculum. But in the process, deliberations regarding what knowledge is of most worth (a critical element of curriculum) (Schubert, 1986)—and why—was side-stepped. This question, however, cannot be avoided (even if submerged) when discussing the education of young children. This state of affairs, though, is not unique to early childhood education, and it is consistent with the general status of curriculum discussions during the sixties and seventies.

Until recently, the field of curriculum focused primarily on the development and management of curriculum. It is only within the last 25 years—basically the life span of systematic dissemination and implementation of early childhood curriculum models—that curriculum studies have begun to move beyond developing and managing curriculum to investigating educational experience in terms of its political, cultural, gender, and historical dimensions (Pinar, 1988). Pinar has labeled this time period one of curricular reconceptualization. This reconceptualization of curriculum is just now beginning to influence discussions of early childhood curriculum.

In addition, as academic school content continues its encroachment on early childhood programs, its legitimacy as a source of early childhood curriculum is being challenged. The clash between advocates of developmental theory and school content regarding which is the most appropriate source for early childhood curriculum is not a new one, of course. But the intensity of this clash has escalated alongside the increasing number of early childhood programs in public schools (see, for example, Bredekamp, 1991; Elkind, 1986, 1989; Hiebert, 1988; Warger, 1988).

Now a third "combatant" has entered the fray: early childhood curriculum theorists. Early childhood curriculum theorists are transferring the premises of the reconceptualized curriculum to discussions of early childhood curriculum (see, for example, Kessler, 1991a; Swadener & Kessler, 1991b). They challenge the appropriateness of *both* developmental theory and academic content as informants for the selection of early childhood curriculum because both limit consideration of the historical, political, and sociological dimensions of curriculum. Early childhood curriculum theorists such as Swadener and Kessler (1991a) argue that early childhood curriculum needs to be analyzed in critical social terms—in terms of whose interests are being served, and marginalized, by curricular decisions. For example, Delpit's (1988) concern that developmentally oriented curricula fail to meet the school readiness needs of low-income minority children is frequently cited to support the argument that curriculum choices cannot be isolated from the community and its concerns.

As a result of these exchanges, curriculum issues are, at last, becoming part of the dialogue in early childhood education. And, as part of this curriculum debate, the soundness of creating and replicating preconceptualized curricula is also being questioned.

Weikart and Schweinhart (1993) asserted that "[d]elivery of high-quality programs is the most important task the early childhood field faces, as programs move from laboratory and demonstration schools into large-scale service to children and their families" (p. 195). As an advocacy statement on behalf of the High/Scope curriculum, their assertion highlights that curriculum models are based on the notion that curricula can be preconceptualized, transported to diverse locations, and uniformly implemented by teachers.

Recent theorizing, however, describes curriculum as knowledge-in-the-making, which differs from the notion of transporting preconceptualized programs. And increasingly, teachers are described as creators and interpreters of curricula, not just as implementors. Arguments in support of the emergent character of curriculum and dynamic quality of teaching, therefore, raise questions regarding the authenticity of curricula developed in laboratories and demonstration schools rather than in the daily interactions between and among children and teachers. They also question the extent to which curriculum models, which were designed to ensure uniformity, can be responsive to children, particular environments, and dilemmas resistive to standardization.

The reconceptualization of curriculum and reassessment of teaching are significant examples of shifts in thinking that have occurred since the era of curriculum models. These and other shifts are the focus of this chapter. When considered as part of an examination of curriculum models, these shifts in thinking uncover structural characteristics of models that offer insight into their educational purpose and function.

■ *Developmental Theory and Early Childhood Curriculum*

According to Spodek (1988), theories of child development have provided the basis for curriculum development in early childhood education since the late 1800s. The relationship between developmental theory and curriculum was reinforced during the 1960s when developmental psychologists assumed a leadership position in developing experimental early childhood programs. It was confirmed when NAEYC approved its far-reaching position statement: Developmentally Appropriate Practice in Early Childhood Programs Serving Children Birth through Age 8 (Bredekamp, 1987).

This relationship is increasingly being challenged, however (Almy, 1988; Biber, 1984, 1988; Kessler, 1990, 1991a; O'Brien, 1993; Silin, 1985, 1987, 1988; Spodek, 1988). Questions regarding developmental theory as a primary source for curriculum development in early childhood education challenge its appropriateness as a teacher guide for promoting child growth (Greene, 1989; Haberman, 1988; Polakow, 1989; Suransky, 1982; Sutton-Smith, 1989), its role in determining practice (Egan, 1983; Fein & Schwartz, 1982), and the extent to which it is value free (Delpit, 1988; Lubek, 1985; O'Brien, 1993; Silin, 1987).

Child development knowledge as an informant for practice is *not* the issue being deliberated. Rather, critics are questioning the dependent—and limiting—relationship between developmental theory and early childhood curriculum. These challenges come from the disciplines of philosophy, sociology, and curriculum studies, as well as early childhood education.

In addition, developmental theory is informed by an ever-expanding knowledge base about child development. Another aspect of this discussion, therefore, concerns the extent to which the assumptions and research that provided the undergirding for developmental theory and early childhood curriculum models during the sixties and early seventies remain valid.

Review of the significant developmental premises that undergird initial construction of curriculum models discloses that the developmental knowledge base has been altered in significant ways. Because, by definition, curriculum models have established parameters, the progressive nature of knowledge is problematic for them. In addition, changing understandings about child development from ongoing research and thought are not easily incorporated into early childhood curriculum models "in the field." Consequently, programs implementing specific models often inadvertently continue to promote practices based on dated understandings (Moore, 1983). This discrepancy provides the basis for Simons and Simons's (1986) conclusion, for example, that "Montessori education, as practiced today, is misguided in its attempt to keep alive a system of education that may have been effective and appropriate in the past, but which, being fossilized, is inappropriate for the children of today" (p. 218). The unavoidable divergence between newly created knowledge and a model's particular frame of reference highlights one of the tensions inherent to reliance on research and theory as templates for practice.

Questioning Old Assumptions and Making New Ones: Changing Understandings about Child Development

Faith in the positive, developmental effect of early childhood programs has largely reflected optimism regarding the impact of children's early experiences on their future success with society's educational and economic systems. Kagan (1983) attributes this linkage to the presumption of connectivity, an assumption that children's earlier experiences are causally related to their later experiences. In the case of early education, children's early experiences have been directly linked with their later abilities to succeed with the public school system and future employment demands.

Embedded within this conclusion are presumed answers to two questions that have existed throughout the history of developmental psychology (Cole & Cole, 1989): (1) Is development explained primarily by heredity or environment? and (2) Is the process of development continuous or discontinuous?

During the sixties and early seventies, bolstered by the conclusions of psychologists such as Hunt (1961) and Bloom (1964) regarding children's intellectual development, environmental influences, in general, and early experiences, in particular, were elevated over heredity as a primary explanation of developmental outcomes and individual differences. Furthermore, these outcomes were believed to be the result of a continuous process of growth. Later developmental outcomes were assumed to be predicated on earlier ones; human development was characterized as a cumulative process.

Under the influence of Freudian psychology and the prevailing assumption that children's intellectual abilities were predetermined by heredity, early childhood programs in the 1940s and 1950s focused primarily on nurturing children's social/emotional development and providing supportive environments for their evolving capabilities. With the emphasis on cognitive development during the sixties, the focus changed from nurturing children's social/emotional development to stimulating their cognitive development. Educationally, this shift was reflected in the then-new programmatic emphasis on providing young children from economically disadvantaged circumstances a "head start" on school success.

According to Bronfenbrenner (1974), interest in early stimulation originated from theory emerging in the early fifties that pointed to the beneficial effects of early stimulation on animal and human development. The change in attitude toward cognitive development is also attributed to the discovery of Jean Piaget's work on cognitive development (in part due to English translations of his work). His work was repeatedly used to emphasize the importance of early, stimulating experiences in the growth of children's mental abilities (White & Buka, 1987).

The assumption that development is continuous was integral to discussions about the detrimental, developmental impact of accumulated negative experiences. Called the cumulative deficit hypothesis, this notion provided a psychological rationale for early intervention programs (Evans, 1975), which, in turn, spawned the development of curriculum models.

Since the heyday of curriculum model development, there is: (1) renewed appreciation for the role of heredity in human development, (2) a more differentiated understanding of the environment's contributions to development, (3) recognition of the social nature of development and children's contributions to the process, and (4) a reassessment of developmental psychology as an objective science. These four shifts reflect changing assumptions and understandings about child development. Because early childhood education and its curriculum models have been so reliant on developmental theory for their design, knowledge of these shifts provides a basis for assessing the theoretical currency of enduring early childhood curriculum models.

The Contribution of Heredity to Child Development.   When enthusiasm for early intervention programs first emerged, it was fueled by the then-new belief that children's intelligence was not fixed; especially for young children living in poverty, there was an expectation that their intelligence could be modified by the provision of enriching experiences. This view credited the environment, rather than heredity, with determining the outcome of cognitive development.

Recent research on the contributions of heredity to individual development, however, has redirected the swing of the pendulum regarding the relative roles of heredity and environment (Cole & Cole, 1989; Horowitz & O'Brien, 1989; Kagan, 1983; Plomin, 1989). According to Plomin (1989), increasing acceptance of hereditary influence on individual differences in development is "one of the most remarkable changes in the field of psychology that has occurred during the decade" (p. 105).

Findings from behavioral genetic research have helped document that genetic influence on individual differences in development is significant and substantial (Plomin, 1989). Individual malleability, consequently, is now understood in a more restricted way (see, for example, Gallagher & Ramey, 1987).

Recognition of the contribution of genetic factors to development does not mean that the importance of environmental contributions is being dismissed, however. Rather, renewed respect for the complex interplay between environmental and genetic variables is emerging.

With respect to the major determinants of behavioral development, a consensus is beginning to emerge. This consensus involves the notion that the general outlines of behav-

ioral development have strong biological bases and will develop in most normal environments. But the specific behaviors that must be acquired are very much influenced by the
availability of opportunities for learning in the child's environment. (Horowitz & O'Brien,
1989, p. 441)

Associated with the concept of plasticity, or malleability, of intellectual development has been the issue of timing, of when best to intervene to compensate for a
poor environment. The concept of *critical period* contends that there are unique
times in a child's growth during which specific environmental or biological events
must occur for development to proceed normally. The work of psychologists, such
as Bloom (1964), helped reinforce the idea of a child's first 5 years as critical to, and
predictive of, later intellectual development.

Developmental psychologists and early educators have used this concept extensively in their advocacy for early childhood programs as a means to offset the cumulative deficit of children placed at risk because of environmental or biological circumstances. But as a result of challenges to the supremacy of the environment as a
predictor of development, the concept of critical periods in intellectual development
has also been reassessed.

Early intervention programs were designed to intervene in the lives of disadvantaged children in order to modify the course of their early development. Hence, the
field of compensatory education contains the majority of experimental studies relevant to the modifiability of intellectual development in young children (Ramey,
Bryant, & Suarez, 1985). Contrary to expectations, these studies indicated that earlier
wasn't always better and that program effects often faded several years after intervention (Clarke, 1984; Ramey, Bryant, & Suarez, 1985; also, see Chapter 7).

As Clarke (1984) has pointed out, exposure to a good early childhood program
might temporarily alleviate some of the difficulties experienced by disadvantaged
children, but it cannot be expected to provide an effective, long-term barrier to
ongoing environmental risks. In their analysis of the issue, Horowitz and O'Brien
(1989) concluded,

> Development is not a disease to be treated. It is a process that needs constant nurtu-
> rance. There is no reason to expect that an intensive program of early stimulation is an
> inoculation against all further developmental problems. No one would predict that a child
> given an adequate amount of vitamin C at 2 years of age will have no vitamin deficiency at
> 10 years of age. Currently, according to the most viable model of development that
> applies to both at-risk and normal children, developmentally functional stimulation is
> desirable at every period of development and not only in the early years. (p. 444)

In addition, findings that an adverse early environment can be mitigated by later,
more supportive experiences have provided challenges to an interpretation of the
early years as a sole predictor of later ability (Clarke & Clarke, 1976; Kagan, 1984;
Rutter, 1985). According to Kessen (1983), "The commitment to the special, even
unique importance of the child's encounters during the infantile years—a commitment old and almost universal—is under such serious attack these days, we can won-
der if it will survive the decade" (p. 31).

Within the classroom setting, renewed appreciation of the significance of hered-ity to children's development can increase early childhood educators' appreciation of, and responsiveness to, individual differences. And, at the level of policy, these more recent understandings can help reframe perceptions regarding the "power" of early childhood education to eliminate the effects of "disadvantaged" environments. More realistic understandings about the contribution of early childhood experiences to later growth and development can help relieve the unrealistic burden often placed on early childhood education to serve as a lone vehicle for social reform (Lazerson, 1970; Woodhead, 1988)—an expectation still held by many within the public school and business sectors who are searching for answers to the dilemmas of economic disadvantage and educational reform.

The Contributions of Environment to Child Development.   When curriculum models were systematically initiated during the late sixties, psychologists and educa-tors focused primarily on constructing environments that would stimulate children's cognitive development. The nature and intensity of the stimulation varied by curricu-lum model, but, in general, "the environment" was a global, undifferentiated con-cept. Few questioned that the home environment of poor children, in comparison to their middle-class peers, was inferior in terms of stimulating their cognitive develop-ment; this assumption, of course, provided justification for early intervention (Clarke-Stewart & Fein, 1983; Evans, 1975; Ramey, Bryant, & Suarez, 1985; Ramey & Suarez, 1984).

The meaning of the term *environment,* however, has now been more deeply analyzed. Initial findings from comparative evaluations of curriculum models, which attributed program variance to site variations rather than differences among specific models, contributed to this reassessment. As a result, the belief that children's learn-ing environments and developmental trajectories could be homogenized if they experienced the same curriculum model was undermined.

Attention was then directed to studying the uniqueness of various environments in which learning and development occur and how, in turn, learning and develop-ment are influenced by their particular context (Bronfenbrenner, 1989; Bruner & Haste, 1987; Cazden & Mehan, 1989; Cole & Cole, 1989; Greeno, 1989; Horowitz & O'Brien, 1989; Rogoff & Moreilli, 1989). In other words, now different environments are studied in terms of how they provide for and promote different kinds of learning opportunities.

This apparently benign statement derives its controversy from the fact that it challenges the universality of development—an assumption inherent to most theo-ries of child development (Gardner, 1990; Lubeck, 1985). Relative to our examina-tion of curriculum models, this reassessment implies that curriculum models are more than simply different approaches to early education—they are sources for cre-ating significantly different learning environments.

Bronfenbrenner (1986) suggests that individuals live simultaneously in multiple environments. He describes these multiple environments as a series of embedded, concentric circles, starting with the closest environment, home and neighborhood, and extending to encompass societal norms, policies, and cultural expectations. This ecological framework attempts to identify various circles of influence and how they interact with each other in complex ways to become the different environments in which we live. Better understanding of the complexity of environmental influences challenges earlier, simplistic faith in the ability of early childhood experiences, structurally organized as early childhood programs, to totally and easily transform children's lives.

Cole and Cole (1989) extend Bronfenbrenner's description of embedded environments by placing these environments within a cultural context. Whereas other theoretical frameworks study development in terms of the interaction of heredity and environment, the cultural context perspective incorporates culture as a third contributor to the developmental process. Bruner (1990) would argue that human development can *only* be understood in light of one's cultural context, a factor almost totally neglected in discussions about curriculum models.

Culture is based on the accumulated knowledge of a people and is reflected in their language, beliefs, values, and customs (Cole & Cole, 1989). It is "a way of life shared by members of a population. It is the socio-cultural adaptation or design for living that people have worked out in the course of their history" (Ogbu, 1987, p.156).

Those who advocate the significance of culture contend that biological or environmental factors will have different consequences for development, depending on the specific cultural context in which they are embedded. And these differences have implications for planning early childhood learning environments (Ogbu, 1987; Tharp, 1989; Tobin, Wu, & Davidson, 1989).

Lubek's (1985) and O'Brien's (1993) ethnographic studies of preschool programs affirm this conclusion in terms of the learning environments provided by teachers from different cultural groups. O'Brien's findings are particularly noteworthy because she studied Head Start teachers who were implementing the High/Scope curriculum in a rural, impoverished community. Despite the use of a highly developed and carefully articulated curriculum model, "[t]he varying social milieus of the teachers seem to have been important to their conceptions of the skills, knowledge, and values they believed ought to be transmitted to the children in their charge" (O'Brien, 1993, p. 15). As a result, children's learning environments varied with the cultural priorities of their teachers.

Current sensitivity to cultural differences contrasts with the interpretations that dominated psychological thinking during the sixties and early seventies. At that time, home environments that differed from those of middle-class families were seen as inferior learning environments for young children. The terms *culturally deprived* or *culturally disadvantaged* were frequently applied, and clearly implied the superiority of the majority culture. Some early intervention programs were designed to provide disadvantaged children with experiences to make up for their presumed deficiencies; the Bereiter-Englemann model, it will be recalled, was an especially strong example of this viewpoint.

In contrast, culturally sensitive approaches attempt to avoid devaluation of cultural differences and to understand variation from the perspective of a cultural group (Rogoff & Moreilli, 1989). Edwards and Gandini (1990), for example, studied teacher expectations about the timing of developmental skills in Italian and American early childhood programs. Their cross-cultural study found that these two cultures had different expectations regarding the ages at which children were expected to master various developmental tasks. Differences in cultural expectations also extend to the function of preschools, as Tobin, Wu, and Davidson (1989) vividly portray in their comparison of preschools in three cultures.

Labov's (1969) classic study of differences in how black children used language in formal (such as the classroom) and informal settings highlights the misconceptions that insensitivity to cultural differences can generate. In informal settings with an interviewer from the same ethnic group, black children were found to have highly complex and differentiated language skills. By studying young black children's language skills in a setting more familiar to them, Labov's study fatally challenged the perception that black youth were deficient in their language and reasoning abilities.

Early childhood curricula, however, have tended to rely on white, middle-class perspectives of society and families (Bloch, 1991). Increased appreciation of culture as a third, and significant, contributor to development suggests that traditional reliance on white, middle-class norms should be re-examined in light of the cultural diversity of American children who now participate in early childhood programs, our expanding understanding of cultural differences, and our increasing appreciation that different cultural settings provide different (vs. deficient) backdrops and opportunities for learning.

The Social Nature of Development.   Bruner and Haste (1987) contend that

> [a] quiet revolution has taken place in developmental psychology in the last decade. It is not only that we have begun to think again of the child as a *social being*—one who plays and talks with others, learns through interactions with parents and teachers—but because we have come more to appreciate that through social life, the child acquires a framework for interpreting experiences, and learns how to negotiate the meaning in a manner congruent with the requirements of the culture. (p. 1, emphasis in original)

Primarily under the influence of Jean Piaget's theory of cognitive development, children's developing understandings about the world are most often described in terms of their independently constructed interpretations of experience. Critics argue that this description presumes that children can construct their views of the world in isolation of its social and cultural context, that context does not significantly inform how one's world can be interpreted (Bruner, 1990; Bruner & Haste, 1987; Lee, 1989; Rogoff & Moreilli, 1989).

Recent interpretations of child development and learning attend to the impact of the social and cultural contexts in which children participate (Vygotsky, 1978); they also incorporate the child as a contributor to his or her own development (Bronfenbrenner, 1989; Iran-Nejad, McKeachie, & Berliner, 1990b; Lerner, 1987). By influencing how others respond to them and thus changing the context that, in turn, influences their own behavior, children are now credited as "producers" of their own development (Lerner, 1987).

Renewed emphasis on the social, versus self-sufficient, nature of child development directs attention to the significance of social relationships in all areas of a child's growth: moral (Gilligan, 1988), social relations with adults and peers (Corsaro, 1988; Hartup, 1984, 1989; Kantor, Elgas, & Fernie, 1989), and intellectual (Bruner & Haste, 1987; Greeno, 1989; Lee, 1989; Rutter, 1985). Appreciation for the social nature of child development highlights the importance of contemplating early childhood curriculum models in terms of the relationships they foster among and between children and teachers.

Developmental Psychology as Objective Science: A Reassessment.   As a science, developmental psychology has attempted to describe general laws of behavior that are applicable regardless of circumstances. As developmentalists have become more aware of the ways in which individual behavior is socially and culturally organized, they have begun to diminish their search for laws of development that apply across circumstances.

This is because such laws can be derived only from study of those things that are culturally and environmentally indifferent (Kessen, 1983; White, 1983b). If different settings can facilitate a variety of developmental outcomes, then developmental laws or principles must be related to the setting(s) in which behavior is occurring. Relative to curriculum models, this is a challenging position for program developers who assume that child development principles can be decontextualized and applied across settings with similar results.

Similarly, insights regarding the significance of cultural circumstances have changed our understanding of childhood. The idea of childhood as a separate developmental period has existed as a concept for little more than 100 years (Postman, 1982). Since then, society, with the help of psychology, has invented different kinds of children. The idea that our notions of childhood are culturally constructed, rather than the natural result of a predetermined developmental process, has become a recurring theme (Cleverley & Phillips, 1986; Kagan, 1983; Kessel & Siegel, 1983; Kessen, 1979, 1983; Postman, 1982).

For example, according to Elkind (1987), during the nineteenth century, the dominance of religious thinking helped create the image of the "sinful" child. In the early twentieth century, which was dominated by Freudian psychology, the concept of the sinful child was gradually replaced by the "sensual" child. Contemporary emphasis on the intellectual ability of children, accompanied by research findings detailing the abilities of infants, has gradually replaced the concept of the sensual child with that of the "competent" child (see also Liljestrom, 1983, and Zelizer, 1985, for in-depth descriptions of changing social conceptions of children and childhood).

Major theorists in developmental psychology, consequently, have "gathered an assembly of vastly different children" (White, 1983b, p. 28). Psychology's attempts to describe these "different" children also have been informed by Darwin's theory of evolution (Bronfenbrenner, Kessel, Kessen, & White, 1986; Weber, 1984; White, 1983a), which proposes that development of the species results from improvements in its adaptability. As a result of this thinking, developmental psychology came to assume that the process of development follows a natural order that results in a known endpoint, a goal toward which development is progressing (Bronfenbrenner, Kessel, Kessen, & White, 1986; Weber, 1984; White, 1983a, 1983b).

Some developmentalists, however, challenge whether the process of development can, in fact, be objectively described as traveling toward a known endpoint. Perhaps, some are suggesting, there is no single, clear endpoint or standard of development toward which all individuals evolve (Bronfenbrenner, Kessel, Kessen, & White, 1986; Greene, 1989; Haberman, 1988; Suransky, 1982; Vandenberg, 1993).

White (1983b) contends that "all technical problems that command our interest and our concern and our enthusiasm and our passion have buried within them questions of value" (p. 15). Even descriptions of the developmental process are statements of value. Silin (1987), for example, notes that Piaget's theory and its concern for the development of rational thought arose "in a world dominated by technological accomplishments and scientific approaches to the management of human problems. What Piaget's theory excludes from consideration are nonrational, but not necessarily irrational, modes of thought: intuitive, mythical, religious" (p. 24). Silin goes on to argue that these omissions are not neutral; they reflect a value system consistent with a highly rationalized, scientifically oriented culture. This value system is present not only in Piaget's focus on the development of rational thought but also in his description of the process of adaptation by which rational thought develops. "The implication is that education, in promoting intelligent behavior, promotes adaptation to the environment. In the end, every psychology is embedded not only in a world view but also in a politic, and the politics of adaptation are certainly not the politics of resistance or revolution" (pp. 24–25).

It is these understandings that are of particular importance to early childhood education. Many early childhood educators unknowingly promote the values implicit in developmental theories as if they were objectively determined endpoints for development. The research of Durkin (1987) and Silin (1987, 1988) demonstrate how early childhood education's dependence on developmental theory has fostered the belief that teachers should use child development knowledge to facilitate a child's developmental progression in ways consistent with a particular developmental theory. As summarized by White (1983a),

> If the summum honum of child development is formal operations (the final stage of Piaget's theory of cognitive development), then it is good to do anything that helps bring about formal operations. . . . If it is decentration—or active play, or taking the role of the other, or metacognitive activities—that drives a child toward formal operations, then we know what is good for educators to do with children. (p. 74)

The High/Scope curriculum model and Kamii-DeVries approach provide examples of how theories of development have been used to construct educational environments designed to promote children's growth along a prescribed developmental trajectory.

But, increasingly, the question is being asked: "Should child development theory serve as the source of educational values for early childhood education" (Greene, 1988; Kessler, 1990, 1991b; Silin, 1987, 1988; Spodek, 1988; Swadener & Kessler,

1991a)? Hence, uncertainty regarding the appropriate relationship between developmental theory and early childhood curriculum is deepened by disputes over the objectivity of developmental theories and their individualist perspectives on learning and development.

Child Development Theories and Early Childhood Curriculum: Challenges to the Status Quo

Developmental Theory as the Source of Education Objectives.   In advocating the pivotal position of developmental theory relative to early childhood education, Sigel (1972) contended that

> [d]evelopmental theory ideally describes patterns of growth in cognitive, social, perceptual, and affect areas. Armed with this knowledge, program builders can proceed to construct programs that follow the course of growth. . . . The rationale for advocating "the match" is that such a match is essential if we are to create curricula that are relevant and appropriate for maximizing the development of young children. (p. 13)

One of the best known arguments for constructing early childhood programs that pursue the course of development was advanced by Kohlberg and Mayer (1972). Their argument makes "explicit how a cognitive-developmental psychological theory can be translated into a rational and viable progressive educational ideology, i.e., a set of concepts defining desirable aims, content and methods of education" (Kohlberg & Mayer, 1972, p. 450).

When Kohlberg and Mayer wrote "Development as the Aim of Education" in 1972, there were, as reflected in the diversity of curriculum models, multiple educational programs and methodologies emphasizing different educational outcomes. The challenge then, as now, was how to choose among these outcomes. Their classic paper supplied a justification for why development, as detailed in Piaget's theory of cognitive development, provided the appropriate aim for education.

Kohlberg and Mayer identified three prevalent educational streams of thought informing the selection of educational outcomes: romanticism, cultural transmission, and progressivism. According to Kohlberg and Mayer, the romantic view, associated with maturational theory, promotes nurturing the innate, predetermined capacities of children. They criticized this perspective because it lacked a clear theoretical rationale for pursuing particular educational outcomes.

The cultural transmission view is associated with behavioral theory that explains growth primarily in terms of environmental inputs. Children, for the most part, were construed as relatively passive recipients of environmental stimuli.[1] Because the source of behavioral change is seen as external to the individual, educational objectives aligned with this approach emanate from social consensus, rather than fulfill-

---

[1] As noted in Chapter 6, behavioral theory has undergone considerable revision since the 1960s. Thus, Kohlberg & Mayer's description of behavioral theory should be considered in light of the authors' arguments regarding educational aims, but not as a current description of behavioral theory.

ment of one's innate capacities. Kohlberg and Mayer censured this view for its failure to recognize ultimate standards of worth in learning and development.

In contrast, according to Kohlberg and Mayer (1972), Piaget's cognitive developmental theory provided a clear theoretical rationale for moving from "is" to "ought" that could withstand the logical and philosophical criticisms that undermined the other two perspectives (also see Kohlberg, 1981). Cognitive developmental theory, according to Kohlberg and Mayer, avoids the cultural relativity associated with the romantic and cultural transmission streams of educational thought. This same reasoning, it will be recalled, undergirds the Kamii-DeVries approach.

Kohlberg and Mayer's (1972) rationale assumes a predetermined direction and outcome for human development that, in light of its universality, is objective and independent of context.

> Searching for the "objective" in human experience, the progressive seeks universal qualitative states or sequences in development. Movement from one stage to the next is significant because it is a sequence in the individual's own development, not just a population average or norm. At the same time, insofar as the sequence is a universally observed development, it is not unique to the individual in question. (p. 463)

This line of reasoning, however, contradicts current thinking regarding the significance of environmental and cultural circumstances. It advances development as context-free and developmental theory as a valid source for educational goals, as long as implicit values are articulated and supported by a complementary philosophical framework (also see Weber, 1984). By relying on this line of reasoning, desired educational outcomes are detached from deliberations regarding preferred, and often conflicting, values.

Challenges to Developmental Theory as the Source of Educational Objectives.   Challenges to development as the aim of education stem, in part, from developmental theory's fall from the pedestal of scientific objectivity; this "fall" derails the possibility of rationalizing the notion of "is" to "ought."

Challengers further argue that emphasis on development as an educational outcome directs attention to what children can do, rather than what they should be doing. Yet, it is the question "What should children be doing?" that is educationally significant, and this question needs to be addressed philosophically and ethically, rather than in terms of developmental theory. Critics also contend that overreliance on developmental theory has prompted early childhood educators to side-step the issue of societal values and to ignore discussion—and responsibility—regarding what outcomes are most educationally worthwhile for young children (Kessler, 1991a; Silin, 1987; 1988; Spodek, 1988).

In addition, it is argued that reliance on developmental theory to determine educational goals obscures the political dimensions of what is taught by implying that curriculum choices should be determined by developmental appropriateness, rather than political and moral priorities (Kessler, 1991a; Silin, 1987, 1988). Moreover, according to Bloch (1991), focusing on individual development places responsibility for change on the individual and "serves (whether intentional or not) to distract attention from structural analyses of the problems that help to maintain oppression and inequities in achievement" (p. 105). Based on this reasoning, it is possible, for example, to construe school readiness as an issue of individual, rather than institutional, responsibility.

Others express concern regarding the ways theories of development limit early education's promotion of children's individuality and self-creation by restraining perceptions of the learner (Greene, 1988, 1989; Haberman, 1988; Suransky, 1982; Sutton-Smith, 1989; Zimiles, 1986). Theories of child development, whether intended or not, provide filters through which we interpret children's behaviors. Kessler (1990) reminds us that most developmental standards are derived from study of white males.

> Applying an ethical criterion to the metaphor, early childhood as development, when the development of a relatively privileged segment of the population is used as the standard, leads one to conclude that seeing early childhood as development is not fair to women, children of the working poor and people of color, whose development may differ.

And Polakow (1989) argues that discussions of child development remake children into objects "conditioned, driven, modeled, matured, or staged" (p. 78). The impact of this perception extends to adults who interact with children. When children become objects of study, adults are placed in the role of developers; and adults, according to Polakow, have become developers of an increasingly rational, controllable, and predictable model of the child.

According to Haberman (1988), any theory of child development makes two implicit assumptions: (1) that what can be explained and predicted about child development and behavior by using a theoretical explanation exceeds that portion of growth and behavior that is unpredictable and may never be explained by any theoretical interpretation and (2) that regardless of the specific theory, there is an acceptance of regularity of behavior undergirded by a systematic set of explanations versus an acceptance of chance forces that are unresponsive to purpose, control, or prediction as explanations of behavior. Consequently,

> [t]eachers committed to a theory of development will hold expectations of what is normal and typical which they will inevitably transform into what is desirable. They will then develop and hold expectations for preferred behavior which supports their particular theory and makes them insensitive to other explanations and understandings. (p. 37)

Such restraints, according to Suransky (1982), deprive children "of their own history-making power, their ability to act upon the world in significant and meaningful ways" (p. 8).

In light of our investigation, these provocative concerns are of more than passing interest. These are troublesome critiques for curriculum models because they depend on a consistent model of the child in order to ease dissemination and replication.

Educational dependence on developmental theory affects teachers as well. By creating the notion that all that needs to be known about children exists in an outside body of knowledge, teachers become defined as consumers of knowledge rather than its creators (Silin, 1987; Zimiles, 1986). As a result, Zimiles (1986) points out, teachers tend to be deflected from doing their own thinking. However, as we learned from examining the history of the Developmental-Interaction approach (see Chapter 4), this dependent, consumer-oriented relationship between practitioner and theory is a relatively new phenomenon.

> Whereas in the past, there was a partnership between early education and developmental psychology in the quest for understanding the young child, the vast expansion and differentiation of developmental psychology have assigned dominance to research and left early education in the role of consumer. Yet the level of analysis of most research and its quest for certainty and substantiation rather than theoretical elucidation and elaboration is more browbeating than useful to the educational practitioner. After intimidating and silencing the educator of young children by their masses of data and pose of authoritative mastery, psychologists rush in to fill the vacuum created by their dominance. This sometimes leads to the development of teacher-proof methods that further diminish the level of initiative and resourcefulness to be expected from teachers. (Zimiles, 1986, p. 201)

Relation between Theory and Practice.   Sigel (1972) described the relationship between developmental theory and early childhood programming as a necessary match between theory and practice. His focus on practice as a mirror of theory assumed a dependent relationship that, as we've now seen, has been challenged empirically, philosophically, and practically. In part, continued acceptance of this relationship derives from the failure to distinguish between the functions of psychology and education.

Generally, psychology's purpose is to describe behavior as it is, not in terms of what it ought to be (Egan, 1983; Fein & Schwartz, 1982; Silin, 1988; Spodek, 1988). In contrast, a theory of education, in addition to addressing individual growth, confronts questions of what kind of person society hopes will result from the educational process. As a result, the function of education is to try and shape the forces that produce desired educational outcomes (Egan, 1983; Fein & Schwartz, 1982; Silin, 1987, 1988; Spodek, 1988).

Whereas psychological theories strive to be descriptive and as value-free as possible, educational theories are intentionally prescriptive and value-laden.

> Educators are not trying to describe a process of development in a value-free way; they are trying to prescribe the best way of actualizing a range of preferred potentials. The value-laden nature of the end does not present a problem for educators; it is a part of the job in hand to deal constantly and explicitly with value matters. (Egan, 1983, p. 8)

Egan (1983) concludes that by failing to recognize this distinction, we confuse psychological with educational development. It is perhaps easier, now, to recognize that Kohlberg and Mayer (1972) were trying to construct a bridge between psychological and educational development. They were uncomfortable, however, with the "subjectively" chosen values associated with the romantic and cultural transmission viewpoints. So, they attempted to demonstrate the "natural" superiority of educational objectives associated with Piaget's cognitive-developmental theory.

But the contention that developmental theory depicts "natural" endpoints of growth—and hence a justifiable source of educational objectives—has been severely challenged by revelations of developmental psychology's subjectivity. Skrtic (1991) contends that we are moving away from belief in the objectivism of science and mechanical change toward a more subjective interpretation of knowledge. He argues that this shifting acceptance of subjectivity is part of a larger paradigm shift being experienced by Western civilization. It is worth recalling at this point that similar insight undermined evaluators' "objective" search for the best early childhood curriculum models.

A shift away from the "objectivity" of science, though, resurfaces the dreaded specter of relativism (Bruner, 1990). Bruner (1990), however, is quick to argue that the complex diversity of value commitments inherent to any culture does not equate with an "anything goes" relativism (p. 25), where every belief is as good as every other (as Kohlberg and Mayer apparently feared). The prevalence of multiple choices need not imply that each is necessarily of equal merit nor eliminate requirements for their justification (Bruner, 1990; Buchmann, 1984, 1990).

This conclusion is consistent with the recommendations of a growing number of early childhood educators and theorists: Determination of educationally worthwhile experiences should be derived from critical discussions of our commitments, including community and societal values, and issues of equity and justice (Egan, 1983; Kessler, 1991a; Silin, 1987, 1988; Spodek, 1988; Swadener & Kessler, 1991a). These issues, however, are rarely raised in discussions of early childhood curriculum models.

In order to avoid misinterpretation of this discussion, it is important to repeat a caution provided previously. These concerns should not be construed as suggesting that developmental theory is educationally irrelevant. The issue under deliberation is not the educational relevance of child development research or developmental theory; nor is the issue the developmental nature of education.[2] It is the legitimacy of developmental theory as sole *determinant* of early childhood curriculum that has been identified as problematic. Expressions of concern regarding the limitations associated with developmental theory, therefore, are frequently accompanied by recommendations that early childhood education broaden its perspective to incorporate other disciplines, including sociology, philosophy, anthropology, and curriculum studies, as additional informants for goal setting, decision making, and practice (Almy, 1988; Greene, 1988; Kessler, 1991a; Silin 1987; Swadener & Kessler, 1991a; Takanishi, 1981).

Research on Teacher Effects: New Judgments on the Nature of Teaching

One of the challenges to the practical conceptualization of early childhood education as birth to age 8 years is the fact that early childhood and elementary education have evolved from different institutional histories. Bloch (1991) proposes that the

---

2   For an interesting discussion of education *as* development, see Blenkin & Kelly, 1987.

histories of early childhood and elementary education's different institutional affiliations explain early childhood education's greater reliance on developmental theory
in comparison to elementary education's dependence on efforts aimed at social efficiency and, to a lesser extent, social reform.

Perhaps elementary education's historical preoccupation with efficiency explains
its search for teacher behaviors that increase student achievement, a search primarily
directed toward improving practice. Opportunities to apply the findings to educational decision making—with hopes of increasing student achievement and teacher
accountability—fueled interest in this research (Zumwalt, 1982). In turn, this interest
was based on faith in the power of scientific knowledge to resolve societal problems.
Under the rubric of teacher effectiveness research (which was especially prominent
from the 1960s through early 1980s), researchers sought to explain relationships
between classroom processes (usually teacher behaviors) and educational outcomes.
The curriculum or subject matter being taught, though, was rarely questioned
(Zumwalt, 1989). Brophy (1986) provides a review of this literature.

Teacher effectiveness research assumed effectiveness could be achieved by
teacher application of those strategies and methods that research had identified as
increasing student achievement. It also assumed that the nature of classroom activity
could be dissected and that teaching consisted of tactics "made rigorous by the
application of scientific theory and technique" (Schon, 1983, p. 21; also Doll, 1988).

Despite intense interest in teacher effectiveness research, Goffin's (1989) search
for a similar body of knowledge specific to early childhood education found it to be
virtually nonexistent. What *was* occurring in early childhood education during this
time were program evaluations of early childhood curriculum models. And similar to
the research on teacher effectiveness, these studies hoped to identify the best means
for promoting student achievement. Whereas educational researchers probed for
the most effective teacher behaviors, evaluators of early childhood curriculum models sought confirmation regarding the best early childhood programs. And, when the
complexities of classroom life confounded the positive identification of programs,
evaluators searched for the best match between program and child by attempting to
tease apart the effects of specific teacher behaviors (see Chapter 7).

Thus, although these two research agendas were designed differently, they were
seeking the same outcomes. This correspondence makes recent assessments of the
teacher effectiveness research pertinent to our own inquiry. These assessments
undermine hope of improving teaching—or the anticipated by-product, educational
achievement—by structuring education as a technical enterprise, whether pursued
via research on teacher effectiveness or evaluations of the differential effects of early
childhood curriculum models.

Based on the premise that findings regarding the effectiveness of elementary
teachers could be translated into effective teaching behaviors, research on teacher
effectiveness became the content for teacher education and staff development programs.[3] Zumwalt (1982) and Darling-Hammond (1985) called this linear process of
directly reinterpreting research results into teacher practices a technological orienta-

---

[3]   I rely heavily on an earlier work (Goffin, 1989) for the conclusions provided in the next several para-
graphs.

tion. This orientation, however, has been severely criticized for assuming that knowledge about effective teaching can be transformed into production rules for making teachers more effective. Similar to program evaluators' failure to consider children's influence on their own development, educational researchers have been criticized for neglecting to consider the extent to which teacher effects are mediated by teacher purposes and values, as well as teacher knowledge (Buchmann, 1984; Fenstermacher, 1979; Kerr, 1981; Macmillan & Garrison, 1984; Shulman, 1987; Stodolsky, 1984; Zumwalt, 1982, 1986).

Critics of the teacher effectiveness research claim that teachers do not become more effective merely by acting differently toward students; if this were so, teaching would be simply a technical vocation (Darling-Hammond, 1985) and learning a passive act. As discussed previously, the notion of children's passivity in their own learning and development has been discarded; so has the notion that teachers are passive in learning how to teach and technical in implementing what they know. To the contrary, it is now argued that teachers become more effective by thinking about and reflecting on what makes the activity of teaching worthwhile (Fenstermacher, 1979; Zumwalt, 1986). Embedded within these arguments is a reformation of the teacher's role. This reformation reflects a shift in thinking that is supported by recent conclusions regarding the nature of teaching.

New Judgments about the Nature of Teaching

New conceptualizations of teachers and teaching are distancing themselves from the technical images portrayed by the teacher effectiveness literature. Revisions are increasingly informed by what is being touted as a central characteristic of teaching: the need to act in an uncertain world (Buchmann, 1984, 1990; Cuban, 1992; Kerr, 1981; Lampert, 1985; Scheffler, 1991; Welker, 1991).

> When the template of technical rationality is laid over a messy social or educational problem, it seldom fits. The entangled issues and their ambiguity spill over. There are no procedures to follow, no scientific rules for making decisions. Worse yet, the template hides value conflicts. These so-called "problems" are complex, untidy, and insoluble. They . . . are dilemmas. (Cuban, 1992, p. 6)

The choices that confront teachers are rarely among clear-cut alternatives; it is this characteristic that defines them as dilemmas. It is not feasible, for example, to choose *either* to build curriculum around children's interests *or* around subject matter or to choose between meeting the needs of the group *or* the needs of individual children (Cuban, 1992; Elliott, 1989; Lampert, 1985). Many of the dilemmas teachers confront are unsolvable; thus teaching requires coping with equally weighted alternatives and attempting to do so in ways that actualize one's educational values (Buchmann, 1984; Lampert, 1985; Welker, 1991). From this perspective, teaching rarely entails making purely rational choices and applying technical solutions.

In her conceptual investigation of the use of research knowledge in teacher education and teaching, Buchmann (1984) extends this notion by distinguishing between the functions of research and teaching. Reminiscent of the distinction between developmental theory and educational practice, Buchmann claims that problems in practice are not the result of deficiencies in knowledge. She argues,

> Good practice, not truth, is the goal of action, and knowledge utilization and wise action are not the same. . . . [P]roblems in the practicing professions do not primarily derive from deficiencies in knowledge. They arise instead because of tensions or deficiencies in the moral framework in which professional practice is embedded. (pp. 421–422)

Although these conclusions have not been articulated specifically for early childhood education, the dilemma has been recognized. Many who have previously analyzed curriculum models have noted that child development theories are not geared to the world of practice. Child development theories provide little guidance for how a "matched" program is to be implemented with differing populations on a day-by-day basis (Day, 1977; Fein & Schwartz, 1982; Peters, Neisworth, & Yawkey, 1985; Spodek, 1973). In addition, given the incompleteness of theories of child development, Day (1977) points out that it is impossible to prescribe an entire curriculum without extensive inferences. Consequently, in reality, most curriculum models eschew precise implementation.

Fein and Schwartz (1982) specifically contrast theories of development with practice. They label theories of child development as passivist in orientation with the objective of describing how certain behaviors develop as a result of specified encounters with the environment. In contrast, theories of practice are activist in orientation. Theories of practice assume that certain behaviors or types of knowledge are more desirable than others and describe for the practitioner how to cultivate desired behaviors. Thus, theories of practice are expected to formulate strategies for constructing environments that ensure the greatest beneficial impact within the particular environment of the practitioner.

As a result of these distinctions, both in and out of early childhood education, there is increasing recognition that advancing teaching involves acknowledging its distinctive context and focusing on the generation of what Elliott (1989) and Buchmann (1984) have independently labeled practical wisdom (see also Kerr, 1981; Schon, 1983). "Wisdom can be defined as a holistic appreciation of a complex practical activity which enables a person to understand or articulate the problems (s)he confronts in realizing the aims or values of the activity and to propose appropriate solutions" (Elliott, 1989, pp. 83–84).

Yet, whether intended or not, curriculum models steer teacher attention away from these complexities of teaching. By presenting teachers with a predetermined curricular framework (regardless of how flexible), curriculum models direct teacher energy toward issues of implementation. A recent study by Walsh, Smith, Alexander, and Ellwin (in press) supports this conclusion. Their case study examined teacher efforts to implement the High/Scope curriculum during the first year of a state-wide pilot prekindergarten program. Walsh, Smith, Alexander, and Ellwin found that teachers never felt secure regarding what they were supposed to be doing and, consequently, constantly sought practical information regarding how to implement the model. One teacher even asked whether it was okay to use scissors!

> Implicit in the very notion of a standard curriculum is the idea that implementing it is a technical process, a process of learning what to *do* rather than how to teach. . . . Whatever the strengths of a curriculum, as long as it is imposed and remains outside the control of teachers, it will always be something to do, not a way to think, or even something to think about. (Walsh, Smith, Alexander, & Ellwin, in press)

Guided by newer interpretations of teaching, "effective" teachers are less frequently defined as those who apply the knowledge of others. The critical shift in thinking about teaching is that expertise develops *in* practice (Buchmann, 1984; Elliott, 1989; Schon, 1983), not from repeated practice of predetermined teaching strategies. According to Elliott (1989), teaching cannot be broken down into constitutive elements and still be teaching.

Reflecting on one's practice to discover better resolution to teaching's complex practical problems is essential to this view of teaching. This element is necessitated because no definitive solutions exist for the practical problems of teaching (Buchmann, 1984, 1990; Cuban, 1992; Elliott, 1989; Lampert, 1985). This conceptualization of teaching explicitly challenges technological interpretations of teacher effectiveness; simultaneously, it seeks to elevate appreciation for teachers' contributions to educational deliberations (see, for example, Cuban, 1992). Within this context, the various specialized disciplines, such as psychology, philosophy, sociology, and so forth, become intellectual resources that enable teachers to become better at realizing educational goals "in their actions" (Elliott, 1989, p. 84; also Scheffler, 1991).

■ *Beyond a Search for Efficacy*

Changing views about the nature of teaching and classroom life challenge the expectation that comparisons among curriculum models will produce an answer regarding the most effective way to educate young children. But even if one model were found to be statistically more effective on any given measure, the important influence of context and values—whether in one's choice of models or one's daily practice—stimulates questions about issues other than efficacy.

The distinction between educational means and ends have been set apart. The notion of teaching as merely a technical activity has been fatally punctured. And acknowledgment of the fact that value decisions are implicit in all of our choices makes attempts to neutralize or "objectify" curriculum options unacceptable. Clearly, our continued inquiry needs to set a different course.

Obviously, early childhood curriculum models have always been characterized by differences in their learning contexts and the values they promote as most worthwhile, but the implications of these differences received limited attention or analysis. Curriculum models emerged and flourished during a period when science was considered an objective and authoritative means for discriminating among educational alternatives. It was assumed that effective models for early education could be identified through research and evaluation and then uniformly implemented.

But, what happens when the outcomes of science are no longer recognized as the sole, authoritative basis on which to decide how to best educate children? Skrtic (1991) contends that the social sciences no longer provide criteria for judging one knowledge claim as superior to another. He suggests that the process of science has become a subjective activity that produces "possible knowledges" (p. 19) that are predicated on a particular frame of reference. Framing an investigation of early childhood curriculum models from this perspective establishes a different landscape for contemplating the multiple curriculum models that co-inhabit early childhood education. Furthermore, if curriculum models cannot be assessed in terms of objective criteria, it becomes essential to assess them in terms of the learning contexts they create and the values that they foster—for both children and teachers.

Bruner (1990) addressed the loss of science as a definitive authority (not to be confused with science as a method of inquiry) by pointing to the importance of open-mindedness (also Buchmann, 1990):

> I take open-mindedness to be a willingness to construe knowledge and values from multiple perspectives without loss of commitment to one's own values. . . . It demands that we be conscious of how we come to our knowledge and as conscious as we can be about the values that lead us to our perspectives. It asks that we be accountable for how and what we know. But it does not insist there is only one way of constructing meaning, or one right way. (p. 30)

■ *For Further Reading*

Horowitz, F. D., & O'Brien, M. (Eds.). (1989). Children and their development: Knowledge base, research agenda, and social policy application. *American Psychologist, 44* (2) [Special Issue].

   This special issue of *American Psychologist* is a comprehensive collection of articles that summarizes the knowledge base about children's social, emotional, and intellectual development. Special effort has been given to relating the topics directly to the well-being of children, especially as related to social policy.

Kohlberg, L., & Mayer, R. (1972). Development as the aim of education. *Harvard Educational Review, 42,* 449–496.

   In this classic and frequently cited article, Kohlberg and Mayer compare various approaches to understanding child development and defend their conclusion that Piagetian cognitive-developmental theory provides a logical and defensible framework for promoting development as the aim of education.

Silin, J. G. (1987). The early childhood educator's knowledge base: A reconsideration. In L. G. Katz & K. Steiner (Eds.), *Current topics in early childhood education* (Vol. 7, pp. 17–31). Norwood, NJ: Ablex.

> Silin challenges early childhood education's reliance on developmental theory as the source for curriculum decisions. He argues that recognition of early childhood education as a profession demands that early childhood educators create their own distinctive knowledge base.

Swadener, B. B., & Kessler, S. (Eds.). (1991). Reconceptualizing early childhood education. *Early Education and Development, 2* (2) [Special Issue].

> This special issue, as stated by the editors, provides a forum for examining issues in early childhood education from the perspective of curriculum studies in hopes of expanding early childhood's theoretical base.

Weber, E. (1984). *Ideas influencing early childhood education: A theoretical analysis.* New York: Teachers College Press.

> In historical sequence, Weber describes the evolution of early childhood education in the United States and the significant ideas that have influenced its growth. Although accepting developmental theory as a source for early childhood curriculum, Weber emphasizes the need to recognize the values inherent in different theoretical interpretations of child development.

Zelizer, V. A. (1985). *Pricing the priceless child: The changing social value of children.* New York: Basic Books.

> In a fascinating analysis, Zelizer chronicles how economic and social events in the United States have directly influenced the cultural meaning of childhood. Special emphasis is given to analyzing the ways in which children's changing "worth" has been framed by social and economic occurrences and in illustrating the social impact of economic events.

■ ■ ■ ■ ■ ■

Chapter 9

Curriculum Models and Early Childhood Education

Some Final Thoughts

■ ■ ■ ■ ■ ■

More than 25 years have passed since curriculum models were a focal point in early childhood education. Following a period of declining interest during the late seventies and early eighties, interest in their use re-emerged during the late eighties (see Chapter 2). In response to this renewed interest, this book initially proposed to provide an updated review of enduring early childhood curriculum models. But as the review proceeded, it expanded to include questions regarding the purpose and function of curriculum models and their impact on the field.

In pursuit of further understanding, the notion of curriculum models and the origin and evolution of individual models were considered in the context of both historical and contemporary issues and concerns. In the process, insights regarding the purpose and function of curriculum models began to emerge. Chapter by chapter, it became increasingly apparent that curriculum models, by intent, are designed to bring uniformity to early childhood programs.

Curriculum models are derived from an industrial notion of standardization that assumes "one size fits all"—a notion now under attack not only within education but also within the private and public sectors as well (see, for example, Osborne & Gaebler, 1992; Senge, 1990; Toffler, 1990). To achieve standardization, curriculum models—regardless of their internal flexibility—operate by using predictable representations of teaching and learning and rely on a fixed interpretation of the nature of children and of teachers. This view of curriculum models has clearly emerged from this investigation. It seems, then, that the early childhood profession would at least question renewed public and professional interest in curriculum models.

As revealed throughout these pages, however, the general notion of curriculum models and the individual histories of enduring models have been profoundly shaped by social and historical circumstances. The question as to whether curriculum model use should be encouraged is similarly bounded. Contemporary characteristics of the early childhood field and their intersection with current societal needs and expectations create a particular frame of reference for considering the value and contribution of curriculum models.

Within this context, curriculum models offer positive and negative educational possibilities. Consequently, their resurgence raises complicated questions for the early childhood field. When these questions are deliberated collectively, it is clear that the field has a dilemma. The intent of this final chapter is to pose this dilemma for public debate and to highlight the circumstances that have generated the context for its creation.

■ An Expanded Agenda for Early Childhood Education

Current interest in curriculum models as a systematic approach to early childhood education, similar to interest during the sixties, is still linked with concerns for the education of young children from economically disadvantaged circumstances. But, in addition, recent interest in early childhood curriculum models also reflects the need to well serve the increasing numbers of children participating in early childhood programs. In the 1960s, public and professional interest in early childhood education converged around concern for the economically disadvantaged and was embedded in the civil rights movement. Now, more than 25 years later, renewed interest in early childhood education and its curriculum models reflects contemporary demographics and is embedded in concerns for retaining our nation's economic viability.

Furthermore, changes since the mid-sixties have not been restricted to demographics and changing societal circumstances. The field of early childhood education has also evolved. Thus, in the nineties, early childhood curriculum models are being implemented in a different societal as well as professional context.

These differences in context are not new to this discussion; they were first introduced in Chapter 2. As part of the book's introduction to curriculum models, descriptions of contemporary interest in early childhood programs and the changing configuration of early childhood education provided an up-to-date backdrop for the subsequent examination of individual curriculum models. When reconsidered in light of what has been learned about curriculum models, this contextual information discloses the circumstances that create tension between what we now know to be the purpose and function of curriculum models and ongoing deliberations within the early childhood profession regarding its course to professionalism.

Changing Societal Context

Current interest in early childhood curriculum models emanates, in part, from renewed faith in their effectiveness as vehicles for ensuring that early childhood education mitigates the effects of poverty. This aspiration, of course, reiterates expectations from the late sixties and early seventies that first spurred development of early intervention programs such as Head Start and the systematic development of early childhood curriculum models.

During the mid-sixties, early intervention programs, in general, and Head Start, in particular, emerged from national concern about alleviating poverty juxtaposed with changing assumptions regarding the malleability of intelligence during the early years of life. This combination of events exploded into an optimism regarding the inoculating power of early childhood education and initiated a search for early childhood models that could most effectively harness this potential.

In the nineties, however, interest in early childhood education and its curriculum models extends beyond concern for the economically disadvantaged. Now attention to early childhood education also reflects the increasing numbers of mothers of all socioeconomic status who are in the work force and have young children, the national spotlight on educational reform, and concern with adequately educating all of America's children because of anticipated labor shortages and the challenge of revolutionary technological change. As a result, ongoing concern for the unequal educational success of economically disadvantaged children primarily originates from economic anxieties regarding the availability of a skilled future labor force and the costs to society of unproductive citizens.

Thus, unlike the 1960s, when interest in early childhood education revolved primarily around the single issue of school readiness as a means for creating equal opportunity for economically disadvantaged children, current attention to early childhood education has coalesced around economic concerns. Although early childhood education is still advocated as a vehicle for resolving societal problems, the list of concerns is more differentiated, targets a larger proportion of young children, and involves a constituency that includes public school officials, parents, policy makers, and corporate and civic leaders. Increasingly, early childhood education is seen as critical not only to minimizing the impact of poverty but also as essential to the success of public schools, the future international competitiveness of American business, and the employability of parents.

This expansion of interest has enlarged the child population being targeted and extended the public's expectations for early childhood education. And these expectations, in turn, are beginning to exert pressure on communities and the early childhood profession to provide high quality early childhood programs.

Changing Professional Context

Before the onset of early intervention programs during the mid-sixties, the availability of early childhood education prior to first grade was sporadic. Nursery education was primarily an optional, enrichment-oriented program mostly for children from middle-class families; "day care" was considered a social welfare program for low-income families, and kindergartens had yet to become a fixture of public school education.

Now, of course, in the nineties, a majority of America's children participate in early childhood programs before entering first grade. Most 5-year-olds attend kindergarten, and a majority of preschoolers with a stay-at-home parent attend nursery school. The most dramatic transformation, however, has occurred in the use of child care. Parents of two-thirds of America's children under the age of 6 are currently in the work force, and their children are attending child care.

These out-of-home experiences prior to kindergarten and first grade are increasingly being recognized as children's first encounter with formal education. In addition, children's educational experiences through third grade are being included under the rubric of early childhood education. The presence of so many children in out-of-home settings has heightened professional concern regarding what children experience when in these settings. Simultaneously, public interest in the contributions of early educational experiences to children's success with later schooling and future productivity places pressure on early childhood programs to fulfill society's mounting expectations for early childhood education.

Preparation of early childhood personnel, however, has not kept pace with either increased demand or changing expectations. Ironically, the present shortage exists in large measure because the general public traditionally has not perceived caring for young children to be an educational and/or professional enterprise.

Consequently, as expectations for better quality have begun to accompany demands for program availability, competition for qualified early childhood personnel has been intensifying. Preparing and keeping qualified personnel, however, is undermined by the inferior compensation offered early childhood educators, especially those who work outside the public school system. Building the cadre of professionally prepared early educators is further hampered by the profession's struggle to define the formal requirements that should be associated with professionalism (see, for example, Bredekamp & Willer, 1993). As a result, depending on whether early childhood education occurs within a family child care setting, public school, nursery school, Head Start, or child care program, expectations for teacher qualifications can range from no prerequisites to a high school diploma to a Child Development Associate credential to a 4-year-degree.

Thus, at the time of this writing, the field of early childhood education lacks the capacity to respond to escalating demands for consistent program quality and accountability. Not surprisingly, the repercussions are disheartening. The National Staffing Study (Whitebrook, Howes, & Phillips, 1989), for example, revealed that the majority of young children in child care centers are in less than adequate settings. Similar concerns have been articulated for Head Start (Hymes, 1985; Zigler & Muenchow, 1992), and discouragement with the consequences of inappropriately academic kindergartens and primary grades abounds (see Chapter 5).

■ *Curriculum Models and Early Childhood Education: A Dilemma*

In the 1960s, curriculum models were specifically developed for disadvantaged child populations as alternatives to traditional, "middle-class" nursery school programs. They were intended to provide disadvantaged children with educational experiences that would enable them to enter public schooling on an equal footing with their middle-class peers. In contrast, in the 1990s, curriculum models are advanced not as alternatives targeted toward children with specialized needs but as a framework for mainstream early education; they are promoted as vehicles for improving the overall quality of early childhood education. Weikart (1992; Weikart & Schweinhart, 1993), in particular, cogently articulates this viewpoint.

Few would disagree that the provision of high quality early childhood programs is the most important task that confronts the early childhood profession. But, herein lies the dilemma.

The greater use of curriculum models might, in fact, improve programmatic quality by providing well-articulated curriculum frameworks that could be employed in place of existing, widely varying routines. Improved program quality, plus greater public accountability, would result from the replacement of existing practices with standard programming across settings. Hence, the dissemination and consistent application of curriculum models could change the *floor* of program quality in early childhood education.

By momentarily disregarding our knowledge of the complexities involved in program implementation (see Chapter 7) and temporarily suspending the critical question of how one selects among available curriculum models (see Chapter 8), it is possible to argue that the consistent implementation of curriculum models might provide a vehicle for raising the standard of care and education experienced by young children. But, as we now know, curriculum models affect not only the lives of children, but also the lives of their teachers. Thus, using curriculum models may improve the daily lives of children (up to a certain point), but this achievement, regardless of the chosen curriculum model, occurs at the expense of the profession's vision for itself and its teachers.

This consequence occurs because curriculum models are also vehicles for lowering expectations regarding the professional responsibilities and possibilities of early childhood teachers. The premises that undergird curriculum models delegate teachers to the role of technicians who implement the educational ideas of others, a role in dramatic contrast with dynamic interpretations of learning and generative views of teaching (see Chapter 8). Furthermore, reliance on curriculum models as a means for achieving program quality restricts discussion about quality to issues of implementation—rather than the vitality of learning and growth being experienced by children and teachers.

Current interest in curriculum models is fueled by the need to improve the quality of existing early childhood education programs in the absence of a sufficiently educated early childhood work force—both in the present and the foreseeable future. But, the decision to use curriculum models as a solution to this quandary promises to affect the field by shaping both public and professional perceptions of early childhood education as a technical enterprise. The dilemma now confronting the early childhood profession is how to improve what a majority of today's children are experiencing in early childhood settings and—at the same time—advocate for a view of professionalism that acknowledges the dynamic complexity of teaching young children.

This dilemma is not new to early childhood education. On reviewing her career, Carolyn Pratt (1948/1990), a pioneer in early childhood education and founder of the City and Country School, stated,

> All my life I have fought against formula. Once you have set down a formula, you are imprisoned by it as surely as the primitive tribesman is imprisoned by the witch doctor's magic circle. I would not be talked into making out any blueprints for education, outside the school or within it. [But] this refusal to formulate a "system" made me a problem to our teachers. (p. 56)

Years later, when asked to respond to the challenge of professionalism within early childhood education, Biber (1988) argued that

> the teacher we are asking for is aware of the complexities of the interaction between intellectual development and affective experience in the developing years. Further, the ideal teacher is aware of the differences in the social codes and styles of interaction among young children from widely different cultural groups. Finally, we are looking for a teacher who can maintain healthy, cohesive group functioning which is so flexibly enacted that individual needs can be sensed, understood and met, with suitable adjustment. (p. 46)

This kind of teaching rarely emerges from learning to implement preconceptualized curricula; in fact, it would be discouraged because such responsiveness could undermine a model's consistent implementation. Thus, we must ask: How, within the current context of contradictory expectations and demands, does the early childhood profession respond to the pragmatic, immediate needs of today's children and practitioners and still realize a vision, like that of Biber's, for future generations of children and early childhood educators?

References

Almy, M. (1988). The early childhood educator revisited. In B. Spodek, O. N. Saracho, & D. L. Peters (Eds.), *Professionalism and the early childhood practitioner* (pp. 48–55). New York: Teachers College Press.

Anderson, V., & Bereiter, C. (1972). Extending direct instruction to conceptual skills. In R. K. Parker (Ed.), *The preschool in action: Exploring early childhood programs* (pp. 339–350). Boston: Allyn & Bacon.

Antler, J. (1982). Progressive education and the scientific study of the child: An analysis of the Bureau of Educational Experiments. *Teachers College Record, 83,* 559–591.

Antler, J. (1987). *Lucy Sprague Mitchell: The making of a modern woman.* New Haven, CT: Yale University Press.

Apple, M. W., & Beyer, L. E. (1983). Social evaluation of curriculum. *Educational Evaluation and Policy Analysis, 5,* 425–434.

Baer, D. M. (1975). In the beginning, there was the response. In E. Ramp & G. Simb (Eds.), *Behavior analysis: Areas of research and application* (pp. 16–30). Englewood Cliffs, NJ: Prentice-Hall.

Barnett, W. S. (1986). Methodological issues in economic evaluation of early intervention programs. *Early Childhood Research Quarterly, 1,* 249–268.

Barnett, W. S., Frede, E. C., Mobasher, H., & Mohr, P. (1987). The efficacy of public preschool programs and the relationship of program quality to program efficacy. *Educational Evaluation and Policy Analysis, 10*(1), 37–39.

Barone, T. E. (1992). On the demise of subjectivity in educational inquiry. *Curriculum Inquiry, 22,* 25–38.

Becker, W. C., Engelmann, S., Carnine, D. W., & Rhine, W. R. (1981). Direct instruction model. In W. R. Rhine (Ed.), *Making schools more effective: New directions from Follow Through* (pp. 95–154). New York: Academic Press.

Belsky, J. (1984). Two waves of day care research: Developmental effects and conditions of quality. In R. C. Ainslie (Ed.), *The child and the day care setting: Qualitative variations and development* (pp. 1–34). New York: Praeger.

Bentley, R. (1964). Publisher's foreword to the 1964 edition. *The Montessori Method* (pp. xvii–xxii). Cambridge, MA: Robert Bentley.

Bereiter, C. (1968). A nonpsychological approach to early compensatory education. In M. Deutsch, I. Katz, & A. R. Jensen (Eds.), *Social class, race, and psychological development* (pp. 337–346). New York: Holt, Rinehart & Winston.

Bereiter, C. (1970). Designing programs for classroom use. In F. F. Karten, S. W. Cook, & J. I. Lacey (Eds.), *Psychology and the problems of society* (pp. 204–207). Washington, DC: American Psychological Society.

Bereiter, C. (1972). An academic preschool for disadvantaged children: Conclusions from evaluation studies. In J. C. Stanley (Ed.), *Preschool programs for the disadvantaged: Five experimental approaches to early childhood education* (pp. 1–21). Baltimore: The Johns Hopkins University Press.

Bereiter, C. (1986). Does direct instruction cause delinquency? *Early Childhood Research Quarterly, 1,* 289–292.

Bereiter, C. (1990). Aspects of an educational learning theory. *Review of Educational Research, 60,* 603–624.

Bereiter, C., & Engelmann, S. (1966a). Observations on the use of direct instruction with young disadvantaged children. *Journal of School Psychology, 4*(3), 55–62.

Bereiter, C., & Engelmann, S. (1966b). *Teaching disadvantaged children in the preschool.* Englewood Cliffs, NJ: Prentice-Hall.

Berrueta-Clement, J. R., Schweinhart, L. J., Barnett, W. S., Epstein, A. S., & Weikart, D. P. (1984). *Changed lives: The effects of the Perry Preschool Program on youths through age 19.* Ypsilanti, MI: The High/Scope Press.

Biber, B. (1967). The impact of deprivation on young children. *Childhood Education, 44,* 110–116.

Biber, B. (1967). A learning-teaching paradigm integrating intellectual and affective processes. In E. M. Bower & W. G. Hollister (Eds.), *Behavioral science frontiers in education* (pp. 112–155). New York: John Wiley & Sons.

Biber, B. (1969). Challenges ahead for early childhood education. *Young Children, 24,* 196–205.

Biber, B. (1977a). Cognition in early childhood education: A historical perspective. In B. Spodek & H. Walberg (Eds.), *Early childhood education: Issues and insights* (pp. 41–64). Berkeley, CA: McCutchan.

Biber, B. (1977b). A developmental-interaction approach: Bank Street College of Education. In M. C. Day & R. K. Parker (Eds.), *The preschool in action: Exploring early childhood programs* (2nd ed., pp. 421–460). Boston: Allyn & Bacon.

Biber, B. (1979a). Introduction to section III: "The preschool education component of Head Start." In E. Zigler & J. Valentine (Eds.), *Project Head Start: A legacy of the War on Poverty* (pp. 155–161). New York: The Free Press.

Biber, B. (1979b). Thinking and feeling. *Young Children, 35*(1), 4–16.

Biber, B. (1981). The evolution of the developmental-interaction view. In E. K. Shapiro & E. Weber (Eds.), *Cognitive and affective growth: Developmental interaction* (pp. 9–30). Hillsdale, NJ: Lawrence Erlbaum.

Biber, B. (1984). *Early education and psychological development.* New Haven, CT: Yale University Press.

Biber, B. (1988). The challenge of professionalism: Integrating theory and practice. In B. Spodek, O. N. Saracho, & D. L. Peters (Eds.), *Professionalism and the early childhood practitioner* (pp. 29–47). New York: Teachers College Press.

Biber, B., & Franklin, M. B. (1967). The relevance of developmental and psychodynamic concepts to the education of the preschool child. *Journal of the American Academy of Child Psychiatry, 6*(1–4), 5–24.

Biber, B., Gilkeson, E., & Winsor, C. (1959, April). Teacher education at Bank Street College. *Personnel and Guidance Journal, 37,* 558–568.

Biber, B., Shapiro, E., & Wickens, D. (1977). *Promoting cognitive growth: A developmental interaction point of view* (2nd ed.). Washington, DC: National Association for the Education of Young Children.

Biber, B., & Snyder, A. (1948). How do we know a good teacher? *Childhood Education, 24,* 280–285.

Bissell, J. S. (1973). Planned variation in Head Start and Follow Through. In J. C. Stanley (Ed.), *Compensatory education for children ages two to eight: Recent studies of educational intervention* (pp. 63–107). Baltimore: The Johns Hopkins University Press.

Blackwell, F., & Hohmann, C. (1991). *High/Scope K–3 Curriculum Series. Science.* Ypsilanti, MI: High/Scope Press.

Blenkin, G., & Kelly, V. (1987). Education as development. In G. Blenkin & A. V. Kelly (Eds.), *Early childhood education: A developmental curriculum* (pp. 1–31). London: Paul Chapman.

Bloch, M. N. (1987). Becoming scientific and professional: An historical perspective on the aims and effects of early education. In T. S. Popkewitz (Ed.), *The formation of the school subjects: The struggle for creating an American institution* (pp. 25–62). New York: Falmer.

Bloch, M. N. (1991). Critical science and the history of child development's influence on early education research. *Early Education and Development, 2,* 95–108.

Bloom, B. S. (1964). *Stability and change in human characteristics.* New York: John Wiley & Sons.

Bredekamp, S. (Ed.). (1987). *Developmentally appropriate practice in early childhood programs serving children from birth through age 8.* Washington, DC: National Association for the Education of Young Children.

Bredekamp, S. (1991). Redeveloping early childhood education: A response to Kessler. *Early Childhood Research Quarterly, 6,* 199–209.

Bredekamp, S., & Willer, B. (1993). Professionalizing the field of early childhood education: Pros and cons. *Young Children, 84*(3), 82–84.

Bronfenbrenner, U. (1974). *A report on longitudinal evaluations of preschool programs. Is early intervention effective?* (Vol. 2). Washington, DC: U.S. Department of Health, Education and Welfare, Office of Child Development.

Bronfenbrenner, U. (1986). Ecology of the family as a context for human development: Research perspectives. *Developmental Psychology, 22,* 723–742.

Bronfenbrenner, U. (1989). Ecological systems theory. In R. Vasta (Ed.), *Six theories of child development: Revised formulations and current issues. Annals of child development: A research annual* (Vol. 6, pp. 187–249). Greenwich, CT: JAI Press.

Bronfenbrenner, U., Kessel, F., Kessen, W., & White, S. (1986). Toward a critical social history of developmental psychology: A propaedeutic discussion. *American Psychologist, 41,* 1218–1230.

Bronfenbrenner, U., & Weiss, H. R. (1983). Beyond policies without people: An ecological perspective on child and family policy. In E. F. Zigler, S. L. Kagan, & E. Klugman (Eds.), *Children, families, and government: Perspectives on American social policy* (pp. 393–414). Cambridge: Cambridge University Press.

Brophy, J. E. (1979). Teacher behavior and its effects. *Journal of Educational Psychology, 71,* 733–750.

Brophy, J. E. (1986). Teacher behavior and student achievement. In M. C. Wittrock (Ed.), *Handbook of research on teaching* (3rd ed., pp. 328–375). New York: Macmillan.

Bruner, J. (1990). *Acts of meaning.* Cambridge, MA: Harvard University Press.

Bruner, J., & Haste, H. (1987). Introduction. In J. Bruner & H. Haste (Eds.), *Making sense: The child's construction of the world* (pp. 1–25). New York: Methuen.

Buchmann, M. (1984). The use of research knowledge in teacher education and teaching. *American Journal of Education, 92,* 421–439.

Buchmann, M. (1990). *Learning and action in research reporting.* Issue Paper 90-8. East Lansing, MI: The National Center for Research on Teacher Education.

Burts, D. C., Hart, C. H., Charlesworth, R., & Kirk, L. (1990). A comparison of frequencies of stress behaviors observed in kindergarten children in classrooms with developmentally appropriate versus developmentally inappropriate instructional practices. *Early Childhood Research Quarterly, 5,* 407–423.

Bushell, D., Jr. (1973). The behavior analysis classroom. In B. Spodek (Ed.), *Early childhood education* (pp. 163–175). Englewood Cliffs, NJ: Prentice-Hall.

Bushell, D., Jr. (1982). The behavior analysis model for early education. In B. Spodek (Ed.), *Handbook of research in early childhood education* (pp. 107–184). New York: The Free Press.

Butler, A. L. (1976). Today's child—Tomorrow's world. *Young Children, 32,* 4–11.

Cahan, E. D. (1989). *Past caring: A history of U.S. preschool care and education for the poor, 1820–1965.* National Center for Children in Poverty, School of Public Health, Columbia University (154 Haven Avenue, New York, NY, 10032).

Caldwell, B. M. (1984). From the president. *Young Children, 39*(6), 53–56.

Caldwell, B. M. (1989). Foreword: Prologue to the past. In E. D. Cahan, *Past caring: A history of U.S. preschool care and education for the poor, 1820–1965* (pp. vii–xi). National Center for Children in Poverty, School of Public Health, Columbia University (154 Haven Avenue, New York, NY, 10032).

Campbell, D. T. (1987). Problems for the experimenting society in the interface between evaluation and service providers. In S. L. Kagan, D. R. Powell, B. Weissbourd, & E. F. Zigler (Eds.), *America's family support programs* (pp. 345–351). New Haven, CT: Yale University Press.

Carnine, D., Carnine, L., Karp, J., & Weisberg, P. (1988). Kindergarten for economically disadvantaged children: The direct instruction component. In C. Warger (Ed.), *A resource guide to public school early childhood programs* (pp. 73–98). Alexandria, VA: Association for Supervision and Curriculum Development.

Case, R., & Bereiter, C. (1984). From behaviourism to cognitive behaviourism to cognitive development: Steps in the evolution of instructional design. *Instructional Science, 13,* 141–158.

Cazden, C. B., & Mehan, H. (1989). Principles from sociology and anthropology: Context, code, classroom, and culture. In M. C. Reynolds (Ed.), *Knowledge base for the beginning teacher* (pp. 47–57). New York: Pergamon Press.

Chattin-McNichols, J. (1992a). What does research say about Montessori? In M. H. Loeffler (Ed.), *Montessori in contemporary society* (pp. 69–100). Portsmouth, NH: Heinemann.

Chattin-McNichols, J. (1992b). *The Montessori controversy.* Albany, NY: Delmar.

Children's Defense Fund. (1991). *The state of America's children 1991.* Washington, DC: Author.

Cicirelli, V. (1969). *The impact of Head Start: An evaluation of the effects of Head Start on children's cognitive and affective development.* Athens, OH: Westinghouse Learning Corporation.

Cicirelli, V. G. (1984). The misinterpretation of the Westinghouse Study: A reply to Zigler and Berman. *American Psychologist, 39,* 915–917.

Clarke, A. M. (1984). Early experience and cognitive development. In E. W. Gordon (Ed.), *Review of research in education* (Vol. 2, pp. 125–157). Washington, DC: American Educational Research Association.

Clarke, A. M., & Clarke, A. D. B. (Eds.). (1976). *Early experience: Myth and evidence.* New York: Free Press.

Clarke-Stewart, K. A. (1987a). In search of consistencies in child care research. In D. A. Phillips (Ed.), *Quality in child care: What does research tell us?* (pp. 105–120). Washington, DC: National Association for the Education of Young Children.

Clarke-Stewart, K. A. (1987b). Predicting child development from child care forms and features: The Chicago Study. In D. A. Phillips (Ed.), *Quality in child care: What does research tell us?* (pp. 21–41). Washington, DC: National Association for the Education of Young Children.

Clarke-Stewart, K. A. (1988). Evolving issues in early childhood education: A personal perspective. *Early Childhood Research Quarterly, 3,* 139–149.

Clarke-Stewart, K. A., & Fein, G. G. (1983). Early childhood programs. In J. Campos & M. Haith (Eds.), *Infancy and developmental psychobiology* (Vol. 2, pp. 917–999). In P. Mussen (Ed.), *Manual of Child Psychology,* 4th ed. New York: John Wiley & Sons.

Clarke-Stewart, K. A., & Gruber, C. P. (1984). Day care form and features. In R. C. Ainslie (Ed.), *The child and the day care setting: Qualitative variations and development* (pp. 35–62). New York: Praeger.

Cleverley, J., & Phillips, D. C. (1986). *Visions of childhood: Influential models from Locke to Spock.* New York: Teachers College Press.

Cohen, D. (1975). The value of social experiments. In A. M. Rivlin & P. M. Timpane (Eds.), *Planned variation in education: Should we give up or try harder?* (pp. 147–175). Washington, DC: The Brookings Institution.

Cohen, S. (1969). Maria Montessori: Priestess or pedagogue? *Teachers College Record, 71,* 313–326.

Cole, M., & Cole, S. R. (1989). *The development of children.* New York: Scientific American Books.

Committee for Economic Development. (1987). *Children in need: Investment strategies for the educationally disadvantaged.* New York: Author.

Committee for Economic Development. (1991). *The unfinished agenda: A new vision for child development and education.* New York: Author.

Committee of Nineteen. (1913). *The kindergarten.* Boston: Houghton Mifflin.

Condry, S. (1983). History and background of preschool intervention programs and the Consortium for Longitudinal Studies. In The Consortium for Longitudinal Studies (Ed.), *As *the twig is bent . . . Lasting effects of preschool programs* (pp. 1–31). Hillsdale, NJ: Lawrence Erlbaum.

Consortium for Longitudinal Studies. (1979). *Lasting effects after preschool.* Washington, DC: U.S. Department of Health, Education and Welfare.

Consortium for Longitudinal Studies. (1983). *As the twig is bent . . . Lasting effects of preschool programs.* Hillsdale, NJ: Lawrence Erlbaum.

Copple, C., Sigel, I., & Saunders, R. (1979). *Educating the young thinker: Classroom strategies for cognitive growth.* New York: D. Van Nostrand.

Corsaro, W. (1988). Peer culture in the preschool. *Theory into Practice, 27*(1), 19–24.

Cremin, L. (1964). *The transformation of the school: Progressivism in American education 1876–1957.* New York: Vintage. (Originally published in 1961 by Alfred A. Knopf)

Cuban, L. (1992). Managing dilemmas while building professional communities. *Educational Researcher, 21*(1), 4–11.

Cuffaro, H. K. (1977). The developmental-interaction approach. In B. D. Boegehold, H. K. Cuffaro, W. H. Hooks, & G. J. Klopf (Eds.), *Education before five: A handbook on preschool education* (pp. 45–52). New York: Bank Street College of Education.

Darling-Hammond, L. (1985). Valuing teachers: The making of a profession. *Teachers College Record, 87,* 205–218.

Day, M. C. (1977). A comparative analysis of center-based programs. In M. C. Day & R. K. Parker (Eds.), *The preschool in action* (2nd ed., pp. 461–487). Boston: Allyn & Bacon.

Day, D. E. (1983). *Early childhood education: A human ecological approach.* Glenview, IL: Scott, Foresman.

Delpit, L. D. (1988). The silenced dialogue: Power and pedagogy in educating other people's children. *Harvard Educational Review, 58,* 280–298.

DeVries, R. (1970). The development of role-taking in bright, average, and retarded children as reflected in social guessing game behavior. *Child Development, 41,* 759–770.

DeVries, R. (1978). Early education and Piagetian theory: Applications versus implications. In J. M. Gallagher & J. A. Easley, Jr. (Eds.), *Knowledge and development: Piaget and education* (Vol. 2, pp. 75–92). New York: Plenum.

DeVries, R. (1984). Developmental stages in Piagetian theory and educational practice. *Teacher Education Quarterly, 11,* 78–94.

DeVries, R. (1991). The eye beholding the eye of the beholder: Reply to Gersten. *Early Childhood Research Quarterly, 6,* 539–548.

DeVries, R. (1992). Development as the aim of constructivist education: How can it be recognized in children's activity? In D. G. Murphy & S. G. Goffin (Eds.), *Project Construct: A curriculum guide. Understanding the possibilities* (pp. 15–34). Jefferson City: Missouri Department of Elementary and Secondary Education.

DeVries, R., & Fernie, D. (1990). Stages in children's play of Tic Tac Toe. *Journal of Research in Education, 4,* 98–111.

DeVries, R., & Goncu, A. (1987). Interpersonal relations in four- year dyads from constructivist and Montessori programs. *Journal of Applied Developmental Psychology, 8,* 481–501.

DeVries, R., Haney, J. P., & Zan, B. (1991). Sociomoral atmosphere in direct-instruction, eclectic, and constructivist kindergartens: A study of teachers' enacted interpersonal understanding. *Early Childhood Research Quarter, 6,* 449–471.

DeVries, R., & Kohlberg, L. (1987). *Programs of early education: The constructivist view.* New York: Longman. (Published in 1990 as *Constructivist education: Overview and com-*

parison with other programs by the National Association for the Education of Young Children)

DeVries, R., Reese-Learned, H., & Morgan, P. (1991). Sociomoral development in direct-instruction, eclectic, and constructivist kindergartens: A study of children's enacted interpersonal understanding. *Early Childhood Research Quarterly, 6,* 473–517.

Dewey, J. (1938). *Experience and education.* New York: Collier.

Doll, W. E., Jr. (1988). Curriculum beyond stability: Schon, Prigogine, and Piaget. In W. F. Pinar (Ed.), *Contemporary curriculum discourse* (pp. 114–133). Scottsdale, AZ: Gorsuch, Scarisbrick.

Dowley, E. M. (1971). Perspectives on early childhood education. In R. H. Anderson & H. G. Shane (Eds.), *As the twig is bent: Readings in early childhood education* (pp. 12–21). Boston: Houghton Mifflin.

Durkin, D. (1987). Testing in the kindergarten. *The Reading Teacher, 40,* 766–770.

Edwards, C. P., & Gandini, L. (1989). Teachers' expectations about the timing of developmental skills: A cross-cultural study. *Young Children, 44*(4), 15–19.

Egan, K. (1983). *Education and psychology: Plato, Piaget, and scientific psychology.* New York: Teachers College Press.

Egan, K. (1988). Metaphors in collision: Objectives, assembly lines, and stories. *Curriculum Inquiry, 18,* 63–86.

Egertson, H. A. (1987). Recapturing kindergarten for 5-year-olds. *Education Week, 6*(34), 19–28.

Eisner, E. (1992). Objectivity in educational research. *Curriculum Inquiry, 22,* 9–15.

Elkind, D. (1970). The case for the academic preschool: Fact or fiction? *Young Children, 25,* 132–140.

Elkind, D. (1986). Formal education and early childhood education: An essential difference. *Phi Delta Kappan, 67,* 631–636.

Elkind, D. (1987). Early childhood education on its own terms. In S. L. Kagan & E. F. Zigler (Eds.), *Early schooling: The national debate* (pp. 98–115). New Haven, CT: Yale University Press.

Elkind, D. (1989). Developmentally appropriate practice: Philosophical and practical implications. *Phi Delta Kappan, 71,* 113–117.

Elliott, J. (1989). Educational theory and the professional learning of teachers: An overview. *Cambridge Journal of Education, 19,* 81–101.

Evans, E. D. (1975). *Contemporary influences in early childhood education* (2nd ed.). New York: Holt, Rinehart & Winston.

Evans, E. D. (1982). Curriculum models. In B. Spodek (Ed.), *Handbook of research in early childhood education* (pp. 107–134). New York: The Free Press.

Evans, E. D. (1985). Longitudinal follow-up assessment of differential preschool experience for low-income minority group children. *Journal of Educational Research, 78,* 197–202.

Fein, G., & Schwartz, P. M. (1982). Developmental theories in early education. In B. Spodek (Ed.), *Handbook of research in early childhood education* (pp. 82–104). New York: The Free Press.

Fenstermacher, G. D. (1979). A philosophical consideration of recent research on teacher effectiveness. In L. S. Shulman (Ed.), *Review of research in education* (Vol. 6, pp. 157–185). Itasca, IL: American Educational Research Journal.

Ferreiro, E., & Teberosky, A. (1982). *Literacy before schooling.* Portsmouth, N.H.: Heinemann. (Original work published in 1979)

Flanagan, O. (1993). *The science of the mind* (2nd ed.). Cambridge, MA: MIT Press.

Flynn, R. (1992). Developing a constructivist framework: A state initiative. In D. G. Murphy & S. G. Goffin (Eds.), *Project Construct: A curriculum guide. Understanding the possibilities* (pp. 3–6). Jefferson City: Missouri Department of Elementary and Secondary Education.

Forman, G., & Hill, F. (1980). *Constructive play: Applying Piaget in the preschool.* Monterey, CA: Brooks/Cole.

Forman, G., & Kuschner, D. (1977). *The child's construction of knowledge: Piaget for teaching children.* Monterey, CA: Brooks/Cole.

Franklin, M. B. (1981). Perspectives on theory: Another look at the developmental-interaction point of view. In E. K. Shapiro & E. Weber (Eds.), *Cognitive and affective growth: Developmental interaction* (pp. 65–84). Hillsdale, NJ: Lawrence Erlbaum.

Franklin, M. B., & Biber, B. (1977). Psychological perspectives and early childhood education: Some relations between theory and practice. In L. G. Katz, M. Z. Glockner, S. T. Goodman, & M. J. Spencer (Eds.), *Current issues in early childhood education* (Vol. 1, pp. 1–32). Norwood, NJ: Ablex.

Frede, E., & Barnett, W. S. (1992). Developmentally appropriate public school preschool: A study of implementation of the High/Scope Curriculum and its effects on disadvantaged children's skills at first grade. *Early Childhood Research Quarterly, 7,* 483–499.

Gallagher, J. J., & Ramey, C. T. (1987). *The malleability of children.* Baltimore: Paul H. Brookes.

Gallagher, J. M., & Sigel, I. E. (Eds.). (1987). Hothousing of young children [special issue]. *Early Childhood Research Quarterly, 2*(3).

Gardner, H. (1990). *Art education and human development.* Occasional paper No. 3. Los Angeles: The Getty Center for Education in the Arts.

Gardner, H. (1991). *The unschooled mind: How children think and how schools should teach.* New York: Basic Books.

Gersten, R. (1986). Response to "Consequences of Three Preschool Curriculum Models through Age 15." *Early Childhood Research Quarterly, 1,* 293–302.

Gersten, R. (1991). The eye of the beholder: A response to "Sociomoral atmosphere . . . A study of teachers' enacted interpersonal understanding." *Early Childhood Research Quarterly, 6,* 529–537.

Gersten, R., Carnine, D., Zoref, L., & Cronin, D. (1986). A multifaceted study of change in seven inner-city schools. *The Elementary School Journal, 86,* 257–276.

Gersten, R., Darch, C., & Gleason, M. (1988). Effectiveness of a direct instruction academic kindergarten for low-income students. *The Elementary School Journal, 89,* 227–240.

Gersten, R., & George, N. (1990). Teaching reading and mathematics to at-risk students in kindergarten: What we have learned from field research. In C. Seefeldt (Ed.), *Continuing issues in early childhood education* (pp. 245–259). New York: Merrill/Macmillan.

Gilkeson, E. C., Smithberg, L. M., Bowman, G. W., & Rhine, W. R. (1981). Bank Street model: A developmental-interaction approach. In W. R. Rhine (Ed.), *Making schools more effective: New directions from Follow Through* (pp. 249–288). New York: Academic Press.

Gilligan, C. (1977). In a different voice: Women's conceptions of self and of morality. *Harvard Educational Review, 47,* 481–517.

Gilligan, C. (1988). *The origins of morality in early childhood.* Working paper series No. 7. The Project on Interdependence at Radcliffe College, Cambridge, MA.

Glaser, R. (1990). The reemergence of learning theory within instructional research. *American Psychologist, 45,* 29–39.

Goffin, S. G. (1983). A framework for conceptualizing children's services. *American Journal of Orthopsychiatry, 53,* 282–290.

Goffin, S. G. (1989). Developing a research agenda for early childhood education: What can be learned from the research on teaching? *Early Childhood Research Quarterly, 4,* 187–204.

Goffin, S. G., & Lombardi, J. (1988). *Speaking out: Early childhood advocacy.* Washington, DC: National Association for the Education of Young Children.

Goodykoontz, B., Davis, M. D., & Gabbard, H. F. (1948). Recent history and present status of education for young children. In N. B. Henry (Ed.), *Early childhood education: The forty-sixth yearbook of The National Society for the Study of Education* (Part 2, pp. 44–69). Chicago: University of Chicago Press.

Gray, S. W., Ramsey, B. K., & Klaus, R. A. (1982). *From 3 to 20: The Early Training Project.* Baltimore: University Park Press.

Greenberg, P. (1987). Lucy Sprague Mitchell: A major missing link between early childhood education in the 1980s and Progressive Education in the 1890s–1930s. *Young Children, 42*(5), 70–84.

Greenberg, P. (1990a). Before the beginning: A participant's view. *Young Children, 45*(6), 41–52.

Greenberg, P. (1990b). *The devil has slippery shoes.* Youth Policy Institute, P.O. Box 40132, Washington, DC. (Originally published in 1969 by Macmillan)

Greenberg, P. (1992). Why not academic preschool? (Part 2). Autocracy or democracy in the classroom? *Young Children, 47*(3), 54–64.

Greene, M. (1988). What happened to imagination? In K. Egan & D. Nadaner (Eds.), *Imagination and education* (pp. 45–56). New York: Teachers College Press.

Greene, M. (1989). Beyond the predictable: Possibilities and purposes. In L. R. Williams & D. P. Fromberg (Eds.), The proceedings of *Defining the field of early childhood education: An invitational symposium* (pp. 153–179). Charlottesville, VA: W. Alton Foundation.

Greeno, J. J. (1989). A perspective on thinking. *American Psychologist, 44,* 134–141.

Gregory, B. C., Merrill, J. B., Payne, B., & Giddings, M. (Eds.) (1908). *The coordination of the kindergarten and the elementary school: Seventh yearbook of the National Society for the Scientific Study of Education* (Part 2). Chicago: University of Chicago Press.

Grubb, W. N. (1987). *Young children face the states: Issues and options for early childhood programs.* Paper prepared for the Center for Policy Research in Education, Rutgers University, New Brunswick, NJ.

Grubb, W. N., & Lazerson, M. (1988). *Broken promises: How Americans fail their children.* Chicago: The University of Chicago Press.

Haberman, M. (1988). What knowledge is of most worth to teachers of young children? *Early Child Development and Care, 38,* 33–41.

Harris, J. D., & Larsen, J. M. (1989). Parent education as a mandatory component of preschool: Effects on middle class, educationally advantaged parents and children. *Early Childhood Research Quarterly, 4,* 275–287.

Hartup, W. W. (1984). Commentary: Relationships and child development. In M. Perlmutter (Ed.), *Parent-child interaction and parent-child relations in child development, The Minnesota Symposia on child psychology* (Vol. 17, pp. 177–184). Hillsdale, NJ: Lawrence Erlbaum.

Hartup, W. W. (1989). Social relationships and their developmental significance. *American Psychologist, 44,* 120–126.

Haskins, R. (1989). Beyond metaphors: The efficacy of early childhood education. *American Psychologist, 44,* 274–282.

Hauser-Cram, P. (1990). Designing meaningful evaluations of early intervention services. In S. J. Meisels & J. P. Shonkoff (Eds.), *Handbook of early childhood intervention: Theory, practice, and analysis* (pp. 583–602). Cambridge, MA: Cambridge University Press.

Hauser-Cram, P., & Shonkoff, J. P. (1988). Rethinking the assessment of child-focused outcomes. In H. B. Weiss & F. H. Jacobs (Eds.), *Evaluating family programs* (pp. 73–94). New York: Aldine DeGruyter.

Hebbeler, K. (1985). An old and a new question on the effects of early education for children from low-income families. *Educational Evaluation and Policy Analysis, 7,* 207–216.

Hewes, D. W. (1983). (Letter to the editor.) *Young Children, 38*(4), 3.

Hiebert, E. H. (Ed.) (1988). Early childhood programs in public schools [special issue]. *The Elementary School Journal, 89*(2).

High/Scope Foundation. (1991). *The Child Observation Record.* Ypsilanti, MI: High/Scope Press.

Hilgard, E. R., & Bower, G. H. (1975). *Theories of learning* (4th ed.). Englewood Cliffs, NJ: Prentice-Hall.

Hodges, W., Branden, A., Feldman, R., Follins, J., Love, J., Sheehan, R., Lumbley, J., Osborn, J., Rentfrow, R. K., Houston, J., & Lee, C. (1980). *Follow Through: Forces for change in the primary schools.* Ypsilanti, MI: The High/Scope Press.

Hodges, W. L., & Sheehan, R. (1978). Follow Through as ten years of experimentation: What have we learned? *Young Children, 34*(1), 4–18.

Hofferth, S. L. (1989). What is the demand and supply of child care in the United States? *Young Children, 44*(5), 28–33.

Hofferth, S. L., & Phillips, D. A. (1987). Child care in the United States, 1970 to 1995. *Journal of Marriage and the Family, 49,* 559–571.

Hohmann, C. (1991). *High/Scope curriculum series. Mathematics.* Ypsilanti, MI: High/Scope Press.

Hohmann, C., & Buckleitner, W. (1992a). *High/Scope K–3 curriculum series. Learning environment.* Ypsilanti, MI: High/Scope Press.

Hohmann, C., & Buckleitner, W. (1992b, Fall). Getting started: Opening the doors to High/Scope's K–3 approach. *High/Scope ReSource, 11*(3), 1, 10–13.

Hohmann, M., Banet, B., & Weikart, D. (1979). *Young children in action: A manual for preschool educators.* Ypsilanti, MI: The High/Scope Press.

Horowitz, F. D., & O'Brien, M. (1989). In the interest of the nation: A reflective essay on the state of our knowledge and the challenges before us. *American Psychologist, 44,* 441–445.

Horowitz, F. D., & Paden, L. Y. (1973). The effectiveness of environmental early intervention programs. In B. M. Caldwell & H. N. Ricciuti (Eds.), *Review of child development research* (Vol. 3, pp. 331–402). Chicago: The University of Chicago Press.

House, E. R. (1990). Trends in evaluation. *Educational Researcher, 19*(3), 24–28.

House, E. R., Hutchins, E. J. (1979). Issues raised by the Follow Through evaluation. In L. G. Katz, M. Z. Glockner, C. Watkins, & M. Spencer (Eds.), *Current topics in early childhood education* (Vol. 2, pp. 1–11). Norwood, NJ: Ablex.

Hunt, J. McV. (1961). *Intelligence and experience.* New York: Ronald.

Hunt, J. McV. (1964). Introduction: Revisiting Montessori. In M. Montessori, *The Montessori Method* (pp. xi–xxxix). New York: Schocken.

Hunter, M. (1976). Teacher competency: Problem, theory, and practice. *Theory into Practice, 15,* 162–171.

Hunter, M. (1977). A tri-dimensional approach to individualization. *Educational Leadership, 34,* 351–355.

Hunter, M. (1979). Teaching is decision making. *Educational Leadership, 37,* 62–64.

Hymes, J. L., Jr. (1978). America's first nursery schools: An interview with Abigail A. Eliot. *Early childhood education living history interviews* (Book 1, pp. 7–25). Carmel, CA: Hacienda Press.

Hymes, J. L. (1985). Head Start: Hopes and disappointments. *Young Children, 40*(6), 16.

Inagaki, K. (1992). Piagetian and post-Piagetian conceptions of development and their implications for science education in early childhood. *Early Childhood Research Quarterly, 7,* 115–133.

Iran-Nejad, A., McKeachie, W. J., & Berliner, D. C. (1990a). The multisource nature of learning: An introduction. *Review of Educational Research, 60,* 509–515.

Iran-Nejad, A., McKeachie, W. J., & Berliner, D. C. (Eds.). (1990b). Toward a unified approach to learning as a multisource phenomenon [special issue]. *Review of Educational Research, 60*(4).

Issacs, S. (1966). *Intellectual growth in young children.* New York: Schocken Books. (Originally published in 1930)

Jacobs, F. (1988). The five-tiered approach to evaluation: Context and implementation. In. H. B. Weiss & F. H. Jacobs (Eds.), *Evaluating family programs* (pp. 37–68). New York: Aldine DeGruyter.

Jordan, T. J., Grallo, R., Deutsch, M., & Deutsch, C. P. (1985). Long-term effects of early enrichment: A 20-year perspective on persistence and change. *American Journal of Community Psychology, 13,* 393–415.

Kagan, J. (1983). Classifications of the child. In P. H. Mussen (Ed.), History, theory, and methods (Vol. 1, pp. 527–560). W. Kessen (Ed.), *Handbook of child psychology* (4th ed.). New York: John Wiley & Sons.

Kagan, J. (1984). *The nature of the child.* New York: Basic Books.

Kagan, S. L. (1987). Early schooling: On what grounds? In S. L. Kagan & E. F. Zigler (Eds). *Early schooling: The national debate* (pp. 3–23). New Haven, CT: Yale University Press.

Kagan, S. L. (1989). Early care and education: Tackling the tough issues. *Phi Delta Kappan, 70,* 433–439.

Kagan, S. L. (1990). *Excellence in early childhood education: Defining characteristics and next-decade strategies.* Washington, DC: Office of Educational Research and Improvement, U.S. Department of Education.

Kagan, S. L. (Ed.). (1991). Editor's Preface. *The care and education of America's young children: Obstacles and opportunities.* The Ninetieth Yearbook of the National Society for the Study of Education, Part I (pp. ix–xiii). Chicago: University of Chicago Press.

Kagan, S. L., & Garcia, E. E. (Eds.). (1991). Educating linguistically and culturally diverse preschoolers [special issue]. *Early Childhood Research Quarterly, 6*(3).

Kagan, S. L., Powell, D. R., Weissbourd, B., & Zigler, E. F. (Eds.). (1987). *America's family support programs.* New Haven, CT: Yale University Press.

Kagan, S. L., & Zigler, E. F. (1987). Preface. In S. L. Kagan & E. F. Zigler (Eds.), *Early schooling: The national debate* (pp. xiii–xviii). New Haven, CT: Yale University Press.

Kamii, C. K. (1971). Evaluation of learning in preschool education: Socio-emotional, perceptual-motor, and cognitive development. In B. S. Bloom, J. T. Hastings, & G. Madaus (Eds.), *Handbook on formative and summative evaluation of student learning* (pp. 281–398). New York: McGraw-Hill.

Kamii, C. (1972). A sketch of the Piaget-derived preschool curriculum developed by the Ypsilanti Early Education Program. In S. J. Braun & E. Edwards (Eds.), *History and theory of early childhood education* (pp. 295–312). Worthington, OH: Charles A. Jones.

Kamii, C. (1975). One intelligence indivisible. *Young Children, 30,* 228–237.

Kamii, C. (1981a). Application of Piaget's theory to education: The preoperational level. In I. E. Sigel, D. M. Brodzinsky, & R. M. Golinkoff (Eds.), *New directions in Piagetian theory and practice* (pp. 231–363). Hillsdale, NJ: Lawrence Erlbaum.

Kamii, C. (1981b). Teachers' autonomy and scientific training. *Young Children, 36*(4), 5–14.

Kamii, C. (1982). *Number in preschool and kindergarten: Educational implications of Piaget's theory.* Washington, DC: National Association for the Education of Young Children.

Kamii, C. (1984). Autonomy: The aim of education envisioned by Piaget. *Phi Delta Kappan, 65,* 410–415.

Kamii, C. (1985). Leading primary education toward excellence. *Young Children, 40*(6), 3–9.

Kamii, C. (1992). Autonomy as the aim of constructivist education: How can it be fostered? In D. G. Murphy & S. G. Goffin (Eds.), *Project Construct: A curriculum guide. Understanding the possibilities* (pp. 9–14). Jefferson City: Missouri Department of Elementary and Secondary Education.

Kamii, C. K., with DeClark, G. (1985). *Young children reinvent arithmetic: Implications of Piaget's theory.* New York: Teachers College Press.

Kamii, C., & DeVries, R. (1976). *Piaget, children, and number.* Washington, DC: National Association for the Education of Young Children.

Kamii, C., & DeVries, R. (1977). Piaget for early education. In M. C. Day & R. K. Parker (Eds.), *The preschool in action: Exploring early childhood programs* (2nd ed., pp. 365–420). Boston: Allyn & Bacon.

Kamii, C., & DeVries, R. (1978). *Physical knowledge in preschool education: Implications of Piaget's theory.* Englewood Cliffs, NJ: Prentice-Hall.

Kamii, C., & DeVries, R. (1980). *Group games in early education: Implications of Piaget's theory.* Washington, DC: National Association for the Education of Young Children.

Kamii, C., DeVries, R., Ellis, M., & Zaritsky, R. (1975). *Playing with rollers: A preschool teacher uses Piaget's theory.* [Film]. Chicago: Office of Instructional Resources Development, University of Illinois at Chicago Circle.

Kamii, C., & Joseph, L. (1989). *Young children continue to reinvent arithmetic, 2nd grade.* New York: Teachers College Press.

Kamii, C. K., & Radin, N. L. (1967). A framework for a preschool curriculum based on some Piagetian concepts. *Journal of Creative Behavior, 1,* 314–324.

Kamii, C. K., & Radin, N. L. (1970). A framework for a preschool curriculum based on some Piagetian concepts. In I. J. Athey & D. O. Rubadeau (Eds.), *Educational implications of Piaget's theory* (pp. 89–100). Waltham, MA: Gina-Blaisdell.

Kantor, R., Elgas, P. M., Fernie, D. E. (1989). First the look and then the sound: Creating conversations at circle time. *Early Childhood Research Quarterly, 4,* 433–448.

Karmiloff-Smith, A. (1992). *Beyond modularity: A developmental perspective on cognitive science.* Cambridge, MA: MIT Press.

Karnes, M. B., Shwedel, A. M., & Williams, M. B. (1983). A comparison of five approaches for educating young children from low-income homes. In The Consortium for Longitudinal Studies (Ed.), *As the twig is bent . . . Lasting effects of preschool programs* (pp. 133–169). Hillsdale, NJ: Lawrence Erlbaum.

Karweit, N. (1988). Quality and quantity of learning time in preprimary programs. *The Elementary School Journal, 89,* 119–133.

Kennedy, M. M. (1978). Findings from the Follow Through Planned Variation Study. *Educational Researcher, 6*(6), 3–11.

Kerr, D. H. (1981). The structure of quality in teaching. In J. F. Soltis (Ed.), *Philosophy and education,* Eightieth Yearbook of the National Society for the Study of Education, Part I (pp. 61–93). Chicago: University of Chicago Press.

Kessel, F. S., & Siegel, A. W. (Eds.). (1983). *The child and other cultural inventions.* New York: Praeger.

Kessen, W. (1979). The American child and other cultural inventions. *American Psychologist, 34,* 815–820.

Kessen, W. (1983). The child and other cultural inventions. In F. S. Kessel & A. W. Siegel (Eds.), *The child and other cultural inventions* (pp. 26–47). New York: Praeger.

Kessler, S. A. (1990, April). *Early childhood education as caring.* Paper presented at the annual meeting of the American Educational Research Association, Boston.

Kessler, S. A. (1991a). Alternative perspectives on early childhood education. *Early Childhood Research Quarterly, 6,* 183–197.

Kessler, S. A. (1991b). Early childhood education as development: Critique of the metaphor. *Early Education and Development, 2,* 137–152.

Key experiences in mathematics. (1990). Mimeographed handout from High/Scope K–3 Training Workshop.

Kilpatrick, W. H. (1914). *The Montessori system examined.* Boston: Houghton Mifflin.

Kliebard, H. M. (1986). *The struggle for the American curriculum 1893–1958.* New York: Routledge.

Kohlberg, L. (1981). From *is* to *ought*: How to commit the naturalistic fallacy and get away with it in the study of moral development. In L. Kohlberg, *The philosophy of moral development: Moral stages and the idea of justice* (pp. 101–189). San Francisco: Harper & Row.

Kohlberg, L. (1984). *The psychology of moral development.* New York: Harper & Row.

Kohlberg, L., & Lickona, T. (1987). Moral discussion and the class meeting. In R. DeVries & L. Kohlberg, *Constructivist early education: An overview and comparison with other programs* (pp. 143–181). New York: Longman. (Published in 1990 as *Constructivist education: Overview and comparison with other programs* by the National Association for the education of Young Children)

Kohlberg, L., & Mayer, R. (1972). Development as the aim of education. *Harvard Educational Review, 42,* 449–496.

Kramer, R. (1988). *Maria Montessori: A biography.* Reading, MA: Addison-Wesley. (Originally published in 1976)

Labov, W. (1969). *The study of non-standard English.* Washington, DC: ERIC Clearinghouse for Linguistics.

Lally, J. R., Mangione, P. L., Honig, A., & Wittner, D. S. (1988). More pride, less delinquency: Findings from the 10-year follow-up study of the Syracuse University Family Development Research Program. *Zero to Three, 4*(4), 13–18.

Lampert, M. (1985). How do teachers manage to teach? Perspectives on problems in practice. *Harvard Educational Review, 55,* 178–194.

Laosa, L. M. (1982). The sociocultural context of evaluation. In B. Spodek (Ed.), *Handbook of research in early childhood education* (pp. 501–520). New York: The Free Press.

Larsen, J. M., & Robinson, C. C. (1989). Later effects of preschool on low-risk children. *Early Childhood Research Quarterly, 4,* 133–144.

Lavatelli, C. (1970). *Piaget's theory applied to an early childhood curriculum.* Boston: American Science and Engineering.

Lavatelli, C. (1971). Introduction to early childhood education series. In E. D. Evans, *Contemporary influences in early childhood education* (pp. vii–viii). New York: Holt, Rinehart & Winston.

Lawton, J. T., & Fowell, N. (1989). A description of teacher and child language in two preschool programs. *Early Childhood Research Quarterly, 4,* 407–432.

Lazar, I. (1980). Social research and social policy: Reflections on relationships. In R. Haskins & J. J. Gallagher (Eds.), *Care and education of young children in America* (pp. 59–71). Norwood, NJ: Ablex.

Lazar, I. (1983). Discussion and implications of the findings. In the Consortium for Longitudinal Studies (Ed.), *As the twig is bent . . . Lasting effects of preschool programs* (pp. 461–466). Hillsdale, NJ: Lawrence Erlbaum.

Lazar, I. (1988). Measuring the effects of early childhood programs. *Early Childhood Family Education, 15*(2), 8–11.

Lazerson, M. (1970). Social reform and early childhood education: Some historical perspectives. *Urban Education, 5,* 83–102.

Lazerson, M. (1972). The historical antecedents of early childhood education. In I. J. Gordon (Ed.), *Early childhood education. The seventy-first yearbook of the National Society for the Study of Education,* Part 2 (pp. 33–53). Chicago: University of Chicago Press.

Lee, P. C. (1989). Is the young child egocentric or sociocentric? *Teachers College Record, 90,* 375–391.

Lee, V. E., Brooks-Gunn, J., & Schnur, E. (1988). Does Head Start work? A 1-year follow-up comparison of disadvantaged children attending Head Start, no preschool, and other preschool programs. *Developmental Psychology, 24,* 210–222.

Lee, V. E., Brooks-Gunn, J., Schnur, E., & Liaw, F-R. (1990). Are Head Start effects sustained? A longitudinal follow-up comparison of disadvantaged children attending Head Start, no preschool, and other preschool programs. *Child Development, 61,* 495–507.

Lerner, R. M. (1987). The concept of plasticity in development. In J. J. Gallagher & C. T. Ramey (Eds.), *The malleability of children* (pp. 3–14). Baltimore: Paul H. Brookes.

Levin, H. M. (1988, June). *Cost-benefit and cost-effectiveness analysis of interventions for children in poverty.* Paper presented for a Working Conference on Poverty and Children, Lawrence, KS.

Liljestrom, R. (1983). The public child, the commercial child, and our child. In F. S. Kessel & A. W. Siegel (Eds.), *The child and other cultural inventions* (pp. 124–157). New York: Praeger.

Lubeck, S. (1985). *Sandbox society: Early education in black and white America.* London: The Falmer Press.

Maccoby, E. E., & Zellner, M. (1970). *Experiments in primary education: Aspects of Project Follow-Through.* New York: Harcourt Brace Jovanovich.

Macmillan, C. J. B., & Garrison, J. W. (1984). Using the "new philosophy of science" in criticizing current research traditions in education. *Educational Researcher, 13*(10), 15–21.

Maehr, J. (1991). *High/Scope K–3 curriculum series. Language and literacy.* Ypsilanti, MI: High/Scope Press.

Mayer, R. S. (1971). A comparative analysis of preschool curriculum models. In R. H. Anderson & H. G. Shane (Eds.), *As the twig is bent. Readings in early childhood education* (pp. 286–314). Boston: Houghton-Mifflin.

McDermott, J. J. (1965). Introduction. In M. Montessori, *The advanced Montessori Method: Spontaneous activity in education* (pp. xi–xxviii). New York: Schocken.

Melton, G. B. (1987). The clashing of symbols: Prelude to child and family policy. *American Psychologist, 42,* 345–354.

Miller, L. B. (1979). Development of curriculum models in Head Start. In E. Zigler & J. Valentine (Eds.), *Project Head Start: A legacy of the War on Poverty* (pp. 195–220). New York: The Free Press.

Miller, L. B., & Bizzell, L. P. (1983a). Long-term effects of four preschool programs: Sixth, seventh, and eighth grades. *Child Development, 54,* 727–741.

Miller, L. B., & Bizzell, L. P. (1983b). The Louisville experiment: A comparison of four programs. In The Consortium for Longitudinal Studies (Ed.), *As the twig is bent . . . Lasting effects of preschool programs* (pp. 171–199). Hillsdale, NJ: Lawrence Erlbaum.

Miller, L. B., Bugbee, M. R., & Hybertson, D. W. (1985). Dimensions of preschool: The effects of individual experience. In I. E. Siegel (Ed.), *Advances in applied developmental psychology* (Vol. 1, pp. 25–90). Norwood, NJ: Ablex.

Miller, L. B., & Dyer, J. L. (1975). Four preschool programs: Their dimensions and effects. *Monographs of the Society for Research in Child Development, 40*(5–6, Serial No. 162).

Mitchell, A., & David, J. (1992). *Explorations with young children: A curriculum guide from the Bank Street College of Education.* Mt. Ranier, MD: Gryphon.

Mitchell, A., Seligson, M., & Marx, F. (1989). *Early childhood programs and the public schools: Between promise and practice.* Dover, MA: Auburn Publishing

Montessori, M. (1913). *Pedagogical anthropology* (F. T. Cooper, Trans.). New York: Frederick A. Stokes.

Montessori, M. (1948). *The discovery of the child* (M. A. Johnstone, Trans.). Adyar, Madras, India: Kalakshetra Publications.

Montessori, M. (1963). *The absorbent mind* (C. A. Claremont, Trans.). Adyar, Madras, India: The Theosophical Publishing House. (Original work published 1949)

Montessori, M. (1964). *The advanced Montessori Method: The Montessori elementary material* (A. Livingston, Trans.). New York: Schocken. (Original work published in English in 1917)

Montessori, M. (1964). *Dr. Montessori's own handbook.* Cambridge, MA: Robert Bentley. (Original work published 1914)

Montessori, M. (1964). *The Montessori Method* (A. E. George, Trans.). New York: Schocken. (Original work published in English in 1912)

Montessori, M. (1965). *The advanced Montessori Method: Spontaneous activity in education* (F. Simmonds, Trans.). New York: Schocken. (Original work published in English in 1917)

Montessori, M. (1966). *The secret of childhood* (M. Joseph Costelloe, Trans.). Notre Dame, IN: Fides (Original work published 1937)

Montessori, M. (1970). *The child in the family* (N. R. Cirillo, Trans.). Chicago: Henry Regnery. (Original work published in English in 1936)

Moore, S. G. (1977). Research in review. Old and new approaches to preschool education. *Young Children, 33*(1), 69–72.

Moore, S. G. (1983). Comments on Weikart's chapter. In M. Perlmutter (Ed.), *Development and policy concerning children with special needs, The Minnesota Symposia on child psychology* (Vol. 16, pp. 197–205). Hillsdale, NJ: Lawrence Erlbaum.

Moskovitz, S. T. (1968). Some assumptions underlying the Bereiter approach. *Young Children, 24,* 24–31.

Murphy, D., & Baker, O. (1990). The approach of a state department. In C. Kamii (Ed.), *Achievement in the early grades: The games grown-ups play* (pp. 101–109). Washington, DC: National Association for the Education of Young Children.

Murray, F. (1979). The generation of educational practice from developmental theory. *Educational Psychology, 14,* 30–43.

NAEYC Organizational History and Archives Committee. (1976). NAEYC's first half century, 1926–1976. *Young Children, 31,* 462–476.

National Association for the Education of Young Children and National Association of Early Childhood Specialists in State Departments of Education. (1991). Position statement: Guidelines for appropriate curriculum content and assessment in programs serving children ages 3 through 8. *Young Children, 46*(3), 21–38.

National Association of Elementary School Principals. (1990). *Early childhood education and the elementary school principal: Standards for quality programs for young children.* Alexandria, VA: Author.

National Association of State Boards of Education. (1988). *Right from the Start.* Alexandria, VA: Author.

National Association of State Boards of Education. (1991). *Caring communities.* Alexandria, VA: Author.

National Commission on Children. (1991). *Beyond rhetoric: A new American agenda for children and families.* Final report of the National Commission on Children. Washington, DC: Author.

Nuthall, G., & Snook, I. (1973). Contemporary models of teaching. In R. M. W. Travers (Ed.), *The second handbook of research on teaching* (pp. 47–76). Chicago: Rand McNally.

O'Brien, L. M. (1993). Teacher values and classroom culture: Teaching and learning in a rural, Appalachian Head Start program. *Early Education and Development, 4,* 5–19.

Ogbu, J. U. (1987). Cultural influences on plasticity in human development. In J. J. Gallagher & C. T. Ramey (Eds.), *The malleability of children* (pp. 155–169). Baltimore: Paul H. Brookes.

Osborn, D. K. (1980). *Early childhood education in historical perspective.* Athens, GA: Education Associates.

Osborne, D., & Gaebler, D. (1993). *Reinventing government: How the entrepreneurial spirit is transforming the public sector.* New York: Plume.

Peters, D. L. (1977). Early childhood education: An overview and evaluation. In H. L. Hom, Jr. & P. A. Robinson (Eds.), *Psychological processes in early education* (pp. 1–21). New York: Academic Press.

Peters, D. L., Neisworth, J. T., & Yawkey, T. D. (1985). *Early childhood education: From theory to practice.* Monterey, CA: Brooks/Cole.

Phillips, D. A. (1987). Epilogue. In D. A. Phillips (Ed.), *Quality in child care: What does research tell us?* (pp. 122–126). Washington, DC: National Association for the Education of Young Children.

Phillips, D. A., & Howes, C. (1987). Indicators of quality child care: Review of research. In D. A. Phillips (Ed.), *Quality in child care: What does research tell us?* (pp. 1–19). Washington, DC: National Association for the Education of Young Children.

Pinar, W. F. (Ed.). (1988). Introduction. *Contemporary curriculum discourses* (pp. 1–13). Scottsdale, AZ: Gorsuch Scarisbrick.

Pitcher, E. (1966). An evaluation of the Montessori Method in schools for young children. *Childhood Education, 42,* 489–492.

Pizzo, P. (1983). Slouching toward Bethlehem: American federal policy perspectives on children and their families. In E. F. Zigler, S. L. Kagan, & E. Klugman (Eds.), *Children, families, and government. Perspectives on American social policy* (pp. 10–32). Cambridge, MA: Cambridge University Press.

Plomin, R. (1989). Environment and genes: Determinants of behavior. *American Psychologist, 44,* 105–111.

Polakow, V. (1986). Some reflections on the landscape of childhood and the politics of care. *Journal of Education, 168*(3), 7–12.

Polakow, V. (1989). Deconstructing development. *Journal of Education, 171*(2), 75–87.

Postman, N. (1982). *The disappearance of childhood.* New York: Delacorte.

Powell, D. R. (1987a). Comparing preschool curricula and practices: The state of research. In S. L. Kagan & E. F. Zigler (Eds.), *Early schooling: The national debate* (pp. 190–211). New Haven, CT: Yale University Press.

Powell, D. R. (1987b). Methodological and conceptual issues in research. In S. L. Kagan, D. R. Powell, B. Weissbourd, & E. F. Zigler (Eds.), *America's family support programs* (pp. 311–328). New Haven, CT: Yale University Press.

Pratt, C. (1990). *I learn from children.* New York: Perennial Library. (Originally published in 1948)

Ramey, C. T., Bryant, D. M., & Suarez, T. M. (1985). Preschool compensatory education and the modifiability of intelligence: A critical review. In D. Ditterman (Ed.), *Current topics in intelligence* (pp. 247–298). Norwood, NJ: Ablex.

Ramey, C.T., & Suarez, T. M. (1984). Early intervention and the early experience paradigm: Toward a better framework for social policy. *Journal of Children in Contemporary Society, 17,* 3–13.

Ramp, E. A., & Rhine, W. R. (1981). Behavior analysis model. In W. R. Rhine (Ed.), *Making schools more effective: New directions from Follow Through* (pp. 155–200). New York: Academic Press.

Random House. (1988). *The Random House College Dictionary* (rev. ed.). New York: Author.

Rashid, H. M. (1984). The role of case studies in the longitudinal evaluation of preschool effects: Some make it, some don't. *Dimensions, 12*(2), 11–14.

Read, K. (1966). *The nursery school: A human relations laboratory.* Philadelphia: W. B. Saunders.

Reese, H. W., & Overton, W. R. (1970). Models of development and theories of development. In L. R. Goulet & P. B. Bales (Eds.), *Life span developmental psychology: Research and theory* (pp. 116–145) New York: Academic Press.

Rescorla, L., Hyson, M. C., Hirsh-Pasek, K. (Eds.). (1991a). Editors' notes. Academic instruction in early childhood: Challenge or pressure? *New directions for child development* (No. 53, pp. 1–4). San Francisco: Jossey-Bass.

Rescorla, L., Hyson, M. C., Hirsh-Pasek, K. (Eds.). (1991b). Academic instruction in early childhood: Challenge or pressure? *New directions for child development* (No. 53). San Francisco: Jossey-Bass.

Reynolds, A. J. (1992). Mediated effects of preschool intervention. *Early education and development, 3,* 139–164.

Rhine, W. R. (Ed.). (1981). *Making schools more effective: New directions from Follow Through.* New York: Academic Press.

Rickover, H. G. (1959). *Education and freedom.* New York: E.P. Dutton.

Rivlin, A. M., & Timpane, P. M. (1975). Planned variation in education: An assessment. In A. M. Rivlin & P. M. Timpane (Eds.), *Planned variation in education: Should we give up or try harder?* (pp. 1–21). Washington, DC: The Brookings Institution.

Rogers, V. R. (1970). *Teaching in the British primary school.* New York: Macmillan.

Rogoff, B., & Moreilli, G. (1989). Perspectives on children's development in cultural psychology. *American Psychologist, 44,* 343–348.

Royce, J. M., Murray, H. W., Lazar, I., & Darlington, R. B. (1982). Methods of evaluating program outcomes. In B. Spodek (Ed.), *Handbook of research in early childhood education* (pp. 618–652). New York: The Free Press.

Rutter, M. (1985). Family and school influences on cognitive development. *Journal of Child Psychology and Psychiatry, 26,* 683–704.

Scheffler, I. (1991). Four languages of education. *In praise of the cognitive emotions and other essays in the philosophy of education* (pp. 118–125). New York: Routledge.

Schon, D. A. (1983). *The reflective practitioner: How professionals think in practice.* New York: Basic Books.

Schubert, W. H. (1986). *Curriculum: Perspective, paradigm, and possibility.* New York: Macmillan.

Schwandt, T. A. (1989). Recapturing the moral discourse in evaluation. *Educational Researcher, 18*(8), 11–16, 35.

Schweinhart, L. J. (1987, Spring–Summer). Child-initiated activity: How important is it in early childhood education? *High/Scope ReSource, 6*(2), 1, 6–10.

Schweinhart, L. J., & McNair, S. (1991). New Child Observation Record (COR) for ages 2½ – 6. *High/Scope ReSource, 10*(3), 4–7.

Schweinhart, L. J., & Weikart, D. P. (1985). Evidence that good early childhood programs work. *Phi Delta Kappan,66,* 545–553.

Schweinhart, L. J., & Weikart, D. P. (1993). Changed lives, Significant benefits: The High/Scope Perry Preschool project to date. *High/Scope ReSource, 12*(3), 1, 10–14.

Schweinhart, L. J., Weikart, D. P., & Larner, M. B. (1986). Consequences of three preschool curriculum models through age 15. *Early Childhood Research Quarterly, 1,* 15–45.

Seitz, V. (1987). Outcome evaluation of family support programs: Research design alternatives to true experiments. In S. L. Kagan, D. R. Powell, B. Weissbourd, & E. F. Zigler (Eds.), *America's family support programs* (pp. 329–344). New Haven, CT: Yale University Press.

Selman, R. (1980). *The growth of interpersonal understanding.* New York: Academic Press.

Selman, R., & Kohlberg, L. (1972a). *First things: Values.* White Plains, NY: Guidance Associates.

Selman, R., & Kohlberg, L. (1972b). *A strategy for teaching values.* Pleasantville, NY: Guidance Associates.

Selman, R., Kohlberg, L., & Byrne, D. (1974a). *A strategy for teaching social reasoning.* Pleasantville, NY: Guidance Associates.

Selman, R., Kohlberg, L., & Byrne, D. (1974b). *First things: Social reasoning.* White Plains, NY: Guidance Associates.

Senge, P. M. (1990). *The fifth discipline: The art and practice of the learning organization.* New York: Doubleday.

Shapiro, E., & Biber, B. (1972). The education of young children: A developmental-interaction approach. *Teachers College Record, 74,* 55–79.

Shapiro, E., & Mitchell, A. (1992). Principles of the Bank Street approach. In A. Mitchell & J. David (Eds.), *Explorations with young children: A curriculum guide from the Bank Street College of Education.* Mt. Ranier, MD: Gryphon.

Shapiro, E. K., & Wallace, D. B. (1981). Developmental stage theory and the individual reconsidered. In E. K. Shapiro & E. Weber (Eds.), *Cognitive and affective growth: Developmental interaction* (pp. 111–130). Hillsdale, NJ: Lawrence Erlbaum.

Shapiro, E. K., & Weber, E. (Eds.). (1981). *Cognitive and affective growth: Developmental interaction.* Hillsdale, NJ: Lawrence Erlbaum.

Shulman, L. S. (1987). Knowledge and teaching: Foundations of the new reform. *Harvard Educational Review, 57,* 1–22.

Siegel, I. (1972). Developmental theory and preschool education: Issues, problems and implication. In I. J. Gordon (Ed.), *Early childhood education,* The Seventy-first Yearbook of the National Society for the Study of Education, Part II (pp. 13–31). Chicago: The University of Chicago Press.

Sigel, A. W., & White, S. H. (1982). The child study movement: Early growth and development of the symbolized child. In H. R. Reese (Ed.), *Advances in child development and behavior* (Vol. 17, pp. 233–285). New York: Academic Press.

Sigel, I. E. (1990). Psychoeducational intervention: Future directions. *Merrill-Palmer Quarterly, 36,* 159–172.

Sigel, I. E. (1991). Preschool education: For whom and why? In L. Rescorla, M. C. Hyson, & K. Hirsh-Pasek (Eds.), Academic instruction in early childhood: Challenge or pressure? *New directions for child development* (No. 53, pp. 83–91). San Francisco: Jossey-Bass.

Silin, J. G. (1985). Authority as knowledge: A problem of professionalization. *Young Children, 40*(3) 41–46.

Silin, J. G. (1986). Psychology, politics, and the discourse of early childhood educators. *Teachers College Record, 87,* 611–617.

Silin, J. G. (1987). The early childhood educator's knowledge base: A reconsideration. In L. G. Katz & K. Steiner (Eds.), *Current topics in early childhood education* (Vol. 7, pp. 17–31). Norwood, NJ: Ablex.

Silin, J. G. (1988). On becoming knowledgeable professionals. In B. Spodek, O. N. Saracho, & D. L. Peters (Eds.), *Professionalism and the early childhood practitioner* (pp. 117–134). New York: Teachers College Press.

Silver Ribbon Panel. (1990). *Head Start: The nation's pride, A nation's challenge.* Alexandria, VA: National Head Start Association.

Simons, J. A., & Simons, F. A. (1986). Montessori and regular preschools: A comparison. In L. G. Katz & K. Steiner (Eds.), *Current topics in early childhood education* (Vol. 6, pp. 195–223). Norwood, NJ: Ablex.

Skeels, H. M. (1966). Adult status of children with contrasting early life experiences. *Monographs of the Society for Research in Child Development, 31*(3, Serial No. 105).

Skeels, H. M., & Dye, H. B. (1939). A study of the effects of differential stimulation on mentally retarded children. *Proceedings and addresses of the American Association on Mental Deficiency, 44,* 114–136.

Skrtic, T. (1991). The crisis in modern knowledge. *Behind special education: A critical analysis of professional and school organization* (pp. 1–24). Denver: Love.

Smilansky, S. (1968). *The effects of sociodramatic play on disadvantaged preschool children.* New York: John Wiley & Sons.

Sonquist, H. D., & Kamii, C. K. (1967). Applying some Piagetian concepts in the classroom for the disadvantaged. *Young Children, 22,* 231–246.

Spodek, B. (1973). *Early childhood education.* Englewood Cliffs, NJ: Prentice-Hall.

Spodek, B. (1977). What constitutes worthwhile educational experiences for young children? In B. Spodek (Ed.), *Teaching practices: Reexamining assumptions* (pp. 5–20). Washington, DC: National Association for the Education of Young Children.

Spodek, B. (1986). Development, values, and knowledge in the kindergarten curriculum. In B. Spodek (Ed.), *Today's kindergarten: Exploring the knowledge base. Expanding the curriculum* (pp. 32–47). New York: Teachers College Press.

Spodek, B. (1988). Conceptualizing today's kindergarten. *The Elementary School Journal, 89,* 203–211.

Spodek, B., & Walberg, H. J. (1977). Introduction: From a time of plenty. In B. Spodek & H. J. Walberg (Eds.), *Early childhood education: Issues and insights* (pp. 1–7). Berkeley, CA: McCutchan.

Stallings, J. A. (1975). Implementations and child effects of teaching practices in Follow Through classrooms. *Monograph of the Society for Research in Child Development, 40,* 7–8.

Stallings, J. A., & Stipek, D. (1986). Research on early childhood and elementary school programs. In M. C. Wittrock (Ed.), *Handbook of research on teaching* (pp. 727–753). New York: Macmillan.

Steiner, G. Y. (1981). *The futility of family policy.* Washington, DC: The Brookings Institution.

Suransky, V. P. (1982). *The erosion of childhood.* Chicago: University of Chicago Press.

Sutton-Smith, B. (1989). Radicalizing childhood. In L. R. Williams & D. P. Fromberg (Eds.), The proceedings of *Defining the field of early childhood education: An invitational symposium* (pp. 77–151). Charlottesville, VA: W. Alton Jones Foundation.

Swadener, B. B., & Kessler, S. (Eds.). (1991a). Introduction to the special issue. *Early Education and Development, 2,* 85–94.

Swadener, B. B., & Kessler, S. (Eds.). (1991b). Reconceptualizing early childhood education [special issue]. *Early Education and Development, 2*(2).

Stodolsky, S. S. (1984). Teacher evaluation: The limits of looking. *Educational Researcher, 13*(9), 11–18.

Takanishi, R. (1979). Evaluation of early childhood programs: Toward a developmental perspective. In L. G. Katz, M. Z. Glockner, C. Watkins, & M. J. Spencer (Eds.), *Current topics in early childhood education,* (Vol. 2, pp. 141–168). Norwood, NJ: Ablex.

Takanishi, R. (1981). Early childhood education and research: The changing relationship. *Theory into Practice, 20,* 86–92.

Tharp, R. G. (1989). Psychocultural variables and constants: Effects on teaching and learning in schools. *American Psychologist, 44,* 349–359.

Tobin, J. J., Wu, D. Y. H., & Davidson, D. H. (1989). *Preschool in three cultures.* New Haven, CT: Yale University Press.

Toffler, A. (1990). *Power shift.* New York: Bantam Books.

Travers, J. R., & Light, R. J. (Eds.). (1982). *Learning from experience.* Washington, DC: National Academy Press.

U. S. Department of Education. (1986). *What works: Research about teaching and learning.* Washington, DC: Author.

U.S. Department of Education. (1991). *America 2000: An education strategy.* Washington, DC: Author.

Vandenberg, B. (1993, March). *Is development an anachronism?* Paper presented at the Society for Research in Child Development, New Orleans.

Vinovskis, M. A. (1993). Early childhood education: Then and now. *Daedalus, 122,* 151–176.

Vygotsky, L. S. (1978). *Mind in society: The development of higher psychological processes.* Cambridge, MA: Harvard University Press.

Wallgren, C. (1990, Spring/Summer). Introducing a developmentally appropriate curriculum in the primary grades. *High/Scope ReSource, 9*(2), 4–10.

Walsh, D. J. (1987). Changes in kindergarten: Why Here? Why Now? *Early Childhood Research Quarterly, 4,* 377–391.

Walsh, D. J., Smith, M. E., Alexander, M,. & Ellwein, M. C. (in press). The curriculum as mysterious and constraining: Teachers' negotiations of the first year of a pilot program for at-risk four-year-olds. *Journal of Curriculum Studies.*

Warger, C. (Ed.). (1988). *A resource guide to public school early childhood programs.* Alexandria, VA: Association for Supervision and Curriculum Development.

Weber, E. (1969). *The kindergarten: Its encounter with educational thought in America.* New York: Teachers College Press.

Weber, E. (1970). *Early childhood education: Perspectives on change.* Worthington, OH: Charles A. Jones.

Weber, E. (1984). *Ideas influencing early childhood education: A theoretical analysis.* New York: Teachers College Press.

Weikart, D. P. (1981). Effects of different curricula in early childhood intervention. *Educational Evaluation and Policy Analysis, 3,* 25–35.

Weikart, D. P. (1983). A longitudinal view of a preschool research effort. In M. Perlmutter (Ed.), *Development and policy concerning children with special needs, The Minnesota Symposia on child psychology* (Vol, 16, pp. 175–196). Hillsdale, NJ: Lawrence Erlbaum.

Weikart, D. P. (1984). Preface. In J. R. Berrueta-Clement, L. J. Schweinhart, W. S. Barnett, A. S. Epstein, & D. P. Weikart, *Changed lives: The effects of the Perry Preschool Program on youths through age 19.* Ypsilanti, MI: High/Scope Press.

Weikart, D. P. (1987). Curriculum quality in early education. In S. L. Kagan & E. F. Zigler (Eds.), *Early schooling: The national debate* (pp. 168–189). New Haven, CT: Yale University Press.

Weikart, D. P. (1988). Quality in early childhood education. In C. Warger (Ed.), *A resource guide to public school early childhood programs.* Alexandria, VA: Association for Supervision and Curriculum Development.

Weikart, D. P. (1989). *Quality preschool programs: A long-term social investment.* New York: Ford Foundation.

Weikart, D. P. (1990, Fall). Celebrating 20 years. *High/Scope ReSource, 9*(3), 11–16, 22–23.

Weikart, D. P. (1992, Winter). "The right stuff": Early childhood programs with lasting impact. *High/Scope ReSource, 11*(1), 1, 10–13.

Weikart, D. P., Hohmann, C. F., & Rhine, W. R. (1981). High/Scope Cognitively Oriented Curriculum model. In W. R. Rhine (Ed.), *Making schools more effective: New directions from Follow Through* (pp. 201–247). New York: Academic Press.

Weikart, D. P., Rogers, L., Adcock, C., & McClelland, D. (1971). *The cognitively oriented classroom—A framework for preschool teachers.* Urbana: University of Illinois.

Weikart, D. P., & Schweinhart, L. J. (1987). The High/Scope Cognitively Oriented Curriculum in early education. In J. L. Roopnarine & J. E. Johnson (Eds.), *Approaches to early childhood education* (pp. 253–268). New York: Merrill/Macmillan.

Weikart, D. P, & Schweinhart, L. (1993). The High/Scope Curriculum for early childhood care and education. In J. L. Roopnarine & J. E. Johnson (Eds.), *Approaches to early childhood education* (2nd ed., pp. 195–208). New York: Merrill/Macmillan.

Weinberg, R. A. (1979). Early childhood education and intervention: Establishing an American tradition. *American Psychologist, 34,* 912–916.

Weiss, B. (1992). Foreword. In J. Chattin-McNichols (Ed.), *The Montessori controversy* (p. iv) Albany, NY: Delmar.

Weiss, C. H. (1983). Ideology, interests, and information: The basis of policy decisions. In D. Callahan & B. Jennings (Eds.), *Ethics, the social sciences, and policy analysis* (pp. 213–245). New York: Plenum.

Weiss, H. B. (1988). Family support and educational programs: Working through ecological theories of human development. In H. B. Weiss & F. H. Jacobs (Eds.), *Evaluating family programs* (pp. 3–36). New York: Aldine DeGruyter.

Welker, R. (1991). Expertise and the teacher as expert: Rethinking a questionable metaphor. *American Educational Research Journal, 28,* 19–35.

White, K. R. (1988). Cost analysis in family support programs. In H. B. Weiss & F. H. Jacobs (Eds.), *Evaluating family programs* (pp. 429–433). New York: Aldine DeGruyter.

White, S. H. (1970). The learning theory tradition and child psychology. In P. H. Mussen (Ed.), *Carmichael's manual of child psychology* (Vol. 1, pp. 657–701). New York: John Wiley & Sons.

White, S. H. (1983a). The idea of development in developmental psychology. In R. M. Lerner (Ed.), *Developmental psychology: Historical and philosophical perspectives* (pp. 55–77). Hillsdale, NJ: Lawrence Erlbaum.

White, S. H. (1983b). Psychology as a moral science. In F. S. Kessel & A. W. Siegel (Eds.), *The child and other cultural inventions* (pp. 1–25). New York: Praeger.

White, S. H., & Buka, S. L. (1987). Early education: Programs, traditions, and policies. In E. Z. Rothkopf (Ed.), *Review of research in education* (Vol. 14, pp. 43–91). Washington, DC: American Educational Research Association.

Whitebrook, M., Howes, C., & Phillips, D. (1989). *Who cares? Child care and the quality of care in America. Final report of the National Staffing Study.* Oakland, CA: Child Care Employee Project.

Willer, B. (1987). *The growing crisis in child care: Quality, compensation, and affordability in early childhood programs.* Washington, DC: The National Association for the Education of Young Children.

Williams, L. R. (1977). The behavioral approach. In B. D. Boegehold, H. K. Cuffaro, W. H. Hooks, & G. J. Klopf (Eds.), *Education before five: A handbook on preschool education* (pp. 53–67). New York: Bank Street College of Education.

Winsor, C. (1973). *Experimental schools revisited: Bulletins of the Bureau of Educational Experiments.* New York: Agathon Press.

Wittrock, M. C., & Lumsdaine, A. A. (1977). Instructional psychology. In M. R. Rosenzweig & L. W. Porter (Eds.), *Annual Review of Psychology* (Vol. 28, pp. 417–459). Palo Alto, CA: Annual Reviews.

Woodhead, M. (1988). When psychology informs public policy: The case of early childhood intervention. *American Psychologist, 43,* 443–454.

Zelizer, V. A. (1985). *Pricing the priceless child: The changing social value of children.* New York: Basic Books.

Zigler, E. (1984). Foreword. In B. Biber (Ed.), *Early education and psychological development* (pp. ix–xi). New Haven, CT: Yale University Press.

Zigler, E. (1984). Meeting the critics on their own terms. *American Psychologist, 39,* 916–917.

Zigler, E. F. (1987). Formal schooling for four-year-olds? No. In S. L. Kagan & E. F. Zigler (Eds.), *Early schooling: The national debate* (pp. 27– 44). New Haven, CT: Yale University Press.

Zigler, E., & Anderson, K. (1979). An idea whose time had come: The intellectual and political climate. In E. Zigler & J. Valentine (Eds.), *Project Head Start: A legacy of the War on Poverty* (pp. 3–19). New York: The Free Press.

Zigler, E. F., & Freedman, J. (1987). Evaluating family support programs. In S. L. Kagan, D. R. Powell, B. Weissbourd, & E. F. Zigler (Eds.), *America's family support programs* (pp. 352–361). New Haven, CT: Yale University Press.

Zigler, E. F., Kagan, S. L., & Klugman, E. (Eds.). (1983). *Children, families and government: Perspectives on American social policy* (pp. 10–32). Cambridge: Cambridge University Press.

Zigler, E., & Muenchow, S. (1992). *Head Start: The inside story of America's most successful educational experiment.* New York: Basic Books.

Zimiles, H. (1977). A radical and regressive solution to the problem of evaluation. In L. G. Katz, M. I. Glockner, S. T. Goodman, & M. J. Spencer (Eds.), *Current topics in early childhood education* (Vol. 1, pp. 63–70). Norwood, NJ: Ablex.

Zimiles, H. (1986). Rethinking the role of research: New issues and lingering doubts in an era of expanding preschool education. *Early Childhood Research Quarterly, 1,* 189–206.

Zimiles, H. (1987). The Bank Street Approach. In J. L. Roopnarine & J. E. Johnson (Eds.), *Approaches to early childhood education* (pp. 163–178). New York: Merrill/Macmillan.

Zuckerman, M. (1987). Plus ça change: The high-tech child in historical perspective. *Early Childhood Research Quarterly, 2,* 255–264.

Zumwalt, K. K. (1982). Research on teaching: Policy implications for teacher education. In A. Lieberman & M. W. McLaughlin (Eds.), *Policy making in education*. Eighty-first yearbook of the National Society for the Study of Education, Part I (pp. 215–248). Chicago: University of Chicago Press.

Zumwalt, K. K. (1986). Working together to improve education. In K. K. Zumwalt (Ed.), *Improving teaching*. Alexandria: VA: Association for Supervision and Curriculum Development.

Zumwalt, K. (1989). Beginning professional teachers: The need for a curricular vision of teaching. In M. C. Reynolds (Ed.), *Knowledge base for the beginning teacher* (pp. 173–184). New York: Pergamon Press.

Index

Absorbent Mind, The (Montessori), 49, 51
Academic-based curriculum models, 27, 116–124
Academic Program for Disadvantaged Children, An (Bereiter), 97
ACEI (Association for Childhood Education International), 18
Achievement tests, 169, 172, 176–177
Active learning, 152–153
Adcock, C., 126, 128, 149
Addams, Jane, 44
Advanced Montessori Method: Spontaneous Activity in Education (Montessori), 48
Advanced Montessori Method: The Montessori Elementary Material (Montessori), 48
Alexander, M., 205–206
Almy, M., 189, 202
American Montessori Association, 45
American Montessori Society, 47, 62
AMI (Association Montessori Internationale), 45, 61
Anderson, K., 18–20, 170
Anderson, V., 102, 106–107
Antler, J., 66–67, 68, 72–75, 77*n*, 95–96
Apple, M. W., 182, 185
Arithmetic instruction. *See* Math instruction
Assessment. *See* Program evaluation; Student assessment
Association for Childhood Education International (ACEI), 18
Association Montessori Internationale (AMI), 45, 61
As the Twig is Bent . . . The Lasting Effects of Preschool Programs, 186
Autonomous ego, 84
Autonomy, 131, 133, 142, 145

Baer, Donald M., 97
Baker, O., 131
Banet, B., 128–129, 149–154, 157, 161
Bank Street approach, 21, 24–25, 66–67, 73. *See also* Developmental-Interaction approach
Head Start and, 78–80
Project Follow Through and, 67–68
Bank Street School for Children, 73, 81
Barnett, S. W., 166, 174
Barnett, W. S., 26, 123, 126, 159, 166, 173–174, 182, 184–185
Barone, T. E., 182
Basal readers, 106
Base-line measures, 171
Becker, W. C., 101, 105, 111–114, 124
BEE (Bureau of Educational Experiments), 66–67, 71–75
Behavioral curriculum models, 81–82, 91, 100–104
compared with Developmental-Interaction approach, 81–82
Behavioral science of education, 138
Behavior Analysis Model, 24–25
Behaviorism, 4, 98, 118, 138, 198*n*
Bereiter-Engelmann model and, 100–104
Direct Instruction model and, 100–104
Behavior modification, 65
Bell, Alexander Graham, 44
Bell, Mary Hubbard, 44
Belsky, J., 25, 27
Bentley, R., 49
Bereiter, Carl, 97–98, 101–111, 178–179
Bereiter-Engelmann model, 98–100, 194. *See also* Direct Instruction model

Bereiter-Engelmann model, *continued*
    behaviorism and, 100–104
    curriculum, 107–108
    evaluation of, 176–178
    goals, 108
    language instruction, 107, 109–110
    math instruction, 107, 110
    reading instruction, 107, 110
    student assessment, 107
    teacher roles, 110–111
    teaching methods, 108–110
Berliner, D. C., 106*n*, 195
Berrueta-Clement, J. R., 26, 123, 126, 159, 173, 184
Beyer, L. E., 182, 185
Biber, Barbara, 17, 21–22, 24, 65–70, 72–96, 99,
    102–103, 110*n*, 124*n*, 129, 180, 189, 214
Bilingual/Bicultural Model, 24
Bissell, J. S., 23, 168–169
Bizzell, L. P., 167, 174–177
Blackwell, F., 150
Blenkin, G., 202*n*
Bloch, M. N., 72, 117, 120, 195, 199, 202–203
Bloom, B. S., 19–20, 47, 190, 192
Blow, Susan, 14
Bower, G. H., 100–101, 104
Bowman, G. W., 74, 91–92
Branden, A., 23, 119
Bredekamp, S., 7, 29–30, 32, 121–122, 188–189, 212
British Infant Schools, 66*n*
Bronfenbrenner, U., 12, 172*n*, 180, 191, 193–197
Brooks-Gunn, J., 183–184
Brophy, J. E., 106*n*, 203
Brown v. The Board of Education of Topeka, 19
Bruner, J., 193–196, 202, 207
Bryant, D. M., 18, 169, 171, 174, 183, 192–193
Buchmann, M., 202, 204–207
Buckleitner, W., 150–151, 154, 157–158
Bugbee, M. R., 27–28, 174–176, 179–181
Buka, S. L., 14–15, 19, 21, 33, 45, 72, 79, 100, 119,
    170, 180, 191
Bureau of Educational Experiments (BEE), 66–67,
    71–75
Burts, D. C., 109
Bush, George, 13
Bushell, D., Jr., 102*n*
Butler, A. L., 24
Byrne, D., 143

Cahan, E. D., 17, 21, 33, 70*n*
Caldwell, Bettye M., 13, 15

Campbell, D. T., 171
Carnine, D., 101, 103, 105, 108, 112–116, 121, 124
Carnine, L., 103, 105, 108, 112–113, 121
Casa dei Bambini, 39–44, 47
Case, R., 98, 101
Cazden, C. B., 193
*Changed Lives: The Effects of the Perry
    Preschool Program on Youths through Age 19,*
    125, 159
Charlesworth, R., 109
Chattin-McNichols, J., 45, 47–48, 54, 61–62, 165*n*
Child care, 25, 27, 29–30, 99
    evaluation, 179
    quality, 12
Child-centered environment, 55–56
Child development, 15, 30–31, 141, 190–198. *See also*
    Developmental theory
    early childhood curriculum models and, 198–202
    environment and, 180, 193–195
    heredity and, 191–193
    Montessori method and, 46
Child Development Associate, 69*n*, 212
Child in the Family, The (Montessori), 51
Children's Defense Fund, 12, 30
Children's House, 39–44, 47
Child-sized furniture, 55–56
Cicirelli, V., 23, 170
Circle time (High/Scope), 156–157
City and Country School, 73, 214
Clarke, A. D. B., 192
Clarke, A. M., 192
Clarke-Stewart, K. A., 16, 20, 22, 25, 27–28, 169–171,
    174, 179–181, 183, 185, 193
Classroom arrangement (Developmental-Interaction
    approach), 92
Clean-up time (High/Scope), 156
Cleverley, J., 196
Clinton, Bill, 13*n*
Cognitive development theory, 22–23, 106*n*, 117,
    190–191, 198–199, 202. *See also*
    Developmental theory
    Developmental-Interaction approach and, 79,
    83–84, 91
    Kamii-DeVries approach and, 134–141
    Montessori method and, 46
    Piagetian theory and, 134–141
Cognitively Oriented Curriculum, 149
*Cognitively Oriented Curriculum: A Framework for
    Preschool Teachers,* 149
Cohen, D., 169, 171, 182

Cohen, S., 39, 43, 45, 61
Cole, M., 190–191, 193–194
Cole, S. R., 190–191, 193–194
Commercial dissemination, 45, 160
Committee for Economic Development, 13, 29–30, 122
Committee of Nineteen, 14, 18, 43
Community action programs, 19, 80
Compensatory education, 18, 22, 91, 110, 117–119, 192
Conceptual Skills Program, 110n
Concrete operational stage, 134, 153
Conditioned responses, 113
Condry, S., 170–172
Connectivity, 190
Consortium for Longitudinal Studies, 26, 123, 170–175, 186
Constructivism, 131–132, 137–141
Constructivist Education (DeVries and Kohlberg), 134, 160–161
Cooperative School for Student Teachers, 75
Copple, C., 126n
Corsaro, W., 196
Cremin, L., 71–73, 75–76, 79–80, 91, 106
Critical period, 192
Cronin, D., 115–116
Cuban, L., 204, 206
Cuffaro, H. K., 91
Cultural context, 194–196
Cultural deficit, 104
Cultural deprivation, 102–104, 194–195
Cultural Linguistic Approach, 24
Culturally Democratic Learning Environmental Model, 24
Culturally disadvantaged, 194–195
Cultural transmission, 198–199, 201–202
Cumulative deficit hypothesis, 103, 191
Curriculum models. See Early childhood curriculum models
Curriculum theorists, 106–107, 120

DAP (developmentally appropriate practice), 121–124, 189
DARCEE program, 78n, 176
Darch, C., 103–105, 112–113, 121–122, 124, 165n
Darling-Hammond, L., 203–204
Darlington, R. B., 182
Darwin's theory of evolution, 196–197
David, J., 90–91

Davidson, D. H., 194–195
Davis, M. D., 70
Day, D. E., 16, 20, 22
Day, M. C., 6, 15, 87–88, 96, 205
Day care, 99, 212. See also Child care
Day nurseries, 16–17. See also Child care
DeClark, G., 146
Delpit, L. D., 188–189
Desegregation, 19, 47
Deutsch, C. P., 78, 177, 184
Deutsch, M., 78, 109, 177, 184
Development
    education as, 202
    social nature of, 152–153, 195–196
Developmental-Interaction approach, 7, 21–22, 65–69, 85, 141, 201
    Bureau of Educational Experiments, 66–67, 71–75
    classroom arrangement, 92
    cognitive development theory and, 79, 83–84, 91
    compared with behavioral models, 81–82
    compared with Direct Instruction model, 98–99, 102–103, 105–106, 119
    compared with Kamii-DeVries approach, 88, 137
    compared with Montessori Method, 66, 81–82, 84, 88
    curriculum content, 90–91
    developmental processes, 86–89
    evaluation of, 169
    as experimental nursery program, 69–80
    goals, 86–89
    instructional principles, 90–91
    materials, 92
    organization, 92–93
    Piagetian theory and, 129
    Project Follow Through and, 80–81
    psychodynamic theory and, 75–77
    psychological rationale, 80–84
    student assessment, 74
    teacher-child relationship, 89–91
    teacher roles, 68, 81, 89–91, 93
    teaching strategies, 89–91
    tenets, 84–85
    theoretical formulations, 86–87
    theory and practice relationship, 93–96
    traditional model and, 78–80
    value priorities, 86
Developmentally appropriate practice (DAP), 121–124, 189
Developmentally Appropriate Practice in Early Childhood Programs, 121, 189

Developmental psychology, 20–21, 76–77, 84, 121
    as objective science, 196–198
Developmental Stages in Piagetian Theory and Educational Practice (DeVries), 125
Developmental theory, 3–5, 22, 31, 82, 120. *See also* Child development; Cognitive development theory
    early childhood curriculum models and, 99, 189–190
    as source of education objectives, 198–201
    teaching, effect on, 200–201
Development as the Aim of Education (Kohlberg and Mayer), 198
Devil Has Slippery Shoes, The (Greenberg), 19
DeVries, Rheta, 6, 27, 109, 125–127, 129, 131–148, 153n, 155, 160–161, 179
Dewey, John, 14, 44–45, 66n, 71, 74, 76, 84, 86, 91, 95
Didactic materials (Montessori Method), 57–60
Direct instruction, 91, 106n, 159
Direct Instruction Follow Through Program, 175, 178–179
Direct Instruction model, 7, 24, 97–100, 111–116, 140n. *See also* Bereiter-Engelmann model; Engelmann-Becker model
    behaviorism and, 100–104
    classroom resources, 114
    compared with Developmental-Interaction approach, 98–99, 102–103, 105–106, 119
    compared with Montessori Method, 99, 105–106, 119
    concepts and tasks, 114–115
    kindergartens and, 111–112
    language instruction, 113
    longitudinal studies, 123–124
    math instruction, 113
    program content, 113
    programmatic design, 113–115
    Project Follow Through and, 98
    psychological framework, 100–107
    in public schools, 105–106, 119
    reading instruction, 113
    science of education and, 104–107
    teaching methods, 105–107, 115–116
    teaching strategies, 114–115
Directress, 53–54
Disadvantaged children. *See* Low-income children
Discovery of the Child, The (Montessori), 49
DISTAR program, 110n, 113–115
Dr. Montessori's Own Handbook, 49, 57, 63

Doll, W. E., Jr., 203
Dowley, E. M., 21
Durkin, D., 197
Dye, H. B., 20
Dyer, J. L., 169, 176–177
Dynamic psychology, 84

Early childhood care and education, 29–30
Early childhood curriculum models, 3–9, 206–207. *See also* Program effectiveness; Program evaluation
    academic-based, 27, 116–124
    behavioral, 81–82, 91, 100–104
    child development and, 198–202
    contemporary backdrop, 27–31
    context of, 14–16
    decline of, 25–26
    defined, 15–16
    developmental theory and, 99, 189–190
    development of, 21–25
    differential impact, 27, 175–185
    early childhood education and, 120, 209–214
    empirical evaluation, 166–175
    Head Start and, 23, 67–68
    implementation accuracy, 166
    policy decisions, 11–14, 182–185
    political setting, 18–19
    psychological insights, 19–21
    quality of, 31–32, 160, 213–214
    source of, 187–189
    systematic variation, 16–18
Early childhood curriculum theorists, 188
Early childhood ecosystem, 30
Early childhood education, 25–26
    agenda for, 210–212
    age span, 30
    availability, 211–212
    configuration, 29–30
    cost-effectiveness, 123, 125, 159, 183–184
    curriculum models and, 120, 209–214
    elementary education and, 119–121
    history, 14–16, 202–203
    knowledge base, 30–31
    models approach, 100
    Piagetian theory and, 128–129
    professional context, 17–18, 30–32, 44–45, 211–212, 214
    program sponsors, 30
    public policy and, 11–14

societal context, 28–29, 211
Early childhood educators, 32, 212. *See also*
 Professionalism
Early Education and Development, 208
Early Education and Psychological Development
 (Biber), 65, 95–96
Early intervention programs, 16, 25–26, 30
 experimental, 19–20, 22
Early Training Project, 20
Economically disadvantaged. *See* Low-income chil-
 dren
EDC Open Education Program, 24–25
Education. *See also* Early childhood education;
 Elementary education
 behavioral science of, 138
 as development, 202
 objectives, 198–201
 science of, 104–107
Education, U. S. Department of, 13, 27, 106*n*
Education, U. S. Office of, 23, 149
Educational gymnastics, 56–57
Educational learning theory, 101, 106
Educational practice, science of, 127
Educational reform movement, 13, 27–28, 211
Educational theories, 84
 psychological theories and, 201–202
Edwards, C. P., 194–195
Egan, K., 31, 118, 189, 201–202
Egertson, H. A., 122
Eisner, E., 182
Elementary education
 early childhood education and, 119–121
 history, 202–203
Elgas, P. M., 196
Eliot, Abigail, 17, 66*n*
Elkind, D., 15, 99, 121, 188, 196
Elliott, J., 31, 204–206
Ellwein, M. C., 205–206
Empirical abstraction, 140
Employment, 16–17, 25, 28–29, 211
Enabler Model, 25
Engelmann, Siegfried, 101, 103–108, 110*n*, 111–114,
 124
Engelmann-Becker model, 25, 111
Environment
 child-centered, 55–56
 child development and, 180, 193–195
 vs. heredity, 47, 190
 prepared, 50–53, 55–56

Epistemology, 134, 137
Epstein, A. S., 26, 123, 126, 159, 173, 184
Erikson, Erik, 84
Escobar, C. M., 185
Evaluation. *See* Program evaluation
Evans, E. D., 3, 15–16, 18–19, 33, 71, 85, 99, 129,
 165*n*, 173–174, 177, 191, 193
Experimental early intervention programs, 19–20, 22
Experimental methodology, 104–105
Experimental nursery program (Developmental-
 Interaction approach), 69–80
Extensions newsletter, 159

Family of theories, 83–84
Federal government, 11–14, 23–24
Fein, G., 16, 20, 25, 169–171, 174, 179–181, 183,
 185,189, 193, 201, 205
Feldman, R., 23, 119
Females, program evaluation for, 177
Feminism, 68–69
Fenstermacher, G. D., 204
Fernie, D., 133, 139, 196
Ferreiro, E., 131, 147
Fixed intelligence, 117, 119, 130, 191
Flanagan, O., 142*n*
Florida Parent Education Model, 24–25
Flynn, R., 131
Follins, J., 23, 119
Follow Through Planned Variation, 168–169, 175
Formal operational stage, 134, 197
Forman, G., 126*n*
Franklin, M. B., 21, 68–69, 81–84, 87, 94, 180
Frede, E., 166, 174
Freedman, J., 183
Free gymnastics, 56–57
Free play, 76
Freud, Anna, 84
Freud, Sigmund, 84
Freudian psychology, 17, 76, 190, 196
Froebel, Friedrich, 14–15, 17, 37–38, 43–44, 66*n*,
 71–72, 120
Full-day early childhood programs. *See* Child care
Furniture, child-sized, 55–56

Gabbard, H. F., 70
Gaebler, D., 209
Gallagher, J. J., 191
Gallagher, J. M., 108
Gandini, L., 194–195

Garcia, E. E., 30
Gardner, H., 127, 193
Garrison, J. W., 204
Gender, and program evaluation, 177
Genetics. *See* Heredity
George, Anne, 44
George, N., 103, 108, 112, 121
Gersten, R., 103–105, 108, 112–113, 115–116,
    121–122, 124, 165*n*, 178–179
Gesell, Arnold, 20, 44
Gesell, Beatrice, 20, 44
Gestalt psychology, 84
Giddings, M., 30
Gilkeson, E., 74, 81, 91–92
Gilligan, C., 142*n*, 196
Glaser, R., 101
Gleason, M., 103–105, 112–113, 121–122, 124, 165*n*
Glockner, M. Z., 186
Goffin, S. G., 12, 33, 100, 182, 203
Goncu, A., 27, 127
Goodykoontz, B., 70
Government involvement, 11–14, 23–24
Grallo, R., 177, 184
Gray, S. W., 19–20, 26, 78, 170, 177, 185
Great Society, 12, 29
Greenberg, P., 19, 21, 68–69, 72–73, 77–79, 96
Greene, M., 189, 197, 200, 202
Greeno, J. J., 193, 196
Gregory, B. C., 30
Group games, 131, 142–145
Group Games in Early Education (Kamii and
    DeVries), 145
Grubb, W. N., 12, 173, 183–184
Gruber, C. P., 179

Haberman, M., 189, 197, 200
Hall, G. Stanley, 44
Hands-on-learning, 132–133
Haney, J. P., 27, 143, 179
Harriet Johnson Nursery School, 73
Harris, J. D., 183*n*
Hart, C. H., 109
Hartmann, Heinz, 84
Hartup, W. W., 196
Haskins, R., 173–174, 182–184
Haste, H., 193, 195–196
Hauser-Cram, P., 167, 171, 180–181
Head Start
    access to, 12

Bank Street approach and, 78–80
beginnings, 11, 16–18, 20–22, 67, 69, 117
as community action program, 19, 80
curriculum models and, 23, 67–68
enrollment, 29
evaluation of, 168–171, 175, 212
High/Scope Curriculum model and, 194
nursery programs, effect on, 99
performance of graduates, 23, 25, 183
purpose, 117–119
Head Start Planned Variation, 104, 168–169
Hebbeler, K., 173, 183
Heredity
    child development and, 191–193
    vs. environment, 47, 190
Heteronomy, 131, 142, 145, 148
Hewes, D. W., 55
Hiebert, E. H., 188
High/Scope Child Observation Record, 155
High/Scope Cognitively Oriented Curriculum Model,
    24–25
High/Scope Curriculum model, 7, 123, 148–154, 188,
    197, 205
    circle time, 156–157
    clean-up time, 156
    compared with Kamii-DeVries approach, 151
    daily routine, 155–157
    evaluation of, 166, 172–173, 177–178
    Head Start and, 194
    history, 128–129
    key experiences, 154–155, 157–158
    K-3 framework, 149–150, 157–158
    math instruction, 153
    parent education component, 184
    Piagetian theory and, 125–128, 151–152
    Plan-Do-Review, 153, 155–157
    planning time, 156
    preschool framework, 154–157
    primary curricula, 149–150, 157–158
    program dissemination, 158–160
    Project Follow Through and, 149–150, 158
    in public schools, 149–150
    reading instruction, 153
    recall time, 156
    student assessment, 155
    teacher roles, 152, 157
    work time, 156
High/Scope Educational Research Foundation,
    126–127, 158

High/Scope Press, 159
High/Scope Registry Conference, 159
High/Scope ReSource, 159
Hilgard, E. R., 100–101, 104
Hill, F., 126*n*
Hill, Patty Smith, 14
Hirsh-Pasek, K., 108, 121
Hodges, W., 23, 119, 168–169
Hofferth, S. L., 29
Hohmann, C., 149, 150–154, 157–158
Hohmann, M., 128–129, 149–154, 157, 161
Home-School Partnership Model, 24
Honig, A., 177, 184
Horowitz, F. D., 18, 20, 104, 180–182, 184, 191–193,
      207
House, E. R., 166–169, 182, 185
Houston, J., 23, 119
Howes, C., 27, 212
Humanists, 120
Hunt, J. McVicker, 19–20, 44–47, 190
Hunter, Madeline, 106*n*
Hutchins, E. J., 166, 168–169, 182
Hybertson, D. W., 27–28, 174–176, 179–181
Hymes, J. L., Jr., 17, 21, 212
Hyson, M. C., 108, 121

I Learn from Children (Pratt), 95
Inagaki, K., 127
Individualized Early Learning Program, 24–25
Infant Schools, 66*n*
Institute for Developmental Studies, 78
Instructional design, 101
Instructional psychology, 101
Instructional theories, 101, 106
Intelligence
      fixed, 117, 119, 130, 191
      malleability of, 191–192, 211
Intelligence tests, 107, 169–172
Interdependent Learning Model, 24–25
International Kindergarten Union, 14, 17–18, 43*n*
IQ scores, 20, 167–169, 172, 176–177
Iran-Nejad, A., 106*n*, 195
Issacs, Susan, 76, 77*n*, 84, 95
Itard, Jean-Marc-Gaspard, 39, 61

Jacobs, F., 174, 181, 183
Jensen, A. R., 109
Johnson, Harriet, 66, 73, 84, 93, 95
Johnson, Lyndon B., 12

Jordan, T. J., 177, 184
Joseph, L., 131, 146

Kagan, J., 190–192, 196
Kagan, S. L., 12–13, 29–30, 122, 183, 187
Kamii, Constance K., 126–129, 131–135, 137–141,
      143–146, 148
Kamii-DeVries approach, 7, 125–128, 131–134, 197,
      199
   cognitive development theory and, 134–141
   compared with Developmental-Interaction
      approach, 88, 137
   compared with High/Scope Curriculum model,
      151
   curriculum and activities, 141–147
      group games, 131, 142–145
      moral reasoning, 142–143
      physical-knowledge activities, 131, 140–144
      traditional school curricula, 145–147
   evaluation of, 179
   history, 128–129
   math instruction, 145–147
   number concepts, 145–147
   Project Follow Through and, 127
   reading instruction, 145–147
   student assessment, 138–139
   teacher roles, 147–148
   traditional model and, 145–147
   writing instruction, 145–147
Kantor, R., 196
Karmiloff-Smith, A., 127
Karnes, M. B., 167, 169, 174–177
Karp, J., 103, 105, 108, 112–113, 121
Karweit, N., 178
Katz, I., 109
Katz, L. G., 62, 186, 208
Kelly, V., 202*n*
Kennedy, M. M., 168
Kerr, D. H., 31, 204–205
Kessel, F., 196–197
Kessen, W., 180, 192, 196–197
Kessler, S., 31, 188–189, 197–200, 202, 208
Key experiences, 154–155, 157–158
Key Experiences in Mathematics, 157
Kilpatrick, William Heard, 44–45, 47
Kindergartens, 14–17, 37–38, 71–72, 99, 117, 120
   Direct Instruction model and, 111–112
   enrollment, 29
Kirk, L., 109

Klaus, R. A., 19–20, 26, 170, 177, 185
Kliebard, H. M., 43, 106–107, 118, 120, 124, 130
Klugman, E., 12
Kohlberg, Lawrence, 6, 127, 131–148, 153*n*, 160–161, 198–199, 201–202, 207
Kramer, R., 38–40, 43–46, 49, 61–62
K-3 curriculum (High/Scope), 149–150, 157–158
Kuschner, D., 126*n*

Labov, W., 195
Lally, J. R., 177, 184
Lampert, M., 204, 206
Language and Literacy (Maehr), 150
Language deprivation, 104
Language instruction
    Bereiter-Engelmann model, 107, 109–110
    Direct Instruction model, 113
    Montessori Method, 59–60
Language use, black children, 195
Laosa, L. M., 183
Larner, M. B., 27, 109, 123, 152–153, 159, 177–179
Larsen, J. M., 177, 183*n*
Laura Spelman Rockefeller Memorial Foundation, 20
Lavatelli, C., 21–22, 126*n*, 137
Lawton, J. T., 166
Lazar, I., 170–172, 182
Lazerson, M., 12, 185, 193
Learning, defined, 100–101
Learning by doing, 133
Learning deficit, 103
Learning theories, 22, 31, 101
Lee, C., 23, 119
Lee, V. E., 183–184
Lerner, R. M., 195
Levin, H. M., 184
Lewin, Kurt, 84
Liaw, F-R., 184
Lickona, T., 143
Light, R. J., 166–167, 174, 181–182
Liljestrom, R., 196
Loeffler, M. G., 62
Logico-mathematical knowledge, 140–143
Lombardi, J., 12
Longitudinal studies, 26–28, 126, 159, 170–175, 186
    Direct Instruction model, 123–124
Louisville experiment, 176
Love, J., 23, 119
Low-income children, 18, 22, 41, 68, 102–103, 107–111. *See also* Poverty

policy decisions and, 182–185
Lubeck, S., 189, 193–194
Lumbley, J., 23, 119
Lumsdaine, A. A., 98, 101

Maccoby, E. E., 119
Macmillan, C. J. B., 204
Macmillan, Margaret, 66*n*
Maehr, J., 150
Magnet schools, 47–48
Making Schools More Effective, 124
Males, program evaluation for, 177
Malleability of intelligence, 191–192, 211
Mangione, P. L., 177, 184
Maria Montessori: A Biography (Kramer), 62
Marx, F., 13, 27, 30
Maternal employment, 16–17, 25, 28–29, 211
Mathemagenic Activities Program, 24
Mathematics curriculum guide (Hohmann), 150
Math instruction
    Bereiter-Engelmann model, 107, 110
    Direct Instruction model, 113
    High/Scope Curriculum model, 153
    Kamii-DeVries approach, 145–147
Maturation theory, 120, 198
Mayer, R., 6, 16, 136, 198–199, 201–202, 207
McClelland, D., 126, 128, 149
McClure, S. S., 44
McDermott, J. J., 47
McKeachie, W. J., 106*n*, 195
McNair, S., 155
Measurement. *See* Program evaluation; Student assessment
Mehan, H., 193
Melton, G. B., 185
Mental health movement, 77
Mental retardation, 20, 39–40
Merrill, J. B., 30
Merrill, Jenny, 44
Method, and science, 104–105. *See also* Teaching methods
Method of Scientific Pedagogy Applied to Child Education in the Children's House, The (Montessori), 49
Middle-class children, 183, 195
Miller, L. B., 22–23, 27–28, 79, 167, 169, 174–177, 179–181
Minorities, 30, 182–183, 194, 200

Missouri Department of Elementary and Secondary Education, 131
Mitchell, A., 13, 27, 30, 67, 84, 90–91
Mitchell, Lucy Sprague, 66–67, 68, 72–75, 77, 84, 93, 95–96, 129
Mobasher, H., 166, 174
Models, defined, 15. *See also* Early childhood curriculum models
Models approach to early childhood education, 100
Mohr, P., 166, 174
Montessori, Maria, 37–63, 66*n*, 160
Montessori, Mario, 45, 61
Montessori, Mario, Jr., 61
Montessori Method, 7, 37–39, 60–62, 190
    child development and, 46
    child's labor concept, 53–54
    cognitive development theory and, 46
    compared with Developmental-Interaction approach, 66, 81–82, 84, 88
    compared with Direct Instruction model, 99, 105–106, 119
    concepts, 49–54
    didactic materials, 57–60
    evaluation of, 175–177
    history, 39–48
    language instruction, 59–60
    method, 48–49
    motor education, 56–57
    obedience, 54
    order, 49, 53–54
    patenting, 45–46
    prepared environment, 50–53, 55–56
    program, 55–60
    psychological concepts, 46–47
    in public schools, 47–48
    reading instruction, 59–60
    schedule, 58
    as scientific pedagogy, 49–51
    sensory education, 57–59
    spontaneous activity, 47, 49, 51–53, 63
    teacher roles, 44
    writing instruction, 59–60
Montessori Method, The (Montessori), 42, 44, 46–49, 58, 63
Moore, S. G., 24, 190
Moral development, stages of, 132
Moral reasoning, 142–143
Moreilli, G., 193–195
Morgan, P., 27, 109, 127, 133, 139, 179

Moskovitz, S. T., 98
Mothers in work force, 16–17, 25, 28–29, 211
Motivation, 84, 91
Motor education, 56–57
Muenchow, S., 212
Murphy, D., 131
Murray, F., 131
Murray, H. W., 182
Mussen, P., 185

National Association for Nursery Education (NANE), 17–18, 21*n*
National Association for the Education of Young Children (NAEYC), 7, 17, 21, 29, 73
    developmentally appropriate practice statement, 121–123, 189
National Association of Early Childhood Specialists in State Departments of Education, 7
National Association of Elementary School Principals, 29, 122
National Association of State Boards of Education, 122
National Center for Montessori Education, 45
National Commission on Children, 30
National Education Association (NEA), 18
National Governors' Association, 13
National Staffing Study, 212
NEA (National Education Association), 18
New School Approach, 24
Nixon, Richard, 171
Nongraded Model, 24
North American Montessori Teachers Association, 45*n*
Number concepts (Kamii-DeVries approach), 145–147
Nursery schools, 16–17, 20–21, 29–30, 120, 211–212
    experimental (Developmental-Interaction approach), 69–80
    Head Start, effects of, 99
Nuthall, G., 16

Obedience (Montessori Method), 54
O'Brien, L. M., 189, 194
O'Brien, M., 180–181, 191–193, 207
Observation, 50, 52, 155
Office of Child Development, 22
Office of Economic Opportunity, 19, 23, 78–79
Office of Education, U. S., 23, 149
Ogbu, J. U., 194

Open approach, 66n
Open Court Kindergarten Program, 110n
Operant conditioning, 117
Operational reasoning, 132
Order (Montessori Method), 49, 53–54
Osborn, D. K., 16, 18, 24
Osborn, J., 23, 119
Osborne, D., 209
Overton, W. R., 83

Paden, L. Y., 18, 20, 104, 181–182, 184
Parent education, 21, 184
Parent participation, 41, 116, 172, 183n
Parent Supported Diagnostic Model, 24
Parker, R. K., 87–88, 96
Patents, 45–46
Payne, B., 30
Peabody, Elizabeth, 14
Pedagogical anthropology, 48, 50
Pedagogical Anthropology (Montessori), 48
Perry Preschool Project, 78, 125, 128, 148–149, 159,
    173–174
  cost-benefit analysis, 183–184
Perspective taking, stages of, 132
Peters, D. L., 166, 169, 205
Phillips, D. A., 27, 29, 181, 186, 212
Phillips, D. C., 196
Physical knowledge, 131, 140–144
Physical Knowledge in Preschool Activities (Kamii
    and DeVries), 144
Piaget, Children, and Number (Kamii and DeVries),
    146
Piaget, Jean, 22, 66n, 77, 83–84, 117, 142, 147, 153,
    191, 195, 197–199, 202
Piagetian mystique, 129–131
Piagetian theory
  adoption of, 129–131
  cognitive development theory and, 134–141
  constructivism and, 131–132, 137–141
  Developmental-Interaction approach and, 129
  early childhood education and, 128–129
  High/Scope Curriculum model and, 125–128,
      151–152
  structural stages, 84–85, 132–139
Pinar, W. F., 188
Pitcher, E., 46
Pizzo, P., 12
Plan-Do-Review (High/Scope), 153, 155–157
Planned Variation, 104, 168–169, 175

Planning time (High/Scope), 156
Plasticity concept, 191–192
Play, 76, 133, 142, 151
Playing with Rollers (film), 144n
Play School, 73
Plomin, R., 191
Polakow, V., 185, 189, 200
Policy decisions
  black children and, 182–183
  low-income children and, 182–185
  program effectiveness and, 182–185
  public policy, 11–14
Political setting, 18–19
Pollitzer, Margaret, 77n
Postman, N., 196
Poverty, 12, 21–23, 28–29, 79–80, 117–118, 211. See
    also Low-income children
Powell, D. R., 11, 14, 16, 22, 25, 27–28, 30, 121, 167,
    169, 173–174, 178–181, 184
Powell, N., 166
Practice, relationship with theory, 201–202, 205
  Developmental-Interaction approach, 93–96
Pratt, Caroline, 66, 73, 84, 95, 214
Prentice Hall Personalized Learning Model, 24
Preoperational stage, 134–135, 153
Prepared environment (Montessori Method), 50–53,
    55–56
Preschool education. See Early childhood education
Primary curricula (High/Scope), 149–150, 157–158
Professionalism, 17–18, 30–32, 44–45, 211–212, 214
Program effectiveness, 174–175
  defining, 180–182
  long-term, 170–173, 192
  policy decisions and, 182–185
  short-term, 167–170
Program evaluation, 155, 165, 180, 203
  Bereiter-Engelmann model, 176–178
  child care, 179
  defined, 164
  Developmental-Interaction approach, 169
  empirical findings, 166–175
  by gender, 177
  Head Start, 168–171, 175, 212
  High/Scope Curriculum model, 166, 172–173,
      177–178
  Kamii-DeVries approach, 179
  Montessori Method, 175–177
  traditional model, 177–178
Program models versus curriculum models, 4–5

Programs of Early Education: The Constructivist View (DeVries and Kohlberg), 132, 134, 160
Program sponsors, 30
Progressive education movement, 66, 69–73, 75–77, 79–82, 91, 198
Progressive movement, 71
Project Construct, 131, 138
Project Follow Through, 22–23, 100, 104
    Bank Street approach and, 67–68
    Developmental-Interaction approach and, 80–81
    Direct Instruction model and, 98
    High/Scope Curriculum model and, 149–150, 158
    Kamii-DeVries approach and, 127
    purpose, 119, 168–169
Psychodynamic theory, 82
    Developmental-Interaction approach and, 75–77
Psychological theories, 22
    educational theories and, 201–202
Psychologist's fallacy, 136
Public policy, 11–14
Public schools, 13, 29
    Direct Instruction model and, 105–106, 119
    High/Scope Curriculum model and, 149–150
    Montessori Method and, 47–48
Punishment, 113

Quality issues, 12, 31–32, 160, 213–214

Radin, N. L., 129
Rambusch, Nancy McCormick, 45, 62
Ramey, C. T., 18, 169, 171, 174, 183, 191–193
Ramp, E. A., 102n
Ramsey, B. K., 19–20, 26, 170, 177, 185
Rashid, H. M., 181
Read, Katherine, 141
Readers, basal, 106
Reading instruction
    Bereiter-Engelmann model, 107, 110
    Direct Instruction model, 113
    High/Scope Curriculum model, 153
    Kamii-DeVries approach, 145–147
    Montessori Method, 59–60
Recall time (High/Scope), 156
Reese, H. W., 83
Reese-Learned, H., 27, 109, 127, 133, 139, 179
Reflective abstraction, 143
Reinforcement, 113
Relativism, 202
Reliability, 170

Rentfrow, R. K., 23, 119
Representation, 153, 155
Rescorla, L., 108, 121
Research, 20–21, 74–75. *See also* Longitudinal studies
    bias in, 200
    ethnographic studies, 194
Responsive Education Program, 24–25
Responsive Environments Corporation Early Childhood Model, 25
Retardation, 20, 39–40
Reynolds, A. J., 172n
Rhine, W. R., 74, 91–92, 101–102, 105, 112–114, 124, 149, 152–153, 158, 165n
Rickover, Hyman G., 80
Rivlin, A. M., 23, 166–169, 182
Robinson, C. C., 177, 183n
Rogers, L., 126, 128, 149
Rogers, V. R., 66n
Rogoff, B., 193–195
Rollers, 144
Romanticism, 198–199, 201–202
Rothkopf, E. Z., 33
Royce, J. M., 182
Rutter, M., 192, 196

Saunders, R., 126n
Scheffler, I., 204, 206
Schnur, E., 183–184
Schon, D. A., 31, 203, 205–206
School readiness, 22, 28, 43, 119, 200, 211
School reform movement, 13, 27–28, 211
Schubert, W. H., 6, 187
Schwandt, T. A., 185
Schwartz, P. M., 189, 201, 205
Schweinhart, L. J., 26–27, 109, 123, 126, 129, 150–156, 159–160, 166–167, 173, 177–179, 184, 188, 213
Science
    as definitive authority, 207
    developmental psychology as, 196–198
    of education, 104–107
    of educational practice, 127
    method and, 104–105
Science curriculum guide (Blackwell and Hohmann), 150
Scientific pedagogy, 49–51
Secret of Childhood, The (Montessori), 49
Seefeldt, C., 33
Seitz, V., 171
Self-creation, 51–52

Self-discipline, 54
Self-esteem, 112, 172
Self-help skills, 56–57
Seligson, M., 13, 27, 30
Selman, R., 132, 139, 143
Senge, P. M., 209
Sensorimotor stage, 134
Sensory education, 57–59
Sensual child, 196
Sequin, Edward, 39, 61
Sergi, Guiseppe, 50
Setting Up the Learning Environment (Hohmann
    and Buckleitner), 150
Shaping, 101, 113
Shapiro, E., 66–67, 69, 75, 80–84, 86, 89, 93–94
Sheehan, R., 23, 119, 168–169
Shonkoff, J. P., 180–181
Shulman, L. S., 174, 204
Shwedel, A. M., 167, 169, 174–177
Siegel, A. W., 21, 196
Sigel, I., 18, 99, 108, 121, 126*n*, 174, 178, 198, 201
Silin, J. G., 15, 31, 95, 189, 197, 199, 201–202, 208
Silver Ribbon Panel, 29–30
Simons, F. A., 61–62, 190
Simons, J. A., 61–62, 190
Simple abstraction, 140, 143
Sinclair, Hermaine, 147
Skeels, H. M., 20
Skinner, B. F., 101–102, 117
Skrtic, T., 202, 207
Small-group instruction, 116, 156
Smilansky, Sara, 151
Smith, M. E., 205–206
Smithberg, L. M., 74, 91–92
Snook, I., 16
Snyder, A., 81
Social-arbitrary knowledge, 141–142
Social development, 152–153, 195–196
Social efficiency, 106–107, 120–121
Socialization, 8, 86, 88
Social meliorists, 120
Social Studies: A Way to Integrate Curriculum for
    Four and Five Year Olds (videotape), 90*n*
Social studies instruction (Developmental-Interaction
    approach), 90–91
Societal context, 28–29, 211
Sociodramatic play, 142, 151
Sociomoral atmosphere, 143–145
Sonquist, H. D., 129

Spencer, M. J., 186
Spodek, B., 4, 14–16, 26, 29, 96, 100, 122, 185, 189,
    197, 199, 201–202
Spontaneous activity, 47, 49, 51–53, 63
Spontaneous Activity in Education (Montessori), 47,
    63
Sputnik, 19, 80, 117, 130
Staff development, 158–159, 203–204
Stages of moral development, 132
Stages of perspective taking, 132
Stage theory, 84–85, 132–139
Stallings, J. A., 167, 169, 175, 178–179, 184
Standardized tests, 107, 169–170, 172, 176–177
Standing, E. M., 38
Stanford-Binet intelligence test, 107
State Orthophrenic School, 39–40
Steiner, G. Y., 12
Steiner, K., 208
Stimulus control, 113
Stimulus-response psychology, 100
Stipek, D., 167, 169, 175, 178–179, 184
Stoddard, George, 21*n*
Stodolsky, S. S., 204
Structuralism, 84–85, 132–139
Student assessment, 104, 169–172, 176–177
    Bereiter-Engelmann model, 107
    Developmental-Interaction approach, 74
    High/Scope Curriculum model, 155
    Kamii-DeVries approach, 138–139
Suarez, T. M., 18, 169, 171, 174, 183, 192–193
Subject matter knowledge, 91, 147
Sullivan, Harry Stack, 84
Suransky, V. P., 180, 189, 197, 200
Sutton-Smith, B., 189, 200
Swadener, B. B., 188, 197–198, 202, 208
Symbolic play, 142

Takanishi, R., 169, 179–183, 185–186
Teacher-child relationship (Developmental-
    Interaction approach), 89–91
Teacher education, 50, 61, 75, 95, 158–159, 203–205
Teacher effectiveness, 106*n*, 181–182, 202–204
Teacher roles, 8–9, 213–214
    Bereiter-Engelmann model, 110–111
    Developmental-Interaction approach, 68–69, 81,
        89–91, 93
    High/Scope Curriculum model, 152, 157
    Kamii-DeVries approach, 147–148
    Montessori Method, 44

Teaching. *See also* Professionalism
    developmental theory and, 200–201
    nature of, 202–206
Teaching Disadvantaged Children in the Preschool, 110*n*
Teaching methods
    Bereiter-Engelmann model, 108–110
    Direct Instruction model, 105–107, 115–116
Teaching moves, 109
Teaching strategies
    Developmental-Interaction approach, 89–91
    Direct Instruction model, 114–115
Teaching the Disadvantaged Child (Bereiter and Engelmann), 106*n*
Teaching the Disadvantaged Preschooler (Bereiter and Engelmann), 103–104
Teberosky, A., 131, 147
Tests. *See* Standardized tests
Tharp, R. G., 194
Theories, family of, 83–84
Theories of instruction, 101, 106
Theory, relationship with practice, 201–202, 205
    Developmental-Interaction approach, 93–96
Thorndike, Edward, 14, 100, 106, 117
Timpane, P. M., 23, 166–169, 182
Tobin, J. J., 194–195
Toffler, A., 209
Traditional model, 22, 159
    Developmental-Interaction approach and, 78–80
    evaluation of, 177–178
    Kamii-DeVries approach and, 145–147
Training, 50, 61, 75, 95, 158–159, 203–205
Travers, J. R., 166–167, 174, 181–182
Tucson Early Education Model, 24–25

University lab schools, 73

Value relative objectives, 136–137
Value system, 15–16, 197–198, 201–202
    Developmental-Interaction approach, 86
Vandenberg, B., 197
Villa, Pancho, 43
Vinovskis, M. A., 184
Vygotsky, L. S., 195

Walberg, H., 26, 96
Walden School, 77*n*, 82
Wallace, D. B., 75, 94
Wallgren, C., 149–150, 157–158

Walsh, D. J., 120*n*, 205–206
Warger, C., 27, 188
War on Poverty, 18–19, 23
Watkins, C., 186
Watson, John, 100, 118*n*
Weber, E., 14–15, 17–18, 33, 37, 44–45, 69, 72–73, 84, 99, 102, 117–118, 120, 129–130, 196–197, 199, 208
Wechsler Intelligence Test, 171
Weikart, David P., 23–24, 26–27, 31–32, 78, 109, 123, 125–129, 148*n*, 149–161, 167, 169, 172–173, 177–179, 184, 188, 213
Weinberg, R. A., 19
Weisberg, P., 103, 105, 108, 112–113, 121
Weiss, B., 47
Weiss, C. H., 182
Weiss, H. B., 174, 181, 183
Weiss, H. R., 12
Weissbourd, B., 30
Welker, R., 204
Werner, Heinz, 84
Wertheimer, Max, 84
Westinghouse Ohio study, 23, 25, 170
What Works, 106*n*
White, K. R., 184
White, S. H., 14–15, 19, 21, 33, 45, 72, 79, 98, 100–101, 104, 117–119, 170, 180, 191, 196–197
Whitebrook, M., 212
Whole child concept, 21, 74, 77, 80–82, 135
Wickens, D., 84
Willer, B., 32, 212
Williams, L. R., 78*n*
Williams, M. B., 167, 169, 174–177
Wilson, Woodrow, 43
Winsor, C., 67, 81
Wittner, D. S., 177, 184
Wittrock, M. C., 98, 101
Woodhead, M., 26, 182, 184–185, 193
Work time (High/Scope), 156
Writing instruction
    Kamii-DeVries approach, 145–147
    Montessori Method, 59–60
Wu, D. Y. H., 194–195

Yearbook of the Society for the Study of Education, 187
Young Children, 96
Young Children in Action, 149–150, 161
Ypsilanti-Carnegie Infant Education Project, 158

Ypsilanti Early Education Program, 128
Ypsilanti Preschool Curriculum Demonstration
    Project, 159

Zan, B., 27, 143, 179
Zelizer, V. A., 196, 208

Zellner, M., 119
Zigler, E., 12, 18–20, 30, 78, 124*n*, 170–171, 183, 212
Zimiles, H., 67, 69, 74, 169, 181–182, 200–201
Zoref, L., 115–116
Zuckerman, Michael, 118
Zumwalt, K. K., 203–204

ISBN 0-675-21154-9

90000>

9 780675 211543

INDEX

architects 10–11
arithmetic 11
armies 12, 13
artifacts 4, 5, 8

body tissues 20

calendars 7
canopic jar 21
chariots 13
cosmetics 12, 18–19
crops 5, 6, 8, 9

decimal system 11

eyes 19

flood 5, 6, 9
funerals 16, 17

harp 16–17
henna 18, 19
hieroglyphs 15

kohl 19

measuring rods 6, 10–11

mummies 20–21
music 16–17

Nile River 4–5, 6

ore 19

papyrus paper 15
processions 17
pyramids 5, 9, 10, 11

reeds 6, 8

scribes 11, 14–15
seasons 6
settled 4
sickles 8–9
soil 5, 9
spears 12

temples 9, 10, 11
tombs 5, 7, 9, 16, 17, 20, 21
tools 8–11, 20, 21
traders 4, 11
treasures 4–5, 20

weapons 12–13
writing palette 14

FURTHER INFORMATION

Web sites

Read more about Ancient Egypt on these fun Web sites:

www.egypt.mrdonn.org

www.historyforkids.org/learn/egypt

www.touregypt.net/kids

Books

Ancient Egypt: Why Were Mummies Wrapped?
    by Catherine Chambers. Miles Kelly Publishing (2010)

Egypt the Culture (Lands, Peoples, and Cultures)
    by Arlene Moscovitch. Crabtree Publishing Company (2008)

Gods and Goddesses of Ancient Egypt
    by Janeen Adil. Capstone Press (2008)

What Did the Ancient Egyptians Do for Me?
    by Patrick Catel. Heinemann (2010)

Life in Ancient Egypt (Peoples of the Ancient World)
    by Paul Challen. Crabtree Publishing Company (2005)